FROMMER'S TOURING GUIDES

BRAZIL

D1453897

Author: **Jean-Louis Péru**
Translation: **Nina de Voogd**
Editor: **Lisa Davidson-Petty, Alexandra Tufts-Simon**
Photo credits: **Explorer:** Boutin, pp. 50, 120-121, 172-173;
Cheuva, pp. 8, 21, 24, 42, 156; Costa, pp. 26-27, 30, 140, 153, 200,
221, 236; Dubois, p. 244; Edouard, pp. 59, 233; Errath, pp. 180-181;
Gohier, pp. 17, 193, 240-241; Kremer, pp. 62, 204-205; Moisnard,
pp. 54-55, 84-85; **La Photothèque S.D.P.:** Robin, p. 81.

This edition published in the United States and Canada in 1990 by
Prentice Hall Trade Division
A Division of Simon & Schuster, Inc.
15 Columbus Circle
New York, NY 10023

© Hachette Guides Bleus, Paris, 1990. First edition.
English translation © Hachette Guides Bleus, Paris, 1990.
Maps © Hachette Guides Bleus, Paris, 1990.

ISBN 0-13-331182-1
ISSN 0899-2800

Printed in France by Mame Imprimeurs (Tours)

FROMMER'S TOURING GUIDES

GUIDES

BRAZIL

PRENTICE HALL

NEW YORK ■ LONDON ■ TORONTO ■ SYDNEY
TOKYO ■ SINGAPORE

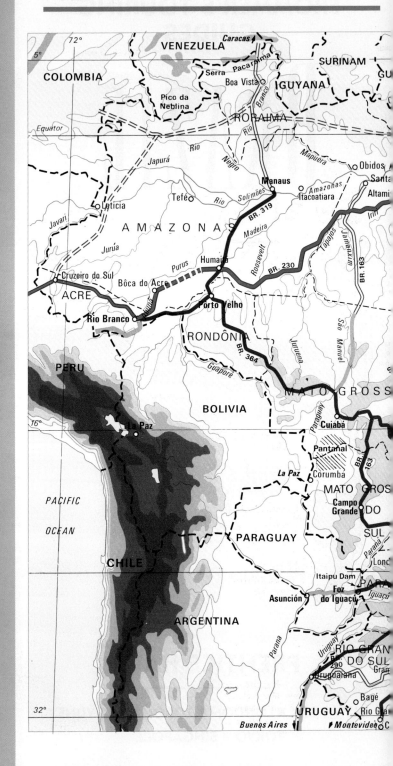

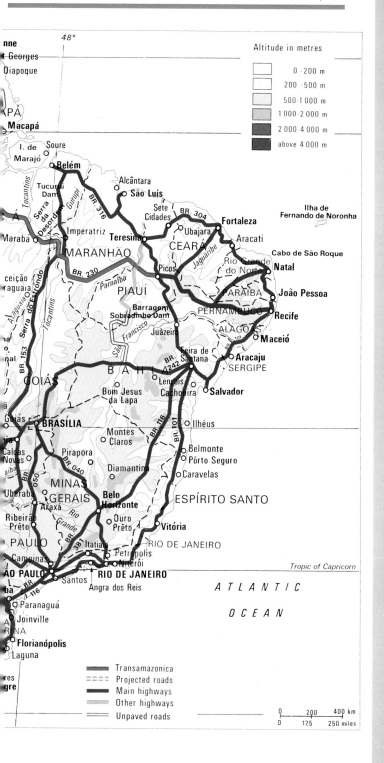

Altitude in metres

0 - 200 m
200 - 500 m
500 - 1 000 m
1 000 - 2 000 m
2 000 - 4 000 m
above 4 000 m

nne
Georges
Oiapoque

PÁ
Macapá

48°

I. de
Marajó
Soure

Belém

Tucuraí
Dam

Alcântara

○ **São Luís**

Sete
Cidades

BR 304

Fortaleza

Ilha de
Fernando de Noronha

Maraba ○
Imperatriz
Teresina

○ Ubajara

CEARÁ

Aracati

Cabo de São Roque

MARANHÃO

Picos

Jaguaribe

Rio Grande
do Norte

Natal

ceição
raguaia

BR 230

Parnaíba

PIAUÍ

Barragem
Sobradinho Dam

São Francisco

Juàzeiro

PARAÍBA

João Pessoa

PERNAMBUCO

Recife

ALAGOAS

○ **Maceió**

nal

BR 153

Serra do Estrondo

Serra da Desordem

Gurupi

Tocantins

Tocantins

Araguaia

BR 316

Feira de
Santana

BR
A242

Aracaju

SERGIPE

GOIÁS

B A H I A

Lençóis ○

Bom Jesus
da Lapa

Cachoeira

○**Salvador**

Goiás ○

BRASÍLIA

Montes
Claros

BR 116

BR 101

○ Ilhéus

ia
Caldas
Novas

Pirapora

BR 040

○ Belmonte

aiba

BR 050

Diamantina ○

○ Pôrto Seguro

MINAS

○Caravelas

Uberaba ○

GERAIS

Araxá

Rio

**Belo
Horizonte**

ESPÍRITO SANTO

Ribeirão
Prêto ○

Grande

○ Ouro
Prêto

○ **Vitória**

PAULO

BR 381

Itatiaia

RIO DE JANEIRO

Campinas

Petrópolis

Niterói

ĀO PAULO

Santos

RIO DE JANEIRO

Tropic of Capricorn

ba

BR 116

Angra dos Reis

○Paranaguá

○ Joinville

RINA

○ **Florianópolis**

Laguna

res
gre

A T L A N T I C

O C E A N

Transamazonica
Projected roads
Main highways
Other highways
Unpaved roads

0   200   400 km

0   125   250 miles

▬ CONTENTS

▬ HOW TO USE YOUR GUIDE

● Before you leave home, read the sections 'Planning Your Trip' p. 11, 'Practical Information' p. 16, 'Brazil in the Past' p. 31 and 'Brazil Today' p. 43.

● The rest of the guide is for on the spot use. It is divided into chapters discussing either **cities** (eg, Rio de Janeiro, São Paulo) or **regions** (eg, Nordeste, Amazonia). Each chapter includes sections pointing out what to see and providing practical information about the particular area (accommodation, useful addresses, etc).

● Practical advice and information on people, places and events can be located quickly by referring to the '**Index**' p. 262. For further information about Brazil, consult the '**Suggested Reading**' section at the back of the guide p. 261.

● To easily locate recommended sites on the maps, refer to the map coordinates printed in blue in the text. Example: II, C3.

▬ SYMBOLS USED

Sites, monuments, museums and points of particular interest

***   Exceptional
**   Very interesting
*   Interesting

Hotels and restaurants

See pp. 16 and 20 for an explanation of classification policy.

▬ MAPS

INTRODUCTION TO BRAZIL

B razil projects a kaleidoscope of images: pristine beaches under a blazing sun; carnival costumes of gaudy feathers and shimmering sequins; throbbing samba dancing in the streets; enthusiastic crowds watching a soccer match; inaccessible Indian territories; dense jungles abundant with plant and animal life; mines bursting with gold and precious stones; the vast expanses of the Amazon basin, five times the size of state of Texas; and the futuristic architecture of the new capital of Brasília.

These images all convey aspects of a country that remains enigmatic. Brazil is a raw country, but also one of sensitivity and sensuality. The racial mixture of its people and its history link it to many civilizations, but it belongs to none. If, at times, it seemed to have been assimilated by one particular culture, in the end it absorbed that culture. Here, in the heart of South America, everything is undergoing rapid change — Brazil is a giant country in the process of developing.

Today, tourism in Brazil is growing at full speed, thanks to the efforts of government and trade organizations. However, because most Brazilians with the means to travel have often chosen to go abroad, you may not always find that the tourist facilities in Brazil are sufficiently developed.

Rio de Janeiro, São Paulo, Salvador and Brasília are the four most-visited cities in Brazil, and are essential stops on any itinerary. If you really want to get a full taste of Brazil, however, you might add a visit to historical Minas Gerais, the jungles of Amazonas, the magnificent waterfalls of Iguaçu or one of the other lesser-known regions.

Wherever you decide to travel, you can be certain that you will meet some real characters in Brazil: an old miner still searching for gold, a thrice-bankrupt businessman on the lookout for the deal of the century, a rich *fazendeiro* whose land comprises thousands of acres, or a young girl waiting impatiently for Carnival.

The Brazilians will amaze you with their *joie de vivre*, their friendliness and their faith in tomorrow. This state of mind is perfectly expressed in a popular Brazilian saying — there is nothing to worry about since God is Brazilian *(Deus e brasileiro)!*

Salvador's Carnival, considered by Brazilians to be the most authentic, attracts visitors from all over the world.

Brazil in brief

Location: Occupies close to half of the South American continent.

Borders: 9,768 mi/15,719 km, bordering every South American country except Chili and Ecuador. To the north (from east to west): French Guiana, Suriname, Guyana, Venezuela, Colombia; to the west (from north to south): Peru, Bolivia, Paraguay, Argentina and Uruguay.

Area: 3,286,470 sq mi/8,511,965 sq km; farthest north-to-south distance: 2,684 mi/4,320 km.

Coastline: 4,605 mi/7,410 km on the Atlantic ocean.

Population: 141,302,000.

Capital: Brasília (pop. 1,720,000).

Major cities: São Paulo (pop. 10,100,000), Rio de Janeiro (pop. 5,600,000), Belo Horizonte (pop. 2,120,000), Salvador (pop. 1,800,000).

Religion: Catholic, although there are numerous occult religions (see p. 50).

Language: Portuguese; some English and Spanish are also spoken.

Government: Multi-party federal republic with two legislative bodies, the Senate and the Chamber of Deputies.

Administrative division: Twenty-three states, three territories and a federal district (Brasília).

Economic activity: Agriculture (coffee, sugar cane, bananas, citrus fruits); mining (iron ore, manganese, chrome ores, bauxite, tin concentrates and gold).

PLANNING YOUR TRIP

This section will provide all the information you need before setting out: the best time to visit, how to get there, customs formalities, currency and many other useful tips.

WHEN TO GO

Any season is a good one to visit Brazil. Why not spend Christmas at the beach? Don't forget that Brazil is situated in the southern hemisphere, and the seasons are the opposite of those in Europe or North America. The coolest months are June, July and August, with average temperatures of 55° F/15° C to 77° F/25° C; the hottest months are December, January and February, with average temperatures of 86° F/30° C to 104° F/40° C.

Because of its vast size, Brazil has several distinct climatic zones. The north of the country is tropical, with heavy rain from June to August (the 'wet' season) and warm winters during the relatively 'dry' season from October to December. In the south, the climate is cooler and temperatures in winter may fall as low as 40° F/5° C.

Average temperatures

	Jan		Mar		May		July		Sept		Nov	
	min	max	min	max	min	max	min	max	min	max	min	max
BELÉM	73	88	73	86	73	88	72	90	72	90	72	90
°F												
°C	23	31	23	30	23	31	22	32	22	32	22	32
BELO HORIZONTE	64	81	63	81	54	77	50	75	57	81	63	81
°F												
°C	18	27	17	27	12	25	10	24	14	27	17	27
BRASÍLIA	64	81	64	82	59	81	55	79	61	86	64	81
°F												
°C	18	27	18	28	15	27	13	26	16	30	18	27
MANAUS	73	86	73	86	75	88	73	90	75	91	75	90
°F												
°C	23	30	23	30	24	31	23	32	24	33	24	32
PORTO ALEGRE	68	88	66	84	55	72	50	68	55	72	63	81
°F												
°C	20	31	19	29	13	22	10	20	13	22	17	27
RECIFE	75	86	75	86	73	84	70	81	72	82	75	86
°F												
°C	24	30	24	30	23	29	21	27	22	28	24	30
RIO DE JANEIRO	73	86	73	84	68	79	64	77	66	77	68	82
°F												
°C	23	30	23	29	20	26	18	25	19	25	20	28
SALVADOR	73	84	75	84	72	81	70	79	70	81	73	82
°F												
°C	23	29	24	29	22	27	21	26	21	27	23	28
SÃO PAULO	64	82	63	81	55	73	50	70	55	77	59	77
°F												
°C	18	28	17	27	13	23	10	21	13	25	15	25

You will find more detailed information on the best times to visit in the sections dealing with the different regions.

▬ GETTING THERE

Plane

There are flights from North America and Europe to Brazil every day of the year. Contact your travel agent, tour operator or airline company (see specific airline addresses below) for reservations and purchase of plane tickets and other tourist services.

Flights from North America

Regularly scheduled flights to Brazil from North America are offered by **Varig, Pan American, Aerolineas Argentinas** and **Japan Airlines**. Varig flies from New York, Los Angeles and Miami to Rio de Janeiro; Pan American flies from New York and Los Angeles to Rio de Janeiro; Aerolineas Argentinas flies from New York to Rio de Janeiro. The non-stop New York to Rio de Janeiro flight by Pan American or Varig takes 9 hr 20 min.

For information and reservations, contact the following airline offices.

Aerolineas Argentinas, 9 Rockefeller Plaza, New York, NY 10020, ☎ (212) 974 3353. A toll-free number is available from the United States and Puerto Rico, ☎ (800) 327 0276.

Japan Airlines, 555 West Seventh St., Los Angeles, CA 90014, ☎ (213) 620 9580. Also has offices in New York, NY, ☎ (212) 838 4400. A toll-free number is available from the United States and Puerto Rico, ☎ (800) JALFONE.

Pan American, 600 Fifth Ave., New York, NY 10020, ☎ (212) 687 2600. Also has offices in: Houston, TX, ☎ (713) 447 0088; Miami, FL, ☎ (305) 874 5000; Newark, NJ, ☎ (201) 643 3172 (in Spanish); Washington, DC, ☎ (202) 845 8000; Toronto, Canada, ☎ (416) 368 2941. A toll-free number is available from the United States and Canada, ☎ (800) 221 1111.

Varig, 634 Fifth Ave., New York, NY 10020, ☎ (212) 682 3100. Also has offices in: Chicago, IL, ☎ (312) 565 1301; Houston, TX, ☎ (713) 651 9804; Los Angeles, CA, ☎ (213) 624 6324; Miami, FL, ☎ (305) 358 4935; Philadelphia, PA, ☎ (215) 567 5380; San Francisco, CA, ☎ (415) 986 5737; Washington, DC, ☎ (202) 331 8913; Montreal, Canada, ☎ (514) 845 5121; Toronto, Canada, ☎ (416) 963 8842. A toll-free number is available from the United States and Canada, ☎ (800) 468 2744.

Flights from Europe

It is possible to fly to Brazil from most European capitals. **Varig** offers direct flights to Rio de Janeiro from London, Paris, Milan, Frankfurt and Madrid. **British Airways** flies non-stop to Rio de Janeiro from London twice weekly. It also offers flights to Rio de Janeiro from Dublin, Glasgow and Edinburgh, although these flights all include stop-overs. Other airlines offering flights to Brazil from Europe include **Air France, KLM, SAS, Lufthansa, Alitalia, Iberia, Swissair** and **Aerolineas Argentinas**.

Great Britain

British Airways, 421 Oxford St., London W1R 1FJ, ☎ (01) 897 4000 (central reservations); 75 Regent St., London W1R 7HG, ☎ (01) 987 4000; 30/32 Frederick Street, Edinburgh EH2 2JR, ☎ (031) 225 2525; 66 Gordon Street, Glasgow G1 3RS, ☎ (041) 332 9666; 60 Dawson St., Dublin 2, ☎ (01) 610 666.

Swissair, Swiss Centre, 10 Wardour St., London W1V 4BJ, ☎ (01) 439 4144.

Varig, 16 Hanover St., London W1R 0HG, ☎ (01) 629 9408.

Ships

It is possible to travel to Brazil by ship, but such a voyage is long, expensive and, increasingly, unusual. Several European shipping lines operate cargo ships to Brazil carrying a limited number of passengers. The trip takes about two weeks.

For information, contact the following shipping companies:

Europe

Continental Shipping & Travel, 179 Piccadilly, London W1V 9DB, ☎ (01) 491 4968.

Nedlloyd, Boompjes 40, 3011 BX, Rotterdam, ☎ 417 7911.

United States

Moore-McCormack Line, ☎ (212) 683 0619.

ENTRY FORMALITIES

If you are a United States citizen, you must produce your passport and visa and a round-trip or continuing-passage ticket upon entering Brazil.

If you are a British subject, you need your passport and a round-trip or continuing-passage ticket upon entering Brazil. No visa is necessary.

Passports must be valid for a period of at least six months after your departure from Brazil.

Visa

United States citizens must obtain a visa prior to arrival in Brazil. A visitor's visa is easily obtained for genuine short-term visits (maximum: 90 days) from the Brazilian Embassy or Consulate nearest you (see 'Before you leave: some useful addresses' p. 14). Visas usually take three days to process and are issued free of charge. They can be renewed for another 90 days within 15 days of expiration of the first visa. For longer stays, you must leave the country to renew your visa (returning immediately if you wish). It is also important to hold on to the emigration permit you receive on entering Brazil. If you lose it, you may have to pay up to US$100 on leaving.

Customs

Visitors over 18 may enter Brazil with US$300 worth of goods duty-free, 400 cigarettes, or an equivalent amount of tobacco or cigars, and two litres of alcohol.

Pets

To bring pets into Brazil, visitors need a health and vaccination certificate from a vet that has been notarized by your local Brazilian consulate.

Vaccinations

No vaccinations are required to enter Brazil. As long as you stay in the large cities, you will have nothing to fear in the way of disease. On the other hand, if you plan to stay any length of time in Amazonas, it is wise to be vaccinated against all the standard tropical diseases (yellow fever, typhoid, etc).

WHAT TO PACK

Clothing

Visitors to the north of Brazil need only pack light clothing, even in winter, because temperatures never fall below 68° F/20° C. If you plan to travel to the south in June, July or August, you should take along some warm clothing.

Medication

Bring a basic medicine kit containing aspirin, Band-Aids, disinfectant and an intestinal remedy of some sort in case the food or the change in climate doesn't agree with you. If you plan to travel to Amazonas, you should include anti-malaria tablets and an insect repellent. If you are under medical treatment, it is best to buy what you need before you depart. Remember to carry your prescription or else certain drugs may be taken from you at customs.

Photographic equipment

Cameras and film are much more expensive in Brazil than in the United States or Great Britain. It is recommended that you bring what you will need.

Miscellaneous

Electricity in Brazil is mostly of the 110-volt variety. Thus, American electrical appliances will work, but European electrical appliances will need an adaptor. Adaptors are sometimes provided by Brazilian hotels.

MONEY

Currency

In February 1986, the cruzado (CzS) replaced the cruzeiro as Brazil's monetary unit. The new cruzado bills are being slowly brought into circulation, but old cruzeiros are still widely in use. A cruzado consists of 100 centavos.

Devaluation

Because of runaway inflation, the Brazilian cruzado is frequently devalued. This means that the prices given in this guide are subject to change and should be used as an approximate guideline.

Credit cards

Brazilian shops accept all well-known credit cards such as American Express, Diners Club and Visa. The amount of your purchase will be calculated according to the official rate of exchange, however, which is always less favourable than the unofficial one. It is preferable to use cash.

Your budget

An average day, for two people, including one night in a moderately priced hotel, one taxi trip, two meals in a restaurant and night-time entertainment costs over US$100. The American dollar is the international currency that is easiest to negotiate in Brazil's unofficial exchange agencies, boutiques and elsewhere. If you are coming from a country other than the United States, we recommend that you change your money into American dollars before entering Brazil.

BEFORE YOU LEAVE: SOME USEFUL ADDRESSES

Great Britain

Embassy
London; 32 Green St., WIY 4AT, ☎ (01) 4990877

Consulate
London: 6 St Albans St., SW1 4SG, ☎ (01) 9309055.

Canada

Embassy
Ottawa: 255 Albert St., Suite 900, ONT KIP 6A9, ☎ (613) 2371090.

Consulates
Montreal: 2000 Mansfield St., Suite 1700, QU 43A 3A5, ☎ (514) 4990968.

Toronto: 77 Bloor St. West, Suite 1109, ONT M5S 1M2, ☎ (416) 922 2503
Vancouver: Royal Center, 1055 Georges St. West, Suite 1700, BC V6E 3P3, ☎ (604) 687 4589.

United States

Embassy

Washington: 3006 Massachusetts Ave., NW, DC 20008, ☎ (202) 745 2700.

Consulates

Chicago: 20 North Wacker Dr., Suite 1010, IL 60606, ☎ (312) 372 2177.
Los Angeles: 3810 Wilshire Blvd., Suite 1500, CA 90010, ☎ (213) 382 3133.
New York: 630 Fifth Ave., Suite 2735, NY 10111, ☎ (212) 757 3080.
San Francisco; 300 Montgomery St., Suite 1160, CA 94140, ☎ (415) 981 8170 or 981 8175.

PRACTICAL INFORMATION

▬ ACCOMMODATION

Hotels

The Brazilian hotel industry is growing rapidly, and its most distinguishing characteristic is its lack of homogeneity. On the one hand, large Brazilian and international hotel chains have built, and are building, expensive luxury hotels. On the other, there are many small, inexpensive hotels where you will have to settle for basic amenities. There is no formal system of evaluating hotels or the rates charged in Brazil.

In this book, we have introduced our own ratings and the highest (▲▲▲▲) has been given to hotels belonging to international or Brazilian chains. They generally provide such amenities as restaurants, swimming pools, boutiques, and so on. The next rating (▲▲▲) goes to hotels with air-conditioning, telephone, and hot and cold running water. Below that (▲▲) are moderate hotels that maintain a comfortable standard. The lowest category (▲) is for hotels without amenities, sometimes without what you may consider as necessities. However, it is important to bear in mind, especially in rural areas, that these hotels may be set in charming localities and give a warm welcome.

Motels

It is against the law in Brazil for a man to invite a woman into his hotel room, and some motels are reputed to serve as places of prostitution. Certain chains, such as **Luxor**, however, are known for their modern comforts and their safe and pleasant atmosphere.

Camping

Camping has become popular in Brazil in the last few years. Even cities with only a modest tourist business now boast camping sites. You can also ask proprietors of large farms for permission to camp.

Brazil's principal camping club is: **Camping Club do Brasil** (CCB), Rua Senador Dantas 75, Rio de Janeiro, ☎ : 262 7172. Here, you can pick up a guide *(Guiá de Areas de Camping)* that lists all Brazil's camping sites.

▬ BUSINESS HOURS

Shops are generally open weekdays from 9am-6:30pm and, except for certain food shops, most stores are closed on Sundays and sometimes on Saturday afternoons.

Banks are open Monday to Friday 10am-4:30pm.

Service stations are closed on Sundays and, in certain regions, on Saturdays also.

▬ CURRENCY EXCHANGE

Do not change more money than you need when you arrive at the airport because the exchange rate is prohibitive there. If you land on a day when the banks are closed (Saturdays, Sundays and holidays), your hotel porter will be able to change a small amount for you at a better rate.

Two of the many small, modest hotels in Brazil.

Because of frequent devaluations, we suggest that you change money as the need arises. The rate of exchange may well keep varying during your stay.

The best places to exchange money are small boutiques (such as jewelry shops), where you will be given the unofficial exchange rate, a far better one than the official (or bank) rate. Other places where you can go to change money are the *casas de cambio*, unofficial establishments that are openly tolerated by authorities.

▬ DO'S AND DON'TS

The best thing to do when you arrive in Brazil is to forget all about your northern habits when it comes to organization and punctuality. Checking into a hotel or boarding public transportation may take some time, so just relax!

Brazilians love to communicate. They are forever soliciting a reaction of some kind — a glance, a smile. If you don't respond you will remain a stranger. You will be offered a *cafezinho* (small cup of coffee) at least 10 times a day — this is a Brazilian ritual. The handshake is the official form of greeting, as is the *abraço*, which consists of friendly little pats on the back while being clutched in a close embrace. Patting someone too hard is considered vulgar.

If you have any trouble finding your way around, don't hesitate to ask directions. You will discover that Brazilians are extremely helpful and they will often go out of their way to lead you to your destination.

▬ EMERGENCIES

The following is a list of emergency telephone numbers that apply throughout Brazil.

Emergency: ☎ 192.
Fire: ☎ 193.
Medical: ☎ 191.
Pharmacy: ☎ 136.
Police: ☎ 190.

FESTIVALS AND HOLIDAYS

Festivals and holidays, rooted in both the Catholic and Afro-Brazilian traditions, abound in Brazil. You will find that even the Catholic holidays are permeated with customs unique to Brazil. The following is a list of some of the country's major celebrations:

January

Jan 1: Bom Jesus dos Navegantes. This ancient Bahai festival, devoted to Jesus the Navigator, is celebrated with colourfully decorated naval processions on the Boa Viagem beach in Salvador.

Third week in January: Feast of Nosso Senhor do Bonfim. One of Salvador's most important and ancient holidays. The women, dressed in traditional Bahian costume and balancing pots of flowers on their heads, wash the steps of Salvador's churches. This is followed by a procession to the sea where they offer the flowers to Yemanjá.

Jan 20: Feast of São Sebastião. Homage is paid to the patron saint of Rio de Janeiro.

February

Four days before Ash Wednesday: Carnival. This is undoubtedly the most important event of the year. The tourist can best experience these four days of delirium in Rio de Janeiro (see p. 61), Salvador (see p. 135) and Recife (see p. 165).

March-April

A week of Catholic celebrations precede Easter. In Nova Jerusalem, near Recife, the Passion of Christ (see p. 170) is reenacted on a grand scale.

April 21: Tiradentes. On the anniversary of his death, Tiradentes, a hero during the struggle for independence, is honoured. Ouro Preto, where he lived and worked, becomes the capital of Brazil for one day (see p. 219).

May

May 1: Festa do Trabaho (Labour Day). National holiday.

May 13: Anniversary of the abolition of slavery.

June-August

June 1-31: Juninas Festas (June holidays). The feast days of St Anthony, St John and St Peter are the occasion of lively celebrations throughout Brazil, particularly in Amazonia.

June 23-Aug 25: Bumba-meu-Boi. The festival, held mostly in the Nordeste, recalls a popular tale about a slaughtered ox that was brought back to life. Songs and music accompany representations of this death and rebirth theme in São Luis.

August 1-30: Folklore Month. Plays, symposia and games are organized throughout the country.

September-October

Sept 7: Brazilian Independence Day. Ceremonial parades are held throughout the country.

Oct 12: Feast of Nossa Senhora Aparecida. Brazil's patron saint is honoured throughout the country and thousands of pilgrims journey to Aparecido do Norte in São Paulo state.

Oct 14-29: Cirio de Nazaré. Some 400,000 people gather in Belém to pay homage to the city's patron saint, Our Lady of Nazareth. Street festivities include a procession during which her statue is paraded throughout the city (held on the second Sunday in October).

November

Nov 2: Dinados (All Souls' Day). National holiday.

Nov 15: Birth of the Republic of Brazil. National holiday.

December

Dec 8-Jan 1: Yemanjá. Several weeks of festivities in homage to Yemanjá, the goddess of the sea. On the night of December 31, the beaches of Rio de Janeiro are ablaze with candles and people gather to offer presents that are thrown into the sea at midnight.

Dec 8: Imaculada Conceiçao (Immaculate Conception). Large processions are held, especially in Salvador.

Dec 24-Jan 6: Reisada. Costumed children go from door to door, receiving presents and exchanging invitations.

Dec 25: Natal (Christmas).

FOOD AND DRINK

Brazilian cuisine is simple, consisting mainly of rice, beans, tapioca and dried meat. Although every ethnic group has contributed its tastes, none of these has really taken hold and ethnic food is mainly confined to the restaurants of Rio and São Paulo. Brazil's only true culinary tradition is that of the black population. As Brazilian Paulo Mendes Campos so aptly put it: 'The food consumed by Brazilian whites improved considerably when blacks came into their kitchens'. This statement does much to explain the excellence of Bahia (Salvador) cuisine.

Bahia cuisine

Based on palm oil, coconut, and pimento, the cuisine of Bahia is delicate and creamy and requires a great deal of preparation. The best and most elaborate dishes were once used as religious offerings in the *candomblé* ceremonies. Bahia is also known for its sweets and pastries, which are Portuguese in origin.

Norte cuisine

The cuisine of Norte is what remains of authentic Indian cuisine. It can be found mainly in Pará and Maranhão. Its basic ingredients are fish, tapioca, regional plants and seaweed. This kind of cuisine may not look or taste appetizing to you, but it offers a golden opportunity for sampling turtle, snake or iguana. Desserts consist of many different tropical fruits.

Gaucho cuisine

It may seem exaggerated to speak of gaucho cuisine, yet in the south of Brazil, where all the livestock is bred and people are traditionally meat-eaters, there is a speciality: *churrasco* or charcoal-grilled meat.

Specialities

In the large cities of Brazil, regional dishes take a back seat to international cuisine, and there are very few restaurants that specialize solely in regional dishes by which is meant Bahia cuisine. However, a dish that originated in Bahia has now become the national speciality — *feijoada*. This is the sort of family dish that every Brazilian eats at least once a week, either at home or in a restaurant.

Feijoada is more than a dish — it is an entire meal. All of its ingredients are put on the table together: black or red beans that have been cooked with sun-dried meat, beef, sausage, pork fat and pig's feet, ears and tails. Separate dishes contain rice, finely shredded green cabbage, slices of ham, and grilled pork ribs. For a modest price, you can eat as much as you want.

Both salt- and fresh-water fish are abundant in Brazil, yet the taste for fish does not seem to have caught on among Brazilians. In seaside restaurants, however, you can order a tasty *pescada* (tiny fish fried in oil) or slices of *badejo* (boneless fish). Squid and octopus are plentiful, and *camarões* (shrimp) and *lagostas* (lobster) are excellent in Brazil. The latter are very expensive because most of them are exported. *Camarões* are served in hundreds of different ways and they are all worth sampling.

Pasteis are a kind of salted pastry filled with meat. Portuguese in origin, they come in many forms, *cochinhas and empadinhas* to name just two. They are sold in special shops known as *pastelarias*.

There is a huge variety of fruit in Brazil. There are seven kinds of banana and over a dozen kinds of orange. Other fruits found in abundance are *abacaxis* (pineapple), mango, guava, watermelon, coconut, fig, grape, pomegranate and avocado. These are all made into delicious *sorvetes* (sherbets).

Restaurants and *lanchonetes*

The large cities all boast good restaurants, especially known for their foreign cuisine. If you want to eat fast and inexpensively, go to a *lanchonete* (luncheonette). They can be found on almost any street corner and serve sandwiches, cold cuts and daily specials.

Prices of restaurants listed in this guide have been classified in four categories, indicated by asterisks:

**** — Very expensive
*** — Expensive
** — Reasonable
* — Inexpensive

Drink

The most popular drink in Brazil is beer, which is light and delicious whether in a bottle, a can or on draught. A popular soft drink is *guarana*, which is made from a fruit that comes from the Amazon region. There is a wide variety of other fruit juices, lemonade and, of course, the ever-present Coca Cola.

Brazilians boast of their *aguardente* (brandy made from sugarcane), and it is excellent. It is drunk neat or as an ingredient in a national aperitif called *caipirinha*, a mixture of brandy, sugar and crushed lemon. *Caipirinhos* are prepared to order and served with ice. *Batidas* are fruit juices mixed with brandy and sugar according to a specific recipe. The most popular of these is the *batida de limão* (lemon), but it is also tasty made with coconut, orange or banana.

▬ *HEALTH*

Hospitals and doctors

Brazilian medicine is among the most expensive in the world. If you have an accident and require emergency treatment, go to a *pronto socorro* (emergency hospital) where treatment is free. However, it may be crowded and you may have to wait.

Pharmacies

Pharmacies stay open until very late in the evening and sell every medicine under the sun. These drugs may vary a great deal in quality and are almost always sold without a prescription. Brazilian pharmacists are not trained in the same manner as pharmacists throughout the United Kingdom and the United States and it is best to be wary. Make sure to check the dates on all drugs that you purchase.

Insects and snakes

Marshy areas should be avoided at all costs because of the risk of tropical diseases. Outside of the cities there are many mosquito species, most of which, however, are not dangerous. *Carapatos* can be a problem in areas where livestock is bred: once they latch onto the skin, the only means to remove the insects without tearing the skin is to kill them first with alcohol. If you are visiting the Amazon basin, beware of snakes. You should bring along a snake-bite serum. Numerous serums are on sale in all major pharmacies, including an all-purpose serum that will protect you from all types of snakes.

Bahia specialities, sold by street vendors and elegant restaurants alike, are considered the best in Brazil.

Drinking water

Tourists, unaccustomed to Brazil's water, often have gastro-intestinal problems after drinking tap water. We recommend that you drink only bottled mineral water or soft drinks.

■ LANGUAGE

Unlike other South American countries, where Spanish is spoken, Brazil's language is Portuguese — the result of its colonization by Portugal in the 16th and 17th centuries. The language as it is used in Brazil, however, is quite different from that of Portugal. The Brazilians pronounce their words more clearly and have added many words from Indian dialects. If you know no Portuguese, don't worry. Many people speak Spanish, and increasingly people working in the tourism industry can speak English. See p. 256 for a glossary of useful words and phrases.

■ MEDIA

Radio and television

Each state has its own stations. São Paulo and Rio have six colour television networks and over 20 radio stations. Brazil's most popular television shows, *novelas*, are series which are broadcast late in the evening. A number of foreign films are also shown on television, sometimes in the original language with Portuguese subtitles.

Newspapers and magazines

Brazil has many newspapers and magazines, and each state publishes its own newspaper. The most widely read newspaper are *O Estado de São Paulo* and *Folha de São Paulo* in São Paulo and *Jornal do Brasil* and *O Globo* in Rio (the latter two carry complete lists of plays and films). Good weekly magazines are sold all over Brazil. The only English-language newspaper in Brazil is the *Daily Post/Brazil Herald*.

■ ORGANIZING YOUR TIME

Brazil is so huge that you would need three to four months to see the whole country. Depending on the length of your trip, you will have to choose which places interest you most. Remember that the distances between regions are vast and the travel time will vary greatly depending on the mode of transportation you select.

Unless you are going on an organized tour, you are bound to encounter unanticipated delays. It is advisable therefore not to organize your voyage too rigidly, but to leave some leeway for the unexpected.

A one-week trip

Concentrate on two places, preferably Rio de Janeiro and Salvador. Alternatively, you can spend the whole week in Rio de Janeiro and take a short excursion either to Brasília (one day) or to Foz do Iguaçu (two days, including traveling time).

A two-week trip

Two weeks are the minimum needed to see the major places of interest to tourists. You should spend four days in and around Rio de Janeiro. Afterward you can visit Foz de Iguaçu (two days), the historical towns of Minas Gerais (two to three days) and Brasília (one day), either using Rio as a base or moving from locale to locale. Finally, save at least three days for Salvador.

Three to four weeks

An extra week or two in Brazil will allow you to see all the places above plus any of the following:

● São Paulo (two days)

- Recife and Olinda (three days)
- an excursion down the São Francisco River (eight to ten days)
- an expedition through the Amazon basin (one week)
- a journey through the Pantanal valley (on week)
- a tour of the southern states (four to six days)

POST OFFICE

Brazil's postal system operates seven days a week throughout the year, except on official holidays. Delivery service, though, is often irregular. Brazilian stamps are so varied and beautiful that they are worth collecting. They can be bought in hotels as well as in post offices. Be sure to mail your letters yourself — people at hotel desks may not always be reliable. Letters to the United States or Europe generally take four to six days. Post offices in certain cities have a general delivery or poste restante service *(lista de correos)* but it is safer to use your consulate.

Telegram and telex

Telegrams can often be sent from hotels. If this service is not available, they can be sent from the post office. To send an international telegram by telephone, dial 000 222.

The only places where telex service is available are in the offices of the **Embratel,** the official Brazilian tourist agency, (see p. 28), and in the big hotels.

SAFETY

The distribution of wealth in Brazil is extremely disparate: a small percentage of the population is rich while millions live in inadequate housing and suffer from malnutrition. The economic recession of the last few years has aggravated the poverty, leading to an outbreak of robberies.

To avoid becoming a victim of theft, keep to the following guidelines: stay clear of the city slums; do not flaunt your jewelry (or better yet, don't wear any); leave your cash and valuables in the hotel safe or, if your hotel doesn't have a safe, carry travelers checks; be especially cautious with your belongings on the beaches and on public transport, favourite haunts of pickpockets.

In general, with a little bit of common sense and tact, the visitor is unlikely to experience any problems.

SHOPPING

Brazil is a wonderful place to shop: there is an enormous variety of things to buy, and most shops will give you an excellent rate of exchange if you make your purchase in US dollars.

Coffee and alcohol

Often, a tourist's favourite purchases are coffee (on sale at the airport) and alcohol — the sugarcane brandy that makes such excellent *batidas* (see p. 20).

Precious and semi-precious stones

Brazil is known for its precious stones, mainly aquamarine, tourmaline, topaz and amethyst. Nearly 90% of these stones come from Brazil. Emeralds and diamonds are also found here but in lesser quantities. Brazil also produces such semi-precious stones as opal, tiger's eye and garnet, which are made into necklaces, rings and bracelets. If you are a collector, there are magnificent stones like rock crystal, quartz and geode. There are shops selling stones throughout Brazil. However, if you prefer to go to the source, you'll have to visit Minas Gerais (see p. 215). The foremost centres are Belo Horizonte, Governador Valadares and Teofilo Otoni.

Hammocks from Nordeste are popular souvenirs.

Sources of various precious and semi-precious stones:
- Diamonds: Minas Gerais, Roraima, Goiás, Mato Grosso, Bahia.
- Emeralds: Bahia, Goiás, Minas Gerais.
- Aquamarines: Paraíba, Rio Grande, Bahia, Minas Gerais, Espirito Santo.
- Tourmalines: Goiás, Ceará, Minas Gerais.
- Topazes: Minas Gerais, Rondonia.
- Opals: Piauí, Rio Grande do Sul.
- Amethysts: Goiás, Mato Grosso do Sul.

Handcrafts

Brazil offers innumerable choices if you are interested in buying handcrafts as souvenirs. You can find, among others:
- Leather goods: workmanship is a bit rough, but there is a good variety, including handbags, belts, cushions, etc.
- Terracotta statues: these may or may not be painted.
- Butterflies: ranking among the most beautiful in the world, sold either

mounted for collectors or encased as souvenirs for tourists.
- Silver objects and jewelry: these come mainly from Salvador.
- Tapestries: these come mainly from Bahia.
- Soapstone *(pedra-sabão)* articles: made in Ouro Preto.
- Hammocks: made in Fortaleza and Natal in Nordeste.
- Crocodile or snake skins: these come from Belém and Manaus.
- Batiks: generally depict colonial scenes.
- Indian artifacts: include bows and arrows, statues, etc.

SPORTS

Soccer

To a Brazilian, the word 'sport' is synonymous with what he calls *futebol*, played year round. Brazilian soccer players are among the best in the world. Every four years the World Cup sends the entire country into a frenzy, and any employer who wants his staff to come to work has no choice but to install a television in the workplace. Brazil has won the World Cup three times, thanks to the one and only Pelé.

Every big city has its own stadium: Rio's Maracanã Stadium (see p. 79) is designed for 155,000 spectators and is the largest in the world. Matches for the national championship are epic events, especially when clubs from the same city or region play against each other. The most famous clubs are located in Rio de Janeiro (Fluminense, Flamengo, Vasco), São Paulo (São Paulo, Corintians, Santos, Palmieras) and Minas Gerais (Atlético, Cruzeiro).

Motor racing

Motor racing is Brazil's second most popular sport. Brazil is home to three world champions. Emerson Fittipaldi won the Formula One world championship in 1972 and 1974; Nelson Piquet outdid him by winning it three times in 1981, 1983 and 1987; and Ayrton Senna was world champion in 1988. The Formula One Grand Prix is held during the third week of March in Rio de Janeiro, although there are plans to move the race to Brasília.

Water-sports

With such an extremely long coast, Brazil offers a tremendous variety of water-sports, although surfing remains the Brazilians' favourite.

TELEPHONE

To make a local call, public booths called *orelhas* are available. You will need a token or *ficha*, on sale at news-stands. To make a long-distance call, go to one of the offices of the telephone company, Compania Telefonica. Rates are half-price after 8pm.

Brazil has several regional telephone companies and they are not integrated into the postal system. You cannot make telephone calls from the post office. Most cities have telephone offices that are often open late, where you can make local or long-distance calls. Where possible, we have given the addresses of these offices under 'Useful addresses' in each city. If the address is not indicated, inquire at your hotel or contact a local tourist office.

To make an international call from Brazil, dial:

Great Britain	44
United States and Canada	1
France	33
Italy	39
Switzerland	41

Brazilian area codes:

Aracaju (079), Belém (091), Belo Horizonte (031), Boa Vista (095), Brasília (0612), Campo Grande (0672), Cuiabá (065), Curitiba (0412),

The siesta is a time-honoured tradition: this kite vendor takes his in the shadow of his wares.

Florianópolis (0482), Fortaleza (085), Foz do Iguaçu (0455), Goiâna (062), João Pessoa (083), Macapá (091176), Maceió (082), Manaus (092), Natal (084), Ouro Preto (031), Porto Alegre (051), Porto Velho (069), Recife (081), Rio Branco (068), Rio de Janeiro (021), Salvador (071), São Luis (098), São Paulo (011), Teresina (086), Vitória (027).

To telephone abroad with the help of an English-language operator, dial 000 111.

For information in English about long-distance calls, dial 000 333.

▬ TIME

Brazil is so large that it encompasses four time zones. The eastern part of the country (as far as Rio Xingu) is, in winter, three hours behind

Great Britain, two hours ahead of New York and five hours ahead of Los Angeles. Thus, in the winter, when it is noon in Rio and São Paulo, it is 3pm in London, 10am in New York and 7am in Los Angeles.

All of Amazonas (to the west of Rio Xingu) and Mato Grosso are one hour behind eastern Brazil. Acre and Rio Branco are two hours behind eastern Brazil. Fernando de Noronha Island, on the other hand, is one hour ahead of eastern Brazil.

In case of doubt, dial 130 for a speaking clock (in Portuguese).

▬ TIPPING

It is customary to tip hotel employees, tour guides, hairdressers, and others, according to your assessment of the service rendered. An average tip in both hotels and restaurants is 10-15% (unless it has been included in your bill). You do not need to tip taxi-drivers, although most people let the driver 'keep the change'.

■ TOURIST INFORMATION

Every Brazilian state and large city boasts a tourist office. It will provide you with the *Guia Quatro Rodas*, which lists hotels, restaurants and camping sites.

The official Brazilian tourist agency is called **Embratur**. Its central office is in Rio de Janeiro, on Rua Mariz e Baros near Praça de Bandeira ☎ (021) 273 2212. They can answer questions in English.

■ TRANSPORTATION

The most important fact to bear in mind when traveling in Brazil is its huge size. Because of this and because so much of the country is rural, it is easy to lose your way. Don't hesitate to ask for directions — it's the only way to make sure that you're going the right way. Not all areas are well marked and you will find that you are given conflicting information quite often.

By air

Air travel is the most practical way to get about in a country as large as Brazil. Flights within Brazil are normally expensive but you can purchase the economical **Brazil Air Pass** from all major airlines and travel agencies handling international flights to Brazil. It must be purchased with your international ticket before you leave home.

The pass is good for 21 days and buys an unlimited number of flights inside Brazil on **Varig/Cruzeiro**. These flights may be either part of an itinerary or may take you back and forth between a given departure point. The Brazil Air Pass costs (at the time of going to press) US$330 for adults, US$165 for children from two to 12 years of age and US$33 for children under two years old.

You can establish your itinerary before you leave for Brazil or upon arrival in the country. Only one Air Pass is allowed per person. Baggage allowance is 44 lb/20 kg per person and the only local cost is an airport arrival tax of approximately US$10. The pass allows you to return to the point of entry, but you can never fly the same route twice. Certain Brazilian hotels will give discounts of up to 30% to people traveling on the Air Pass.

Regular flights within Brazil are very expensive. For instance, a round-trip from Rio to Manaus costs more than an entire Air Pass. From Rio, there are daily shuttle flights to São Paulo (44 per day), Brasília (20 per day) and Belo Horizonte (15 per day). There is also regular jet service between Rio and São Paulo.

The domestic market is served by three companies: Varig/Cruzeiro, Vasp and Transbrasil. All have offices in major cities and all are reliable. Small regional companies, also reliable, include **Nordeste** (for Nordeste region), **Riosul** (for south), **Taba** (for Amazonas), and **Tam** and **Votec** (both for the south-eastern and central regions).

By train

Because service is uncomfortable and slow, few people travel by train in Brazil. Trains connect all the large cities, but the only ones recommended are the night train from Rio to São Paulo and the day train from Rio to Belo Horizonte. If, however, you enjoy train travel and have time to spare, Brazil's antiquated trains offer the unique experience of traveling as in days gone by. The following routes pass through the loveliest parts of the country.

● São Paulo to Santos (down the Serra to the sea).
● São Paulo to Corumba (at the Bolivian Border).

- Rio to Belo Horizonte (up the slopes of the Serra).
- Curitiba to Paranaguá (down the Serra to the sea).

By bus

Travel by bus is both economical and relatively fast. Tickets cost about one-fifth the price of going by air (one-third if you buy a sleeper ticket). These buses are generally less comfortable than their counterparts in the United States or Great Britain, except for those that travel the main highways between Rio and São Paulo. They are generally not air-conditioned.

Surprisingly, given the large distances involved, buses do usually run to schedule. From São Paulo to Rio you can get direct buses to all of the large cities. In all large cities local buses provide service (not nearly so comfortable or punctual, though) to the smaller cities and towns.

Tickets are sold either in bus stations or in certain travel agencies. It is wise to reserve a seat at least one day ahead of time.

By car

Some of the Brazilian road network is well developed, especially in the southern regions. Generally, the roads between the major cities are paved. You will, however, find simple dirt roads that cannot be avoided on a trip into the interior. In addition, certain areas become inaccessible when the rains cause floods.

If you choose to travel by car, note that driving is on the right and that the speed limit on highways is 50 mi/80 km per hour. You will need an international driver's license.

Always check before starting out to make sure that your car is in good condition and that the roads leading to your destination are open. Try to fill up as often as possible since service stations can be 60 mi/100 km apart. Note, too, that practically all of them are closed on Sundays. Most Brazilian cars run on sugarcane-based ethanol, which is cheaper than petrol.

In general, we do not recommend using a car to get around the major cities. Brazilians have a reputation for reckless driving, the cities abound in one-way streets, and parking is often difficult to find. On the other hand, a car can be useful to visit the environs of Rio and São Paulo, for example.

Tourist maps of Brazil are few and fairly rudimentary. In the major cities you can buy detailed city maps at news-stands. If you are coming to Brazil from the United Kingdom, you might pick up a copy of the **Bartholomew** World Travel Series Map of *Brazil and Bolivia*.

In the event of an accident, no matter how slight, the police must be called (for insurance purposes).

Car rental

All the larger cities have branches of companies like Hertz and Avis. Renting a car from them means that you will have a car that is properly insured and in good condition. The cost is approximately the same as in Europe or North America. Note there is a regional tax of about 5%.

By boat

Despite the large number of Brazilian waterways, they are seldom used for transportation. The most established routes, if you wish to see the countryside by boat, are :

- From Belém to Manaus (via the Amazon River).
- From Pirapora to Juazeiro (via the São Francisco River).
- Smaller stretches on the rivers Paraná, Paraguai and Araguaia.

All of the large cities on the coast are connected by regular, but infrequent, boat services. There are also cruises (25-30 days) that sail from Santos or Rio to Argentina or northwards towards Belém.

BRAZIL IN THE PAST

Officially, Brazil was discovered on April 22, 1500, by Pedro Alvares Cabral, who was looking for a western route to India. He landed at Porto Seguro (between Salvador and Rio de Janeiro). There is evidence, however, that Brazil's coast may have been explored long before by the Phoenicians, and it is almost certain that its existence was known to navigators after Christopher Columbus's first voyage in 1492.

In 1494, with the Treaty of Tordesillas, the pope designated a meridian 370 leagues to the west of the Cape Verde Islands, dividing the New World in half. According to this treaty, all land west of the line was to be Spain's, all land east Portugal's. This line ran close to the mouth of the Amazon River not far from Belém, which meant that Brazil was designated as Portuguese before it had even been explored.

THE COLONIZATION OF BRAZIL

During the first quarter of the 16th century, the Portuguese, continuing their lucrative trade with India, paid scant attention to the new territory. The French, meanwhile, who did not recognize the Treaty of Tordesillas, were smuggling out vast quantities of *pau-brasil,* a kind of redwood tree containing a much-sought-after dye. These early traders or *brasileiros* referred to the new territory as the 'land of brazil' and before long it came to be known simply as Brazil.

In 1530, a Portuguese expedition was sent to Brazil to counter the French presence. Most of the coastline was explored and two permanent settlements were founded, one in the south at São Vicente (near Santos), the other in the north at Olinda (near Recife). In 1534, Portugal further secured its hold on the territory by setting up the same colonial system that had proved successful in its other possessions. The country was divided into 15 provinces, known as captaincies, which were given to 12 of the king's subjects. The system was meant to establish Portuguese

A Portuguese bandeirante *in Goiâna — these explorers opened up the Brazilian interior in the 17th century.*

control over Brazil without using the funds of the royal treasury. Each donee was responsible for the prosperity and defense of his tract of land.

Fifteen years later, with all but two captaincies in complete ruin, a central authority was set up with Tomé de Souza as governor-general, and Bahia (now Salvador) as the seat of the colonial government. Bahia was to remain the capital of Brazil for the next 214 years.

Sugarcane soon became an important crop and slaves from Africa were imported to work on the sugar plantations.

SPANISH RULE
AND THE QUEST FOR LAND

In 1580, Philip II of Spain also became King of Portugal. The two countries lived under the same rule until 1640. At that time Portugal regained its sovereignty under the Duke of Braganza, who was proclaimed King of Portugal as Dom João IV. During the 60-year period of Spanish rule, Spain's enemies also became the enemies of Portugal — and did all they could to establish a foothold in Brazil.

In 1587, English pirates attacked Salvador and went on to ravage Santos, São Vicente, Olinda and Recife. In 1612, the French took possession of Maranhão and founded São Luis, but they were driven out in 1615.

The most devastating invasions, however, were made by the Dutch, whose West India Company was searching for lands on which to plant sugarcane. The Dutch were defeated in Salvador in 1624, but succeeded in settling in the region of Pernambuco (Recife and Olinda) in 1637. They stayed in this area for 17 years, during which time they were responsible for an astonishing degree of economic expansion. Their presence prompted Indians, blacks and Portuguese to join together for the first time.

As long as Portugal and Spain were united under one crown, the boundaries between their overseas colonies ceased to exit. Groups of adventurers known as *bandeirantes* progressed further and further into Brazil in search of gold, gems and Indians. The largest of these expeditions set out from São Paulo, Salvador, Olinda, São Luis and Belém, with the blessing of the Portuguese government. In 1637, Pedro Texeira traveled up the Amazon with 2000 men and managed to reach Quito, now the capital of Ecuador.

Expeditions organized to conquer the Norte and Nordeste regions set out from Recife and went as far as French Guiana. Jesuit missionaries, who had launched a full-scale venture to convert the natives, helped penetrate the country's interior. However, in south and central Brazil, the Spanish Jesuits were blamed for much of the trouble with the Indians and were driven out of Brazil. In 1674, Fernão Dias Paes explored the Minas Gerais region, opening the way for the discovery of gold, which was found there 20 years later.

THE SUPREMACY OF GOLD
AND THE EARLY UPRISINGS

The same spirit of unity that had once focused all Brazilians' energy against the Dutch now turned against Portugal. Feelings of discontent about slavery, labour conditions and Jesuit activities began to converge. The first uprisings against the colonial government took place in Pernambuco in 1666, followed shortly after by those in Maranhão in 1684.

Many slaves took advantage of these upheavals and fled to the interior, where they set up a tribal hierarchy. They built fortified villages known as *quilombos* and often set out in armed bands to attack towns or farms. The largest of these settlements was Quilombo dos Palmares in Alagoas (see p. 163). It was razed in 1694 on orders of the Governor of Pernambuco.

Between 1700 and 1720, the taxes levied by the Portuguese on gold and the rivalry between Paulistas (residents of São Paulo), Mineiros (residents of Minas Gerais) and Portuguese merchants led to a new series of rebellions, which included the wars of Emboadas (Minas Gerais), Mascates (Olinda), the Bahia mutiny and the mutiny at Vila Rica (now Ouro Preto).

The gold mines were among Portugal's main source of wealth at this time. They also brought prosperity to Brazil's southern provinces where the cities of São Paulo and Rio de Janeiro developed as the ports that shipped gold overseas. Other provinces also benefited by providing the economic underpinning for the gold-mining area.

During the 18th century, Brazil was once again at war with France and Spain because Portugal had become allied with England in the struggle for the Spanish succession. The French attacked Rio de Janeiro in 1710 and in 1711, while the Spanish invaded the south and founded the *colonia do Sacramento*. A series of treaties with France and Spain finally brought an end to the border skirmishes. In 1762, Brazil became a Portuguese dominion governed by a viceroy, and in 1763 Rio de Janeiro was declared the capital of Brazil.

REVOLUTIONARY MOVEMENTS
AFTER 1789

The American and French revolutions and the liberal ideas encountered by the sons of wealthy families sent to Europe for their education contributed to a movement for independence. The principal ideas of this movement were behind the *Inconfidência Mineira* and the *Inconfidência Baiana*.

The *Inconfidência Mineira* rebellion of 1789 grew out of Portugal's insistence that a specific yearly quantity of gold be handed over, despite the mines' having been gradually depleted. The ideas of José da Silva Xavier, known as Tiradentes, served to focus the rebellion. Tiradentes, who was based in Vila Rica (present-day Ouro Preto), advocated the abolition of slavery and the creation of a republic, among other things. This rebellion was betrayed by one of its members, and Tiradentes was hanged and then beheaded in Rio de Janeiro on April 21, 1792.

The *Inconfidência Baiana* uprising of 1797 was a reaction against the harsh rule of the Portuguese governors. Once again, it was betrayed before it could get off the ground, and the rebels were executed.

THE ARRIVAL OF THE KING AND THE DECLARATION OF INDEPENDENCE

Napoleon invaded Portugal in 1807. On the advice of the British, Dom João VI fled to Brazil with his entire court and settled in Rio de Janeiro in 1808. His arrival marked the beginning of a new era of prosperity for Brazil: its ports began to welcome foreign ships (only Portuguese vessels had been admitted up until then), immigration was permitted, and new industries (previously forbidden) were established. Schools and universities were created, printing presses established and, with them, books and newspapers. A modern economy suddenly came to life and made rapid progress.

In 1808, Brazil invaded and annexed French Guiana (returning it to France in 1817, two years after Napoleon's fall). Dom João VI also annexed Uruguay (then the *Provincia Cisplatina*) in 1821. There were two uprisings at this time, in Ceará and Pernambuco, which were ruthlessly suppressed.

In 1820, a revolution suddenly flared up in Portugal, forcing the king to return and draw up a new constitution. On April 26, 1821, Dom João VI sailed for Portugal, taking his entire family except for his son, Dom Pedro, who stayed behind as regent. He also took the Bank of Brazil's gold reserves. Once again Brazil was a Portuguese colony.

In his role as regent, Dom Pedro did all he could to lessen colonial animosity toward the home country, introducing liberal measures that were frowned upon by the Crown. Dom Pedro was ordered to return home, but in a historic proclamation made on January 9, 1822, he refused. One month later, he declared that no measure decreed by Portugal was to be enacted without his approval. An attempted revolt by a Portuguese general, Avilez, was put down, and Portuguese reinforcements were repelled as they tried to land. Upon his return from a military inspection in the São Paulo region, Dom Pedro was informed by a messenger that Portugal had cancelled all his decrees and had declared him a mere governor answerable to the Crown. He was so angry that he declared independence on the spot, in the presence of his guard of honour, on September 7, 1822.

After he was crowned emperor of Brazil, Dom Pedro had to contend with insurgents, both Portuguese rebels and others whose aim was to transform Brazil into a republic. A year of armed struggle finally drove the Portuguese from Brazil. The United States was the first country to recognize Brazilian independence in 1824. Portugal followed suit in 1825.

THE FIRST EMPIRE

Serious internal conflicts and Dom Pedro's dissolution of the Constituent Assembly led to a host of problems. The Provincia Cisplatina seceded from Brazil and became the Eastern Republic of Uruguay in 1828. Upon the death of his father, Dom João VI, Dom Pedro I decided to accept the Portuguese crown, which tarnished his image in Brazil and gave rise to further revolutionary movements. To avert a civil war, he abdicated in favour of his five-year-old son.

A succession of regents took over, and the government was faced with one revolutionary movement after another: the *Cabanagem* in Pará, the *Sabinada* in Bahia, the *Balaiada* in Maranhão and the famous *Farrapos* or *Farroupilha* revolt in Rio Grande do Sul, which lasted ten years.

Finally, in 1840, Dom Pedro II turned 15 and ascended the throne. At this time, the precarious Brazilian economy was based on slave labour, the export of its crops, and the import of manufactured goods. In the south, however, coffee was on its way to becoming an important source of revenue, while in the northern forests the first rubber trees were being tapped.

THE SECOND EMPIRE

The reign of Dom Pedro II marked a turning point for Brazil. Thanks to its production of coffee, it was about to become an economic force to be reckoned with on the international market.

No sooner had Dom Pedro II been crowned emperor than he had to pacify the same provinces that had rebelled against his father: the *Balaiada* revolt in Maranhão was crushed in 1840 and the *Farroupilha* rebellion in 1845. He also had to contend with upheavals in Minas Gerais in 1842 and in Pernambuco in 1845. In 1850, Brazil went to war against the Argentinian dictator, Rosas, in defense of Uruguay, and in 1864, Brazil had to fight against Uruguay over border violations.

All of these events culminated in the great war against Paraguay that lasted from 1865 to 1870. The dictator of Paraguay, Francisco Solano Lopez, was anxious for his country to have an outlet to the sea and invaded Argentina, Uruguay and Brazil. This resulted in a triple alliance of the offended countries and a resounding defeat for Paraguay. The curious fact is that Brazil was magnanimous in victory and claimed neither territorial nor financial damages.

THE ABOLITION OF SLAVERY

The war with Paraguay led to a string of social upheavals inside Brazil. Ever since 1831, the British had been advocating the abolition of the slave trade. In 1850, Dom Pedro II had put a halt to the importation of slaves despite strong opposition from coffee and sugar planters. Subsequently, when whites and blacks fought side by side against Paraguay, the notion of abolition gained such headway that, once the fighting was over, black veterans were set free. On September 28, 1871, a law known as *Ventre Libre* stipulated that all children of slaves born after that date would be free. Soon, all slaves over the age of 65 were also given their freedom and, on May 13, 1888, Princess Isabella, acting as regent while Dom Pedro II was in Europe, signed the Aurea Decree, which put an end to all slavery.

Brazil, meanwhile, had become such an important coffee producer that by 1870 it held a world monopoly. Sugar production was on the wane, although it still ranked second among exported crops. Other important crops included tobacco, cocoa and, as the Second Empire drew to a close, rubber.

Politically, the old republican ideas had never really died. In the aftermath of the war with Paraguay, the resentment of the large landowners over the abolition of slavery was such that it came as no surprise when, on November 15, 1889, Marshall Deodoro da Fonseca, with solid army backing, proclaimed Brazil a republic. The imperial family had no choice but to flee to Europe. Brazil's first constitution was drawn up, modeled on that of the United States.

THE FIRST REPUBLIC

The first republic lasted from 1889 to 1930. Of all the governments that held sway during this time, the one headed by Rodrigo Alves (1902-1906) was the most progressive. His Minister for Foreign Affairs, Baron de Rio Branco, managed to solve all of the age-old border issues with outstanding skill — he is particularly remembered for persuading Bolivia to give up the Acre territory. Other famous presidents of the first republic include Floriano Peixoto, Alfonso Pena, Epitácio Pessoa and Washington Luís.

The republic had to contend with many rebellious situations: the Federalist Revolution and the army revolt in the south (1893-1895), the Canudos campaign in Bahia (1897), the Contestado campaign in Santa Catarina (1915), the Juazeiro rebellion (1914) and the revolutions of 1923, 1924 and 1930. This last revolution brought to power Getúlio Vargas, who was to alter the very character of the regime.

During the 19th century, Brazil grew into an important economic power thanks to its production of rubber. After 1910, however, this production was gradually abandoned because of British competition from rubber plantations in Asia.

The country entered World War I in 1917, after Germany had sunk a fair number of its merchant ships. The end of the first republic was marked by an economic recession caused by the crash of the stockmarkets of 1929. This resulted in, among other things, the end of Brazil's coffee monopoly.

THE SECOND REPUBLIC
AND GETÚLIO VARGAS

From 1930 until 1945, Brazilian politics were dominated by Getúlio Vargas. He first headed the second republic's provisional government (1930-1934), then was given a three-year presidential mandate (1934-1937) after being elected by the Constituent Assembly and, finally, went on to extend that mandate by establishing a military dictatorship. This last period was known as the *Estado Novo* (new state). It took the form of a strongly centralized bureaucracy, body politic and economy.

There were a number of social upheavals that shook the country during this time, such as the communist uprising of 1935 and the *integraliste* movement of 1938. The most famous of these, however, was the regime's 20-year war in the Nordeste region against the *cangaceiros.* These *cangaceiros,* whose name derived from the way they overloaded their shoulders with weapons (*canga* means 'yoke'), were well-organized gangs of outlaws who operated more or less at the behest of local politicians, looting villages and bringing death and destruction to the whole region until 1940. The most notorious *cangaceiro* was Virgulino Ferreiro, known as Lampião. He was finally caught and put to death in 1940.

Brazil entered World War II on August 22, 1942. Navy and air force bases were built in the Nordeste region, and Brazilian forces were instrumental in keeping the Axis out of the southern Atlantic. In 1944, Brazilian soldiers joined forces with American troops in Italy.

The slump in the coffee market, which began under the first republic, worsened during the second. To maintain prices, the government went as far as ordering the burning of all coffee reserves. Fortunately, the downturn in the economy was compensated for by the industrial expansion of Rio de Janeiro and São Paulo and by growth in the agricultural sector in northern Paraná.

THE NEW REPUBLIC
AND THE COUP D'ETAT OF 1964

After the fall of Getúlio Vargas, the foundations were laid for the *república nova* (new republic) — foundations still in place today. The 1946 constitution turned Brazil into a federal republic comprising 23 states, three territories and one federal district (Brasília). Each state has its own government and administration.

Several great figures have presided over this republic. Getúlio Vargas made a triumphal comeback in 1951, only to commit suicide on August 24, 1954, after having been accused of ruling like a dictator.

From 1956 to 1961, Juscelino Kubitschek, a popular president, inaugurated a series of ambitious enterprises, including the construction of Brasília. In 1960, this became the nation's capital — an amazing feat considering that Brasília sits on an arid plain in the state of Goiás. This and other praiseworthy projects were executed, however, at the expense of the economy, which was beset with runaway inflation (up to 500% a year).

After Kubitschek, João Goulart seemed to be leading the country towards a form of socialism. He nationalized the major industries and made plans for allowing illiterates to vote. Accused of setting the country on the road to communism, he was forced to step down in 1964 when the army seized power in a bloodless coup. Goulart was driven out of the country, and many of his followers also went into exile.

THE MILITARY REGIME AND ECONOMIC BOOM

The government of Castelo Branco, who was president from 1964 to 1967, marked the beginning of an era of army rule and strong presidential powers. Existing political parties were dissolved. The new regime came to power with the backing of the United States, which also provided financial aid to help get the economy back on its feet. Political activity was channeled into two officially sanctioned parties: the ARENA, which backed the regime, and the MDB, which constituted the legally authorized opposition.

Gradually, however, the regime hardened its stance when Marshall Costa e Silva (1967-1969) and General Emilio Garrastazu Medici (1969-1974) came to power. On December 13, 1968, Institutional Act V gave the president the power to govern by decree. Strict censorship was imposed and purchasing power was curtailed on the grounds that inflation must be curbed. The opposition retaliated with kidnappings and muggings of foreign diplomats, bank robberies, and other acts of subterfuge. Repressive countermeasures by the government were ruthless. Paramilitary death squads began to sow terror, and on the initiative of Dom Helder Camara, Archbishop of Recife, a number of the clergy joined the opposition.

While all this political terror was going on, the Brazilian economy prospered. Foreign capital poured in, multinational companies invested in Brazil, and the rate of inflation dwindled from 140% to 20% a year. Brazil's economic boom led the government to launch various ambitious projects like the 2175 mi/-3500 km Transamazonica Highway, from the Bolivian frontier to the east coast, and Mobral, an educational project launched to wipe out illiteracy. Opponents of the government accused it of using these projects to flatter national pride, divert attention from its social policies, and unite public opinion around the notion of nationalism. Brazil was now in the forefront of South America and had become a serious competitor of Europe in African and Middle Eastern markets. Its annual rate of economic growth was more than 10%.

1974 — A WATERSHED YEAR

While the generals' economic triumphs enjoyed broad support, their politics and censorship did not. When General Ernesto Geisel came to power in March 1974, he declared that it was time to liberalize the political system and reintroduce democracy. In February 1979, João Batista Figueiredo became president and followed in Geisel's footsteps. This change in the regime is known as the *abertura* (the 'opening up'). Censorship was lifted, the notorious Institutional Act V of 1968 was abolished, Brazilians living in exile were allowed to return, strikes became legal once again, and the two-party system was scrapped.

Unfortunately, however, the worldwide economic recession brought hardship and unemployment to Brazil, and social unrest followed. During the legislative elections of 1974 and 1978, the opposition won a number of seats, and by November 1982, it held a majority in Parliament. São Paulo metalworkers went on strike, the church hardened its stance, and even Pope John Paul II's visit in 1980 did nothing to quell the turmoil. Street violence was on the rise. Big-city shops and supermarkets were looted every day. People were hungry. By September 1983, the government had no choice but to comply with the demands of the International Monetary Fund and institute austerity measures. One of these measures was to discontinue linking wages to the rates of inflation (over 30% in 1984). As a result of this, the currency's value hit an all-time low.

The economic crisis was coupled with a serious political crisis resulting from the gradual but relentless political awakening of the electorate. The PDS, the party in power and the heir to ARENA, was now faced with a host of opposition parties. Foremost among them were the PMDB, which had grown out of the earlier MDB, the PTB, a right-of-centre party, the PDT, led by Brizola, Governor of Rio de Janeiro, the PT, headed by union leader, Lula, and the PP, a centrist party, led by Tancredo Neves, Governor of Minas Gerais.

Aware of its broad popular support, the opposition sought to promote a direct voting system for presidential elections, organizing mammoth demonstrations of more than one million people in Rio de Janeiro and São Paulo under the slogan *Direitas Ja!* ('Direct Elections now!'). Parliament rejected the proposal on April 25, 1984, but nonetheless, on January 15, 1985, Tancredo Neves became the first civilian elected President of Brazil since 1964. Brazil had turned another page in its long and tumultuous history.

RETURN TO DEMOCRACY: AN OBSTACLE COURSE

Old and ailing, Tancredo Neves never governed. On March 14, 1985, a mere few hours before his ceremonial investiture, he was rushed to the hospital and died after a five-week-long illness, leaving the presidency to his running mate,

Chronology of historical events

1494	Treaty of Tordesillas: the pope designates Brazil Portuguese
1500	Pedro Alvares Cabral discovers Brazil, landing at Porto Seguro
1530	Portugal starts colonization
1532	São Vicente founded, near what is now Santos
1537	Papal bull forbids using Indians as slaves
1548-1850	More than two million Africans brought to Brazil as slaves
1549	Jesuits arrive; Bahia founded (now Salvador)
1624	First Dutch invasions
1674	First *bandeirantes* expedition into Minas Gerais in search of treasure
1700-1800	The gold era
1759	Expulsion of Jesuits
1763	Rio de Janeiro becomes the capital
1789	*Inconfidência Mineira* revolt led by Tiradentes
1808	King Dom João VI of Portugal flees to Brazil
1820	Beginning of Portuguese immigration
1822	Proclamation of Brazilian Independence on September 7; Dom Pedro I installed as emperor
1824	Beginning of German immigration, which continues up until World War II
1827-1915	The rubber boom
1840	Dom Pedro II ascends the throne
1840-1929	The coffee boom
1871	Law known as *Ventre Libre* declares that all children born to slaves will be free
1872	First Brazilian census: 9,930,478 inhabitants
1884	Beginning of Italian immigration, which continues until 1954
1888	*Aurea* law abolishes slavery
1889	Marshall Deodoro da Fonseca proclaims Brazil a republic
1908	Beginning of Japanese immigration
1929	Serious economic crisis; coffee reserves are destroyed
1930-1945	Getúlio Vargas comes to power in a palace revolution; in 1934 he is elected president and in 1937 installs *Estado Novo*
1946	New constitution turns Brazil into a federal republic
1950	Vargas re-elected as president but commits suicide in 1954
1960	Brasília is founded by President Kubitschek (1956-1961)
1964-1985	President João Goulart's fall from power and flight; the armed forces take over
1964-1974	Brazil's economic 'miracle': a growth rate of 10-15% yearly
1968	Promulgation of Institutional Act V giving absolute power to the president, limiting individual liberty, imposing censorship and closing down Congress; period marked by urban guerilla warfare, kidnappings and death-squad raids; many Brazilian intellectuals go into exile
1972	Brazil's population reaches 100 million
1978	Abolition of Institutional Act V; amnesty declared for political exiles
1979-1984	Nordeste hit by a severe drought
1985	Tancredo Neves is elected president but dies on April 21 a few hours before he is to be inaugurated; he is succeeded by Vice President José Sarney
1986-1987	Cruzado Plan, designed to curb inflation and boost economy, fails. Brazil's foreign debt is more than US$114 million; it is in the midst of a severe financial crisis.
1988	The popularly elected Constitutional Assembly of 559 members draws up a new constitution, providing a foundation for Brazil's future development.

Vice President José Sarney. Although an erstwhile supporter of military rule and known as a late-comer to progressive ideas, President Sarney adopted a democratic stance and tackled such issues as land reform, the establishment of a Constituent Assembly and the fight against inflation. He soon ran into many obstacles. Land reform, or the distribution of land to poor, landless peasants, is relentlessly opposed by landowners (4% of whom control 85% of the land). The Catholic Church, on the other hand, openly sympathizes with the poor. The Constituent Assembly has only been in session since February 1987 and is having a hard time making any headway amid widespread public indifference. On December 17, 1989, Fernando Collor was elected president of the country on a platform offering pragmatic solutions to the troubled economy — reduction in the number of civil servants and privatization of State companies. Collor is facing serious problems — the failure of the 1986 Cruzado Plan to lower inflation and the mammoth foreign debt (US$114 billion in 1988) have pushed the country into a recession.

Nevertheless, Brazil's economy continues to grow. With a US$275 billion gross national product, Brazil ranks as the world's 10th largest economy. What's more, with its wealth of natural resources from minerals to hydroelectric power, the country possesses enormous potential. Equally important for future development is its human potential: Brazilians have a strong sense of national pride and determination. These assets will all prove essential in Brazil's struggle to overcome its economic and social difficulties.

BRAZIL TODAY

Foremost among the charms of Brazil are its people and their easy way of expressing their emotions. Joys and sorrows, likes and dislikes, are all expressed with an exuberance that matches the lush and tropical environment. For Brazilians, to live means to feel. They prefer to tolerate any excesses rather than appear aloof and cool.

You'll often hear the following idiomatic expressions — which convey great depth of feeling — applied to many everyday situations:

● *saudade* is the feeling of loss or longing for someone or something that has touched you profoundly and is no longer at hand. On your return home you may well look back on your trip with a heart full of *saudade do Brasil.*

● *bagunça* is the state of everyday confusion that Brazilians like to think they can resolve — thus making them feel that they are coping.

● *dar un jeito* means 'to muddle through', thanks to the brainstorm that will miraculously cure any problems caused by the usual *bagunça.*

Another very appealing facet of Brazilian life is that music is everywhere. Almost any event — an anniversary, a national or religious holiday, a soccer match, an electoral or advertising campaign — provides an excuse to dance to the beat of the samba.

The country's customs also add to its charm — the fascination with the occult and a total *joie de vivre.* Brazilians feel that life is a game in which everyone is given a chance.

Daily life in Brazil has elements of the Baroque: witness the houses painted in flamboyant colours, the handcrafted goods, and the decorations you will see on trucks all around the country. It will not take you long to find out that Brazil is a country where anything can happen and usually does. Nothing ever stands still and nothing ever lasts, yet it is a country of extraordinary resilience.

There is nothing delicate about the natural environment either, which is still largely untamed. Hundreds of miles of beach

Over seven varieties of bananas are grown in Brazil, the world's leading producer of this fruit.

lie utterly deserted, and 60% of the land is still in a pristine state. It is a country rife with opportunity for anyone prepared to take a chance. People still prospect for gold and precious minerals.

The very monotony of such vast and uninhabited space makes every town seem like a unique enclave with its own special charm — its physical arrangement, its architecture and its way of life. Whatever you're looking for — adventure or something more sedate — each state has myriad charms.

REGIONS OF BRAZIL

Brazil is divided into 27 administrative units: 23 states, three federal territories and the federal district of Brasília. All of these units fall into five main areas, each of which has its own geographical and cultural characteristics:

• *Norte* region consists of the Amazon basin, with the cities of Belém and Manaus.

• *Nordeste* region comprises all of the small states along the northern coast, including the cities of Salvador, Recife, Natal, Fortaleza and São Luís.

• *Sudeste* region covers what is known as the industrial trio of São Paulo, Rio de Janeiro and Belo Horizonte.

• *Centro-Oeste* region consists of the country's central plateau, containing Mato Grosso and the capital, Brasília.

• *Sul* region comprises the southern states and their cities, Curitiba, Porto Alegre and Florianópolis.

POPULATION

In 1987, the Brazilian population was estimated at 143 million. A little more than 25% of the national territory is inhabited — the rest is virtually empty. Close to 40% of the population inhabits a strip of land along the coast some 60 mi/100 km wide that amounts to only about 8% of the country's territory. São Paulo and Rio de Janeiro with their suburbs alone account for 20 million inhabitants — that's six times more than all of the Amazon region, which covers over 1.3 million sq mi/3.4 million sq km.

More than half of Brazil's population is under the age of 25, and in the poorer areas, families with 10 to 15 children are common. The population of Brazil has grown very quickly due to a high birthrate and successive waves of immigration. In 1872, the population was less than 10 million; in 1900 the census yielded a figure of over 17 million. By 1940 the figure exceeded 41 million and had reached 71 million ten years later. The 1970 census reported over 94.5 million, and today the population grows by 3.7 million a year.

GEOGRAPHY

The first thing to understand about Brazil is that its territory is truly huge. With a surface area of 3,286,470 sq mi/ 8,511,965 sq km, it is the fifth largest country in the world. It covers over half of the South American continent. Its border is 9768 mi/15,719 km long and every South American country except Chile and Ecuador is its neighbour. Its coastline is about 4605 mi/7410 km long.

Brazil consists of one vast plateau, which stretches all along its east coast, and declines gradually towards the west, where it blends into the Amazon and Paraná river basins. At its northern extremity its contours rise and form the boundary with the Guianas and Venezuela. Brazil's mountains are not spectacularly high — the Andes Mountains lie well beyond its borders. Its highest summits are in Minas Gerais, where the tallest peak of the Serra da Mantiqueira range is the Pico da Bandeira (9482 ft/2890 m), and near the Venezuelan border, where the Pico da Neblina rises to 9888 ft/3014 m.

The main water basins are those of the Amazon, São Francisco and Paraná rivers. About 3728 mi/6000 km long, the Amazon is the longest river in the world. It has an estuary 62 mi/100 km long and pours up to 4,942,000 cubic ft/ 140,000 cubic m of water into the Atlantic per second. It sweeps along an average of 3,924,000 cubic yd/3,000,000 cubic m of alluvium per day. The river bed hardly slopes at all, for it only descends by about 213 ft/65 m over a 1864 mi/3000 km distance. The river's main tributaries are the Negro, Purus, Madeira, Tapajos and Xingu, as well as the Tocantins River and its tributary, the Araguaia River, dear to fishermen, which share the Amazon's estuary. Transatlantic ships can sail up the Amazon as far as Manaus, and the river basin has a network of navigable waterways totalling some 10,560 mi/17,000 km in length.

The São Francisco River, 1926 mi/3100 km long, is the second longest river in Brazil and flows through the states of Minas Gerais and Bahia before pouring anywhere between 1076 and 14,352 cubic ft/900 and 12,000 cubic m of water per second into the Atlantic Ocean. Its middle course is navigable for over 620 mi/1000 km. The São Francisco River has always been a crucial factor in the Nordeste region's development.

Together with the Uruguai River, the Paraná River irrigates the southern part of the country. Its main tributary, the Paraguai River, irrigates all of Mato Grosso's south-west before joining the Paraná in Argentina. The Paraná River's rate of flow can be anywhere between 13,080 and 78,480 cubic yd/10,000 and 60,000 cubic m per second.

Temperatures in the Amazon basin are more or less constant and rarely rise above 80° F/27° C. Hardly a day goes by without rain. Along the Nordeste coast (Recife, Salvador), rainfall is also heavy, and summers tend to be hot and humid. The Sertão in the country's interior, where it is very hot, is known for its appalling droughts. In Rio de Janeiro and São Paulo, the humidity hovers around 80% and both temperatures and weather vary considerably. The south has a more temperate climate; rainfall is heavy and temperatures may even drop to freezing point. There are years when, during a single season, Brazil must contend with devastating floods in the Amazon region, drought in Nordeste and a bitter cold wave in the south.

Brazil's vegetation is the product of many different kinds of soil and climate. The result has been diversification and considerable differences in landscape and regional characteristics.

The Amazon basin's equatorial forest takes on different forms. It comprises the *caaeté,* the *varzea* and the *igapo.* The *caaeté* is tall and dense with trees of 130-160 ft/40-50 m tall, rooted in solid earth. The *varzea* consists of thickets of shrubs rooted in moist soil that is periodically flooded. The *igapo* is an area of impenetrable shrubs that grow under the odd tree in soil that is flooded all year round.

● The *mata,* the coastal tropical forest, grows along the central plateau from north to south.

● The *pinheiral* is the pine forest of the south, dominated by the majestic *pinheiro do Paraná,* Paraná pine.

● The *cerrados* or savannas with scattered, stunted trees, lie in the Brazilian heartland, where droughts alternate with heavy seasonal rains. These fairly open spaces, when properly irrigated, can be turned into fertile agricultural land.

● *Caatingas,* areas of thorny shrubs and various kinds of cacti, are found in very dry regions such as the *Sertão* of Nordeste.

● *Palmeirais de babaçus* are lovely palm groves that lie in the northern regions near the Amazon forest.

● *Pantanal,* the area of Mato Grosso that lies in the river basins of the Paraguai and the Araguaia, is flooded for six months of the year.

● *Campos* are vast stretches of grassland that are used for grazing in the southern part of Brazil.

● The coastal areas have a vegetation of their own. Various plants grow on dunes and along the shores of lagoons formed by sandbanks.

ANIMAL LIFE

Brazil's animal life is remarkably varied, especially in the Amazon region and Mato Grosso. The Amazon forest is a huge natural reserve with an incredible number of insects, birds and reptiles. Because of the stable climate, even a few primitive species have been able to survive. The high degree of humidity and high temperatures have led to the development of giant species as well, such as the mygales spider, the steel-blue morpho butterfly, and the anaconda, the largest snake in the world.

The tropical climate has also resulted in extraordinary diversification in other animal life, particularly fish. The best known are the formidable piranhas, a carnivorous species, and the gymnotes (electric eels), which kill their prey with electric shocks. Birds are also spectacular: toucans with red and yellow beaks, multicoloured parrots and hummingbirds. Monkeys come in all shapes and sizes. Hunting is illegal, but allowed in the case of dangerous species such as snakes and crocodiles.

THE BRAZILIAN MELTING POT

The Brazilian people derive from many different ethnic groups and racial mixes — European, African and Indian. Brazilians have specific terms for the various racial mixtures: *mulatos* have black and white ancestors; *caboclos* (or *mamelucos*) are descended from whites and Indians; *cafuzos*'s ancestors are Indian and black. Asians born in Brazil are called *niseis*.

Brazilian authorities have always favoured immigration but have not always managed to control it, and so, large numbers of convicts and various kinds of adventurers poured in for years. Every immigrant was given a plot of land to cultivate but then had to fend for himself. Immigration has now become strictly regulated, and the only applicants allowed to settle are skilled workers needed in particular industries.

The Portuguese were the first to settle in Brazil. By the early 19th century, more than 500,000 had arrived, but the main wave of Portuguese immigration did not occur until 1820. Over one million Portuguese moved to Brazil between 1820 and 1920, and the overall figure since the country's discovery is said to exceed two million. Brazilians have much in common with the Portuguese in the way they live and adapt to their environment. They have inherited the Portuguese's fervent Catholic faith, artistry and gift for building.

Some two million Africans were brought to Brazil between 1548 and 1850, the period of slavery. They came from Guinea, the Congo, Angola and Mozambique and brought with them their own traditions and beliefs. The Portuguese spoken in Brazil is all the richer for the many African words in its vocabulary.

Italians arrived in several waves between 1884 and 1954, almost 1.5 million in all. The first wave came from northern Italy and settled in the southern part of Brazil (Rio Grande do Sul), where they planted wheat and maize and established vineyards. Later arrivals came from southern Italy and settled in São Paulo state, where they worked on the coffee plantations.

Around 1824, Germans were invited to come and till the land, particularly in parts of Rio Grande do Sul. Their traditional Germanic way of life did not integrate with Brazil's and even today entire villages remain adamantly German. The Germans founded two cities in Santa Caterina state that have prospered: Blumenau and Joinville. Later waves of German immigrants joined the industrial sector.

A sizeable group of immigrants from the Near East (Turks, Syrians, Lebanese) live in Brazil and are mostly involved in trade.

The Japanese have been immigrating to Brazil since 1908, settling mostly in São Paulo state, where they have specialized in market gardening and the cultivation of tea, rice, cotton and soya. They have joined forces in vast cooperatives such as the Cotia Agricultural Cooperative in São Paulo. Their integration into the Brazilian community has not been smooth and even today the Japanese colony in Brazil remains a closed one. Japanese are increasingly found in big business circles.

In southern Brazil, large groups of Poles and Russians have settled and there are descendants of the early Dutch colonists living in the north.

THE INDIANS

In the early days of colonization, as the French and Portuguese fought over possession of the land, they exploited existing rivalries between various Indian tribes. Once the Portuguese had triumphed, however, they tried to put the Indians to work on the land as slaves. They organized hunts for Indians on a massive scale. However, the Indian cultures were such that the Indians could not endure slavery — if there was no chance to escape, many preferred to commit suicide.

After the Portuguese had solved their labour needs by bringing in African slaves, they regarded the Indians as obstacles to the development and expansion of their plantations. The Indian tribes were virtually decimated as a result of murderous raids and their lack of resistance to European diseases such as influenza, measles and smallpox. Consumption of alcohol further ravaged the tribes.

It is estimated that, when the Portuguese arrived, Indians numbered between two and three million. Some tribes, such as the Tupinambas, the Tamoios and the Carijos, are extinct, while others have been greatly reduced. Today, there are approximately 100,000 Indians (optimists put the figure as high as 250,000). Of the estimated 143 known tribal groups, 33 live in the Amazon region, 29 in Mato Grosso, 22 in Pará and the rest in Maranhão, Nordeste and the south. The best known tribes are the Xavantes, the Xingus, the Karajas, the Guaranis, the Kayapos, the Kaingangas and the Araras.

Ethnologists distinguish 11 cultural divisions among present-day Indian tribes. However, these ethnic categories do not necessarily correspond with linguistic ones. It is customary to classify the following linguistic groups.

● Aruaks in southern Mato Grosso and along the Colombian border ((23 tribes).
● Tupis in southern Mato Grosso and Maranhão (26 tribes).
● Macro-jes in the south, the central plateau and Maranhão (18 tribes).
● Panos near the Peruvian border and in the western part of the Amazon region (12 tribes).
● Kirianas (five tribes).

Thirty-seven other tribes have never been classified linguistically.

The treatment of Indians has been the subject of much controversy. Even in the early days of colonization some Brazilians raised their voices against the slaughter of Indians. Chief among them were the Jesuit Father Antonio Vieira, the writer-politician José Bonifacio de Andrade, and the philosopher Texeira Mendes, all of whom felt that Indians should be protected under the Brazilian Constitution. Their protests had little effect and progress was only made when Marshall Candido Rondon arrived.

Candido Rondon (1865-1958) was commissioned to set up a telegraph network in the Brazilian interior (Mato Grosso). In the course of this work, it was inevitable that he would come across various Indian tribes. Through his interaction with the Indians, he grew to love and respect their cultures. His travels (covering some 30,000 mi/50,000 km throughout the Mato Grosso and the Amazon region) and the extensive contact he had with the Indians made him acutely aware of and enormously sympathetic to the Indians' plight. In 1910, he persuaded the Brazilian government to set up a Service for the Protection of Indians.

Francisco Meireles (1908-1968) was also active on behalf of the Indian cause. As a civil servant with Rondon's Service for the Protection of Indians, he did outstanding work for the Indians throughout his life. His son, Apoema, has followed in his footsteps.

The brothers Villas Boas (Claudio, Alvaro, Leonardo and Orlando) devoted their lives to the protection of Indians and were responsible for the creation of the first Indian reservation, Xingu Park, in 1961. Claudio, in fact, spent nine years there, never leaving once. The Villas brothers have done a mammoth job of helping Indians in the Amazon region, building airfields and setting up bureaus.

In 1967, a government body, Fundação Nacional do Indio (FUNAI), was founded to defend the indigenous population. It assists Indians in medical and educational matters, in their dealings with the police, and with administration of land and civil rights. FUNAI has established numerous hospitals, schools and welfare centres. The Indian situation is highly complex, however, and FUNAI routinely comes under fire. Its resources are very limited and its specialists are asked to perform miracles.

In an effort to preserve tribal groups, FUNAI has created special reservations with educational and health facilities. A large number of tribes live in each of these reservations, although, sadly, some of them were transported there by force. The reservations are off-limits to virtually all outsiders. Exceptions are made for scholars, who must apply to FUNAI. Visitors tempted to go on an organized tour from Manaus or Belém to an 'Indian village', should be aware that these villages are fakes, constructed specifically for tourists. An unauthorized visit to an actual Indian habitat is punishable by law.

The following are Brazil's primary Indian reservations:

- Xingu Park in Mato Grosso (7,410,000 acres/ 3,000,000 hectares).
- Araguaia Park on Bananal Island in the state of Goias (4,940,000 acres/2,000,000 hectares).
- Tumucumaque Park near the border with Guyana in the state of Pará (7,000,000 acres/2,800,000 hectares).
- Aripuana Park in Mato Grosso (4,200,000 acres/ 1,700,000 hectares).

An Indian of the Xingu reservation in Mato Grosso.

• Yanomani Park in Roraima (5,430,000 acres/ 2,200,000 hectares).

There are also 17 smaller reservations that shelter a few Indian groups without providing specialized facilities. FUNAI operates 144 offices that maintain contact with isolated groups of Indians.

OCCULT RELIGIONS

Brazil is the largest Catholic country in the world. Magic and spiritualism, however, also play a very large part in Brazilian life. These occult practices mirror the complexities of the Brazilian culture, forming a unique national blend of Christianity, spiritualism and African cults.

Afro-Brazilian cults used to be forbidden by the government, but as the cults persisted and became the subject of a number of sociological studies, the government decided to bow to both the Brazilians' need for a past and to the requirements of the tourist industry. It first accepted these creeds as major components of Brazilian folklore and, subsequently, as bona fide religions. A Brazilian will often tell you that he doesn't know a thing about any of this nonsense and then volunteer the odd detail or explain why he thinks one or the other of these beliefs might deserve serious consideration, even though he, himself, of course, has nothing to do with it. Then he will tell you that he just happens to know someone who… and so forth.

Candomblé is a cult that was brought to Brazil by African slaves. It is an age-old religious tradition rooted in African culture. Although the Portuguese were strict Catholics, they didn't interfere in the beliefs of their slaves. Often, black nannies taught their white charges to revere spirits and the forces of nature, particularly on the sugar plantations of Nordeste.

Little by little these more or less secret practices turned into ceremonies, and it seems that, around 1830, they began to take the form of scheduled seances in Salvador, a city that remains the most important centre of *candomblé*.

The focus of *candomblé* is on the invocation of the forces of nature. These forces enter the body of a medium and speak through him in an African tongue. In return for any help provided, the faithful are asked for gifts and animal sacrifices. The ritual is elaborate and full of mystery, with much ceremony and opulent costumes.

Having learned about the occult from their servants, whites were open to different religions or spiritual experiences. Around 1860, they rushed to read the texts written by Frenchman Allan Kardec, whose books influenced spiritualism all over the world. Levitation and contacting the dead came into fashion, taking hold especially in Rio de Janeiro and São Paulo. It has now developed to such a point that spiritualism societies even run their own schools and hospitals. The spiritualism ritual is simple, requires no particular ceremony or costume, and no offerings are given.

Umbanda dos Caboclos was born about 50 years ago as a system of belief rooted in Indian folklore. A purely national phenomenon, *umbanda* has been very successful and now boasts followers at every level of Brazilian society. There are more than 95,000 officially registered *umbanda* centres, and the doctrine is gaining ground throughout Latin America. Its followers invoke spirits who express themselves via a medium. Offerings are requested but there is no animal sacrifice. The ritual and the doctrine contain elements of Catholicism, *candomblé,* indigenous beliefs, spiritualism and cabalist theories and add up to a form of religious practice that is uniquely Brazilian. *Umbanda* is also known as white magic.

Quimbanda is a cult whose origins are obscure, but it seems to have evolved around the same time as *umbanda* and is its very opposite. While *umbanda* aims to do good, *quimbanda*'s goals are purely evil. It operates in secret because it is illegal. Cases of bewitchment and evil spells cast by *quimbanda* practices can be countered by the power of *umbanda*. Quimbanda is also known as black magic.

Macumba is a broad term covering all religious practices rooted in Afro-Brazilian cults, whatever their nature. To understand Brazil and the national mentality, it is important to understand the population's preoccupation with the occult. It is in Rio de Janeiro and Salvador that the Afro-Brazilian cults are most highly developed. Visitors are certain to be dazzled by the rituals, trances and cases of possession, the costumes and the music.

ART AND ARCHITECTURE

Indigenous art

Unlike the Incas and the Aztecs, Brazilian Indians led a semi-nomadic existence in a tropical habitat and, thus, left virtually no traces of their way of life. Any structures that they built consisted of wood and foliage and the only knowledge we have of these constructions comes from observations written by explorers.

Today, body-painting seems to be the last link with the ancient traditional art of the Indians.

Colonial architecture

Colonial architecture dates back to the 16th century. The first colonial houses were made of adobe and wood, and later ones were constructed of stone with whitewashed walls and tiled roofs. They were designed with slavery in mind. On the big plantations, or *engenhos,* a great deal of care was lavished on the master's house; the slaves' quarters on the other hand, were plain. In the cities, wealthy citizens built two-storey houses, or *sobrados,* using the ground floor as a warehouse or slave quarters.

Jesuit missionaries built sober, almost windowless convents and churches, and along the coast, huge fortresses went up. By the end of the 17th century, a number of Brazil's most impressive churches had been built, like the cathedral in Salvador. Around this time, architecture began to show regional characteristics and statuary made of terra cotta or wood, came into vogue.

Baroque art

Baroque art flowered in the 18th century as the rational style of the Renaissance gave way to a new flamboyance. In Brazil this exuberance coincided more or less with the discovery of gold, which led to ornate gilding in Brazilian decoration. It is curious that hardly any of the gold mined in Minas Gerais was used to decorate its local churches, and that the foremost examples can be found in Salvador.

The rush for gold and diamonds in the early 18th century resulted in the construction of many towns in Minas Gerais. The wealth of these towns accounted for the vast number of religious edifices erected in them during the second half of the century. Many of them show the work of Brazil's greatest sculptor, Aleijadinho (see p. 219).

After 1770, the Baroque style gave way to Rococo. Façades became more willowy, interiors less heavily gilded and decorated and structures more sophisticated. Many magnificent examples can still be seen in Ouro Preto.

From the early 19th century, many townhouse façades were covered with *azulejos* (Portuguese-style multi-coloured tiles) and neo-Classical ornaments in stone and ironwork. About this time, the first great farmhouses or *fazendas* were built, as were the 'little palaces' or *palacetes* of the coffee barons.

Historical painting was very much in vogue in the 19th century. The most famous of its practitioners were Meireles, Aleida Junior, Decio Vilares, Belmiro and Visconti.

20th-century trends

Until well into the 1930s, the focus of Brazilian architecture was on town planning and its problems. The arrival of Le Corbusier in 1937 heralded a revolution. His design for Rio de Janeiro's Ministry of Education was executed by a team of young architects who soon became renowned in their own right as leaders in post-war Brazilian architecture: Oscar Niemeyer, permanently associated with Brasília even though he also left his mark on Rio de Janeiro, Belo Horizonte and São Paulo; Lucio Costa, Brasília's designer; Alfonso Reidy and Jorge Machado Moreira. Landscape architect Roberto Burle-Marx was responsible for a revolution in gardening concepts.

The paintings of Anita Malfatti — similar to those of the German Expressionists — were exhibited as early as 1917. It was not, however, until the 1922 Week of Modern Art that the period's novel aesthetic theories found expression in two distinct trends firmly rooted in the Brazilian experience. One of them was lyrical in character and showed up in the landscapes of Tarsila do Amaral and in the sensuous portraits of women by Emiliano di Cavalcanti; the other was Expressionist in character and took form after the economic crisis of 1929, in such socially oriented work as that of Lasar Segall, a Lithuanian who had settled in Brazil in 1924, and, even more so, in the regional scenes depicted by Candido Portinari.

Since World War II Brazilian painting has increasingly echoed the abstract trends of European and American artists.

LITERATURE

Brazilian literature in the 17th century was only a pale reflection of literature on the Iberian peninsula, except for Gregorio de Matos Guerra's satirical poetry about Bahia. In the 18th century though, academies were founded throughout the country. The celebrated Minas Gerais school at Ouro Preto, which included poets Manual da Costa, Basilio da Gama, Alvarenga Peixoto and Antonio Gonzaga, also flourished.

Brazilian literature did not really come into its own until the 19th century when fine novels were written about Brazilian life and history, by such people as José de Alencar *(O Guarani, Iracema),* Joaquim Manuel de Macedo *(A Moreninha),* Antonio de Almeida, Casimiro de Abreu and José Bonifacio de Andrade, all of whom were defenders of the blacks and Indians.

The most remarkable figure in late 19th-century Brazilian literature was the great mulatto novelist Machado de Assis, best known for *Dom Casmurro, Memorias Postumas de Bras Cubas, Quincas Borba* and *Reliquias de Casa Velha.* Other good writers included Raul Pompeia *(O Ateneu),* Aluizio Azevedo, Coelho Neto, Euclides da Cunha, Lima Barreto, Graça Aranha, and the political writer Rui Barbosa. Among poets were Alberto de Oliveira, Vicente de Carvalho, and Cruz e Souza.

In the 20th century, it took the 1922 Week of Modern Art for a modern movement influenced by Cocteau and Cendrars to come to the fore. It was then that such names as Mário

Immaculate white dresses are traditional attire for festivities in Salvador.

de Andrade *(Pauliceia Desvairada* and *Clã do Jabuti)*, Alcantara Machadon, Oswald de Andrade, Guilherme de Almeida and Manuel Bandeira first became familiar to the public.

By 1930, Brazilian literature began to focus on socio-economic issues and regional nuances. Historian and sociologist Gilberto Freyre's classic work on the slave system and the fusion

of Brazil's cultures, *Casa Grande e Senzala*, dates from this period. Novelists wrote passionately about the regions where they were born: Rachel de Queiroz about Ceará, José Lins de Rego about Paraíba, Graciliano Ramos about Alagoas and Erico Verissimo about Rio Grande do Sul. The most famous of them all, Jorge Amado, immortalized Bahia in his books, *Mar Morte,*

Capitães de Areia, Gabriela Cravo e Canela and *Bahia de Todos os Santos.*

The post-war period has produced two outstanding writers, Clarice Lispector and João Guimarães Rosa. Among the important contemporary poets are Carlos Drummond de Andrade, Murilo Mendes, Jorge de Lima, Cecilia Meireles, João Cabral de Melo Neto and Vicinius de Morais.

MUSIC

Brazil's most widespread form of artistic expression is music. It is one of the cornerstones of most Brazilians' lives. First of all there is the *samba.* Hundreds are written for every Carnival, and the best become hits. There are many variations, including the *samba-canção,* in which words and music are crucial to success, and others that include elements of jazz *(bossa nova)* or of rock.

Every region has preserved its musical traditions, as for example the Nordeste *forro* or *frevo* accordion music. Famous names in *musica popular* include João Gilberto, Caetano Velaso, Tom Jobin, Gilberto Gil, Elis Regina, Gal Costa, Milton Nascimento, Chico Buarque and Luís Gonzaga.

In the field of classical music, the first composer of any merit was Carlos Gomes (1836-1896), who was very influenced by Italian opera. Around the same period, Alexander Levy and Henriques Oswald tried to create a specifically Brazilian form of music, something which Alberto Nepomuceno (1864-1920) did with more success later.

It was left to the most outstanding figure in Brazilian music, Heitor Villa-Lobos (1887-1954), to make creative use of popular material. He traveled up and down the country in search of traditional themes, instruments and rhythms. He also had a keen ear for the Amazon region's birdsongs. He wrote music of every description and left a huge body of work. His best known works include *Amazonas, Poems, Rude,* various *choros,* his brilliant chamber-music études and his wonderful *Bachianas Brasileiras.*

Modern composers include Radames Gnatalli, Brasilio Itibere, Camargo Guarnieri, Carlos Nobre, J.A. Almeida Prado, Guerra Peixe, Francisco Mignone, Luís Cosme and Lourenço Fernandez, among others. Two famous Brazilian pianists are Nelson Freire and Magda Tagliaferro.

CINEMA

The most prominent pre-war filmmaker was Humberto Mauro, but very little of his work has survived. The Brazilian film industry did not really come into its own until the 1960s, with the birth of a radical new movement called *cinema novo,* which took a firm stand against the dreary, ordinary productions of the day. Strongly influenced at first by the neo-realism of Italian films, *cinema novo* addressed Brazil's social problems, in particular those of the Nordeste. As early as 1953, a film called *O Cangaceiro* by Lima Barreto had already focused on the peasants' plight and paved the way for *cinema novo*. The hardships plaguing the 'land of drought' served as an inspiration for Rui Guerra's film *Os Fuzis* (1962), Nelson Pereira dos Santos's *Vidas Secas* (1964), and Glauber Rocha's *Deus e Diabo na Terra do Sol* (1964) and *Antonio das Mortes* (1969).

By 1968 when total censorship was imposed, *cinema novo* began to lose vitality. Films became blandly mediocre if not downright vulgar. As the country's political situation has improved, the film industry has begun to revive. Two films made in 1976 leave no doubt about the country's potential: Carlos Diegues' *Xica da Silva* and Bruno Barreto's *Dona Flor e Seus Dois Maridos* (based on a novel by Jorge Amado). Other noteworthy recent films are *O Amuleta de Ogum* by N.P. dos Santos and *Iracema* by J. Bodensky. Now that censorship is a thing of the past, films are making a huge impact on the Brazilian public and they are attracting international attention as well.

SOAP OPERAS

Novelas, as Brazilian soap operas are called, have much in common with this genre and with Cuban and Mexican radio programs as well. In the hands of the powerful Brazilian television company, TV Globo, the fourth largest in the world, the *novela* has been turned into a national obsession. Scheduled to last from six months to one year, these serials are followed closely by all sorts of Brazilians. Full of melodrama and convoluted plots, they blend dream and reality and contain references to national problems and daily events. Others recapture the nostalgic era of colonial Brazil.

Most of the *novelas* have highly original plots. Episodes are shot only a few days before being aired and plots may be modified as the result of an opinion poll or a wave of viewer protests. Their fame has spread beyond Brazil and a number of these programs have been bought by other countries.

THE ECONOMY

Brazil's gross national product (GNP) for 1987 was US$275 billion, ranking it as one of the world's major economic powers (10th largest worldwide, first in Latin America). Yet its gross per capita income is only US$1510, which puts it behind such countries as Venezuela, Argentina and Uruguay. While Brazil is one of the world's 'relatively poor' countries, it has vast natural resources and an extremely diverse economy.

The Brazilian economy runs on a system that combines liberalism with state intervention and is in the process of being thoroughly restructured. The country's massive foreign debt has led those in power to call for an all-out effort to increase exports.

Growth was very high until 1980 but has dwindled since

1981 when the interest on the foreign debt and soaring inflation (227% in 1985) became the most visible symptoms of what was a world crisis rather than a Brazilian one. In February 1986, the Cruzado Plan sought to curb inflation by imposing a wage-price freeze, a move that was greeted with overwhelming approval from the public at large. However, this actually led to a rise in demand and a fall in supply, especially in agricultural products because farmers refused to sell below cost. In 1986, when the situation became critical, prices were freed and inflation hit the sky again. In 1987 Brazil declared a moratorium on interest on its foreign debt.

The inflation rate, more than 10% a month in 1989, continues to be a major concern. Two plans instituted in 1988 and again in 1989 to check it, failed. By mid 1989, strikes became increasingly frequent with workers demanding higher wages to keep up with soaring prices. Fears mounted that the poorer segments of society would turn to rioting and violence, as they had in Argentina in the spring of 1989. Yet, despite Brazil's worrying rate of inflation and enormous foreign debt, many experts remained optimistic. Brazil's economy has its strong points, not the least of which is an enormous productive capacity that translated into a trade surplus of US$19 billion in 1988.

Agriculture

Brazil is second only to the United States as a food exporter. Accounting for approximately 10% of the country's GNP, the country's agricultural production is going through a period of reorganization. Crops such as coffee, soya, sugarcane, orange juice and corn have all been boosted, largely at the expense of staple crops such as beans, rice and cassava. Today, Brazil ranks as one of the world's leading producers of coffee, soya, sugarcane, orange juice, cocoa, corn, cassava, bananas and tobacco. Grain production rose from 50 million tons in 1980 to 70 million in 1989, and with over 130 million head of cattle and 32 million pigs, livestock raising is another important source of income. Finally, with timber covering some 40% of the territory, Brazil's lumber industry is highly developed though deforestation of the Amazonian rain forests over the last two decades has caused worldwide concern (see p. 227). Recently, the Brazilian government has adopted a series of measures destined to control land use in the Amazon.

Mineral deposits

Brazil is the third-largest producer of iron ore in the world (90 million tons a year). The mining of the Carajas deposits in the state of Pará has more than doubled in the last few years. Among other large mineral reserves are manganese, bauxite and tin. Uranium reserves are thought to be large, though not enough is known about these to hazard a guess. As for gold, smuggling makes it difficult to assess the size of its production, but Brazil is certainly one of the world's largest producers.

Industry

Brazil produces about 12 million tons of steel a year. The

Sacks of rubber, once the source of fabulous wealth in Manaus, awaiting transport in Guyana.

industry is largely state-run, but most of its investment comes from foreign sources (US Steel, Thyssen, etc). Until 1981, the automobile industry turned out over one million cars a year, but this industry has been badly hit by the economic crisis and is only now regaining its earlier level. The engineering industry is expanding rapidly and gearing to meet the country's needs of keeping imports at a minimum. Thanks to a protectionist policy, the electronics and telecommunications industries are doing well. The aeronautics industry has scored several successes on the international market with its small reconnaissance planes. The arms industry also does well on the international market for such items as light tanks and spare parts.

Sources of energy

Petrobas, the state-run company in charge of prospecting, refining and distributing oil products, has instituted a large-scale development project. The country's production of crude oil has risen considerably in the last few years: it is now over 30 million tons a year.

The vast hydroelectric potential (over 520 billion kilowatt-hours) of Brazil's great rivers has only been partially harnessed. The gigantic plant at Itaipu on the Paraná River alone produces some 70 billion kilowatt-hours per year. As for nuclear energy, the reactor built at Angra dos Reis has begun to produce electricity, and on September 4, 1987, President Sarney announced to the world that Brazil had mastered the technique of enriching uranium.

Problems and prospects

Brazil has now become a major economic power. It has an infrastructure that has few equals in the Third World and has made remarkable industrial progress. Such success has had its price: the foreign debt now stands at over US$114 billion. Large-scale expansion has also led to huge disparities among regions and social classes. The Nordeste, for example, remains an enclave of poverty compared to the dynamic south. The great landowning class continues to hold power over the rural sector. People living on the fringes of large industrial cities are desperately poor and have no opportunities to share in the country's economic growth. The 1985 election brought a civilian to power, and the country's return to democracy now very much depends on the success of its economy.

RIO DE JANEIRO

In Brazil they say that 'God created the world in six days; the seventh he devoted to Rio'. Today, even the aggressive-looking skyscrapers do little to mar the amazing natural beauty of this city, which lies between vast mountains blanketed by tropical forests and a majestic coastline that boasts some of the most beautiful beaches in the world.

Portuguese navigator Gonçalo Coelho was the first to discover the area on January 1, 1502. Sailing into Guanabara Bay, where Rio is now situated, he was impressed by the force of the current and immediately assumed he had entered a river, and so named it *Rio de Janeiro* ('January River').

Surprisingly, the Portuguese initially paid little attention to the area. It was the French, under Admiral Villegaignon, who first settled here in November 1555. The admiral had high hopes of turning the region into a colony, but the dream was short-lived. In 1565, Mem de Sá, the third governor of Brazil, reclaimed the territory and, in the same year, founded the town of São Sebastião do Rio Janeiro, named in honour of the king of Portugal, Dom Sebastião.

By the 17th century, Rio had become a prosperous city, thanks to its thriving sugar trade. The area's wealth and status increased with the discovery of gold in Minas Gerais, and in 1763 the city became the seat of the viceroy. Then, following Brazil's independence in 1834, Rio became the capital of the country. It remained so until Brasília took its place in 1960.

The arrival of the exiled King Dom João VI in 1808 brought European culture to Rio in abundance. The city became obsessed with building and still is today. As a result, Rio is made up of an extraordinary mélange of ornate 18th- and 19th-century architecture — most prominent along the Avenida Rio Branco — and Brazilian modern architecture, which became prominent in 1937 with the construction of Rio's controversial Ministry of Education by Oscar Niemeyer. Perhaps the best example of this unique style is the lovely Museum of Modern Art, which was built by Alfonso Reidy in 1958 and serves as a focal point of the city. Meanwhile, along the Avenido República do Chile, you will find examples of Rio's penchant for futuristic architecture, such as its new 263-ft/80-m-high cone-shaped cathedral.

Rio is indeed a stunning city, yet it is not the beauty and gaiety of the city that will first attract the attention of visitors flying into Rio de Janeiro International Airport. It is the gap between the rich and poor neighbourhoods that the traveler sees first. On the north side of the city lies a labyrinth of dismal streets lined with factories and makeshift housing, while in the southern zone rises the legendary world of luxury hotels, chic cafés that never close, and magnificent beaches like Copacabana and Ipanema. Here on the south side, the sound of samba vies with the din of the traffic. Despite the frenetic atmosphere of this city, the Cariocas (inhabitants of Rio) are a relaxed, easy-going people. For natives and tourists alike, a perfect day in Rio has three parts: the beach in the morning, a stroll through streets lined with art galleries and elegant boutiques in the afternoon, followed by samba and good conversation in the evening.

Unquestionably the most important event of the year in Rio is Carnival, which takes place in late February or early March (see p. 72). From Saturday to Tuesday, the city is one enormous explosion of colour, music and dance. Sumptuous decorations line the streets depicting Carnival themes, all of which have a religious base or else derive from Brazilian folklore.

During Carnival, exotic parades follow one another night and day. Normally, these begin with the *blocos,* small neighbourhood groups. Afterward come the samba schools, which represent different quarters of the city and may consist of up to 3000 people. These parades are the high point of Carnival. The people taking part will have been preparing for at least six months and may have saved all year to pay for their costumes.

For the inhabitants of Rio, Carnival is their reward for a year of hard work — a time when they can forget all their worries and let the sound of samba lift their spirits sky high.

Umbanda (white magic)

The ceremonies of *umbanda,* religious rites that derive from Afro-Brazilian mystical traditions, are practiced throughout Rio and are an important part of Brazilian culture. The main ceremonies take place in *terreiros,* of which there are hundreds throughout the state.

The mediums who preside over the ceremonies wear different coloured necklaces depending on which saint they represent — there are seven main divinities worshipped by Brazilians. After various purifying rites, the mediums are 'possessed' by their divinity and go into a trance. They are then ready to give advice to people in the audience who ask for help. In return, votive offerings are left for the divinities such as candles, food and drink. You will come across them everywhere — on street corners, beaches and in forests. Be careful not to disturb these offerings as they are a sacred part of *umbanda* ritual.

Parades by the samba schools are the major attraction of Rio's Carnival.

▬ PRACTICAL INFORMATION

Telephone area code: 021

When to go

Rio's climate is pleasant year round. In winter (June to August), temperatures average between 63° F/17° C and 72° F/23° C. From September to November the weather is variable, with frequent short downpours almost every day. Summers (December to March) are humid (which makes the beaches extremely crowded). Temperatures average between 72° F/23° C and 95° F/35° C.

Access

Plane

Rio de Janeiro is the main gateway to Brazil from Europe and North America. Its new and technologically advanced international airport, **Rio de Janeiro International Airport** (☎ 398 5050), is served by all major airlines and has direct air service with many cities in the United States, Canada and Europe (see p. 12). It also offers connecting flights to all South American capitals.

From the airport regularly scheduled buses run into the city, stopping at all major hotels. So do fixed-rate taxis.

Another airport, **Santos Dumont**, Centro, II, D2 (☎ 220 7728), five minutes from downtown Rio de Janeiro, has a shuttle link-up with São Paulo.

Aerolineas Argentinas, Rua São José 40, ☎ 221 4255.
Air Canada, Av. Mal Câmara 160, Centro, ☎ 240 1622.
Air France, Av. Rio Branco 257, Centro, I, C2, ☎ 220 8661.
Alitalia, Av. Presidente Antonio Carlos 40, Centro, I, D2, ☎ 210 2192.
American Airlines, Rua da Assembléia 10, Centro, I, C2, ☎ 221 9455.
British Airways, Av. Rio Branco 108, Centro, I, C2, ☎ 242 6020.
British Caledonian, Rua Uruguaiana 10, Centro, I, C2, ☎ 252 9728.
Continental Airlines, Rua da Assembléia 10, Centro, I, C2, ☎ 222 5161.
Cruzeiro, Av. Alm Silvio de Noronha 365, ☎ 297 5141.
Iberia, Rua Pedro Lessa 41, ☎ 262 8885.
Pan Am, Av. Presidente Wilson 165, Centro, I, C2, ☎ 240 6662.
SAS, Av. Presidente Wilson 231, Centro, I, C2, ☎ 210 1222.
Swissair, Av. Rio Branco 99, Centro, I, C2, ☎ 203 2152.
Tap, Av. Rio Branco 31, Centro, I, C2, ☎ 210 2414.
Transbrasil, Av. Atlântica 1998, Copacabana, II, C3, ☎ 236 7475.
United Airlines, Av. Beira-Mar 406, Castelo, ☎ 220 3397.
Vario, Av. Alm Silvio de Noronha 365, ☎ 297 5141 or 220 9242.
Vasp, Av. N.S. de Copacabana 291, Copacabana, II, C3, ☎ 292 2112.
Western Airlines, Av. Rio Branco 161, Centro, I, C2, ☎ 220 1484.

Train

In Brazil, it is better to travel by road or by air because trains are slow and, increasingly, services are being closed down. Trains are generally on time, however, and are inexpensive.

Estação Barão de Mauá, Av. Francisco Biscalho, São Cristóvão, ☎ 273 3198, provides service to Vitória and Rio's suburbs.
Estação dom Pedro II, Praça Cristiano Ottoni, Centro, I, A2 ☎ 233 3277, provides service to São Paulo and Rio's suburbs.

Bus

Brazilian buses are very comfortable and clean. Almost all the principal cities of Brazil are connected by bus routes.

Estação Mariano Prócopio, Pça. Maua, Centro, I, C1, ☎ 291 5151, provides service to cities in the state of Rio de Janeiro.
Estação Novo Rio, Av. Francisco Bicalho 1, São Cristóvão, ☎ 291 5151, provides service to all the state capitals and large cities.

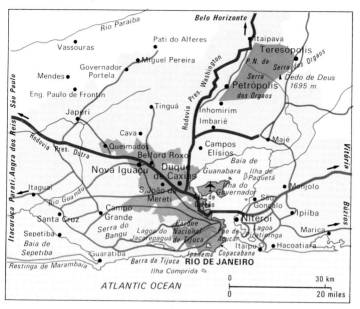

Environs of Rio.

Ship

It is possible to go to Rio by ship. From the United States, regular services are offered by the **Moore-McCormack Line** (☎ 212 683 0619).

From Europe, it is possible to take a **NedLloyd of Rotterdam** cargo ship from Rotterdam to Rio. This trip takes about two weeks.

Shipping lines in Rio include:
Delta Line, Rua Uruguaiana 174, Centro, I, C2, ☎ 242 8020.
Linea C, Av. Rio Branco 109, Centro, I, C2, ☎ 232 4309.
Lloyd Brasileira, Rua do Rosário 1, Centro, I, C2, ☎ 221 3176.

Accommodation

Hotels

The most luxurious hotels in Rio are situated along the beaches. They all belong to international chains and are all expensive. Farther inland, at the edge of the southern zone and close to Centro, such areas as Botafogo, Laranjeiras, Flamengo, and Glória have hotels that are comfortable yet charge less than those on the beaches. Certain hotels located between Barra da Tijuca and Alto da Boa Vista are also comfortable, but these lie far from most sites of interest. We do not recommend them unless you have a car. Finally, the hotels in Centro, the business district, cater principally to business people. This area offers very little activity for the tourist after the offices close. The explanation for the rating system of the following hotels can be found on p. 16.

▲▲▲▲ **Caesar Park**, Av. Vieira Souto, Ipanema, II, B4, ☎ 287 3122. The Caesar Park prides itself on its first-rate service, which includes a rooftop swimming pool, two restaurants, three bars and various boutiques. 221 rooms.

▲▲▲▲ **Copacabana Palace**, Av. Atlântica 1702, Copacabana, II, CD3, ☎ 255 7070. This former palace dating from 1930 has been completely remodeled. It contains all the standard amenities, as well as an art gallery and a theatre. 222 rooms.

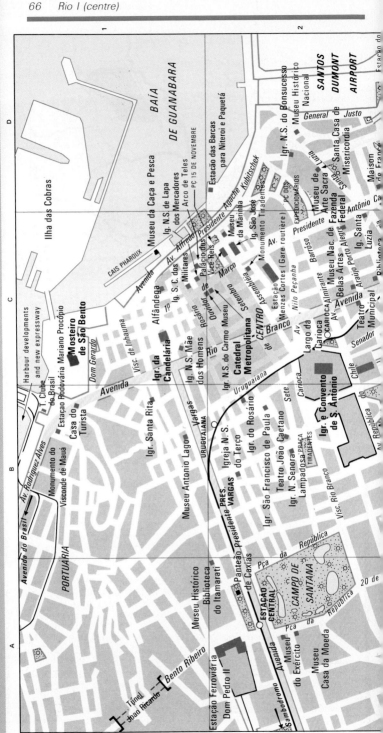

SANTOS
DUMONT
AIRPORT

BAÍA
DE GUANABARA

Ilha das Cobras

Estação das Barcas
para Niteroi e Paquetá

Museu da Caça e Pesca

Ig. N.S. de Lapa
dos Mercadores

Arco de Teles
PÇ 15 DE NOVEMBRE

Museu Histórico
Nacional

General de Justo

Maison
de France

Museu de
Arte Sacra

Santa Casa de
Misericordia

CAIS PHAROUX

Av. Alfredo Presidente Agache Kubitschek

Ig. São José

Museu da Marinha

Monumento Tiradentes

PÇ DOS
EXPEDICIONÁRIOS

Ig. Santa
Luzia

Ig. Santo
Antônio Ca

Museu Nac. de Fazenda
Federal

Palácio dos
Vice-Reis

Av.
Presidente

Barroso

Araújo Porto Alegre

Museu de
Belas Artes

Avenida

Almirante

Av.
de
Março

Av. S. C. dos
Militares

Avenida

Alfândega

1º de
Março

Estação
Wenzes Cortes (Gare routière)

Av. Nilo Peçanha

Senador

CARIOCA

Harbour developments
and new expressway

Av. Rodriguez Alves

Mosteiro
de São Bento

Dom Gerardo

Visc. de Inhauma

Ouvidor

Rio
de
Janeiro

Museu

Setembro

CENTRO

Branco

Largo da
Carioca

Chile

Teatro
Municipal

T. Clube
do Brasil

Estação Rodoviária Mariano Procópio

Casa do
Turista

Ig. da
Candelária

Ig. N.S. Mãe
dos Homens

Ig. N.S. do Carmo

Catedral
Metropolitana

Assembléia

de Uruguaiana

Av.
República
do

Monumento do
Visconde de Mauá

Avenida

Ig. Santa Rita

Museu Antonio Lago

Igreja N. S.
do Terço

Ig. do Rosário

Carioca

Sete

Ig. e Convento
de S. Antônio

PORTUÁRIA

Avenida do Brasil

Vargas

URUGUAIANA

Ig. São Francisco de Paula

Teatro João Caetano

Ig. N. Senora
Lampadosa

PRAÇA
TIRADENTES

Visc. Rio Branco

PRES.
VARGAS

Museu Histórico
Biblioteca
do Itamarati

Panteão Presidente
de Caxias

ESTAÇÃO
CENTRAL

Pça
da

CAMPO DE
SANTANA

Pça
da

Av.
República

da
República

República

20 de

Túnel
João Ricardo

Estação Ferroviária
Dom Pedro II

Bento Ribeiro

Sambódromo

Avenida

Museu
do Exército

Casa da Moeda

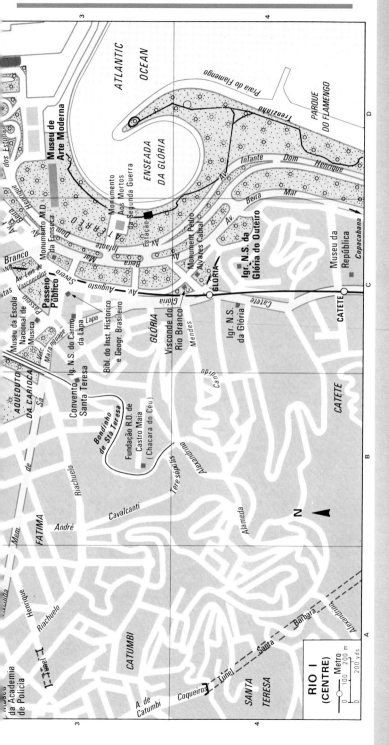

ATLANTIC

OCEAN

Museu de Arte Moderna

ENSEADA DA GLÓRIA

Praia do Flamengo

Trenzinho

PARQUE DO FLAMENGO

Monumento Aos Mortos da Segunda Guerra

Monumento M.D.

Av. Beira Mar

Av. Infante Dom Henrique

Av. Infante Dom Henrique

Av. Beira Mar

Av. Augusto Severo

Monument Pedro Alvares Cabral

Igr. N.S. da Glória do Outeiro

GLÓRIA

Museu da República

Branco

Av. Luis de Vasconcelos

Passeio Público

Museu da Escola Nacional de Música

Lapa

Ig. N.S. do Carmo da Lapa

Matarazupe

Bibl. do Inst. Historico e Geogr. Brasileiro

Visconde da Rio Branco

Mendes

Glória

GLÓRIA

Igr. N.S. da Glória

Catete

CATETE

Copacabana

AQUEDUTO DA CARIOCA

Sá

Convento Santa Teresa

Bondinho de Sta teresa

Fundação R.O. de Castro Maia (Chacara do Céu)

Teresópolis

Canário

CATETE

Riachuelo

André

Cavalcanti

Alexandrino

Alameda

N

FATIMA

Mem

Henrique

Riachuelo

CATUMBI

Santa

Barbara

Alexandrino

A. de Catumbi

Coqueiros

Tunel

SANTA TERESA

RIO I (CENTRE)

Metro

0   100   200 m

0   200 yds

Museu da Academia de Policia

Tunel

dos Estudos

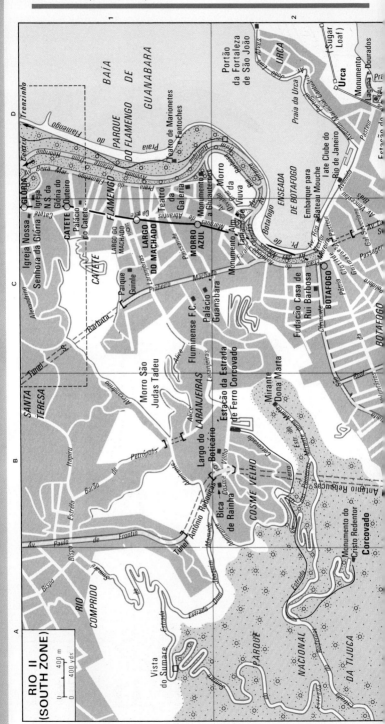

RIO II
(SOUTH ZONE)

0   400 m
0   400 yds.

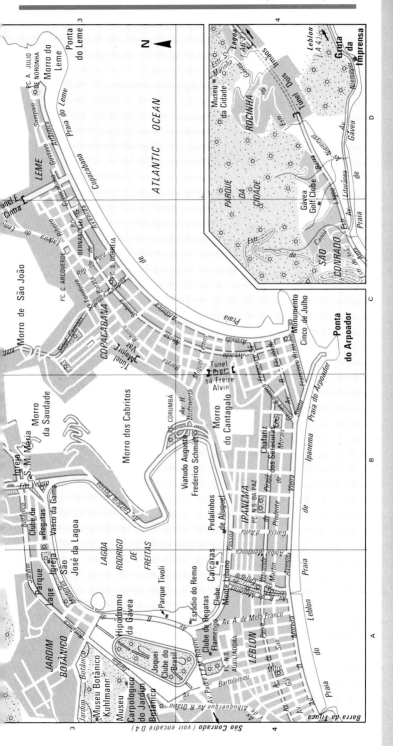

▲▲▲▲ **Inter-continental Rio**, Av. Pref. Mendes de Morais 222, São Conrado, II, D4, ☎ 322 2200. This high-quality hotel sits in a lovely garden, near a golf course. It has a restaurant, four bars, three swimming pools, a piano bar, boutiques and tennis courts. 463 rooms.

▲▲▲▲ **Méridien**, Av. Atlântica 1020, Leme, II, CD3, ☎ 275 9922. The truly French ambience here extends to a restaurant directed by the famous Paul Bocuse. Cinema, piano bar and boutiques number among the many tourist pleasures. 496 rooms.

▲▲▲▲ **Nacional Rio**, Av. Niemeyer 769, São Conrado, II, A4, ☎ 322 1000. Built by architect Niemeyer, this is one of Rio's great meeting places. Two restaurants, four bars and two swimming pools are only some of the amenities you'll find here. 520 rooms.

▲▲▲▲ **Othon Palace**, Av. Atlântica 3264, Copacabana, II, CD3, ☎ 255 8812. This hotel's typical Brazilian charm includes a seaview, a rooftop swimming pool, a restaurant and several boutiques. 581 rooms.

▲▲▲▲ **Rio Palace**, Av. Atlântica 4240, Copacabana, II, CD3, ☎ 521 3232. Four bars, two restaurants, two swimming pools, piano bar, boutiques, gym, tennis courts — the list of pleasures goes on and on. 418 rooms.

▲▲▲▲ **Rio Sheraton**, Av. Niemeyer 121, Vidigal, II, A4 off map, ☎ 274 1122. This is the only hotel in Rio that has its own private beach. It also boasts two restaurants, four bars, three swimming pools and many boutiques. 571 rooms.

▲▲▲ **Everest Rio**, Rua Prudente de Morais 1117, Ipanema, II, B4, ☎ 287 8282. This is a very good hotel that includes a restaurant, two bars, several boutiques and a swimming pool. 169 rooms.

▲▲▲ **Glória**, Rua do Russel 632, Glória, I, C4, ☎ 205 7272. One of Rio's oldest hotels, the Glória overlooks Flamengo beach. Besides a swimming pool in the open air, there are also a restaurant, four bars, a piano bar and a couple of boutiques. 616 rooms.

▲▲▲ **Leme Palace**, Av. Atlântica 656, Leme, II, CD3, ☎ 275 8080. This was at one time the best hotel in Rio, and still retains its charms. In addition to a restaurant and two bars, you'll also find a coffee shop. 193 rooms.

▲▲▲ **Marina Palace**, Rua Delfim Moreira 630, Leblon, II, A4, ☎ 259 5212. This hotel is located on the beach in a residential area of Leblon. It includes a restaurant, three bars, a swimming pool, a coffee shop and a boutique. 160 rooms.

▲▲ **Carlton**, Rua João Lira 68, Leblon, II, A4, ☎ 259 1932. The Carlton offers good service, but it is not located at the beach. It does have a restaurant and a bar. 45 rooms.

▲▲ **Luxor Continental**, Rua Gustavo Sampaio 320, Leme, II, CD3, ☎ 275 5252. Although the rooms are small, they are very comfortable. You'll find a restaurant, a bar, a coffee shop and several boutiques. 283 rooms.

▲▲ **Luxor Regente**, Av. Atlântica 3716, Copacabana, II, CD3, ☎ 287 4212. The rooms here are well kept and the hotel contains a restaurant and a bar. 261 rooms.

▲▲ **Ouro Verde**, Av. Atlântica 1456, Copacabana, II, CD3, ☎ 542 1887. Besides a seaview and one of the best restaurants in Rio, this hotel has a bar and a boutique. 66 rooms.

▲▲ **Praia Ipanema**, Av. Vieira Souto 706, Ipanema, II, B4, ☎ 239 9932. The rooms, public areas and services all of a first-rate quality. It offers a restaurant, two bars and a swimming pool. 105 rooms.

▲▲ **Savoy Othon**, Av. N.S. de Copacabana 995, Copacabana, II, CD3, ☎ 257 8052. This hotel is situated on the main commercial street of Rio and has a restaurant and bar. 153 rooms.

▲▲ **Sol Ipanema,** Av. Vieira Souto 320, Ipanema, II, B4, ☎ 267 0095. A high standard of comfort reigns in the rooms, and the service is of the very best. There is a restaurant and a bar. 78 rooms.

▲ **Acapulco Copacabana,** Rua Gustavo Sampaio 854, Leme, II, CD3, ☎ 275 0022. This hotel is clean and comfortable, but the service is sometimes lacking. There is a bar but no restaurant. 118 rooms.

▲ **Aeroporto,** Av. Beira-Mar 280, Centro, I, C1-2, ☎ 210 3253. Because this hotel is downtown, it is conveniently located if you have come to Brazil to do business. Its restaurant and bar are convenient, too. 80 rooms.

▲ **Ambassador,** Rua Sen. Dantas 25, Centro, I, C1-2, ☎ 297 7181. In the downtown area, this hotel is air-conditioned and includes a garage and a hairdresser. 178 rooms.

▲ **Argentina,** Rua Cruz Lima 30, Flamengo, II, CD1, ☎ 225 7233. The Argentina is clean and acceptable and includes a restaurant and bar. 80 rooms.

▲ **Castro Alves,** Av. N.S. de Copacabana 552, Copacabana, II, CD3, ☎ 257 1800. Good quality in this air-conditioned hotel. 74 rooms.

▲ **Debret,** Av. Atlântica 3564, Copacabana, II, CD3, ☎ 521 3332. This comfortable hotel is air-conditioned and has a bar. 104 rooms.

▲ **Excelsior,** Av. Atlântica 1800, Copacabana, II, CD3, ☎ 257 1950. Two-thirds of the rooms in this hotel are air-conditioned, and there is a bar and a restaurant. 186 rooms.

▲ **Grande Hotel São Francisco,** Rua Visc. de Inhauma 95, Centro, I, C1-2, ☎ 223 1224. This hotel provides good service for people on business trips. It has a restaurant and bar. 163 rooms.

▲ **Miramar Palace,** Av. Atlântica 3668, Copacabana, II, CD3, ☎ 247 6070. This good hotel has air-conditioning, a restaurant and several bars. 144 rooms.

▲ **Novo Mundo,** Praia do Flamengo 20, Flamengo, II, CD1, ☎ 225 7366. With a reputation for consistent good quality, the Novo Mundo offers a restaurant, a bar and a piano bar. 213 rooms.

▲ **Olinda,** Av. Atlântica 2230, Copacabana, II, CD3, ☎ 257 1890. This is an adequate small hotel with a restaurant and a bar. 98 rooms.

▲ **Plaza Copacabana,** Av. Princ. Isabel 263, Copacabana, II, CD3, ☎ 275 7722. This is a good hotel with air-conditioning, a restaurant and a bar. 166 rooms.

▲ **Trocadero,** Av. Atlântica 2064, Copacabana, II, CD3, ☎ 257 1834. This hotel has air-conditioning, a restaurant and a bar. 120 rooms.

Camping

Camping Clube do Brasil (CCB), RJ-9, Av. Sernambetiba 3200, Bara da Tijuca, ☎ 399 0628.

Camping Clube do Brasil (CCB), RJ-10, Estr. do Pontal 5900, Recreio dos Bandeirantes, ☎ 327 8400.

Novo Rio, Av. das Américas, Recreio dos Bandeirantes, ☎ 327 8213.

Pousada da Serra, Rua Crescêncio Mendes Nascimento 608, Vargem Grande, ☎ 232 4825.

Sitio Paulista, Estr. do Pacui, Vargem Grande, ☎ 327 8779.

Private houses and apartments

If you don't want to stay in a hotel, you can rent a private house or apartment by the season (one to three months). The official tourist agency, Riotour (see p. 82), can provide you with information. The newspaper, *Jornal do Brasil,* also lists advertisements for places to rent.

Entertainment and cultural life

Rio boasts a fairly high level of cultural and artistic activity. It has some 40 theatres, including the **Teatro Municipal** at Praça Floriano, I, C1, ☎ 262 6322, which stages operas, ballets and concerts featuring internationally acclaimed artists. Very good concerts are also held at the **Sala Cecilia Meireles**, Largo da Lapa 47, Centro, and at the **School of Music**, Rua do Passeio 98, Lapa, I, C3.

Rio has close to 60 cinemas that feature Brazilian and foreign films. Shows take place every two hours starting at noon. There are midnight shows in the larger cinemas at weekends.

Copacabana and Ipanema have a number of art galleries situated near the Rua Visconde de Piaja. There are also excellent permanent exhibitions at the **Museu de Arte Moderna** (Museum of Modern Art), Av. Infante Dom Henrique, Flamengo, I, D3, ☎ 210 2188 (closed for renovation at publication), and the **Museu Nacional de Belas Artes** (National Museum of Fine Arts), Av. Rio Branco 199, Centro, I, C2, ☎ 240 0068 (open Tues-Fri 10am-5:30pm, Sat and Sun 3-6pm).

Rio is also well-known as a convention centre. Most conventions are held in the big hotels, such as the **Hotel Nacional** or the **Hotel Glória,** or in the **Riocentro Convention Centre.**

Carnival

Beginning on the Saturday before Ash Wednesday, Carnival transforms Rio into one enormous explosion of colour, music and dance. At least six months of preparations precede the official opening, and the activity becomes increasingly feverish in the weeks before the actual celebration.

This is the best time to visit one of Rio's samba schools. For a modest entrance fee you can watch the members rehearse to compete in the main parades. The following is a list of the most popular schools:

Beija-Flor, Rua Pracinha Wallace Paes Leme 1652, Nilópolis, ☎ 791 1353.

Império Serrano, Av. Ministro Edgar Romero 114, Madureira, ☎ 359 4944.

Mangueira, Rua Visconde de Niterói 1082, Mangueira, ☎ 234 4129.

Mocidade Independente de Padre Miguel, Rua Cel. Tamarindo 38, Padre Miguel, ☎ 332 5823.

Portela, Rua Clara Nunes 81, Madureira, ☎ 390 0471.

Salgueiro, Rua Silva Teles 104, Tijuca, ☎ 238 5564.

Neighbourhood samba groups, known as *blocos,* begin to parade in various parts of the city on Saturday and continue night and day throughout Carnival. There are about twenty blocos in Rio, which are regrouped into five larger divisions for Carnival. Each year they organize a show around a theme — complete with costumes, music and dancing — in an attempt to propel their group into the ranks of the top category of samba schools. Most of the first-rate schools started out as blocos. They parade in the centre (mostly along Av. Rio Branco and its side-streets), Ipanema (around Av. Vieira Souto) and Copacabana (around Av. Atlântica).

The official competition of the samba schools is held on Sunday and Monday in the **Sambadrome,** a structure that was built in 1984 especially for Carnival. Designed by Oscar Niemeyer (the architect of Brasília), it consists of a long avenue with seating for spectators on either side, ending at the judges' stand at Praça da Apoteose. The parade begins at 7pm each night and continues until the following morning. On the Saturday following Carnival a parade of the three winning schools is held.

Tickets for the assigned seats in the special tourist bleachers must be bought in advance through a travel agency. They cost about US$100 to US$150 per person. Tickets for the other bleachers are less expensive (between US$30 and US$50) but the view is not as good and the seats are unmarked. Here, it is advisable to arrive around 4pm to secure a good spot.

Costumed balls take place in many of Rio's major hotels and nightclubs. Some of the better known Carnival balls are given at the following places:

Canecão (see p. 78)

Champagne, Rua Siqueira Campos 225, Copacabana, II, C3 ☎ 255 7341

Club Monte Libano, Av. Borges de Medeiros 701, Lagoa, ☎ 239 0032

Iate-Clube do Rio de Janeiro, Botafogo, II, D2 (the renowned Hawaï ball is held on Saturday one week before Carnival)

Palace Club, Hotel Rio Palace (see p. 70)

Palace Copacabana (see p. 65)

Scala (see p. 78)

Teatro Municipal (see p. 88)

For a complete list of the scheduled events, pick up any of Brazil's major newspapers or the weekly *Este Mes no Rio*.

Food

Rio is full of restaurants catering to all tastes and pocketbooks — from lunch-counters known as *lanchonetes* to the more traditional restaurants listed below. Rio's speciality is *feijoada,* a stew made with beef and black beans. You will also find huge shrimp *(camarões),* often as big as your hand, served in every possible way. Top-quality grilled meats *(churrasco),* succulent, fresh pineapples *(abacaxis)* and avocados, and sherbets *(sorvetes)* made from tropical fruits are other gastronomical delights found in Rio. For an explanation of restaurant categories, see p. 20.

**** **Adegão Português,** Campo S. Cristóvão 212, São Cristóvão, ☎ 580 7288. Very good Portuguese cuisine in a pleasant, simple atmosphere. Open daily 11am-11:30pm.

**** **Antiquarius,** Rua Aristides Espinola 19, Leblon, II, A4, ☎ 294 1049. Excellent Portuguese specialities in an elegant setting. Open daily noon-2am.

**** **Barracuda,** Marina da Glória, Parque do Flamengo, II, D1, ☎ 265 3997. This lively restaurant situated at the Glória marina serves a wide variety of delicious seafood dishes. Open daily 11:30-1am.

Rio's cuisine

The favourite dish in Rio is *feijoada,* a thick soup made with black beans, beef, pork and sausages and served with rice, greens and slices of orange. Originally, it is said, it was a dish given to slaves. Now a national rite, the meal is usually eaten on Saturday at lunchtime. Afterward, you will only have the energy to collapse into a hammock and enjoy a well-deserved siesta. Another popular dish is *cozido* — a stew of boiled meat and vegetables.

For those who like the exotic, there is *xinxim de galinha* — an unlikely but delicious combination of chicken cooked with chocolate and palm oil in a peanut and ginger sauce.

A favourite drink is *caipirinha* — made from fermented sugar cane with lemon juice and sugar. Variations on this are *caipirosca* (made with vodka) and *caipirissima* (made with rum).

**** Clube Gourmet, Rua Gen. Polidoro 186, Botafogo, II, C2, ☎ 295 3494. Excellent French cuisine in a relaxed setting. Open Mon-Fri noon-3pm, 8pm-12:30am, Sat 8pm-12:30am, Sun noon-3pm.

**** Enotria, Rua Constante Ramos 115, Copacabana, II, C3, ☎ 237 6705. The best Italian restaurant in Rio. Open Mon-Sat 8pm-12:30am.

**** Grottammare, Rua Gomes Carneiro 132, Ipanema, II, B4, ☎ 287 1596. This very good restaurant combines seafood with Italian fare and is consistently pleasing. Open Mon-Sat 7pm-2am.

**** Mosteiro, Rua S. Bento 13/15, Centro, I, C2, ☎ 233 6426. Good Portuguese cooking in a charming dining room. Open Mon-Fri 11am-4pm.

**** Negresco, Rua Barão da Torre 348, Ipanema, II, B4, ☎ 287 4842. Portuguese cuisine in a lively ambience. Open daily 7pm-2am.

**** Pré Catelan, Rio Palace Hotel, Av. Atlântica 4240, Copacabana, II, C3, ☎ 521 3232. Fabulous French food—especially the desserts. Open Mon-Fri noon-3pm, 7:30pm-midnight, Sat and Sun 7:30pm-midnight.

*** A Lisboeta, Rua Frei Caneca 5, Praça da República, Centro, I, C2, ☎ 232 2611. Good Portuguese cooking in a modest setting. Open Mon-Sat 11am-9pm.

*** Bar do Arnaudo, Rua Alm. Alexandrino 316B, Santa Teresa, I, A4, ☎ 252 7246. Tasty Brazilian cuisine in simple surroundings. Open daily noon-10pm.

*** Casa da Suiça, Rua Candido Mendes 157, Glória, I, C4, ☎ 252 2406. This charming restaurant serves Swiss cuisine. Open Sun-Fri noon-3pm, 7pm-midnight, Sat 7pm-midnight.

*** Champs-Elysées, Av. Pres. Antônio Carlos 58, Centro, I, D2, ☎ 220 4129. An elegant restaurant serving French cuisine. Open Mon-Fri noon-5pm.

*** Ficha, Rua Teofilo Ottoni 98, Centro, I, B1, ☎ 233 8496. Modest restaurant serving good German cooking. Open Mon-Fri 11am-3:30pm.

*** Florentino, Av. Gen. San Martin 1227, Leblon, II, A4, ☎ 274 6841. International cuisine in an agreeable setting. Open daily noon-2am.

*** Monseigneur, Av. Pref. Mendes de Moraes 222, São Conrado, II, CD4, ☎ 322 2200. French cuisine in an elegant setting. Open daily 7-11:30pm.

*** Mr. Zee, Av. Gen. San Martin 1219, Leblon, II, A4, ☎ 294 0591. You will find the best Chinese food in Rio here, in a refined ambience. Open Mon-Sat 7:30pm-1am.

*** Neal's, Rua Sorocaba 659, Botafogo, II, C2, ☎ 266 6577. This restaurant specializes in spare ribs and other North American-style items. Open Tues-Fri noon-3pm, 7:30-11:30pm, Sat and Sun 7:30-11:30pm.

*** Ouro Verde, Av. Atlântica 1456, Copacabana, II, D3, ☎ 542 1887. Very good French cuisine in a charming setting overlooking Copacabana beach. Open daily noon-12:30am.

*** Petronius, Caesar Park Hotel, Av. Vieira Souto 460, Ipanema, II, B4, ☎ 287 3122. Very good seafood in an elegant dining room. Open daily 7pm-1am.

*** Quadrifoglio, Rua Maria Angélica 43, Jardim Botânico, II, A3, ☎ 226 1799. This attractive restaurant serves simple Italian fare. Open Mon-Fri 12:30-3:30pm, 8pm-1am, Sat 8pm-1am, Sun 12:30-3:30pm.

*** Saint-Honoré, Méridien Hotel, Av. Atlântica 1020, Leme, II, D3

☎ 275 9922. The view from this restaurant on the top floor of the hotel is superb and the French cuisine (after recipes of Paul Bocuse) is very good. Open Mon-Fri noon-3pm, 8-11:30pm, Sat 8-11:30pm.

*** **Satiricon,** Rua Barão do Torre 192, Ipanema, II, B4, ☎ 521 0627. Italian cuisine in a pleasant setting. Open daily 7pm-2am.

*** **Shirley,** Rua Gustavo Sampaio 610, Leme, II, D3, ☎ 275 1398. Simple Spanish cooking in pleasant ambience. Open daily noon-1am.

** **A Cabaça Grande,** Rua do Ouvidor 12, Centro, I, C1-2, ☎ 231 2301. This modest luncheon restaurant offers a wide variety of seafood. Open Mon-Fri 11:30am-4pm.

** **Arataca,** Rua Figueiredo de Magalhães 28A, Copacabana, II, C3, ☎ 255 7448. Simple Brazilian food in a relaxed atmosphere. Open daily 11:30-2am.

** **Bec Fin,** Av. N.S. de Copacabana 178, Copacabana, II, C3, ☎ 542 4097. Good French cuisine in an elegant dining room. Open 7pm-3am.

** **Bife de Ouro,** Copacabana Palace Hotel, Av. Atlântica 1702, Copacabana, II, D3, ☎ 255 7070. This charming restaurant offers excellent international cuisine. Open daily 11:30am-4pm, 7pm-1am.

** **Café de la Paix,** Méridien Hotel, Av. Atlântica 1020, Leme, II, D3, ☎ 275 9922. Located in the lobby of the hotel, this is the only brasserie in Rio. Simple dishes prepared in the French manner. Open daily noon-11pm.

** **Café do Teatro,** Av. Rio Branco, Centro, I, C2, ☎ 262 4164. Good international cuisine in a remarkable decor. Open for lunch only Mon-Fri 11am-4pm.

** **Chalé,** Rua da Matriz 54, Botafogo, II, C2, ☎ 286 0897. Simple Brazilian food in a lively setting. Open daily noon-midnight.

** **El Cordobés,** Av. Borges de Medeiros 3207, Lagoa, II, B3, ☎ 246 7431. Charming Spanish restaurant with a terrace overlooking the lagoon. Open daily noon-2am.

** **Escondidinho,** Beco dos Barbeiros 12A, Centro, I, C2, ☎ 242 2234. Welcoming Brazilian restaurant in a simple setting. Open Mon-Fri 11am-4pm.

** **Gattopardo,** Av. Borges de Medeiros 1426, Lagoa, II, B3, ☎ 274 7999. One of the best pizzerias in Rio. Open daily 6pm-midnight.

** **Majorica,** Rua Sen. Vergueiro 11/15, Flamengo, II, C2, ☎ 245 8947. This is a good address to sample the famous Brazilian barbecue, *churrasco.* Open daily noon-midnight.

** **Mariu's,** Av. Atlântica 290B, Leme, II, D3, ☎ 542 2393. Another good address for *churrasco.* Open daily 11:45-2am.

** **Mazot,** Rua Paula Freitas 31A, Copacabana, II, C3, ☎ 255 0834. Swiss specialities, especially fondues, in this charming little restaurant. Open daily noon-2am.

** **Miako,** Rua do Ouvidor 45, Centro, I, C2-3, ☎ 222 2397. This restaurant offers traditional Japanese cooking. Open Mon-Sat 11:30am-3pm, 6-10pm.

** **Nino,** Rua Domingos Ferreira 242, Copacabana, II, C3, ☎ 255 9696. International cuisine in a sophisticated setting. Open daily noon-2am.

** **Pantagruel,** Rua Maria Angélica 51, Jardim Botânico, II, A3, ☎ 246 2982. This attractive dining room has music and good international cuisine. Open daily noon-4pm, 7pm-1am.

** **Rei do Bacalhau,** Rua Guilhermina 596, Encantado, ☎ 249 0988.

Simple Brazilian cooking in a simple, pleasing setting. Open Mon-Sat 11am-11pm.

** Rio Minho, Rua do Ouvidor 10, Centro, I, C1-2, ☎ 231 2338. Excellent seafood served at this well-located restaurant. Open Mon-Sat 11am-4pm.

** Sal e Pimenta, Rua Barão da Torre 368, Ipanema, II, B4, ☎ 521 1460. This is a popular *churrascaria* that features music as well as delicious barbecues. Open daily noon-4pm, 8pm-3am.

** Tarantella, Av. Sernambetiba 850, Barra da Tijuca, ☎ 399 0632. Good Italian cuisine in a charming restaurant with a lovely view. Open daily noon-1am.

* Buffalo Grill, Rua Rita Ludolf 47, Leblon, II, A4, ☎ 274 4848. This is one of the best *churrascarias* in Rio. Open daily noon-3am.

* Carreta, Praça S. Perpétuo 116, Barra da Tijuca, ☎ 399 4055. This *churrascaria* offers good cooking and music. Open daily 11-1am.

* Castelo da Lagoa, Av. Epitácio Pessoa 1560, Lagoa, II, B3, ☎ 287 3514. Good international cooking in a relaxed setting. Open daily noon-4am.

* Copacabana, Av. N.S. de Copacabana 1144, Copacabana, II, C3, ☎ 267 1497. This popular *churrascaria* offers music as well as meat. Open daily 11-2am.

* Gaucha, Rua das Laranjeiras 114, Laranjeiras, II, C1, ☎ 245 2665. Lively *churrascaria* with music and dancing. Open daily 11:30-1am.

* Jardim, Rua República do Peru 225, Copacabana, II, C3, ☎ 235 3263. Good meat and music in this lively *churrascaria*. Open daily noon-1:30am.

* Maria Thereza Weiss, Rua Visconde Silva 152, Botafogo, II, C2, ☎ 286 3098. Tasty Brazilian food in a pleasant ambience. Open daily noon-1am.

* Parque Recreio, Rua Marqûes de Abrantes 92A, Flamengo, II, C1, ☎ 552 1748. Well located and lively *churrascaria*. Open daily noon-2am.

* Porcão de Ipanema, Rua Barão da Torre 218, Ipanema, II, A4, ☎ 521 0999. Good *churrascaria* located near the beach. Open daily 11-1am.

* Real, Av. Atlântica 514A, Leme, II, D3, ☎ 275 9048. This restaurant offers a good variety of seafood. Open daily noon-2am.

* Vice Rey, Av. Mons. Ascâneo 535, Barra da Tijuca, ☎ 399 1683. Original seafood dishes in this pleasant setting. Open daily noon-2am.

Getting around Rio

Rio can be divided into three basic areas: the northern zone (Zona Norte), downtown (Centro) and the southern zone (Zona Sul).

The northern district, which includes Maracanã, São Cristóvão, Tijuca, Bonsucesso, Meier, Madureira, Penha and Vila Isabel, is full of factories and run-down housing. These are fairly dismal-looking neighbourhoods stretching out endlessly along the Avenida do Brasil, which until 1974 was the only road into Rio de Janeiro. It is very easy to lose your way here, and no matter how helpful the locals may be, these dark, narrow, deserted streets are best avoided at night.

Centro (see map pp. 66-67), or downtown, is both the historical centre and the business district of the city. Very lively during office hours, the area is utterly deserted at other times. Nearby, the runways of Santos-Dumont Airport jut out into the bay. The proximity of the airport offers obvious commercial advantages to Rio's business community.

The southern zone (see map pp. 68-69), with its elegant streets, hotels and restaurants, is the more fashionable part of town. The beaches of Leme, Copacabana, Ipanema and Leblon curve around the prettiest shores of Guanabara Bay. Copacabana and Leme lie on either side of Avenida Princesa Isabel, the main avenue leading to the city centre; Leblon and Ipanema lie on either side of a canal linking the Rodrigo de Freitas lagoon *(lagoa)* to the sea.

Other fashionable, mostly residential neighbourhoods of the southern zone include Urca, Botafogo, Jardim Botânico, Laranjeiras, Flamengo, Glória and Santa Teresa. The southwestern part of the southern zone, between Barra de Tijuca and Alto da Boa Vista, offers a lovely setting for walks. The recently constructed Barra da Tijuca housing developments are a sign that Rio is spreading in this direction.

On foot

Walking is a great way to explore specific districts. You will, however, have to rely on other modes of transportation to cover the distances between one area and another.

By car

Rio is a difficult city for visitors to drive in, even for the most experienced driver. Brazilians tend to drive in an uninhibited manner and pedestrians cross busy roads with never a glance to the right or left. With many one-way streets, finding your way around can be extremely hazardous and parking facilities are few and quite expensive.

If you nevertheless decide that you want a car, hiring one in Rio is easy. Remember that many filling stations are closed on Saturdays and Sundays. Often the rental agencies can supply fuel on the weekend.

Avis, Av. Princ. Isabel 150-A, Copacabana, II, C3, ☎ 542 4229.
Hertz, Av. Princ. Isabel 334-B, Copacabana, II, C3, ☎ 275 4996.
Localiza, Av. Princ. Isabel 214-A/B, Copacabana, II, C3, ☎ 275 3340.

By underground

At present the underground *(metrô)* consists of a main line that operates between Tijuca in the centre and Botafogo in the southern zone. It also serves the northern zone via Maracanã Stadium. The *metrô* runs from Monday to Saturday 6am-11pm.

By taxi

Regular yellow taxis can be hailed on the streets. Although these taxis have a meter, your fare will be based on a rate chart that your driver will consult on arrival at your destination. Fares go up between 11pm and 7am and on Sundays. Radio taxis can be summoned by phone or on the street.

If you want more luxury, special taxis *(taxis especial)* are also available. These are larger, fancier and more expensive. You can find these *taxis especial* at airports, outside the large hotels or by telephoning.

You should also be aware that taxi drivers drive at rapid speeds and that it is often impossible to find a taxi on the streets between 5:30 and 7:30pm.

Central de Taxi, ☎ 593 2598.
Coopatax, ☎ 249 5896, 248 1951.
Cootramo, ☎ 270 1442.
Transcoopass, ☎ 270 4888.

Excursions

Rio abounds in tour opportunities. The following are some of the agencies that handle excursions:

Adam Tours, Rua México 111, Centro, ☎ 240 5646.
Bel Air Viagens, Av. Almirante Barroso 81, ☎ 292 1212.
Embratur, Rua Mariz e Barros 13, ☎ 273 2212.
GB International, Av. Princ. Isabel 7, Copacabana, II, CD3 ☎ 275 8148 or 286 9697.
Hotur, Av. General San Martin 360, ☎ 239 9695 or 239 8144.

Kontik Franstur, Estrada da Gávea 899, ☎ 3220404.
Meliá Turismo, Rua Francisco Sá 23, Copacabana, II, C4, ☎ 267 7515.
Metropol, Rua São José 46, ☎ 224 5010.
Sun Flower Turismo, Av. Franklin Roosevelt 115, ☎ 220 1711 or
262 6614.

Boat tours

Several companies offer boat excursions around Rio. **Bateau Mouche** tours the harbour and beaches of Guanabara Bay, passing under the Rio-Niterói bridge and stopping at the island of Paquetá. Departures are from Av. Nestor Moreira 11, Botafogo, II, C2.

Transtur and **Conerj** both operate hydrofoil and ferry services leaving from Praça 15 de Novembro, Centro, I, C1, to Niterói and Paquetá islands.

Bateau Mouche, ☎ 295 1997.
Conerj, ☎ 232 6633.
Transtur, ☎ 231 0339.

Nightlife

Rio has numerous discos, nightclubs and bars, some of which offer shows or live music. Most charge a cover fee that includes the first drink. Many of the restaurants along the beaches provide live background music. The hottest nightspots, at the moment, are found in São Conrado and Barra da Tijuca.

Samba shows

The best samba shows can be seen at:
Oba Oba, Rua Humaitá 110, Botafogo, II, B2, ☎ 286 9848.
Plataforma I, Rua Adaberto Ferreira 32, Leblon, II, A4, ☎ 274 4022.
Scala I and II, Av. Afrânio de Mello Franco 296, Leblon, II, A4, ☎ 239 4448. This is one of Rio's largest clubs.

Samba clubs

You can dance the samba at any of the numeros *sambões* in São Conrado and Barra da Tijuca (**Aldeja, Bem, Cassino Royale, Ilha dos Pescadores, New Joá** and many more).

Concerts

A great place to watch major performing artists, Brazilian and international, is at **Canecão**, Av. Venceslau Bras 215, Botafogo, II, CD2, ☎ 295 3044. The cover charge is reasonable and you can eat and drink while watching the show. On certain nights you can dance the samba here. Other shows featuring Brazilian or international performers are presented at:
Fossa, Rua Ronald de Carvalhau 55, Copacabana, II, C3, ☎ 275 7728.
Golden Room, Copacabana Palace Hotel, II, CD3, ☎ 257 1818.
Hotel Nacional, Av. Niemeyer 769, São Conrado, II, A4, ☎ 399 1000.

Live Brazilian and international dance music

Barba's, Rua Alvaro Ramos 408, Botafogo, II, C2, ☎ 541 8396.
Biblos, Av. Epitácio Pessoa 1484, Lagoa, II, B4, ☎ 521 2645.
Chiko's, Av. Epitácio Pessoa 1560, Lagoa, II, B4, ☎ 287 3514.
Mistura Fina Studio, Rua Garcia D'Avila 15, Ipanema, II, B4, ☎ 259 9394.

Discotheques and nightclubs

Assyrius, Av. Rio Branco 101, Centro, II, C3, ☎ 220 1298.
Caligola, Rua Prudente de Morais 129, Ipanema, II, B4, ☎ 287 1363.
Circus, Rua Gen. Urquiza 102, Leblon, II, A4, ☎ 274 7895.
Mykonos, Rua Cupertino Durão 177, Leblon, II, A4, ☎ 294 2295.
Xatou da Barra, Rua Conde d'Eu 113, Barra da Tijuca, ☎ 399 8344.

Shopping

Rio offers the best shopping in Brazil. With world-famous designer boutiques, fabulous jewelry shops and an amazing variety of handcrafted items, Rio's shopping opportunities can easily be a high point of your stay. You should also bear in mind that the relative strength of European and North American currencies to the Brazilian currency creates wonderful bargains. If you take the time to shop around you will go home with some great buys.

Handcrafts

● Copacabana boutiques: located along the eastern side of the Avenida N.S. de Copacabana and its adjacent streets, shops display all sorts of semi-precious stones in every possible setting — necklaces, pendants, bracelets, ashtrays, and more. There are also shops full of attractive leather goods, sculpture and a host of other items from all over Brazil.

● Handcrafts fairs called *Feiras de Artes e Artesanato* (or *Feirarte*): the best of these is held on the Praça General Osório, II, B4, in Ipanema every Sunday (9am-6pm). Other fairs well worth a visit are the *Feirarte* held on Thursdays and Fridays on the Praça 15 de Novembre, I, C2, in the city centre (8am-6pm) and the fair that takes place on Saturdays on the Praça Lamartine Baba in Barra da Tijuca, II, A4 (8am-6pm).

● The São Cristóvão market: typical of the Nordeste region of Brazil, this market sells regional produce and handcrafts near the Pavilhão de São Cristóvão (open Sun dawn-1pm).

● O Sol: this small, permanent fair features pottery and other handcrafts in wood, straw, etc. It is held in Jardim Botânico, Rua Corcovado 231, II, A3 (Mon-Fri 9am-6pm, Sat 9am-noon).

● Feiras de Antiguidades (antiques fairs): the main ones are located at Praça Marechal Ancora (Saturdays) and Avenida Alvorada 2150 in Barra da Tijuca, II, A4 (Sundays).

● Indian handcrafts are sold in two shops run by FUNAI. One is at Rio de Janeiro International Airport and the other at the Museu do Indio (Indian Museum), Rua das Palmeiras 55, Botafogo, II, C2, ☎ 286 8799 (open Tues-Fri 10am-6pm, Sat and Sun 1-5pm).

Jewelry and precious stones

Most of Rio's jewelers and gem dealers have their shops in Copacabana. If you are interested in seeing stones being cut, contact the main office of the famous jewelry house of **H. Stern**, Av. Rio Branco 173. Brazil mines almost all gemstones — the array of sapphires, emeralds, amethysts, etc., on display is truly impressive.

Luxury goods

Copacabana and Ipanema abound in fashionable boutiques (Rua Visconde de Piaja, in Ipanema, is an essential stop for those interested in high fashion). Designer boutiques offer such well-known names as Yves Saint-Laurent and Pierre Cardin, as well as chic Brazilian creations.

Sports

Soccer *(futebol)* is Brazil's favourite sport. Try to attend at least one match. You will discover that the spectators are as much a part of the show as the players. With every goal scored, the crowd goes wild with enthusiasm, and shredded paper (among other things) rains down from the stands. The best-known stadium is the **Maracanã Stadium**, Rua Prof. Enrico Rabello, São Cristóvão, ☎ 264 9962 (Rio's metro stops here), followed by **São Januario Stadium**, Rua Gen. Almério de Moura 131, São Cristóvão, ☎ 580 7373.

Rio has two golf courses: **Gávea Golf Club**, Estrada de Gávea 800, São Conrado, II, CD4, ☎ 322 4141 (18 holes); **Itanhanga Golf Club**, Estrada da Barra 2005, Barra da Tijuca, ☎ 399 0507 (27 holes).

For hang-gliding, contact the **Associação Brasileira de Vôo Livre**, Rua Marques de São Vicente 140, Gávea, ☎ 259 8798.

The visitor can play tennis at any one of the following addresses: **Clube Canaveral**, Barra da Tijuca, ☎ 399 2192; **Play Tennis**, Barra da Tijuca,

---

Sports

Due to the powerful waves along the coast, surfing is one of the most popular sports in Rio. The best place is on the aptly named Devil's Beach, which although too dangerous for swimmers, is perfect for surfing. Another good surfing beach is the tiny Prainha beach not far from Barra da Tijuca.

Sailing is also a popular pastime in Rio, especially at Arpoador, where you can rent various types of boats. People also sail in the Rodrigo de Freitas lagoon.

Brazilians are particularly keen on hang-gliding. Indeed, the city lends itself to the sport, with its range of mountains and flat plateaux for easy landing. A favourite spot is the solitary mountain of Pedra da Gávea near São Conrado. From here hang-gliders fly across the city to Rio de Janeiro Airport, much to the displeasure of pilots who are forced to dodge them as best they can.

Because of Rio's long flat stretches you will see lots of cyclists on the roads to Ipanema, Arpoador and other beaches. If you can take the heat it's certainly a good way of getting around.

☎ 342 3500; **Quadra Tennis**, Barra da Tijuca, ☎ 399 3778. A few of the major hotels also have tennis facilities. There are squash courts at: **Squash Centre**, Barra da Tijuca, ☎ 208 1697, and **Smash Squash**, Laranjeiras, ☎ 245 3758.

Horse-racing fans can attend races at the **Gávea Racecourse**, Parça Santos-Dumont, ☎ 274 0055, on Thursday evenings and Saturday and Sunday afternoons. The most important race is the Grand Prix of Brazil, which is held on the first Sunday in August. You can go horseback riding at **Sociedade Hipica Brasileira**, Av. Borges de Medeiros 244, Lagoa.

There are four places at the Marina do Glória, Aterro do Flamengo, where you can rent boats (rowboats, canoes, sailboats or fishing boats): **Allmar**, ☎ 205 1047; **Assessoria Náutica Lineo**, ☎ 267 0797; **Marine**, ☎ 205 8646; and **SP Náutica**, ☎ 285 2247. In Copacabana, **Camargo** operates two rental outlets: Av. Princ. Isabel 181 and Av. Prado Junior 160.

Useful addresses

Banks

The headquarters of the main international banks are all located in the city centre.

Banco Chase Manhattan, Rua do Ouvidor 98, I, C2, ☎ 222 2651.
Banco do Boston, Av. Rio Branco 110, I, C2, ☎ 291 6123.
Banco do Brasil, Rua Augusto Severo 84, I, C3, ☎ 277 5454.
Banerj, Av. Nilo Peçanha 175, I, C2, ☎ 221 0667
Bradesco, Rua Barão de Itapagipe 225, ☎ 264 1544.
Citibank, Av. Rio Branco 95, I, C2, ☎ 296 1222.
Lloyds Bank, Rua do Ouvidor 91, I, C1-2, ☎ 222 8804.

Consulates

Australia, Rua Voluntários da Pátria 45, Botafogo, II, BC2, ☎ 286 7922.
Canada, Rua D. Gerardo 35, Centro, I, C2, ☎ 233 9286.
Great Britain, Praia do Flamengo 284, Flamengo, II, D1, ☎ 552 1422.
Ireland, Rua Fonseca Teles 18, S. Cristóvão, ☎ 254 0960.
United States, Av. Presidente Wilson 147, Centro, I, C2, ☎ 292 7117.

Currency exchanges

There are other exchanges on Avenida Rio Branco in Centro, I, C2, near the ones listed below.

Rio's famous statue of Christ the Redeemer stands high atop Hunchback Mountain.

Agencia São Jorge, Av. Rio Branco 31, ☎ 233 0676.
Exprinter, Av. Rio Branco 57A, ☎ 233 3980.
Promoçoes Modernas, Av. Rio Branco 124, ☎ 231 1800.

Emergencies
Pronto Socorro, ☎ 222 2121 or 274 2121.
Tourist Police, Av. Humberto de Campos 135, Leblon, II, A4, ☎ 259 7048.

Post offices
Central Post Offices, Rua Primeiro de Março, at corner of Rua do Rosário, Centro, I , C1; Av. N.S. de Copacabana 540, Copacabana, II, CD3-4; Rua Visconde de Piraja 452, Ipanema, II, AB4.
Santos-Dumont Airport, Senador Salgado Filho Sq., I, D2-3, ☎ 220 9228.

Telephone offices
Av. N.S. de Copacabana 642, Copacabana, II, CD3-4 (open 24 hours).
Rua Visconde Piraja 111, Ipanema, II, AB4 (open daily 6am-midnight).
Praça Tiradentes 41, Centro, I, B2 (open 24 hours).

Tourist information
Embratur (Brazilian Tourist Office), Rua Mariz e Barras 13, ☎ 273 2212.
Riotur (Rio de Janeiro Tourist Office), Rua da Assembléia 10, Centro, I, C2, ☎ 297 7117.
24-Hour Tourist Information, ☎ 580 8000 (in Portuguese, English, and Spanish).

▬ GETTING TO KNOW RIO DE JANEIRO

Even if you have only a few hours to spare, you should at least try to get a taste of Rio's unforgettable, indolent atmosphere. Taxi-drivers are happy to act as guides and will take you on the quickest route to see the city and its beaches. Rio, though, deserves at least a four-day stay — there is enough to do and see here to spend three weeks and still find it hard to leave.

Start your visit at the Praça Maua and head down the Avenida Rio Branco, through the business centre, and all the way to the Aterreo along Guanabara Bay. From here you have a splendid view of Sugarloaf and, on your way to Copacabana, of Corcovado in the distance. On Avenida Atlântica, alongside Copacabana's famous beach, it is worth stopping for a drink or a meal before continuing to Ipanema and the Rodrigo de Freitas lagoon. On the way back, the route passes by Laranjeiras and Santa Teresa as it heads for the Aqueduto da Carioca and Santo Antônio monastery.

If you have time, go up Corcovado for the magnificent view of Sugarloaf and the whole city. Or if you admire Baroque architecture, you may prefer a visit to the Mosteiro de São Bento. To experience the milling Brazilian crowds, go for a walk in the pedestrians-only streets in the city centre on any weekday at lunchtime.

Pão de Açúcar*** (Sugarloaf) II, D2

No tour of Rio is complete without a visit to Sugarloaf, the city's symbol. A huge cone-shaped rock, 1297 ft/395 m high, it stands at the tip of Guanabara Bay. Two cable-cars (which run from 8am-10pm) take you to the top. The first one leaves from the Praça General Tiburcio in Urca (you can get there by taxi or buses 107 and 511) to the Morro da Urca; from there the second goes to Sugarloaf.

From the summit a panoramic view of Rio and its bay opens up before you, and you will feel as if you are right in the heart of town. In a way you are, for the Portuguese founded Rio at Sugarloaf's foot, at Urca.

To the south-west you can see Copacabana and Botafogo. These lie across from the Morro do Macaco and Niterói, and at the base of

Corcovado, with its majestic statue of Christ. To the north lie Laranjeiras, Flamengo, the city centre and the gigantic Rio-Niterói bridge spanning the 250-sq-mi/647-sq-km bay. Behind you lies the sea, dotted with innumerable tiny islands.

One startling aspect of this vantage point is that all of Santos-Dumont Airport's runways point towards Sugarloaf, so that, after takeoff, planes come flying towards you. They then circle Sugarloaf, often far below the summit.

Sugarloaf seems no less strange when viewed from afar. It is visible from the express motorway, from the beaches of Botafogo and Flamengo, from Niterói, from departing and arriving flights and, above all, from the summit of Corcovado.

At the top of Sugarloaf you will find a restaurant, a bar and a souvenir shop.

Corcovado*** (Hunchback Mountain) II, A2

Corcovado, 2331 ft/710 m high, towers above the city and can be seen from every part of Rio. The position of the sun, the shimmering light or an odd cloud formation often make the peak — with its enormous statue of **Christ the Redeemer**, arms outstreched — look strange and mysterious.

If you plan to visit Corcovado by car there are three ways to get to the top: via Laranjeiras and Cosme Velho; via Santa Teresa; or via Alto da Boa Vista through the Tijuca forest. For the most picturesque approach, though, take the small trolley-car (open 8am-6pm; ☎ 285 2533). This climbs the mountain and crosses several curious-looking bridges. As you slowly make your way up and take in the breathtaking view below, you will forget that Rio's hectic tempo even exists.

From the top, you will not only see all of Rio in its full glory, but you will also be better able to grasp the city's topography. All of the districts surrounding the lagoon (Ipanema, Leblon, Jardim Botânico and Gávea) lie at your feet. You can even catch a glimpse of the Hotel Nacional's top floors just behind the mountains. You can also recognize the various parts of town around the bay (Botafogo, Flamengo, Glória, Centro) and you can see that Sugarloaf is an integral part of the landscape. To the north is Maracanã Stadium in São Cristóvão and, in the distance, the Ilha do Governador (Governor's Island) inside the bay.

The statue of Christ the Redeemer stands on the summit on an imposing platform. The statue was completed in 1931 after five years of work by French sculptor Paul Landowski. At night, the statue is lit by powerful floodlights, which make it look even more impressive. Unfortunately, the lights attract swarms of bugs and butterflies but that shouldn't stop you from appreciating the view. Here, too, are a restaurant and a souvenir shop.

The beaches

Rio's beaches are among the city's foremost attractions, and *Cariocas* (natives of Rio) spend the better part of their lives here. They go to the beach before and after work and at lunchtime. It is here that they meet, chat (what they call *bater um papo*), sunbathe and relax.

The beaches are especially crowded on weekends and they are not ideal for swimming. Those inside the bay are not terribly clean, and on the oceanfront beaches the powerful waves, undertows, and whirlpools can be downright dangerous. We advise you to do as most Brazilians do — simply play in the water to cool off. Don't forget to leave your valuables at the hotel and keep an eye on your belongings.

Beaches inside the bay

Flamengo beach is man-made and sits parallel to the Aterreo gardens by the express motorway. Few tourists frequent this beach — it is used mostly by local residents.

Botafogo beach is another man-made beach covered with white sand. It owes its charm to its splendid views of Sugarloaf and the private boats

Rio's beaches, popular with tourists and Brazilians alike, offer a wonderful haven from hectic city life.

bobbing up and down by the late Clube de Rio de Janeiro.

Urca beach is small and sits at the foot of Sugarloaf. Aside from the fact that it is an essential part of Urca's landscape, it is not especially remarkable.

Oceanfront beaches

Praia Vermelha is a small beach with coarse sand. The easiest way to get here is via Urca, from the bottom of the Praça General Tiburcio.

Leme beach to the east of Copacabana beach is far quieter than its neighbour. These two are the city's best beaches. **Copacabana** beach

is nearly 3 mi/5 km long and forms a perfect curve inside the bay. All of the houses along the curve are of the same height, except for the Hotel Méridien and the Hotel Othon at either end. The beach itself is very wide and is divided into sections by signs bearing the numbers zero to six. These are the remains of rescue stations from days gone by. The ocean is usually smooth, but the tide can sometimes be quite dangerous, especially for children. It is best to forget about swimming and just play about in the water like everyone else. The pedlars hawking coffee, *maté* (herbal tea) and lemonade can be quite annoying at first, but in no time you find that you would miss them if they were not there. You can visit one of the nearby cafés in your bathing suit if you feel so inclined.

Ipanema beach is now considered by Brazilians to be more chic than Copacabana, perhaps because the lower skyline of its housing and the proximity of trees make it look less spoiled. There are hardly any cafés, yet all of Rio society and its best-known artists and writers gravitate here.

Castelinho and **Arpoador** beaches lie east of Ipanema. Castelinho is as popular as Ipanema, with the advantage of two sidewalk café-restaurants (Barril 1800 and Castelinho) that are always full of young people and chic Rio crowds. Arpoador attracts mostly surfers.

Leblon beach lies west of Ipanema, beyond the canal from the lagoon to the ocean. It is a fairly quiet place, predominantly used by families.

Outlying beaches

Vidigal beach is the small beach below the Hotel Sheraton.

Gávea and **São-Conrado** beaches form the curve in front of the Hotel Nacional and the Hotel Inter-continental, midway between the chic beaches of Ipanema and Leblon and the unspoiled one at Barra da Tijuca.

Barra da Tijuca beach lies beyond the new housing complex at Jacarépagua and is 22 mi/35 km long. It is surrounded by flat marshes where vegetation is sparse. During the week you might think you had landed on a desert island but it becomes very crowded on weekends. The ocean is especially dangerous here.

Neighbourhoods near the beaches

The districts near the beaches are the most fashionable in Rio. All the activity in these neighbourhoods centres on the beaches, which cater to tourists and vacationing Brazilians. The streets are full of carefree, joyous crowds clad in bathing suits who seem only to be waiting for music to break into a samba.

Copacabana II, C3-4

Copacabana is the oldest of the areas near the beach. Brazilians feel that its time is past, but it still retains a 1930s elegance. It has hotels galore, as well as bars, restaurants and nightclubs — a tourist's paradise.

Unfortunately, Copacabana's inner streets are very noisy and crowded. The main arteries are all one-way, and the constant rush of cars and buses reverberates between the high concrete and stone walls of the buildings. The Avenida N.S. de Copacabana and the Avenida Barata Ribeiro are certainly nice places to visit — but you wouldn't want to live here! You will find all the souvenirs, precious stones and luxury goods you could want in the shops located in the eastern part of the Avenida N.S. de Copacabana. Its central and western parts have shops with more variety. Way to the east, on the other side of the Avenida Princesa Isabel, is Leme, a much quieter neighbourhood.

Ipanema II, B4

Ipanema is Rio's most exclusive residential area. It is far more pleasant than Copacabana because of its greenery and new housing. Along the oceanfront there are only small apartment buildings, and along the lagoon only private houses.

Ipanema has less commercial activity than Copacabana, yet there are still plenty of shops and boutiques selling luxury goods of flawless taste, with price tags to match. Apart from the main streets, Ipanema is a quiet place where throngs of carefree young people divide their time between the beach and the local bars and nightclubs.

Leblon II, A4

Leblon is a good deal less exclusive than Ipanema and, consequently, doesn't have the same fashionable crowd. There is an out-of-the-way feeling here, perhaps due to the proximity of the mountains. The suburbs are also nearby.

Leblon's natural setting is magnificent. On one side is the beach beneath the Morro des Dois Irmãos (Two Brothers) and on the other are the lagoon and the towering Corcovado peak.

The city centre

At first sight the city centre may not seem too appealing. Like all business districts, it is a hectic place, but don't let that stop you from doing some sight-seeing here. There are interesting 18th- and 19th-century buildings, now administrative offices or museums, that are well worth seeing. Speculation about the area's original layout is quite useless; it has been thoroughly changed since the day when the city was founded.

Avenida Rio Branco I, BC1-3

The main avenue of the city centre, Avenida Rio Branco was laid out fairly recently (1905). It leads through the heart of Rio, and its little side-streets have retained their 19th-century charm. It also links two very different landmarks: the Praça Mauá, which might be described as the centre's northern gate, and the Praça Deodoro, which leads into the southern zone.

Shops offering luxury goods can be found in cross-streets such as the Rua Visconde de Inhauma (which turns into the Avenida Marechal Floriano), the Ruas Teófilo Otoni, da Alfândega, Buenos Aires, do Rosário, do Ouvidor, 7 de Setembro, da Assembléia, São José and Almirante Barroso.

Avenida Getúlio Vargas intersects the Avenida Rio Branco beyond the Rua Teófilo Otoni. It is Rio's longest (2.5 mi/4 km) and widest (nearly 300 ft/90 m) street. Going down the Avenida Rio Branco, you will be able to spot the following :

Nossa Senhora da Candelária*** (Praça Pio X), an imposing church that was built in the late 18th century. Monumental in size, it has a Rococo façade; the cupola was added in the 19th century.

São Francisco de Paula** (Largo São Francisco) is a lovely church which was built in 1759. The interior contains works by Mestre Valentim and Manuel da Cunha. A wonderful fountain stands at the back of the church. The first anniversary of Brazilian independence was celebrated here. In the same square there is a statue of José Bonifácio de Andrada e Silva.

Nossa Senhora do Rosário e São Benedito* (Rua Uruguaiana) was built in 1770. Inside is a tomb that is the work of the sculptor Mestre Valentim. This church also houses the **Museum of the Negro** (open Mon-Fri 8am-5pm), which relates the history of slavery. Two other interesting churches in the area are **Santa Rita** (Rua Visconde de Inhaúma) and **Nossa Senhora Mae dos Homes** (Rua de Alfândega).

Praça Mauá I, B1

This square lies near the northern gate into the city centre and is one of the liveliest spots in town. The Mariano Procopi bus terminal for transportation to the northern zone and suburbs and the harbour station are located here. We recommend that you visit the nearby **Mosteiro de São Bento***** (Rua Dom Gerardo 85, ☎ 2917122). Built by Benedictine monks on the Morro de São Bento between 1633 and 1641, this monastery is one of the most beautiful examples of Brazilian religious architecture. While the exterior is quite austere, the interior is a veritable masterpiece of Baroque art, with flamboyantly gilded woodwork, sculpture by Mestre Valentim and paintings by Ricardo do Pilar. Its vast library boasts a great number of ancient works.

Praça Floriano and Praça Mahatma Gandhi I, C2-3

These two pleasant squares, with trees and statues, lie at the southern tip of the Avenida Rio Branco, just before you reach Praça Deodoro. This part of town is a good deal less congested than the rest of the centre, and many of Rio's cinemas and theatres are located in this district. Nearby places worth visiting include the following:

Museu Nacional de Belas Artes*** (National Museum of Fine Arts, Av. Rio Branco 199, ☎ 2400160; open Tues-Fri 10am-5:30pm, Sat and Sun 3-6pm) was first created in 1816 for works brought to Brazil by a delegation of French artists that included Debret, Montigny and Taunay, among others. It also houses Italian paintings of the 17th, 18th and 19th centuries, 19th-century French paintings, and Flemish, Dutch and Portuguese oil paintings. Brazilian art displayed here includes paintings by Rodriguès de Sá, Zeferino da Costa, Araújo Porto Alegre, Visconti, R. Bernardelli Meireles, José de Paulá and di Cavalcanti, as well as sculptures by De Vilares, H. Bernardelli, Veloso and Giorgi.

Biblioteca Nacional** (National Library, Av. Rio Branco 219, ☎ 240 8229) is without a doubt the best library in South America. It contains more than three million works, some of which are extremely rare.

Teatro Municipal** (Municipal Theatre, Praça Floriano) was completed in 1909 and is one of the foremost artistic centres in Brazil. At Carnival time, the most important ball is held here. There is also a theatrical museum on the premises.

The area has various other monuments and places of interest that you might like to visit:

Instituto Histórico e Geográfico* (Historical and Geographic Institute, Av. Augusto Severo 8, ☎ 252 4430; open Mon-Fri 9am-5pm) has a library and a historical museum and presents interesting exhibits on Brazilian handcrafts.

The equestrian statue of Marshall Deodoro da Fonseca* (Passeio Público) commemorates the statesman who proclaimed Brazilian independence.

The statue of Marshall Floriano Peixoto* (Praça Floriano) honours the second president of the Brazilian republica.

The Obelisk* commemorates the inauguration of the Avenida Rio Branca in 1906.

Passeio Público* (Rua do Passeio) is Rio's oldest public park, dating from 1783. It was designed by Mestre Valentim, who also executed the bronze gate.

Praça XV (Quinze de Novembro) I, C2

This is Rio's oldest square and was for a long time the centre of the city. When the Portuguese royal family fled to Brazil in March 1808, they disembarked at the Pharoux quay *(cais)*, which used to be the only landing stage in town before the new harbour in Praça Mauá was built. Today it only serves for navigation inside Guanabara Bay. Since the overhead expressway, Avenida Presidente Kubitschek, was built, the neighbourhood has not been as quiet as it once was.

There are several sights to see in this area.

Convent of Carmo** (Praça XV) is the oldest foundation in Rio. Built in 1590, it now houses part of a university.

Catedral Metropolitana** (Metropolitan Cathedral, Av. Chile) was built by the Carmelites in 1761 and was the former cathedral to the Portuguese royal court. It was completely overhauled in 1890 and a new tower was added in 1905. The remains of many famous men rest in this cathedral, including those of Pedro Alvares Cabral, the man who discovered Brazil.

Nossa Senhora do Carmo** (Rua Primeiro de Março) stands adjacent to the Metropolitan Cathedral, and dates from 1770. The novitiate's chapel and altar are by Mestre Valentim.

Paço Imperial** (Praça XV, ☎ 232 8333; open Tues-Sun 10am-6:30pm) was originally the royal palace and now houses the Department of Posts and Telegraphs. It is a fine example of vintage colonial architecture.

Other places in the area are worth visiting if you have the time.

Alfândega Antiga* (Rua Visconde de Itaborai 78) is the customs building. It is the only surviving building of the architect Montigny.

Arco de Teles* (Praça XV) is an 18th-century construction; the arch is the only vestige of a Senate building.

The statue of General Manuel Luís Osório* (Praça XV) honours the man who won the war against Paraguay. It was sculpted by R. Bernardelli.

Santa Cruz dos Militares* (Rua Primeiro de Março 36, ☎ 2211878) is a small, beautiful church that was constructed between 1780 and 1811 during the colonial period. It now houses a small historical museum (open Mon-Fri 1-4pm).

Castelo I, D2

This is a new neighbourhood built on the site of the Morro do Castelo, which was destroyed in 1922. There are several interesting buildings and monuments to visit here that date from the days of the Morro do Castelo.

Museu Histórico Nacional*** (National Historical Museum, Praça Marechal Ancora, ☎ 2407878; open Tues-Fri 10am-5:30pm, Sat and Sun 2-6pm) is one of the most interesting museums in Rio. It stands on the site of a former 18th-century barracks, which, itself, was built upon an old fortress dating from 1683. The museum's collection of paintings, furniture, china, royal objects, weapons and torture instruments traces the history and way of life in Brazil from its discovery until its proclamation as a republic.

Museu da Imagem e do Som** (Museum of Image and Sound, Praça Rui Barbosa 1, ☎ 2620309; open Mon-Fri 1-6pm) houses documents, films, photographs (100,000 of which are of pre-1940 Rio) and tapes about the city's life and history. It also contains a sizeable collection of musical scores.

Nossa Senhora de Bonsucesso** (Rua Santa Luzia 206, ☎ 2203001) is a lovely church that dates from 1708. The elaborate altars are of particular interest.

Palácio da Cultura** (Palace of Culture, Rua Araújo de Porto Alegre) contains sculptures by Giorgi and paintings by Portinari. The building was designed by Le Corbusier; its construction was begun in 1937. It once housed the Ministry of Education.

Villa-Lobos Museum** (Rua Sorocaba 200, ☎ 2663845; open Mon-Fri 9am-5:30pm) contains various objects and memorabilia that once belonged to the famous composer.

If you have extra time, you might also like to visit some of the following:

The statue of Dom Pedro I* (Praça Tiradentes) honours the first emperor of Brazil.

Santa Casa de Misericordia Hospital* (Rua Santa Luzia) was founded in 1582 and rebuilt in the 19th century.

Santa Luzia* (Rua Santa Luzia 490, ☎ 2204367) is a charming little church that dates from 1752.

The Aterreo I, C3

Between Avenida Beira Mar and Guanabara Bay is the Aterreo 'landfill'. This area, which is the site of the Museum of Modern Art and the War Memorial, was reclaimed from the bay and the adjacent Parque do Flamengo created. Near the memorial is the main station for the little train *(trenzinho)*, which runs through the area.

Museu de Arte Moderna*** (Museum of Modern Art, Av. Infante Dom Henrique, ☎ 2102188; open Tues-Sun noon-5:30pm) was built in 1958 by Alfonso Reidy. Until 1978, when a fire destroyed the building and much of its collection, this was Brazil's finest showcase of contemporary art. The museum is undergoing renovation at the time of publication.

National War Memorial* (opposite Praça Paris) honours Brazil's dead in World War II. It is a simple modern monument that blends in well with its surroundings. Near the monument there is a small museum commemorating the role played by Brazil in World War II (☎ 2401283; open Tues-Sun 8am-5pm).

Avenida República do Chile I, BC2

This avenue runs through a neighbourhood that, today, is constantly undergoing change. Here, you will find monuments and buildings of every conceivable architectural style. A handful of old buildings have survived in their original form, but others, like the ancient Largo da Carioca, have been changed beyond recognition. Sights worth visiting in this area include:

Carioca Aqueduct*** (Largo das Pracinhas) is nearly 800 ft/243 m long. Completed in 1750, it was originally built to channel the water of the Carioca River. Today, it serves as a viaduct for the Santa Teresa tramway.

São Francisco da Penitência*** (Largo da Carioca, ☎ 2620197) is a church that was built in 1656. It boasts one of the most opulent interiors in Rio: jacaranda wood paneling and a ceiling by Caetano Costa Coelho. It also contains a museum of religious art.

Convento de Santo Antônio** (Largo da Carioca, ☎ 2620129), adjacent to São Francisco, was founded in 1619 and contains many tombs of members of the imperial family.

Catedral Nova* (New Cathedral, Av. República do Chile) is not completely finished. Dedicated in 1976, its most spectacular feature is four stained-glass windows.

Petrobas Building* (Av. República do Chile) is the headquarters of a Brazilian oil company. The cube-shaped construction, with lovely indoor gardens created by Burle-Marx, is a fine architectural achievement.

Praça da República I, AB2

Although part of the city centre, this is a fairly quiet neighbourhood. The streets around the central railway station, Estaçao Dom Pedro II, are however quite lively. This area offers many interesting sights.

Campo de Santana** (Av. Presidente Vargas), a huge park, was the site of two of the most important events in Brazilian history: in 1822, Dom Pedro I proclaimed Brazil an empire, and in 1889, Marshall Deodoro proclaimed Brazil a republic.

Museu do Palácio do Itamarati** (Av. Marechal Floriano 196, ☎ 2914411; open Tues-Fri 11am-5pm), built in 1852 by Baron Itamarati, became the home of the first president of Brazil when the republic was declared in 1889. Used as the headquarters of the foreign ministry from 1897 to 1970, it now contains a museum dedicated to Brazilian history and its own past. Check to find out if it is open, because at time of publication it was closed for renovation.

Arquivo Nacional* (National Archives, Praça da República) is the largest public archives in Brazil.

Casa da Moeda* (Mint, Rua Azeredo Coutinho 77, ☎ 2522617; open Mon-Fri 9am-5pm) now houses the Museum of Numismatics and Philately.

The equestrian statue of the Duque de Caxias* (Praça Duque de Caxias) was erected in 1899 in honour of one Brazil's great soldiers.

The southern zone

The neighbourhoods of Rio's southern zone are the city's prime residential areas. They offer some lovely walks and interesting sites. Tour them when you want a break from the beaches or from the frenetic pace of the city centre.

Santa Teresa II, B1

One of Rio's most picturesque neighbourhoods, Santa Teresa is situated on a small hill adjacent to the foothills of the Tijuca forest. It is a quiet place with almost no traffic. The streets, known as *ladeiras*, climb tortuously up the slopes and offer splendid views of Rio below.

Santa Teresa's residents consider themselves a class apart. Many foreigners live here, as do artists, writers and other public figures. The best way to get here is to take the famous tramway *(bonde eletrico)* from its terminal in the city centre near the Petrobas Building behind the Largo da Carioca. The tramway, which crosses the Carioca Aqueduct, was built in 1896. Local activism has kept it from being demolished. Don't miss a visit to the following:

Museu Chácara do Céu*** (Rua Martinho Nobre 93, ☎ 2248981 ; open

Tues-Sat 2-5pm, Sun 1-5pm) was a gift from the renowned patron of the arts and collector, Raymundo Ottoni da Castro Maya. This museum houses many interesting works of art by great Brazilian painters like Portinari and Visconti, as well as works by foreign painters such as Matisse, Dali and Vlaminck. It also contains 18th- and 19th-century Brazilian and Oriental objects and furniture, plus a collection of ancient china. Perhaps its best feature is an enormous garden with a view that includes most of Rio.

Convento de Santa Teresa* (Ladeira de Santa Teresa 52, ☎ 224 1040) was founded in 1753 and is still home to a community of Carmelite nuns. It is a sober-looking building in the colonial style.

Glória, Catete and Flamengo II, CD1

Leaving the Avenida Rio Branco and heading south along the express motorway, you will come across three entrancing neighbourhoods. All along the bay you will have an excellent view of Sugarloaf. The construction of the underground has taken a considerable toll on these streets, yet vestiges of the area's residential past remain. The following sights are worth your attention:

Palácio do Catete*** (Rua do Catete 153, ☎ 225 4302), which dates from 1867, was originally the seat of the federal government. It later became the mansion of several of the republic's presidents. It now houses the **Museu da República**, with a collection of furniture, arms and documents bearing on the history of the republic, and the **Museu Folclore**, with its extensive collection of items on Brazilian folklore and the influence of African cults.

Nossa Senhora da Glória do Outeiro** (on Glória hill, ☎ 225 2869) can be reached either by steps or a tiny funicular up the Ladeira de Nossa Senhora da Glória. This is a charming little church that was once the favourite of the imperial family. It is elliptical in shape and its wooden altar was carved by Mestre Valentim. Adjacent is a small museum of religious art.

Parque do Flamengo** is about 2.5 mi/4 km long and stretches from Santos-Dumont Airport along Guanabara Bay all the way to Botafogo. It covers about 300 acres/121 hectares and sits on land reclaimed from the bay. Designed by Burle Marx, it opened in 1965 during the 400th anniversary of Rio's founding. It contains several sights that can be visited on a little train (the station is near the National War Memorial, see p. 89). There are sports fields, a puppet theatre, gardens, a boat basin and spots for dancing.

Laranjeiras and Cosme Velho II, BC1-2

Laranjeiras is a handsome residential area where the 'coffee barons' built magnificent townhouses *(palacetes)*. Cosme Velho is a less select neighbourhood that lies at the bottom of a valley close to Corcovado (see p. 83). The train station for the trip to Corcovado is located here. Sights to see in this area include:

Palácio Guanabara** (Rua Pinheiro Machado) was built in 1865 for Princess Isabel, the daughter of Dom Pedro II. Today, it is the residence of the Governor of the state of Rio de Janeiro.

Largo do Boticário** (Rua Cosme Velho 822) is an attractive little square of colonial buildings, with many little antique shops.

Parque Guinle** (Rua Gago Coutinho) is a park of handsome residential buildings designed by Lucio Costa. **Laranjeiras Palace**, where the president lives when he is in Rio, stands in the centre of it.

Bica de Rainha* (Rua Cosme Velho) is a spring that is famous because of the high iron content in its water.

Botafogo II, C2

Botafogo is a charming, quiet neighbourhood with a low skyline and many old buildings. It lies between Guanabara Bay and the Rodrigo de Freitas lagoon. Take a stroll in the area and visit the **Casa de Rui Barbosa**** (Rua

São Clemente 134, ☎ 286 1297; open Tues-Fri 10am-4:30pm, Sat and Sun 2-5pm), formerly the home of the celebrated jurist and legislator, Rui Barbosa. It is now a museum exhibiting his personal belongings, documents and furniture — a fine example of a 19th-century private house.

Urca II, D2

You can visit this tiny neighbourhood at the foot of Sugarloaf before taking the cable-car up to the top. The **Monumento aos Herois de Laguna e Dourados*** (Praça General Tiburçio) is an interesting sight. It was raised in memory of the heroes of the war with Paraguay.

Lagoa, Jardim Botânico and Gávea II, AB3

Wedged between the mountains and the sea, these neighbourhoods are, together with Ipanema, Copacabana and Leblon, among the most prestigious districts of the southern zone, especially Jardim Botânico. They are less than 2 mi/3 km from the sea on one side and close to the lagoon, the mountains and the lush vegetation of Tijuca forest.

Jardim Botânico* (Botanical Garden, Rua Jardim Botânico 920, ☎ 274 4898; open daily 8am-5pm) is a magnificent park of approximately 350 acres/141 hectares. It contains some 5000 trees and thousands of plant species. There are particularly beautiful collections of orchids, as well as bromeliads and cacti and a number of plants from the virgin forests of Amazonia. Note, too, the imperial palm grove where the first tree known as Palma Mater was planted in 1809 (the ancestor of all others in the area). The Botanical Garden is also the home of the **Museu Carpológico**, with a collection of more than 150,000 seeds and varieties of fruit, and the **Museu Kuhlmann**, another important botanical museum (both open same hours as Botanical Garden).

Parque da Cidade (Estrada da Santa Mariana, ☎ 322 1328) was formerly the property of the Guinlé family, who donated it to the city. It consists of 75 acres/30 hectares of unspoiled virgin forest, as well as a very beautiful collection of orchids. The mansion in the grounds is now the **Museu da Cidade** (☎ 322 1328). It houses art, furniture and documents relating to the history of Brazil.

Rodrigo de Freitas lagoon is the only remaining lagoon of old Rio. All the districts surrounding it benefit from its unusual character. It is connected to the sea by a tree-lined canal, which is a wonderful place to take a stroll.

Joquei Clube de Gávea* (Jockey Club, Praça Santos Dumont, ☎ 274 0055) holds races day and night. It is a very lively place, especially on the first Sunday of August when the main horse-race of the year, the Grand Prix of Brazil, is held.

Parque Lage* (Rua Jardim Botânico 414) has lovely gardens, lakes and playgrounds for children. The Institute of Fine Arts is housed here.

Planetarium* (Av. Padre Leonel Franco 240, ☎ 274 0096; open Mon-Fri 8am-10pm, Sat and Sun 10am-10pm) was opened in 1970.

São Conrado II, CD4, Joá and Barra da Tijuca

These neighbourhoods are on the outskirts of Rio just beyond the Dois Irmãos mountain near Leblon. There are three ways to get to São Conrado: via the Dois Irmãos tunnel, on Avenida Niemeyer; via the picturesque coastal route; or through the Rocinha slum. São Conrado is residential, but it also boasts a good many bars and restaurants, several fine hotels and the Golf-Clube de Gávea.

From the residential district of Joá, which straddles the foothills of the Pedra da Gávea mountain, you will have a splendid view of Barra da Tijuca. Along the lagoon a number of luxury motels have gone up in the last few years, and their many neon signs make the area look like a miniature Las Vegas.

In Barra da Tijuca you'll find nightclubs, bars, restaurants and samba dance halls (sambões), all of which are packed on weekends. Beyond it are the arid wilds of Restinga de Jacarepagua, a large stretch of marshy plain where the Brazilians are thinking of putting up a modern city designed by Niemeyer. Still farther west is the gigantic Barra da Tijuca beach stretching all the way to the Recreio dos Bandeirantes peninsula. Beyond are the secluded Prainha and Grumari beaches.

Tijuca forest II, A2

This magnificent forest starts almost in the heart of Rio. It began with an outstanding job of reforestation undertaken in 1857 by Major Manuel Archer and continued in 1874 by Baron d'Escragnolle. It has seven different entrances (open 8am-8pm).

From the city centre and the southern zone

Caboclos gate, via Cosme Velho, leads to nearby Corcovado peak and the Mirante de Dona Marta. Following this route a bit farther, you will reach the Estrada do Redentor, which cuts through the forest and comes out at Alto da Boa Vista. Along the way there is a breathtaking panorama. **Mirante de Dona Marta***** is a foothill of Corcovado and stretches almost into town. It doesn't offer as extensive a view as Corcovado, but it does have a good view of the entire bay, Sugarloaf and the city centre.

Macacos gate leads via the Jardim Botânico to the Estrada Dona Castorina and hence to the Estrada da Vista Chinesa. **Mesa do Imperador**** offers another superb view. Dom Pedro II used to be a frequent visitor here, thus its name. **Vista Chinesa**** got its name during the reign of Dom João VI when Chinese farmers tried to grow tea here. The view is remarkable.

Sumaré gate leads from the Estrada de Sumaré to the Estrada do Redentor. This is a long route. **Mirante do Sumaré**** is located near this entrance into the forest and affords a wide view over the northern zone.

Via Alto de Boa Vista

The roads to the other four gates all run through this tiny village on the opposite side of the forest from the city centre. It can be reached from the north via Maracanã and Tijuca or from the south via São Conrado or Barra da Tijuca.

Floresta gate is the main entry into the forest and can be reached from the Estrada do Imperador. It leads to the most interesting part of the forest — a jumble of waterfalls, panoramas, peaks, rivers and spots to picnic. Places worth seeing include **Cascatinha Taunay****, a waterfall that tumbles two storeys; **Açude da Solidão***, a charming small lake; **Bom Retiro***, the departure point for walks to Pico do Archer, Pico da Tijuca and Pico do Papagaio; **Capela Mayrink***, a tiny chapel on the Alto de Mesquita that features art by Portinari; and **Vista Excelsior***, which affords a magnificent view of northern zone.

There are also numerous beautiful grottos and small waterfalls, as well as three restaurants.

Açude gate, after a detour, leads to the Estrada do Imperador.

Sapucaia gate lies at the far end of the Estrada do Redentor.

Passo da Pedra gate is at the end of the Estrada da Vista Chinesa.

The northern zone

The northern zone is a vast area that stretches for over 15 mi/24 km beyond the Avenida do Brasil all along the Santa Cruz railway line. Most of this zone is without interest for the tourist, except for the district of São Cristóvão where there are a few important sites that should not be missed.

Parque de Quinta da Boa Vista*** (Av. Dom Pedro II; open daily 7am-7pm) was once the residence of Dom João VI and his three children, Dom Miguel, Dom Pedro and Dona Maria Tereza. It was given to him in 1818 by Elias Antônio Lopes, a wealthy Portuguese merchant. The palace itself, Quinta Boa Vista, houses the National Museum. The gardens are well kept and can be explored in a horse-drawn carriage. In the park you can visit:

- **Museu Nacional***** (National Museum, ☎ 2648262; open Tues-Sun 10am-4:45pm) is the largest natural history museum in Brazil and one of the most important in South America. It houses zoological, archaeological, ethnographic and mineralogical collections, with over one million specimens. It contains items from other South American countries as well as Brazil. The reference library has more than 300,000 books.

- **Zoological Garden***** (☎ 2542024; open daily 7am-7pm) is an enormous zoo (22 acres/9 hectares) that specializes in birds of every sort. In particular, see the royal hawks.

- **Museu da Fauna**** (Fauna Museum, opposite the entrance to the zoo, ☎ 2280556; open Tues-Sun noon-4:30pm) has a collection of birds and mammals from regions throughout Brazil.

Other sights that you may want to visit in the nearby area include:

Maracanã Stadium** (Av. Maracanã) is the largest stadium in the world. It was built in 1950 for the fourth World Soccer Championship. Designed to hold 155,000 spectators, it sometimes has to accommodate 200,000 on days when there is an important match (see p. 79).

Museu do Índio** (Indian Museum, Rua das Palmeiras 55, ☎ 2862097) houses a collection of over 12,000 artifacts created by the indigenous tribes from Amazonia, Xingu, Pará, Maranhão, Nordeste, Sul and Paraguay. It was inaugurated in 1953 and, in 1967, became part of FUNAI (see p. 49).

Guanabara Bay

This famous bay stretches 18 mi/30 km inland and its shores are some 88 mi/140 km in length. Rio lies on its western shore, Niterói on its eastern. Going around the bay used to be a 93 mi/150 km trip. Now, you can cross it in a few minutes via the Rio-Niterói bridge. Built in 1975, it is over 4 mi/6 km long.

Although the bay's waters are polluted, it retains its charm. It has 84 islands of considerable variety. There are boat tours of the bay that start from Avenida Nestor Moreira in Botafogo (☎ 2951997). Ferry service to Paquetá and Ilha do Governador is offered by **Conerj** (☎ 2310396), and hovercraft service to Paquetá is offered by **Transtur** (☎ 2310339).

Ilha de Paquetá** is the most beautiful of the bay's islands. With 270 acres/110 hectares, it is also the second largest. It was called 'Isle of Love' by Dom João VI. The great Brazilian novelist, Joaquim Manuel de Macedo, extolled its virtues in his novel, *A Moreninha*. Paquetá is a haven of peace free of the noise and pollution of automobiles since bicycles and horsedrawn carriages are the only means of transportation available. Vegetation is lush and the coast consists of one lovely beach after another, interspersed with rugged rock formations. There are some interesting old colonial houses here, such as those of Dom João VI and José Bonifacio, the father of Brazilian independence.

Other sights worth visiting are the tiny **São Roque** church and its cemetery and the nearby islands of **Brocoió** and **dos Lobos**.

Ilha do Governador* is the largest island in the bay, with a surface of over 12 sq mi/32 sq km and a length of over 6 mi/10 km. It is connected to the mainland by a bridge. There are some handsome old private houses to see here, plus restaurants and hotels.

▬ ENVIRONS OF RIO

See maps pp. 65, 104.

Outlying beaches

Costa Verde

This is a verdant stretch of coast that runs south-west of Rio all the way to São Paulo state. It curves around the gigantic Sepetiba Bay and has become much easier to visit since the Rio-Santos highway was built in 1974-1975. If you follow the coast down from Guaratiba to Parati (the last town reached before leaving Rio de Janeiro state), you can stop at the following places:

Guaratiba* provides access to the sandbanks of Restinga do Marambaia, which jut out into Sepetiba Bay.

Itacuruçá** is an appealing little village that also serves as a base for excursions around the bay.

Sepetiba Bay*** is around 62 mi/100 km long and enclosed by a large sandbank called Restinga do Marambaia and a picturesque island called Ilha Grande. There are over 300 islands of varying sizes in the bay, most of which are covered with lush tropical vegetation. They can be reached from several of the bay's ports. Fish are plentiful here, and at certain times of year you can see giant skate swimming near the surface of the warm, shallow water. There are also facilities for every kind of water sport. Places worth visiting around the bay include:

- **Ilha Grande**** (60 sq mi/155 sq km) is the largest island in the bay. It is a former penal colony, now covered with untamed vegetation. It can be reached by boat from Mangaratiba, Angra dos Reis and Parati. Odd vestiges of colonial architecture, such as an aqueduct, remain. The beaches are very attractive, and boat rides that circle the island are available.

- **Ilha do Jaguanum*** is an unspoiled small island.

- **Sepetiba*** is a picturesque little fishing village.

- **Mongaratiba*** is a lovely town with beautiful beaches, splendid views and interesting colonial architecture.

Angra dos Reis* is a booming resort, industrial centre and harbour all rolled into one, which is located 105 mi/169 km south-west of Rio. The town is quite a historical place, with colonial buildings and churches, including two you should try to see: **Nossa Senhora da Concieçao**, dating from 1625, and **Nossa Senhora do Carmo**, dating from 1620. There is also a convent that is well worth a visit, **Convento de São Bernadino de Sena**** (Morro de Santo Antônio, open Tues-Sun 8-11:30am, 1-5pm). Built in 1653, the convent has been abandoned since 1763. Some noteworthy vestiges remain, and the site offers a stupendous view of the town and the harbour.

The areas surrounding the town are still wild, with myriad miniature creeks trickling down the mountainside. The ocean water around Angra dos Reis is of a transparency rarely seen in Brazil. From its harbour you can visit such islands as Ilha Grande, Garaguases, Gipóia, Comprida and Bonfim.

Parati*** is a small town that lies 161 mi/260 km south-west of Rio. It was 'discovered' by tourists when the 60 mi/100 km road from Angra dos Reis was paved. Its sober colonial architecture has survived intact because the town was isolated for so long. The entire town, with its 455 houses, has now been declared a national treasure. There are two lovely churches to see here, Rosário and Santa Rita de Cassia, both dating from 1722. There is also a fort that dates from 1822.

About 6 mi/10 km from Parati are some good beaches. You can also take interesting excursions from here to Ilha do Algodão, Ilha do Arauko and Cedros.

Costa del Sol

The Sun Coast stretches east of Rio from Niterói and ends at the Lagoa Feia (lagoon), slightly above the city of Macaé. The ocean has closed off all of the existing bays with huge sandbanks, creating magnificent lagoons. Since the construction of the Rio-Niterói bridge this area has become a tourist attraction.

Niterói** is the former capital of Rio de Janeiro state. Founded in 1573, it was long known as an Indian village called São Lourenço. In 1835, its name changed to Niterói, which means 'smooth waters'. Two old churches, **Nossa Senhora de Boa Viagem** (1663) and **São Francisco Xavier** (1572), are well worth visiting. Niterói also boasts two forts, **Imbui** (1863) and **Santa Cruz** (1555), as well as a museum devoted to the Brazilian painter Antônio Parreiras (Rua Tiradentes 47).

There are a good many beaches along Niterói's bay, such as Flechas, Icaraí, Boa Viagem and Saco de São Francisco. The most unspoiled and beautiful ones are on the ocean, however, some 12 mi/20 km away. Parallel to them run splendid lagoons called **Piratininga, Itacoatiara** and **Itaipu**, names that are typically Indian (*ita* means stone).

Marica* and **Saguarema*** are small residential towns and tourist centres.

Araruama* is a small resort 75 mi/120 km east of Rio that faces the ocean and a lagoon. It is a centre for mud baths that are purported to cure rheumatism. The town of Araruama lies inland on the shores of the Araruama lagoon (18 mi/30 km long, the largest in the area) but all the good hotels and restaurants are located along the oceanfront beach, the Praia Seca.

Cabo Frio**, 105 mi/170 km to the east of Rio, is a resort much appreciated by Brazilians and by the inhabitants of Rio who come here for their holidays and for Carnival. After being discovered in 1503 by Amerigo Vespucci, the cape became a landmark for navigators and grew into a small colony. Today, the town depends almost exclusively on the tourist industry. At the height of the tourist season it can accommodate as many as 200,000 visitors, thanks to facilities in the town itself, in nearby **Arraial do Cabo**, 6 mi/10 km south, and in **Armaçao dos Buzios**, a fishermen's village about 12 mi/20 km north.

The town boasts a number of old churches, including **Nossa Senhora da Assumpçao** (1615) and **Nossa Senhora Dos Anjos** (1686). It also has an interesting harbour, **São Mateus**, constructed in 1615. Arraial do Cabo has two well-preserved 16th-century churches, **Nossa Senhora dos Remedios** and **Nossa Senhora dos Sagrados**.

Cabo Frio is best known, however, for its remarkable setting and wonderful beaches, including:

● in Cabo Frio itself, Praia do Forte, Praia das Conchas and Praia do Pero.
● at Armação dos Buzios, Praia de Azeda, Brava, Praia dos Buzios, Praia da Ferradura, Praia da Foca, Jeriba and Joçâo Fernandes.
● at Arraial do Cabo, Praia do Forno, Praia dos Anjos, Prainha.

These three tourist centres offer good excursions. You can visit the **Bufalo** and **Cabo islands** and the **Bufalo** and **Azul grottos**.

Rio das Ostras* is a small community located approximately 118 mi/191 km from Rio. Although it is practically devoid of tourist facilities, it is still an interesting place to visit. There are beautiful, unspoiled beaches between Rio das Ostras and Barra de São João.

Macaé** is located approximately 136 mi/220 km from Rio. It is not a tourist centre despite its good beaches (in particular Imbetiba to the south), its lagoons (Imboassica and Carapebus), its islands and its handful of handsome colonial buildings, mainly churches and private mansions. There is also the **Monte Eliseo Castle** dating from 1866.

Accommodation

▲▲▲ **Nas Rocas Club**, Armação dos Búzios, ☎ (0246) 23 1303. In a superb location, this hotel has a wonderful view. It includes a restaurant, three bars, a discotheque and facilities for water sports. 70 rooms.

▲▲ **Angra Inn**, Estr. do Contorno 2629, Angra dos Reis, ☎ (0243) 65 1299. A restaurant, two bars and a swimming pool distinguish this modest hotel. 100 rooms.

▲▲ **Lagos Copa Hotel**, Av. Elias Agostinho 500, Macaé, ☎ (0247) 62 1405. This comfortable hotel has a restaurant, a bar and a swimming pool. 74 rooms.

▲▲ **Pescador**, Av. Beira-Rio, Parati, ☎ (0243) 71 1466. Modest and comfortable, this hotel includes a restaurant, a bar and a swimming pool. 23 rooms.

▲▲ **Porto Aquarius,** Angra dos Reis, ☎ (0243) 65 1642. In an excellent location, with a wonderful view, a restaurant, bar, swimming pool and water sports facilities. 96 rooms.

▲▲ **Pousada do Ouro,** Rua Dr. Pereira 145, Parati, ☎ (0243) 71 1311. In a superb location, this hotel includes a restaurant, a bar and a swimming pool. 23 rooms.

▲▲ **Pousada Pardieiro,** Rua do Comércio 74, Parati, ☎ (0243) 71 1370. A nicely situated hotel with a restaurant, two bars and a swimming pool. 22 rooms.

▲ **Acapulco,** Praia das Dunas, Cabo Frio, ☎ (0246) 43 0202. A restaurant, a bar and a swimming pool are offered by this modest hotel. 40 rooms.

▲ **Cabo Frio Bangalos,** Rua Roma 101, Cabo Frio, ☎ (0246) 43 3828. This hotel is simple but comfortable and includes a restaurant, a bar and a swimming pool. 108 rooms.

▲ **Caribe,** Rua da Concieçao 255, Angra dos Reis, ☎ (0243) 65 0033. A simple hotel with all the basic amenities — telephone, television. 55 rooms.

▲ **Coxixo,** Rua do Comércio 362, Parati, ☎ (0243) 71 1460. This nicely located hotel has a bar and a swimming pool. 27 rooms.

▲ **Malibu Palace,** Av. do Contorno 900, Cabo Frio, ☎ (0246) 43 3131. This modest hotel has a restaurant, a bar and a swimming pool. 102 rooms.

▲ **Mercado de Pouso,** Largo Santa Rita, Parati, ☎ (0243) 71 1114. A simple hotel with a bar. 23 rooms.

▲ **Niterói Palace,** Rua Andrade Neves 134, Niterói, ☎ (021) 719 2155. This comfortable hotel has a restaurant and bar. 60 rooms.

▲ **Panorama,** Av. Elias Agostinho 290, Macaé, ☎ (0247) 62 4455. A modest hotel with a simple restaurant and bar. 58 rooms.

▲ **Parque Hotel Araruama,** Rua Argentina 502, Araruama, ☎ (0246) 65 2129. This lovely hotel sits in a park and offers a nice view, as well as a restaurant, a bar and a swimming pool. 17 rooms.

▲ **Senzala,** Rua Amaral Peixoto, Araruama, ☎ (0246) 24 2230. A comfortable hotel with a restaurant, a bar and a swimming pool. 25 rooms.

Food

** **Adamastor,** Rua José Bento Ribeiro Dantas 712, Armaçao dos Búzios. This restaurant provides delicious seafood and a lovely view. Open daily 2pm-midnight.

** **Au Cheval Blanc,** Rua José Bento Ribeiro Dantas 181, Armaçao dos Búzios, ☎ (0246) 23 1445. French cuisine in a superb setting. Open daily 1pm-midnight.

** **Chez Dominique,** BR-101 Sul, Angra dos Reis. This charming restaurant offers excellent French cuisine. Open daily 1-5pm, 7-11pm.

** **Copa de Ouro,** Hotel Pousada do Ouro, Rua Dr. Pereira 145, Parati, ☎ (0243) 71 1378. Good seafood in simple surroundings. Open daily 11am-4pm, 7-11pm.

** **Fazenda Murycana,** Estr. Cunha, Parati, ☎ (0243) 71 1153. Brazilian cuisine in a lovely park location. Open daily 11am-6pm.

** **Veleiro,** Av. dos Namorados, Cabo Frio. A delicious variety of seafood is served in this pleasant restaurant. Open daily 11-2am.

* **Hiltinho,** Rua Mal. Deodoro 233, Parati, ☎ (0243) 71 1432. Modest seafood restaurant. Open daily 11am-midnight.

* **Picolino**, Rua Mal. Floriano 319, Cabo Frio, ☎ (0246) 43 2436. This modest restaurant specializes in international cuisine. Open daily noon-midnight.
* **Riomar**, Av. Pres. Sodré 406, Macaé, ☎ (0247) 62 0532. This pleasantly located restaurant offers good seafood. Open Mon-Sat 11am-10pm.
* **Le Streghe Búzios**, Av. José Bento Ribeiro Dantas 201, Armaçao dos Búzios. Good Italian cooking in a pleasant location. Open Mon-Fri 8pm-2am.
* **Taberna 33**, Av. Raul Pompéia 110, Angra dos Reis. Modest Italian restaurant. Open Mon-Fri 6pm-1am.
* **La Tavola**, Av. Pres. Sodré 736, Macaé. Modest little seafood restaurant. Open Sun-Fri 11am-4pm.

RIO DE JANEIRO STATE

See maps pp. 65.

Although one of Brazil's smallest states (17,092 sq mi/44,268 sq km), Rio de Janeiro has a population of more than 13.3 million. Its economy is predominantly industrial (metallurgy, steel and chemicals), with agriculture consisting mostly of sugarcane production. Also, much of Brazil's oil comes from off-shore sites around the Campos area.

The production of coffee, long the major crop of the region, has shifted to the south and west. This has led to the economic decline of the state, which largely owes its survival to its proximity to the city of Rio.

If you are interested in finding out what Brazil is really like, the best way is to take a trip into the countryside. Heading for the interior, you will soon catch sight of the magnificent mountain ranges known as *serras*, which moderate the area's temperatures and account for the region's many resorts. Some of these lie in the Serra dos Orgãos, some 62 mi/100 km from Rio. Farther west on the border with Minas Gerais (see p. 215), the foothills of the Serra da Mantigueira blend into a plateau known as *Agulhas Negras* (Black Needles). This pleasant region, although only 31 mi/50 km from the sea, reaches an altitude of 9144 ft/2787 m.

Petrópolis**, at an altitude of 2756 ft/840 m and 43 mi/70 km north of Rio, is one of the most popular mountain resorts with an invigorating climate and an interesting historical past. Originally a small hamlet called Corregeo Seco, it appealed to Dom Pedro I, who bought a home here in 1814. During the reign of Dom Pedro II the community grew due to an influx of German immigrants. Dom Pedro II had a summer house built here that became an imperial palace.

The area is known for its abundant flowers. It also has many interesting sights, including the **Palácio Imperial**, which houses the **Museu Imperial**** (Rua da Imperatriz 220; open Tues-Sun noon-5pm). The museum exhibits art, documents, furniture and costumes that belonged to the imperial family. You might also take a look at the **Casa de Santos Dumont**, which was the home of the celebrated Brazilian aviator; the **Palácio de Cristal**, a copy of London's Crystal Palace, and the **Quitandinha**, a Norman-style former private home. If you like flowers, there are three horticulturists that you can visit: **Florilândia** (roses) and **Floralia** and **Binot** (orchids).

Teresópolis**, at an altitude of 2986 ft/910 m and 59 mi/95 km north-east of Rio, is becoming more fashionable than Petropolis. It is a peaceful spot with a mountainous terrain.

If you like mountain-climbing, this is an ideal area. The best-known peak is one that you can see from Rio, the **Dedo de Deus** (God's Finger). Other peaks in the region include **Dedo de Nossa Senhora** (4330 ft/1320 m), **Nariz do Frade** (6299 ft/1920 m), **Agulho do Diablo** (6627 ft/2020 m) and **Pedra do Sino** (7424 ft/2263 m). These are all in the **Parque Nacional da Serra dos Orgãos**, which has hiking trails. At nearby **Comari** and **Guarani** there are public parks, lakes and waterfalls.

Nova Friburgo**, at an altitude of 2778 ft/847 m and 87 mi/140 km north-east of Rio, lies in the Rio Bengale valley. Originally settled by the Swiss, it has glorious gardens, well-tended parks and several waterfalls.

Parque Nacional de Itatiaia*** is some 109 mi/175 km north-west of Rio in the district of Resende. It stretches 75 mi/120 km to the border with Minas Gerais. Altitudes here vary between 2723 ft/830 m and 9144 ft/2787 m. It is one of the most beautiful national parks in the country.

The easiest way to enter the park is via Itatiaia or Engenheiro along the Via Dutre. If you wish to visit Prateleira peak (8333 ft/2540 m), there is a road that goes up to an altitude of 7874 ft/2400 m; the rest of the trip must be undertaken on foot or on horseback. There are lovely waterfalls and a virgin forest on the route.

About 12 mi/20 km east of the park you can stop at the small village of **Penedo*** which was founded by Finnish settlers. A bit farther, at 31 mi/50 km, is the little town of **Visconde de Maua*** which nestles inside a green valley. **Miguel Pereira*** (70 mi/112 km north-west of Rio), **Vassouras** (73 mi/118 km north-west of Rio) and **Mendes** (87 mi/140 km north-west of Rio) are all small tourist centres in the foothills of the Serra de la Mantigueira.

Eastern Rio state

This area has less to offer tourists and is consequently less popular. Nevertheless, some of the towns are well worth a visit.

Campos*, 174 mi/280 km north-east Rio, is a large city located on the Rio Paraiba. It serves as the economic centre of the state. Take a look at the church of **Nossa Senhora do Carmo** (Rua 13 de Maio 44), dating from 1752.

There are several interesting little towns in the vicinity. You can stop at **Farol de São Tome*** (30 mi/49 km southeast of Campos) and **São João da Barra*** (25 mi/40 km northeast of Campos), both of which have lovely beaches, and the colonial-period villages of **Mussurepe*** (20 mi/32 km from Campos) and **Goitacazes** (8.5 mi/14 km from Campos). Also in the area is the **Lagoa de Cima*** (lagoon), 17 mi/28 km south of Campos.

Farther to the north you will find a handful of spas, including **Raposo**** (89 mi/143 km from Campos) and **Santó Antônio de Pádua*** (66 mi/106 km from Campos).

Accommodation

▲▲▲ **Alpina**, Av. Pres. Roosevelt 2500, Teresópolis, ☎ (021) 742 5252. This lovely hotel has a fabulous view, a restaurant, a bar, a swiming pool and various sports facilities. 42 rooms.

▲▲▲ **Bucsky**, Estr. Niterói, Nova Friburgo, ☎ (0245) 22 5052. Situated in a quiet park, this hotel has a restaurant, a bar, four swimming pools and tennis courts. 94 rooms.

▲▲▲ **Riverside Parque**, Rua Hermogêneo Silva 522, Petrópolis, ☎ (0242) 42 3704. An attractive hotel in the middle of a park, with a restaurant, a bar and a swimming pool. 13 rooms.

▲▲▲ **Sans Souci**, Rua Itajaí, Nova Friburgo, ☎ (0245) 22 7752. Lying in an extensive park, this hotel has a restaurant, three bars, three swimming pools, miniature golf and horseback riding. 70 rooms.

▲▲▲ **São Moritz**, Estr. Teresópolis, Teresópolis, ☎ (021) 742 4360. A charming hotel that sits in a park and offers a nice view, a restaurant, two bars, two swimming pools and horseback riding. 32 rooms.

▲▲▲ **Simon**, Parque Nacional, Itatiaia, ☎ (0243) 52 1122. Situated in the Itatiaia National Park, this hotel affords wonderful views. It has a restaurant, two bars, a swimming pool and various sports facilities, 58 rooms.

▲▲ **Antares**, Rua Vig. João Carlos 19, Campos, ☎ (0247) 22 4055. This comfortable hotel has a restaurant and a bar. 60 rooms.

▲▲ **Cabanas de Itatiaia**, Parque Nacional, Itatiaia, ☎ (0243) 52 1328. A modest hotel, located in the Itatiaia National Park, it offers a restaurant, a bar and a swimming pool. 7 rooms.

▲▲ **do Ypé**, Parque Nacional, Itatiaia, ☎ (0243) 52 1453. This hotel, in the Itatiaia National Park, has a lovely view. On the premises are a restaurant, a bar, a swimming pool and a boutique. 7 rooms.

▲▲ **Garlipp**, Estr. Niterói, Nova Friburgo, ☎ (0245) 42 1330. Situated in a park, this hotel has a restaurant, a bar, a swimming pool and tennis courts. 7 rooms.

▲▲ **Mury Garden**, Estr. Niterói, Nova Friburgo, ☎ (0245) 42 1120. In a charming park, this hotel has a restaurant, two bars and two swimming pools. 24 rooms.

▲ **Casablanca Center**, Rua Gen. Osório 28, Petrópolis, ☎ (0242) 42 2612. This modest hotel has a restaurant and a bar. 69 rooms.

▲ **Casablanca Palace**, Rua 16 de Março 123, Petrópolis, ☎ (0242) 42 0162. A simple hotel without restaurant but with a bar. 15 rooms.

Food

****La Belle Meunière**, Estr. União-Indústria 2189, Petrópolis, ☎ (0242) 21 1573. This lively restaurant serves very good French cuisine. Open daily noon-5pm, 7pm-midnight.

** **Chez Gigi**, Estr. Niterói, Nova Friburgo. Delicious French cuisine accents this charming restaurant. Open daily noon-1am.

** **Irene**, Rua Yeda 730, Teresópolis, ☎ (021) 742 2901. Excellent Russian cuisine in a friendly ambience. Open Mon-Sat noon-2:30pm, 8-11pm.

** **Oberland**, Rua Fernando Bizzolo 63, Nova Friburgo, ☎ (0245) 22 9838. Excellent Swiss cooking in a pleasant atmosphere. Open Mon-Sat noon-3pm, 7-10pm.

** **Parrô do Valentim**, Estr. União-Indústria 10289, Petrópolis, ☎ (0242) 22 1281. Very good Portuguese food, very lively restaurant. Open daily 11:30am-10pm.

** **Simon**, Hotel Simon, Parque Nacional, Itatiaia, ☎ (0243) 52 1122. International cuisine served in a hotel dining room with a great view of the park. Open daily noon-3pm, 7:15-10pm.

* **Itati**, Rua Pres. Dutra Norte, Parque Nacional, Itatiaia, ☎ (0243) 52 1133. Good international cuisine in a simple restaurant. Open daily 11am-11pm.

* **Kantão do Libano**, Av. Pelinca 400, Campos ☎ (0247) 23 2744. This interesting little restaurant serves good Arab cuisine. Open daily 11am-midnight.

* **Lareira**, Av. Feliciano Sodré 221, Teresópolis, ☎ (021) 742 5860. This lively restaurant serves international cuisine. Open daily 11-2am.

* **Majórica**, Praça Getúlio Vargas 74, Nova Friburgo, ☎ (0245) 22 0358. This is a lively little *churrascaria*. Open daily 11am-11pm.

* **Pagode**, Rua André Luis 13, Campos, ☎ (0247) 22 6277. A lively restaurant with a pleasant view and good international cuisine. Open daily 11-3am.

Useful addresses

Airline

Rio Sul, Av. Alberto Torres 109, Campos, ☎ (0247) 22 0205.

Airport

Bartholomeu Lysandro, Campos, ☎ (0247) 22 1672.

Bank

Banco de Brasil, Rua Paulo Barbosa 81, Petrópolis, ☎ (0242) 43 2052.

Bus terminals

Praça da Republica, Campos, ☎ (0247) 22 9849.
Av. Alberto Braune, Nova Friburgo, ☎ (0245) 22 0400.
Rua Dr. Porciuncula 75, Petrópolis, ☎ (0242) 43 1703.
Rua 1 de Miao 100, Teresópolis, ☎ (021) 742 3352

Car rental

Localiza, Av. Alberto Torres 329, Campos, ☎ (0247) 23 4766.

Tourist offices

Parque São Benedito, Praça Nilo Peçanha, Campos.
Centro de Turismo, Praça Dr. Demerval B Moreira, Nova Friburgo, ☎ (0245) 22 0116.
Petrotur, Av. Br. do Amazonas 98, Petrópolis, ☎ (0242) 42 1466.
Praça Olimpica, Teresópolis, ☎ (021) 742 3352.

ESPIRITO SANTO

Espirito Santo is a tiny, little-known state that is really just an extension of Rio de Janeiro state. It lies wedged between the Atlantic Ocean and the Serra that forms the boundary with Minas Gerais. The lovely wide beaches are free from Rio de Janeiro's crowds. Its main source of revenue is coffee. The only industry is the activity surrounding the tanker harbour in Vitória. This was built in 1983 for the transport of iron ore from Minas Gerais to Europe and Japan.

Vitória* is the capital city. Besides the harbour, other sights include the Colonial Museum and the Historical Museum, Anchieta's tomb and the magnificent beaches to the north.

Inland there are several places worth visiting. **Guarapari**** (34 mi/55 km from Vitória) is a well known resort. **Anchieta*** (53 mi/85 km from Vitória) has beautiful beaches and an interesting church, Nossa Senhora de Assumpção.

Domingos Martins (24 mi/39 km from Vitória) is a charming little spa. There is also the **Parque Nacional do Caparão**** (155 mi/250 km from Vitória), which lies in the foothills of the Pico da Pandeira, at 9479 ft/2890 m the second highest peak in Brazil.

Accommodation

▲▲▲ **Porto do Sol,** Av. Beira-Mar 1, Guarapari, ☎ (027) 261 0011. The attractions of this charming hotel include a restaurant, two bars, a swimming pool and various sports facilities. 88 rooms.

▲▲▲ **Senac Ilha do Boi,** Rua Braulio Macedo 417, Vitória, ☎ (027) 227 3222. This lovely hotel offers a fine view in addition to its restaurant, four bars and two swimming pools. 82 rooms.

▲▲ **Novotel,** Av. Adalberto Simão Nader 133, Vitória, ☎ (027) 227 9422. This comfortable hotel has a restaurant, a bar and two swimming pools. 107 rooms.

Food

*** **Pedra do Porto,** Hotel Porto do Sol, Av. Beira-Mar 1, Guarapari, ☎ (027) 261 0011. Excellent international cuisine is served in this beautiful dining room. Open daily noon-midnight.

*** **Tour d'Argent,** Senac Hotel, Rua Braulio Macedo 417, Vitória, ☎ (027) 227 3222. A wide variety of international cuisine is served in this hotel dining room. Open daily 11:30am-11pm.

** **Lai,** Av. Saturnino Rangel Mauro 165, Vitória, ☎ (027) 227 2734. Good Chinese cooking served festively. Open daily 11am-3pm, 6pm-midnight.

** **Monte Fuji,** Rua Manoel Carneiro Gonçalves 21, Vitória ☎ (027) 235 1494. Good Japanese food in a simple restaurant. Open Mon-Fri 6-11:30pm.

* **Adega do Tejo,** Rua Joaquim Lyrio 817, Vitória, ☎ (027) 227 1814. Good Portuguese fare, lively times. Open Mon-Sat 6pm-midnight.

* **Minuano,** Av. Dante Michelini 337, Vitória, ☎ (027) 227 1877. An excellent *churrascaria*. Open daily 11am-3:30pm, 6pm-midnight.

Useful addresses

Airlines

Transbrasil, Rua 7 de Setembro 215, Vitória, ☎ (027) 223 6488.
Varig, Av. Gov. Bley 186, Vitória, ☎ (027) 227 1353.

Airport

de Vitória, ☎ (027) 227 6811.

Bus terminal

Saida BR-101, Vitória, ☎ (027) 222 3366.

Car rental

Interlocadora, Av. Vitória 727, Vitória, ☎ (027) 222 4155.
Locarauto, Av. Fernando Ferraz 3501, Vitória, ☎ (027) 227 0656.

Post office

Av. Fernando Ferrari 1878, Vitória.

Railway terminal

CVRD, Estaçao Pedro Nolasco, Vitória, ☎ (027) 226 4169.

Tourist office

Emcatur, Rua Br. de Monjardim 30, Vitória, ☎ (027) 222 0711.

Travel agencies

Biotur, Av. Gov. Bley 186, Vitória, ☎ (027) 222 5911.
Estur, Av. Jeronimo Monteiro 1000, Vitória, ☎ (027) 223 9043.

SÃO PAULO

São Paulo was founded by two Jesuit missionaries, Manuel da Nobrega and José de Anchieta. Eager to spread their teaching to the inhabitants of Brazil's interior, rather than simply along the coast where the Portuguese had already established towns, they traveled across the ridge of the Serra do Mar, finally reaching the plateau of Piritininga. Here, they founded seven villages, all named after saints. Among these was São Paulo, which was established on January 25, 1554, the birthday of Saint Paul.

Unlike the other six towns, São Paulo flourished. This was because it was situated on the Tiété, a powerful river that flows through hundreds of miles of central Brazil and eventually links up with the great Paraná River. Due to its strategic location, São Paulo, throughout the 17th century, was used as a base by the *bandeirantes,* adventurers who explored neighbouring regions in search of gold and precious jewels. It was from São Paulo that the state of Minas Gerais, Mato Grosso and the southern territories were discovered.

Up until the late 19th century São Paulo was a quiet, mildly prosperous area with a good trade in sugar cane. Then, around 1885, it underwent a complete transformation when coffee plantations were established in the Paraíba valley. The red earth in this area, it turned out, was perfect for growing coffee beans.

The discovery immediately started a boom in the coffee industry. Huge numbers of Italians, Portuguese, Spaniards, Japanese and people from other regions of Brazil began flooding into the territory. As a result, by the end of the century, the town had changed beyond all recognition.

Today the state of São Paulo covers 95,713 sq mi/ 247,898 sq km and has 25 million inhabitants. It is Brazil's most important state in size, population and economic output. The region accounts for 20% of Brazil's agricultural produce (coffee, cotton, sugar and fruit are its main resources), 90% of Brazil's motor vehicles and 60% of its machinery and tools.

Proud of their city, the residents of São Paulo tend to be disdainful of Rio, considering it a city of slackers. The inhabitants of Rio, on the other hand, say that São Paulo is like hell on earth, filled with workaholics who never take time off to relax.

São Paulo is certainly a daunting city to live in, with its traffic, pollution and breakneck pace. However, Brazilians in

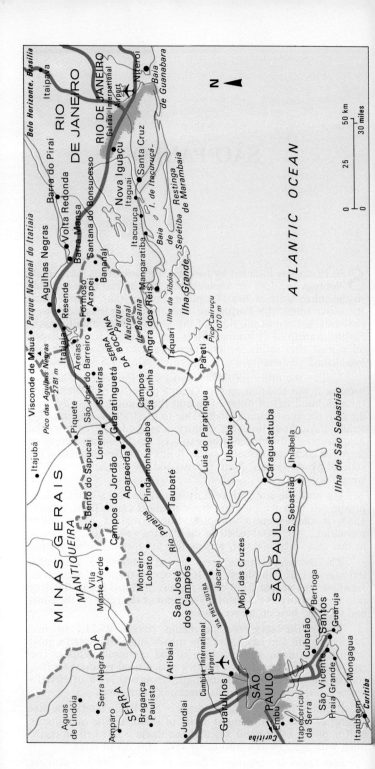

Rio-São Paulo.

general are extremely proud of the city because it is one of the biggest industrial centres in the world.

One reason for the city's prosperity is the state's huge reserve of hydro-electric power. Another is simply the formidable energy of its inhabitants, a legacy perhaps from the city's pioneer days when getting rich was the aim of every adventurer.

Despite its preoccupation with making money, São Paulo has much to offer in the way of culture. There are a number of important museums as well as elegant shops, restaurants and nightclubs. It is certainly a city well worth a visit.

▬ PRACTICAL INFORMATION

See maps pp. 109, 112.

Telephone area code: 011

When to go

São Paulo can be enjoyed at any time of year. You should bear in mind, however, that because of its altitude — around 2600 ft/800 m — it is swept by cold winds from the north and Mato Grosso. The summer months (December-March) are warm.

Access

Plane

About 15 mi/25 km from São Paulo is **Cumbica International Airport,** which handles international and domestic flights (other than to Rio). ☎ 945 2111.

Shuttle flights from Rio and private aircraft arrive at **Congonhas Airport,** I, B3, 5 mi/8 km south of the centre of town. ☎ 531 7444.

Both airports have taxis and buses to take you into town. There is also a bus service between the two airports.

National and international airlines:

Pan Am, Av. São Luis 29, II, A3, ☎ 257 6655.

Rio Sul, Cumbica International Airport, ☎ 543 7261.

Tam, Rua da Consolação 257, II, A3, ☎ 258 6211.

Transbrasil and Nordeste, Av. São Luis 250, II, A3, ☎ 259 7066.

Varig, Rua da Consolação 362, II, A3, ☎ 258 2233.

Vasp, Rua Libero Badaró 106, II, B3, ☎ 37 1161.

Train

São Paulo is accessible by train from all corners of Brazil. It has three railway stations, which serve different areas.

Luz, Jardim da Luz, II, B2, ☎ 227 3299 (Corumba, Brasília, Rio and various cities in São Paulo state).

Prestes, Praça Júlio Prestes, ☎ 223 7211, II, B2 (south-western São Paulo state).

Roosevelt, Praça Agente Cicero, ☎ 292 5417 (eastern São Paulo state and Mogi das Cruzes).

Bus

There are buses to São Paulo from all the main cities in Brazil, as well as from the major South American capitals.

Terminal do Jabaquara, Jabaquara, I, B3, ☎ 235 0322 (coastal destinations).

Terminal do Tiétê, Tiétê, I, B2, ☎ 235 0322 (all of Brazil and South American capitals).

Accommodation

Hotels

Most of the good hotels are in the city centre and are fairly expensive. Several new hotels built by international chains are near the São Bernardo do Campo and Santa Amaro industrial zones. They have all the amenities expected of big chain hotels and are also fairly expensive. In the Santa Efigenia district near the railway and bus stations, there are less expensive hotels but their level of comfort and service are correspondingly lower. The explanation for the categorization of the following hotels can be found on p. 16.

▲▲▲▲ **Brasilton São Paulo,** Rua Martins Fontes 330, Centro, II, AB3-4, ☎ 258 5811. The Brasilton São Paulo has all the amenities of a luxury hotel, including an excellent restaurant, two bars and a swimming pool. 250 rooms.

▲▲▲▲ **Caesar Park,** Rua Augusta 1508, Cerqueira César, I, B2, ☎ 285 6622. Japanese-owned, Caesar Park is a refined hotel decorated with beautiful paintings in many of its room. It has two restaurants, a bar, a swimming pool and a gymnasium. 177 rooms.

▲▲▲▲ **Grand Hotel Ca'd'Oro,** Rua Augusta 129, Centro, II, AB3-4, ☎ 256 8011. Particularly renowned for its superb Italian restaurant, the hotel's other amenities include four bars, two swimming pools, a gymnasium, a bookshop and a drugstore. 290 rooms.

▲▲▲▲ **Maksoud Plaza,** Al. Campinas 150, Bela Vista, II, A4, ☎ 251 2233. An excellent reputation for quality service and comfort plus three restaurants, four bars, a swimming pool, a solarium, a theatre and many shops. 416 rooms.

▲▲▲▲ **Mofarrej Sheraton,** Santos 1437, Cerqueira César, I, B2, ☎ 284 5544. Recently built, this hotel is extremely comfortable and offers a wide range of amenities, including two restaurants, two bars, two swimming pools and various boutiques. 247 rooms.

▲▲▲▲ **São Paulo Hilton,** Av. Ipiranga 165, Centro, II, B3, ☎ 256 0033. Located in the middle of the business area, this hotel offers the high standards consistent with the Hilton chain. A good restaurant, five bars, a swimming pool and several boutiques are some of the services you will find here. 407 rooms.

▲▲▲▲ **Transamerica,** Av. das Naçoes Unidas 18591, Santa Amaro, I, A4, ☎ 523 4511. An ideal holiday centre, equipped with two restaurants, two bars, a swimming pool, tennis and squash courts and many shops. 211 rooms.

▲▲▲ **Crowne Plaza,** Rua Frei Caneca 1199, Cerqueira César, I, B2, ☎ 284 1144. A well-appointed hotel situated on the most beautiful street in Saõ Paulo. It has a good restaurant, two bars and a swimming pool. 223 rooms.

▲▲▲ **Eldorado Boulevard,** Av. S. Luis 234, Centro, II, A3, ☎ 256 8833. A restaurant, two bars, a swimming pool and comfort are offered by this hotel. 141 rooms.

▲▲▲ **Novotel,** Rua Min. Nélson Hungria 450, Morumbi, I, A3, ☎ 553 1211. This French-owned hotel has a restaurant, two bars and a swimming pool. 192 rooms.

▲▲▲ **Othon Palace,** Rua Libero Badaro 190, Centro, II, B3, ☎ 239 3277. This fine hotel has two restaurants, a coffee shop, a bar and several boutiques. 250 rooms.

▲▲▲ **Samambaia,** Rua 7 de Abril 422, Centro, II, B3, ☎ 231 1333. This excellent small hotel boasts attentive service. 65 rooms.

▲▲▲ **São Paulo Center,** Largo Sta. Efigenia 40, Centro, II, B3, ☎ 228 6033. A quality hotel with a restaurant, two bars and several boutiques. 112 rooms.

▲▲ **Bristol,** Rua Martins Fontes 277, Centro, II, AB3-4, ☎ 258 0011. A good medium-sized hotel with a restaurant and a bar. 90 rooms.

▲▲ **Cambridge,** Av 9 de Julho 216, Bela Vista, II, A4, ☎ 239 0399. This pleasant hotel has a good reputation. It contains a restaurant and a bar. 116 rooms.

▲▲ **Danúbio,** Av. Brig. Luis Antônio 1099, Bela Vista, II, A4, ☎ 239 4033. A simple and comfortable hotel with a restaurant and a bar. 137 rooms.

▲▲ **Eldorado Higienopolis,** Rua Mq. de Itu 836, Higienopolis, ☎ 222 3422. This good hotel is located at the city limits. It includes a restaurant, three bars, a swimming pool and several boutiques. 156 rooms.

▲▲ **Excelsior,** Av. Ipiranga 770, Centro, II, B2, ☎ 222 7377. This hotel offers all that the tourist expects, including a restaurant and a bar. 180 rooms.

▲▲ **Gran Corona,** Rua Basilio da Gama 101, Centro, II, B3, ☎ 259 8177. This hotel offers personalized, friendly service. It has a restaurant and a bar. 100 rooms.

▲▲ **Nobilis,** Rua Sta. Efigenia 72, Centro, II, B2, ☎ 229 5155. A comfortable hotel with a modest restaurant and a bar. 150 rooms.

▲▲ **Normandie,** Av. Ipiranga 1187, Centro, II, B2-3, ☎ 228 5766. Modest and adequate, this hotel has a bar and a restaurant. 200 rooms.

▲▲ **Planalto,** Av. Casper Libero 117, Santa Efigenia, II, B2, ☎ 227 7311. You will be greeted warmly at this hotel, which offers a restaurant and a bar. 267 rooms.

▲▲ **Vila Rica,** Av. Vieira de Carvalho 176, Centro, II, AB3-4, ☎ 220 7111. This small and charming hotel will make you feel at home. It has a bar, but no restaurant. 61 rooms.

▲ **Alfa,** Av. Ipiranga 1152, Centro, II, B2, ☎ 228 4188. This little hotel has a restaurant and a bar. 62 rooms.

▲ **Columbia Palace,** Av. S. João 578, Centro, II, B3, ☎ 220 1033. A modest hotel with a restaurant and a bar. 90 rooms.

▲ **Delphos,** Av. Casper Libero 133, Centro, II, AB3-4, ☎ 228 6411. Delphos is a small hotel with a pleasant bar. 41 rooms.

▲ **Lord Palace,** Rua das Palmeiras 78, Santa Cecilia, I, B2, ☎ 220 0422. Modest but tasteful, this hotel has a restaurant and a bar. 125 rooms.

▲ **Menache,** Rua Prates 322, Bom Retiro, ☎ 228 1611. This small hotel doesn't offer much in the way of extras, but is an acceptable lodging. 54 rooms.

▲ **San Marino,** Rua Martinho Prado 173, Consolaçao, I, B2, ☎ 258 7833. Satisfactory if not fancy, this hotel has a modest restaurant and a bar. 76 rooms.

▲ **Solar Paulista,** Rua Francisca Miquelina 343, Bela Vista, II, A4, ☎ 257 2800. The hotel, its restaurant and its bar are modest but acceptable. 59 rooms.

▲ **Términus,** Av. Ipiranga 741, Centro, II, B3, ☎ 222 2266. This simple hotel has a modest restaurant. 70 rooms.

▲ **Windsor,** Rua dos Timbiras 444, Centros, II, AB3-4, ☎ 220 5411. A decent little hotel with a restaurant and a bar. 42 rooms.

Camping

It is cheapest to camp along the coast, but that means being more than 45 mi/70 km from São Paulo. We recommend a well-equipped campsite that is fairly close by the city:

Cemucam, Estr. Raposo Tavares, Cotia, ☎ 492 2126.

A complete list of campsites is available from:

Camping Clube do Brasil, Rua Minerva 156, Perdizes, ☎ 26 3024.

Entertainment and cultural life

São Paulo has a highly developed cultural life — the most sophisticated in all Brazil. It is home to around 30 theatres, the most outstanding of which is the **Teatro Municipal** on Praça Ramos de Azevedo. The Teatro Municipal hosts plays, operas, ballets and concerts by top Brazilian and international entertainers. Other concerts are held in the auditoriums of the **Museu de Arte** (Av. Paulista, I, B2) and the **Museu de Arte Contemporânea** (Parque do Ibirapuera, I, B3).

São Paulo also has plenty of cinemas, both in the city centre and along the Avenida Paulista and its adjacent streets.

Regular exhibitions of Brazilian and foreign art are presented in the more than 20 galleries in the southern zone, around Rua Augusta, Rua Haddock Lobo and various side streets. The museums also have special exhibitions, the most important of which is the Biennale de São Paulo, held every two years from September to November at the Museu de Arte Contemporânea.

São Paulo's Carnival is small compared to Rio's. It offers the advantage, however, of being more intimate, because practically all tourists are in Rio and most Brazilians are on vacation at this time. If you choose to stay in São Paulo for Carnival, note that the main parade is on Avenida Tiradentes, II, C1. Carnival sambas take place in all the nightclubs and the samba schools (see p. 114). There are two gigantic balls at the **Parque do Ibirapuera** (Av. Pedro Álvares Cabral, I, B3, ☎ 544 2511) and **Parque Anhembi** (Av. Olavo Fontoura 1209, Santana, I, B1, ☎ 267 2122).

Festivals of particular interest in São Paulo include the Feast of São Jorge-Ogum (god of war), held at the Parque do Ibirapuera in April and May, the Folklore Festival, at the Parque do Ibirapuera and Praça Roosevelt in August, and the Feast of Yemanjá (goddess of the sea). This last festival, which takes place on the seashore on New Year's Eve, is especially fascinating. To get a good view, go to Guaruja, Santos or Praia Grande — here you will see the coastline lit up by thousands of candles. The Corrida de São Silvestre, a traditional midnight footrace down the Avenida Paulista and the Rua da Consolaçao, also takes place on New Year's Eve.

Not a week in São Paulo goes by without either a national or international fair or convention of some kind. The most important of these are held at the Parque Anhembi, South America's largest fairground. Livestock fairs and domestic animal shows are held at the Parque Fernando Costa in Agua Branca.

Food

São Paulo is celebrated for its restaurants. Every type of cuisine is represented, at every conceivable price. Servings tend to be so generous that one order will often be enough for two people with average appetites. Restaurants specializing in foreign cuisine abound, and make sure to visit one of the many excellent pizzerias.

São Paulo's *churrascarias* (restaurants serving grilled beef) claim to serve the best-quality meat in Brazil, and one of them (Baby-Beef Rubaiyat) even goes so far as to raise its own livestock and advertise the animals' diet and age at slaughter.

If you are interested in inexpensive meals, don't forget the luncheon-ettes *(lanchonetes)* that offer daily specials.

**** **Abril em Portugal,** Rua Caio Prado 47, Centro, II, B3, ☎ 256 5160. Excellent Portuguese cuisine in a lively atmosphere. Open Mon-Sat 8pm-2am.

**** **Baby-Beef Rubaiyat,** Av. Vieira de Carvalho 116, Centro, II, B3, ☎ 222 8333. This is the best *churrascaria* in São Paulo. Open daily 11-1am.

**** **Ca'd'Oro,** Grand Hotel Ca'd'Oro, Rua Augusta 129, Centro, II, AB3-4, ☎ 256 8011. This Italian restaurant is one of the best restaurants in Brazil. Open daily noon-2:30pm, 7-10:30pm.

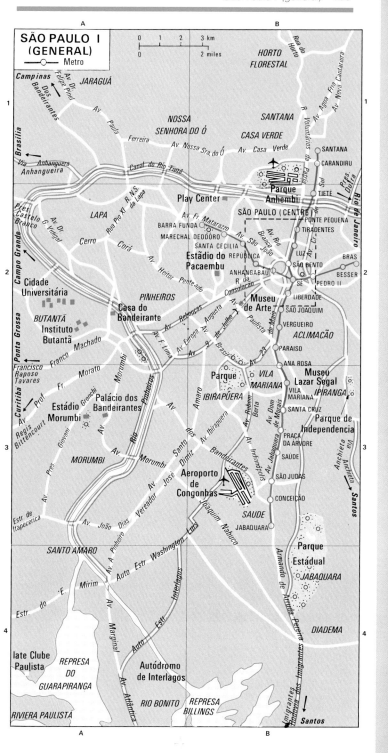

**** **La Casserole,** Largo do Arouche 346, Centro, II, A2, ☎ 220 6283. This charming restaurant serves delicious French cuisine. Open daily noon-3pm, 7pm-midnight.

**** **China Massas Caseiras,** Rua Mourato Coelho 140, Pinheiros, I, A2, ☎ 853 7111. A first-rate Chinese restaurant. Open daily 11:30am-2:45pm, 6-9:45pm.

**** **La Cocagne,** Rua Amaral Gurgel 378, Centro, II, AB3-4, ☎ 256 0938. This very good restaurant offers a wide variety of French cuisine. Open Mon-Sat noon-2:30pm, 7pm-midnight.

**** **Le Coq Hardy,** Av. Adolfo Pinheiro 2518, Alto da Boa Vista, ☎ 246 6013. Superb French cuisine is served in this refined dining room. Open daily noon-2:30pm, 7pm-midnight.

**** **La Cuisine du Soleil,** Hotel Maksoud Plaza, Al. Campinas 150, Bela Vista, II, A4, ☎ 251 2233. French cuisine in a lively ambience. Open Mon-Sat noon-2:30pm, 7:30pm-12:30am.

**** **Dinho's Place,** Largo do Arouche, Centro, II, A2, ☎ 221 2322. An excellent address for *churrasco*. Open daily 11-12:30am.

**** **Marcel,** Rua Epitacio Pessoa 98, Centro, II, A2, ☎ 257 6968. This very good French restaurant specializes in soufflés. Open Mon-Sat noon-2:30pm, 7pm-midnight.

**** **Marquês de Marialva,** Rua Haddock Lobo 1583, Cerqueira César, I, B2, ☎ 852 1805. Excellent Portuguese cuisine in a refined atmosphere. Open daily noon-3pm, 7:30pm-1am.

**** **Paddock,** Av. Brig. Faria Lima 1541, Jardim Paulista, I, A2, ☎ 814 3582. International cuisine in a lively atmosphere. Open Mon-Sat 11:30am-4pm, 6pm-1am.

**** **Roanne,** Rua Henrique Martins 631, Jardim Paulista, I, A2, ☎ 887 4516. Superior French cooking in this handsome restaurant. Open Mon-Sat 7:30pm-12:30am.

**** **La Tambouille,** Av. 9 de Julho 5925, Jardim Europa, I, B2, ☎ 883 6276. International cuisine in an impressive setting. Open daily noon-3:30pm, 7pm-1am.

**** **La Truite Cocagne,** Rua Campos Bicudo 153, Jardim Paulista, I, A2, ☎ 883 2770. A good variety of seafood is offered in this charming restaurant. Open daily noon-3pm, 7pm-1am.

*** **L'Arnaque,** Rua Oscar Freire 518, Cerqueira César, I, B2, ☎ 280 0081. This French-style bistro specializes in nouvelle cuisine. Open daily noon-3pm, 8pm-1am.

*** **A Baiuca-Jardins,** Av. Brig. Faria Lima 609, Jardim Paulista, I, A2, ☎ 212 6341. Interesting international cuisine in a lively setting. Open Mon-Sat noon-3pm, 7pm-4am.

*** **Bassi,** Rua 13 de Maio 334, Bela Vista, II, A4, ☎ 34 2375. A *churrascaria* with delicious food and plenty of atmosphere. Open daily 11am-3:30pm, 7pm-1am.

*** **Bîstro,** Av. S. Luis 258, Centro, II, A3, ☎ 257 1598. This charming restaurant specializes in international cuisine. Open Mon-Sat 11:30am-3pm, 6-11pm.

*** **Chamonix,** Rua Pamplona 1446, Jardim Paulista, II, A2, ☎ 287 9818. A good Swiss restaurant enlivened by French-style accordion music. Open Mon-Sat 7pm-2am.

*** **Don Curro,** Rua Alves Guimarães 230, Pinheiros, I, A2, ☎ 852 4712. An excellent selection of Spanish cuisine is offered in this charming restaurant. Open Mon-Sat noon-3pm, 7pm-midnight.

*** **Freddy,** Praça D. Gastão Liberal Pinto 111, Itaim Bibi, ☎ 852 7339. French cooking in a pleasant atmosphere. Open daily noon-3pm, 7-11:30pm.

*** **Golden Plaza,** Rua Luis Gonzaga de Azevedo Neto 263, Morumbi, I, A3, ☎ 533 7334. This excellent restaurant offers a wide selection of Chinese dishes. Open daily 11:30am-3pm, 6:30pm-midnight.

*** **Kin Kon,** Rua Peixoto Gomide 1066, Cerqueira César, I, B2, ☎ 289 2595. Excellent Chinese cooking served by an attentive staff. Open daily 11:30am-3pm, 6:30pm-midnight.

*** **Massimo,** Al. Santos 1826, Cerqueira César, I, B2, ☎ 284 0311. This restaurant has superior decor, Italian cuisine and service. Open daily 11:30am-3pm, 7pm-midnight.

*** **Los Molinos,** Rua Vasconcelos Drumond 526, Vila Monumento, ☎ 215 8211. Excellent Spanish cuisine in a simple setting. Open Mon-Sat noon-3pm, 7pm-midnight.

*** **La Paillote,** Av. Nazaré 1946, Ipiranga, I, B3, ☎ 63 3626. Good French cooking in a lively restaurant. Open Mon-Sat noon-2:30pm, 7:30-10:30pm.

*** **Rodeio,** Rue Haddock Lobo 1498, Cerqueira César, I, B2, ☎ 883 2322. This lively *churrascaria* serves very good meat. Open daily 11:30am-3pm, 7pm-1:30am.

*** **Rose Room,** Av. Casper Libero 65, Centro, II, AB3-4, ☎ 229 1935. A vide variety of international dishes in a modest decor. Open Mon-Sat noon-3pm, 7-10pm.

*** **Saint Germain,** Rua Pe. João Manoel 190, Cerqueira César, I, B2, ☎ 883 1139. A refined restaurant offering French cuisine. Open Mon-Sat noon-3pm, 7pm-1am.

*** **Saint Jô,** Al. Arapanés 1456, Indianópolis, ☎ 543 6506. This atmospheric French restaurant specializes in soufflés. Open Mon-Sat 7pm-1am.

*** **Sino Brasileiro,** Rua Alberto Torres 39, Perdizes, ☎ 67 4653. This very good Chinese restaurant integrates many Brazilian ingredients in its dishes. Open daily noon-2:30pm, 7-11;30pm.

*** **Spaghetti Notte,** Rua Bastos Pereira 71, Vila Nova Conceiçao, I, B3, ☎ 887 8790. Reservations are advisable for this superb Italian restaurant. Open Mon-Sat 7:30pm-1am.

*** **Suntory,** Al. Campinas 600, Jardim Paulista, I, A2, ☎ 283 2455. Excellent Japanese cuisine in a well-appointed dining room. Open Mon-Sat noon-2:15pm, 7-11:45pm.

*** **Sushi-Yassu,** Rua Tomás Gonzaga 110A, Liberdade, II, B5, ☎ 279 6622. This restaurant offers an interesting variety of Japanese cuisine. Open daily 11:30am-2:30pm, 6pm-midnight.

*** **Terraço Italia,** Av. Ipiranga 344, Centro, II, A3, ☎ 257 6566. Situated on the 41st floor, this restaurant offers a superb view of São Paulo as well as good international cuisine. Open daily noon-2am.

*** **La Trainera,** Av. Brig. Faria Lima 511, Jardim Europa, ☎ 282 5988. Excellent seafood is served in this lively restaurant. Open daily noon-12:30am.

** **A Baiuca,** Praça Franklin Roosevelt 256, Centro, II, A3-4, ☎ 255 2233. Excellent variety of international cuisine in a pleasant ambience. Open Mon-Sat noon-4am.

** **Amaralina,** Rua Borges Lagoa 803, Vila Clementino, ☎ 549 1552. Good Brazilian cooking in a simple atmosphere. Open daily 11:30am-3pm, 6pm-midnight.

** **Andrade,** Rua Artur de Azevedo 874, Pinheiros, I, A2, ☎ 64 8644. Delicious Brazilian dishes are served in this restaurant, which also offers live music. Open Mon-Sat noon-3pm, 7pm-2am.

** **Bolinha,** Av. Cid. Jardim 53, Jardim Europa, ☎ 852 9526. Simple but good Brazilian food in a modest setting. Open daily 11-1am.

** **Cabana,** Av. Rio Branco 90, Centro, II, A2, ☎ 223 9942. A good *churrascaria* with music. Open Sun-Fri 11:30am-11pm.

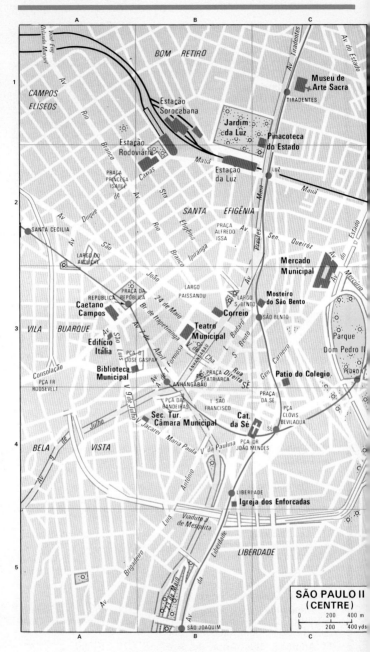

SÃO PAULO II
(CENTRE)

0   200   400 m
0   200   400 yds

** **Colonna**, Rua Maranhão 540, Higienopolis, ☎ 670547. Italian cuisine in a modest restaurant. Open daily 11:30am-3pm, 6pm-midnight.

** **Elio**, Rua Gabriel dos Santos 370, Santa Cecilia, I, B2, ☎ 678399. Good Italian cuisine in a simple setting. Open daily 11am-3pm, 6pm-midnight.

** **Jardim de Napoli,** Rua Dr. Martinico Prado 463, Higienopolis, ☎ 66 3022. Superior Italian cooking in a modest restaurant. Open daily noon-2:30pm, 6:30pm-midnight.

** **Komazushi,** Av. Brig. Luis Antônio 2050, Centro Commercial Paulista. This little restaurant serves very good Japanese cuisine. Open Mon-Fri noon-2pm, 6-10pm.

** **Manhattan,** Rua Bela Cintra 2238, Cerqueira César, I, B2, ☎ 852 0947. This restaurant, which serves international dishes, specializes in crepes. Open daily noon-3:30pm, 7pm-2am.

** **Mexilhao,** Rua 13 de Maio 626, Bela Vista, II, A4, ☎ 288 2485. This restaurant offers a good variety of seafood. Open daily 11:30am-3pm, 6:30pm-1am.

** **Nelore,** Rua Pinheiros 355, Pinheiros, ☎ 64 6823. A lively *churrascaria*. Open daily 11:45am-3:30pm, 6:45pm-midnight.

** **Pagos,** Al. Santos 2395, Cerqira César, I, B2, ☎ 852 3375. A self-service *churrascaria*. Open Sun-Fri 11:30am-3pm.

** **St Peter's Pier,** Al. Lorena 1160, Cerqueira César, I, B2, ☎ 881 2413. Large choice of seafood in this well-appointed restaurant. Open daily noon-3pm, 7pm-2am.

** **Sushigen,** Rua da Consolação 3447, Cerqueira César, I, B2, ☎ 883 0755. Sushi, sashimi and other Japanese specialities are served here. Open daily 6pm-2am.

** **Taquaral,** Av. Adolfo Pinheiro 2546, Alto da Boa Vista, ☎ 522 1899. Live music adds to the ambience in this *churrascaria*. Open daily 11am-midnight.

* **O Profeta,** Al. dos Aicás 40, Indianópolis, ☎ 549 5311. This restaurant serves Brazilian food in a pleasant ambience. Open daily 11:45-1am.

Getting around São Paulo

São Paulo is a modern city where new buildings are being built all the time. It has been called the Chicago of the southern hemisphere. It lies at the confluence or three rivers: the Tietê, the Pinheiros and the Tamanduateí. Sadly, they are now all polluted.

The **city centre,** from Sé to Santa Efigenia, is all that you expect a business district to be, heavily polluted and paralyzed with traffic. It is, however, where all the good hotels are located and where all the nightlife is centred.

In the **southern zone,** the districts of Cerqueira Cesar, Jardim Paulista, Jardim America and Morumbi are partly residential and partly commercial. Situated even farther south of the centre are Ibirapuera, Indianópolis, Santa Amaro and Jabaquara. There is great disparity among these districts. While Ibirapuera and Indianópolis resemble the southern zone's residential districts, Santo Amaro is strictly proletarian. West of Santo Amaro lie Jabaquara and the four suburban townships that make up the vast industrial complex known as ABCD: Santo André, São Bernardo do Campo, São Caetano do Sul, and Diadema.

In the **western zone,** which includes Consolação, Perdizes, Sumaré, Lapa, Pinheiros and Butanta, the neighbourhoods also vary considerably. The area around Lapa is industrial and desolate.

The districts of the **northern zone,** Santana and Casa Verde, and the **eastern zone,** Bras, Moca, Ipiranga and Tatuapé, are heavily industrialized and offer nothing in the way of tourist interest.

On foot

The most practical way of getting around in the heart of São Paulo is on foot. Because of the maze of one-way streets and pedestrian malls, it is virtually impossible to get around in a car. Taxis have the same difficulty.

By bus

There are plenty of buses to choose from in São Paulo. You will have to be patient for they are fairly slow; on the other hand, they are inexpensive.

By underground

São Paulo's first underground line was inaugurated seven years ago and runs north-south through Santana, Sé and Jabaquara. Some bus lines have connections with the underground line, at no extra charge (ask for underground-bus listings in underground stations). The city centre has two stations, at São Bento and Sé.

A second underground line is still under construction, although it operates some services. It runs east-west between Pencha and Marechal Deodoro, with convenient stops at Praça da Sé, Praça da Republica, Bras, Estação Pedro II and Sé. The underground runs from 5am-midnight.

Turismetrô offers organized visits to the city's principal sites on the integrated bus-underground system. Departures are at 9am and 2pm from the Praça da Sé station (☎ 284 8877).

By taxi

Taxis are available in São Paulo but, as already mentioned, are not practical for getting around because of the traffic snarls and the multitude of one-way streets.
Catumbi, ☎ 229 7688.
Coopertaxi, ☎ 941 2555.
Ligue-Taxi, ☎ 270 4211.
Radio-Taxi, ☎ 251 1733.

Excursions

Excursions in comfortable buses are offered by most travel agencies.
Abreutur, Av. Ipiranga 795, Centro, II, AB3, ☎ 222 6233.
Exprinter, Rua Barão de Itapetininga 243, Centro, II, B3, ☎ 259 3622.
Prodetur, Rua Barão de Itapetininga 298, Centro, II, B3, ☎ 230 5422.
Soletur, Av. São Luis 192, Centro, II, A3, ☎ 255 1322.
Toulemonde, Av. Ipiranga 313, Centro, II, AB3, ☎ 231 1329.
Wagon-Lits, Av. São Luis 258, Centro, II, A3, ☎ 256 3121.
Weekend Turismo, Av. Ipiranga 104, Centro, II, AB3, ☎ 257 4188.

Nightlife

São Paulo offers a wide range of nightlife. You can spend a pleasant evening strolling along the Largo de Arouche or Praça Dom José Gaspar, and stop for a drink in one of the sidewalk cafés. The main streets of the city centre stay crowded until late at night. Many restaurants feature a show of some kind or other in the form of music or dancing.

If you are interested in organized entertainment, the following are some of the available choices:

Samba clubs

Spend an evening dancing the samba in one of the clubs known as *casas de samba* or *sambões*. There are hundreds of them nestled around the Avenida Ibirapuera. They are packed on Friday and Saturday nights, but this just adds to the atmosphere. We recommend the following:
Barração de Zinco, Av. Ibirapuera 2411, Moema, ☎ 531 6240.
República do Samba, Rua Santo Antônio 1025, Bela Vista, II, A4
Vila, Av. Ibirapuera 2201, Moema, ☎ 543 2764.

Samba schools

Here, you can watch mainly outdoor performances of the samba to the accompaniment of drums.
Camisa Verde e Branca, Rua James Holland, Barra Funda, I, B2
Mocidade Alegre, Av. Casa Verde 3498, Casa Verde, I, B1
Rosas de Ouro, Rua Rosas de Ouro, Vila Brasilandia, I, B2

Nightclubs

São Paulo boasts several chic nightclubs that offer excellent food. Most

of them also feature floor shows. They are not recommended for singles.
150 Night Club, Maksoud Plaza Hotel, Av. Campinas 150, Bela Vista, II, A4, ☎ 251 2233.
Saint Paul, Av. Lorena 1717, Cerqueira César, I, B2, ☎ 282 7697.
Ta Matete, Av. 9 de Julho 5725, Jardim Paulista, I, A2, ☎ 881 3622.
Tecciro Uisque, Rua Santo Antônio 573, Bela Vista, II, A4, ☎ 347 031.

Bars featuring ao vivo (live) Brazilian music

Halleluyah, Rua Henrique Schaumann 431, Pinheiro, I, A2, ☎ 282 5371.
Ludwig II, Av. Juscelino Kubitschek 985, Itaim Bibi, ☎ 64 6221.
Trianon Piano, Maksoud Plaza Hotel, Av. Campinas 150, Bela Vista, II, A4, ☎ 251 2233.

Bars featuring rock music

Calabar, Rua Pamplona 1213, Cerqueira César, I, B2, ☎ 287 6137.
Woodstock, Rua da Consolação 3247, Jardim Paulista, I, A2, ☎ 883 5419.

Chic bars with music

Absinthe, Rua Bela Cintra 1862, ☎ 853 7212.
Piano, Hotel Ca d'Oro, Rua Augusta 129, Centro, II, AB3-4, ☎ 256 8011.
Santo Colombo, Rua Pe. João Manoel 667, Cerqueira César, I, B2, ☎ 883 2692.

Karaoké

This is a restaurant with an orchestra where customers are expected to sing a song. These are very amusing places, especially recommended on Friday and Saturday evenings.

Kyoto, Rua da Glória 295, Liberdade, II, BC5, ☎ 270 5306.
Lullaby, Rua Cons. Furtado 719, Liberdade, II, BC5, ☎ 279 3942.

Shopping

São Paulo offers a grand assortment of shopping but you should bear in mind that it is more expensive than in Rio. Don't forget that bargaining is expected.

Handcraft

Handcrafts available in São Paulo include tooled leather goods, carved wood items, jewelry made from gems and crystal and many Indian creations.

● Handcrafts fairs called *Feiras de Artes e Artesanato:* the best of these are held on Sunday mornings on the Praça da Republica (the main fair), on Saturday afternoons in the Parque Ibirapuera and on Sunday afternoons at Embu, a small colonial-style village about 15 mi/24 km outside São Paulo on the road to Curitiba. Less important fairs take place on Saturday afternoons on the Praça Roosevelt and on Sunday mornings on the Largo São José de Belém.

● Boutiques: these are scattered along the Rua 7 de Abril, the Rua Barão de Itapetininga, the Rua 24 de Maio and in all of the nearby pedestrian-only streets and shopping arcades.

● Indian handcrafts: these consists of a variety of ornaments, tools and other items made by the Surui, Gavao, Cinta-Larga and Pakanova tribes in particular. FUNAI sells these in shops that they run at Rua Augusta 1371, Centro, and Rua Condé de Itu 390, Santo Amaro, I, A4.

Jewelry

Precious and semi-precious stones, mounted and unmounted, are available in the jewelry shops on the Praça da República, the Rua 7 de Abril, the Rua Barão de Itapetininga and their cross-streets. The famous jeweler, H. Stern, is located at Praça da República 242, II, A3.

Luxury goods

Fashionable clothes and other luxury items are sold in the chic shops along the Rua Augusta, between Avenida Paulista and Avenida dos Estados Unidos.

Shopping centres and department stores

The most fashionable shopping centres include:
Eldorado, Marg. Pinheiros, I, A2.
Ibirapuera, Av. Ibirapuera, I, B3.
Iguatemi, Av. Brig. Faria Lima, I, A2.
Morumbi, Av. Roque Petroni Junior, I, A3.

Department stores are mostly located in the centre of the city, II, B3 Some of the biggest names are **Mappin, Mesbla** and **Sears.**

Flea market

Every Sunday from 8am to 5pm there is an interesting flea market held near the Museu de Arte. Here you'll find good bargains.

Sports

Soccer is just as popular in São Paulo as it is in Rio, and crowds here are just as wild with enthusiasm when their most important clubs (Corinthians, Palmeiras, São Paulo, among others) play a match. There are several large stadiums, including Morumbi (Praça Roberto Gomes Pedrosa, I, A3, ☎ 842 3377), Pacaembu (Praça Charles Müller, I, B2, ☎ 256 9111) and Antártica (Rua Turiaçu 1840, Água Branca, ☎ 263 6344).

Car racing is another sport dear to the Paulistas. Races are held at the internationally renowned Interlagos circuit (Av. Sen. Teotônio Vilela 259, Interlagos, ☎ 521 9911).

The following events are held regularly:

- Formula One Grand Prix (Mar)
- Brazilian soccer championship games (Sept-Dec)
- São Paulo Jockey Club Grand Prix (Oct)
- Latin American Boxing Tournament (Nov)
- São Paulo Derby (Nov)

For further information about sports events, contact the tourist office (see p. 117).

Sports are not limited to spectator events. While there are no public facilities for tennis, swimming or horseback riding, there are a number of excellent clubs that you can apply to join. Members may also invite you in with a guest pass. São Paulo has three public golf courses: two 18-hole courses (Santo Amaro and São Fernando Golf Clubs) and one nine-hole course (São Francisco Club). You can also sail on any of the reservoir-lakes.

Useful addresses

Banks

The following banks are located in the city centre, II, AB3
Banco do Brasil, Av. São João 32, ☎ 239 1533.
Banco Holandes Unido, Rua 15 de November 150.
Banco Internacional, Rua 15 de November 240.
First National Bank of Boston, Rua Libero Badaro 487.
Lloyds Bank, Rua 15 Novembro 143-165.

Car rental

The following car rental agencies are located in the city centre, II, A3
Avis, Rua da Consolação 335, ☎ 256 4166.
Hertz, Rua da Consolação 439, ☎ 256 9722.
Rent-A-Car, Rua da Consolaçao 438, ☎ 256 0201.

Chambers of commerce

American Chamber of Commerce, Av. Vieira de Carvalho 172, Centro, ☎ 222 5676.
British Chamber of Commerce, Rua Formosa 367, Centro, ☎ 222 6377.

Consulates
Canada, Av. Paulista 854, Bela Vista, II, A4, ☎ 287 2122.
Great Britain, Av. Paulista 1938, Cerqueira César, I, B2, ☎ 287 7722.
Ireland, Av. Paulista 2006, Cerqueira César, I, B2, ☎ 287 6362.
United States, Rua Padre João Manuel 933, Jardim América, I, A2
☎ 881 6511.

Currency exchanges
Casa Faro, Av. São Luis 157, Centro, II, A3, ☎ 257 7077.
Exprinter, Rua Br. de Itapetininga 243, Centro, II, B3, ☎ 257 2255.
Kingstur, Rua Alvares Penteado 215, Centro, ☎ 32 9184.

Emergencies
Emergency aid: ☎ 71 8673 or 71 0757.
Police: ☎ 228 2276 or 190.
Pronto socorro (emergency hospital), Av. 9 de Julho 3368, Jardim
América, I, A2, ☎ 883 4455.

Post office
Correio Central, Praça da República 390, Centro, II, A3

Telephone offices
Telesp, Av. 7 de Abril 295, Centro, II, B3 (open 24 hours).
Other telephone offices in the city centre can be found at Praça Dom
José Gaspar 22, Rua Benjamin Constante 200 and Rua Martins Fonte
150 (all open 6:30am-10:30pm).

Tourist offices
Praça da República 154, Centro, II, A3, ☎ 259 2000.
Praça da Sé, Centro, II, C4, ☎ 259 2000.

Travel agencies
Gol-Tour, Av. São Luis 187, Centro, II, A3, ☎ 256 2388.
Panorama, Av. São Luis 47, Centro, II, A3, ☎ 257 7155.
Prodetur, Rua Barão de Itapetininga 298, Centro, II, B3, ☎ 255 5422.
RTT, Lgo. do Paiçandu 72, Centro, II, B3, ☎ 220 6356.

▬ GETTING TO KNOW SÃO PAULO

If you have only a few hours to spare you should try to choose between:
● a walk through the city centre from the Praça da República to the Praça
da Sé via the pedestrian walkways and the Viaduto do Cha;
● a taxi-ride along the Avenida Paulista, past the Parque Ibirapuera and
Morumbi's residential districts.

If you have a morning to devote to sightseeing, one very interesting visit
— as long as you aren't too squeamish — is to the **Instituto Butanta.** It
is world-famous for its research into snakes. An alternative would be to
visit São Paulo's magnificent **Museu de Arte.** If you're free on Sunday
morning, don't miss the **Feira do Artisanato** on the Praça da República
(see p. 115).

If you are fortunate enough to have an extra day, or better still, a
weekend, you can make the 45-mi/73-km trip down the Serra to the
beach resorts of Santos or Guarujá.

The city centre

The city centre is above all a business and trade centre, and although
this is not quite as clear-cut as in Rio, it is generally a place that people
invade in the morning and flee in the evening. Yet it never looks deserted.
This is because all the good hotels are here and because there are
many small apartments where employees in the tourist businesses live.
The hustle and bustle of these streets is not really that different from any
large city, and ultra-modern buildings have sprung up right next to turn-
of-the-century buildings with not a thought for architectural harmony.

The city centre has its natural boundaries. To the west and south is the

Avenida Presidente Artur da Costa a Silva, an enormous street bordered by old, somber-looking buildings. To the east is the Parque Dom Pedro II, which is actually a huge traffic circle in the middle of town. In the north is the railroad station, Estaçao da Luz, with all its surrounding tracks. A narrow valley called Anhangabau, which was once a tea plantation, cuts through the city centre, more or less from north to south, dividing it into two: to the east lies Sé, the oldest neighbourhood of all, and to the west, the Praça da República.

Several bridges connect the two halves. The most well-known of these is the **Viaduto do Cha** (Tea Viaduct), from which you have the best view of the centre. Thousands of pedestrians cross it every day on their way from the Praça Ramos de Azevedo to the Praça da Patriarca.

Sé is a shopping district and a number of its streets, such as the Rua Direita and its cross-streets, are pedestrian-only malls. Most banks have their main offices in Sé. East of the Praça da Sé, gigantic buildings are being constructed.

Tourists tend to be more familiar with the area west of Anhangabau, where the famous **Avenida Ipiranga**, the main artery, leads to all the other main roads, the Avenida Rio Branco, Avenida São José and Avenida São Luis. All of these avenues are connected by pedestrian-only cross-streets, and this area is full of shopping malls where you can find high-quality goods at reasonable prices. The Avenida Ipiranga runs past the **Praça da República**, which is a central landmark in the city.

You are now in the heart of São Paulo, where you will see the three buildings that postcards have made world-famous: the **Alitalia building**, the highest in São Paulo at 42 storeys with a restaurant and terrace offering a panoramic view; the residential **COPAN building**★★ with its gigantic curved wall of concrete (constructed by architect Oscar Niemeyer in 1953); and the **Hilton Tower**.

Certain areas near the centre, such as **Liberdade**, **Bela Vista**, **Consolação** and **Higienópolis**, form a transition to the more residential districts to the south and west. Areas to the north and east of the city centre offer nothing in the way of tourist interest.

Among sights to see in São Paulo's centre are the following.

Basilica de São Bento★★ (Largo de São Bento, II, B3, ☎ 228 3633) was built in 1912 and stands next to a convent dating from 1598. Inside the basilica are 17th- and 18th-century paintings.

Catedral Metropolitana★★ (Praça da Sé, II, BC4, ☎ 37 6832) is a modern building that was begun in 1914, even though it is Gothic in style. It is São Paulo's most important church and houses an impressive 10,000-pipe organ.

Bibliotéca Monteiro Lobato★ (Rua General Jardim 485, II, A3) is a children's library consisting of about 20,000 titles. It also has 5000 books in braille for the blind.

Bibliotéca Municipal★ (Rua da Consolação 94, II, A3) has more than one million works, many of them ancient texts.

Capela da Santa Cruz dos Enforcados★ (Praça da Liberdade 345) was built in 1902 in memory of Francisco das Chagas, whose death on the scaffold had been a miscarriage of justice.

Capela de Anchieta★ (Pátio do Colegio 84) is said to have been built in 1554 on the very site where the city was first founded. A museum, the **Casa de Anchieta**★ (☎ 239 5722; open Tues-Sun 1-5pm), devoted to the city's history, is also at the same address.

Largo do Arouche gardens★, II, A2, are an extremely pleasant place to go and have a drink in the evenings.

Nossa Senhora da Consolação★ (Rua da Consolação 585, II, A3) is a church that was founded in 1799 but rebuilt in the 20th century.

Ordem Terceira de São Francisco★ (Largo de São Francisco, II, B4) was built in stages from 1676 to 1791. The convent retains some elements of the original decoration, although the gilding dates from the 1950s.

There are some interesting old paintings and furniture.

Ordem Terceira do Carmo★ (Av. Rangel Pestana) is a Baroque church dating from 1648. It holds paintings by Brother Jessuino de Monte Carmelo.

Praça da República gardens★, II, A3 , are the scene of an arts and crafts fair that is held every Sunday morning.

Santo Antônio★ (Praça da Patriarca, II, B3) is a church that was founded in 1592, twice demolished and twice rebuilt. Much of its vintage Baroque colonial architecture has survived.

São Francisco★ (Largo de São Francisco, II, B4) is a perfect example of colonial architecture. Built in 1644, this church stands next to the São Francisco convent and boasts some fine Portuguese paintings.

Teatro Municipal★ (Praça Ramos de Azevedo, II, B3) is the site of many cultural activities (see p. 108). It was built in 1903.

Several other churches worth visiting in this area are **Nossa Senhora do Rosário★** on Largo Paissandu, II, B3 , **Santa Cecilia★** on Largo Santa Cecilia, II, A3 , and **Santa Efigenia★** on Largo Santa Efigenia, II, B2

The southern zone

This mostly residential area is progressively becoming the new commercial centre of São Paulo. Some 20 years ago, the Avenida Paulista was a wide and handsome thoroughfare lined with colonial-style palaces *(palacetes)* built by coffee barons. Today, it is just another boulevard of skyscrapers.

At the other end of the southern zone is the Avenida Brig. Faria Lima. During the course of the last five years it, too, has become a commercial street. Between these two streets lie residential areas where grand private houses are being either renovated and turned into executive offices or demolished to make way for luxury apartment buildings. It is here that you will find the Rua Augusta with its chic expensive shops.

In fact, this entire area is full of good restaurants, bars, art galleries and interior-decorating boutiques. The Parque do Ibirapuera, a little farther on, offers a bit of fresh air. On the far side of Pinheiros River lies the Norumbi hill, where the mansions of São Paulo's wealthiest citizens overlook the city. There are many sights to see in this area.

Museu de Arte de São Paulo★★★ (São Paulo Art Museum, Av. Paulista 1578, I, B2 , ☎ 2515644; open Tues-Fri 1-5pm, Sat and Sun 2-6pm) is the most important museum in São Paulo and one of the foremost museums in South America. It was built in 1970 by Lino to a spectacular design. It now looks dreary, however, because its concrete has not aged well. It consists of an underground theatre and film library (films are shown on weekdays at 6:30 and 8:30pm) and upper floors that are used for the exhibitions and offer a magnificent view of São Paulo. It houses about 1000 works, but they are displayed only periodically.

The museum is known for its sculptures (such as the large group of *Dancers* by Degas), but above all it has an outstanding collection of paintings. A sample of some of the fine works included here are:

● Italian: Bernardo Daddi's *Virgin* (the oldest canvas in the museum), Mantegna's *Saint Jerome in the Desert*, Bellini's *Virgin* and Titian's portrait of *Cardinal Cristoforo Madruzzo.*

● Flemish: Hieronymus Bosch's *Temptation of Saint Anthony.*

● Dutch: Frans Hals's portrait of *Andries van der Horn* and Rembrandt's *Self-Portrait.*

● German: portraits by Hans Holbein the Younger and Lucas Cranach the Elder.

With its many skyscrapers, São Paulo's business district resembles any other major city. ▶

● Spanish: El Greco's *Annunciation*, Velasquez's portrait of the *Duke of Olivares* and Goya's portrait of *Cardinal de Bourbon*.

● English: Gainsborough's *Drinkstone Park* and Constable's *Salisbury Cathedral*.

● French: Poussin's *Offering to Priapus*, Fragonard's *Education Is All*, Delacroix's *Four Seasons*, Manet's *Amazone*, Renoir's *Bathers*, Monet's *Le Pont de Giverny*, Gauguin's *Poor Fishermen*, Cézanne's *Portrait of Madame Cézanne* and Matisse's *Plaster Torso*.

Many major European and American contemporary artists, (Modigliani, De Chirico, Arp, Grosz, Matisse, Kandinsky, Chagall, Picasso, Laríonov, Soutine, Max Ernst, Miró, and others) are represented here, as are modern Brazilian painters such as Malfetti, Cavalcanti, Portinari, Segall and Tarsila do Amaral.

Museu de Arte Contemporânea** (Museum of Contemporary Art, Parque do Ibirapuera, I, B3, ☎ 571 9610; open Tues-Sun noon-6pm) was founded in 1963 on the initiative of Brazilian industrialist, Francisco de Matarazzo. He was also responsible for part of its collection. The museum has several thousand works, only one-tenth of which are ever on display.

Casa Brasileira** (Av. Brig. Faria Lima 774, Jardim Europa, I, A2, ☎ 210 2564; open Tues-Sun 1-5pm) is a historical museum of Brazilian furniture.

Museu de Arte Moderna** (Museum of Modern Art, Parque do Ibirapuera, I, B3, ☎ 549 9688; open Tues-Fri 1-7pm, Sat and Sun 11am-7pm) contains works by contemporary Brazilian artists. It also organizes the Bienal de Artes Plasticas, one of South America's top artistic events.

Museu Lasar Segall** (Rua Alfonso Celso 388, Vila Mariana, I, B3, ☎ 572 8211; open Tues, Wed, Thurs and Sun 2:30-6:30pm, Sat 2:30-8pm) is practically the only repository of the works of Russian artist Lasar Segall, who immigrated to Brazil and became a Brazilian citizen.

Parque do Ibirapuera**, I, B3, extends over approximately 395 acres/160 hectares. It was designed and landscaped by architect Oscar Niemeyer and landscape architect Burle-Marx in honour of the fourth centennial of São Paulo's founding. Every Saturday afternoon there is an arts and crafts fair underneath a big tent, and on Sunday afternoons there are outdoor music concerts near the Museum of Modern Art. An aeronautics museum, a planetarium and several monuments can also be visited on the park grounds.

Casa do Sertanista* (Praça Dr. Ennio Barbato 21, Caxingui, I, A3, ☎ 211 5341; open Tues-Sun 9am-5pm) is a museum dedicated to Indian handcrafts and folklore. It was created by the well-known Indian authority, Orlando Villas Boas.

Jardim da Aclimação* (Rua Muniz de Souza 1119, Aclimação) is a restful little park (open 5am-8pm).

Palácio des Bandeirantes* (Av. Morumbi, I, A3) was originally designed as a university building. It has been the seat of São Paulo's government since 1966.

There are two lovely churches in this area, **Nossa Senhora do Perpetuo Socorro*** (Rua Honorio Libero 90, Jardim Europa, I, A2) and **São Judas Tadeu*** (Av. Jabaquara 2682).

The western zone

The west side of São Paulo lies at the confluence of the rivers Tieté and Pinheiros. The Avenida Heitor Penteado cuts across it over a hill that affords some unexpected views of São Paulo. Some of its neighbourhoods, such as Pinheiros and Sumaré, still look like villages, with their shops clustered around their small churches. At the westernmost tip of this area, however, such recent designs as the Instituto Butanta, the Cidade Universitaria and the covered market *(ceasa)* have completely changed the landscape.

Instituto Butantã*** (Av. Vital Brasil 1500, I, A2, ☎ 2118211; open Tues-Sun 9am-5pm, Mon 1-5pm) is a remarkable institution and one of the best of its kind anywhere in the world. It is mainly concerned with the study of Brazil's many snakes. It buys over 30,000 reptiles per year from farmers and hunters and extracts the venom needed for the manufacture of serum and vaccines. If you are really courageous, you can look into a snakepit writhing with poisonous specimens! There is also a museum with collections of live snakes, giant spiders and scorpions. Daily venom-extracting sessions, which usually take place between 10 and 11am and between 3 and 4pm, are among São Paulo's most popular tourist attractions.

Casa do Bandeirante** (Praça Monteiro Lobato, I, A2, ☎ 2110920; open Tues-Sun 9am-5pm) is a typical example of 18th-century São Paulo rural architecture. A pioneer's home has been reconstructed, complete with period items and furniture.

Cidade Universitaria** (Av. Afranio Peixoto, I, A2) is an interesting example of Brazilian architecture and use of space. It includes several noteworthy constructions, in particular the Instituto História e Geográfica and the Faculdadé de Arquitetura e Urbanismo, and several museums including the Museum of Archaeology and Ethnology and the Museum of the American Man.

Ceasa (Rua Aruaba, Jaguaré, I, A2) is São Paulo's central market for vegetables, fruit, flowers and fish.

Consolação Cemetery* (Rua da Consolação) contains remarkable examples of grandiose and opulent funerary art. It belongs mostly to the Italian community.

Museu de Arte Brasileira* (Rua Alagoas 903, Pacaembu, I, B2, ☎ 8264233; open Tues-Fri 2-10pm, Sat and Sun 1-6pm) houses approximately 300 works by modern Brazilian artists.

Parque Fernando Costa* (Av. Francisco Matarazzo 455, Agua Branca, I, B2; open 8am-5pm) is a vast park with a children's playground and numerous exhibitions, in particular of domestic animals and livestock. The atmosphere is reminiscent of a country fair, with entertainers and every imaginable homemade product.

Playcenter* (Rua Dr. Rubens Meirelles 380, I, B2; open Mon, Wed-Fri 10am-7pm, Sat and Sun 10am-8pm) is the site of a year-round fair.

This area also has several churches of interest, including **Calvario** (Rua Cardeal Arcoverde 950, Pinheiros, I, A2), **Nossa Senhora de Fatima** (Av. Dr. Arnaldo 1831), **Nossa Senhora do Monte Serrate** (Rua Pe. Carvalho 853, Pinheiros, I, A2), **Santa Teresinha*** (Rua Maranhão 617) and **São Domingos*** (Rua Caiubi 164, Perdizes, I, B2).

The eastern zone

This part of town is best avoided by the tourist. Except for the few sights listed, which are all close to the boundary of the northern and southern zones, there is nothing worth visiting in this area.

Japanese quarter** is in the area of Liberdade around Rua Galvão Bueno, II, C4-5. It is a great place to visit for its restaurants and shops selling interesting oriental goods.

Parque da Independência*** (Av. Dom Pedro I, Ipiranga, II, C3) is a formal French garden that lies in the hills of Ipiranga. It was here that Dom Pedro I declared Brazilian independence in 1822. There are many things to see here.

● **Independence Monument**** was raised in 1922. Constructed from granite and bronze, it commemorates Brazilian independence. It bears a reproduction in relief of Pedro America's painting *O Grito do Ipiranga (Proclamation of Ipiranga).*

● **Museu Paulista**** (☎ 2154588; open Tues-Sun 9am-5pm) is housed in a huge palace in the Italian Renaissance style. It contains collections of arms, documents and furniture that formerly belonged to famous Brazilians.

● **Caso do Grito*** is an 18th-century herdsman's cottage where Dom Pedro I spent the night before delivering his famous cry of 'Independence or death'.

● **Imperial Chapel*** contains the tomb in which Dom Pedro I and his wife are buried.

The northern zone

The northern zone, like the eastern zone, offers very little of interest to the tourist. There is, of course, the Museum of Sacred Art, and sometimes there are intriguing exhibitions in the Parque Anhembi.

Museu de Arte Sacra*** (Museum of Sacred Art, Av. Tiradentes 676, II, C1, ☎ 227 7694; open Tues-Sun 1-5pm) has been established inside the former Luz monastery, which was built in 1774 by Brother Antônio Santana Galvão. It is one of Brazil's foremost museums of religious art, containing objects from São Paulo state, Rio, Minas Gerais and Salvador. Particularly noteworthy are the sculptures by Frei Agostinho de Jesus, Francisco-Xavier de Brito (and his illustrious disciple, Aleijadinho) and Mestre Valentim, the paintings by Frei Jesuino do Monte Carmelo, handsome Baroque altars, Rococo oratories and a sumptuous gold plate.

Horto Florestal* (Rua do Horto, I, B1; open daily 7am-5:30pm) is a 430 acre/174 hectare park where you can enjoy picnics and outings.

Jardim da Luz* (Praça da Luz, Bom Retiro, II, B1; open daily 7am-6pm) is one of São Paulo's oldest parks.

Parque Anhembi* (Av. Olavo Fontoura 1209, Santana, I, B1, ☎ 267 2122) is one of South America's most important exhibition centres. Ask for a program of events at your hotel because many of its exhibitions are great fun to visit.

Pico do Jaragua*, I, A1, is a peak that is over 3722 ft/1135 m high and affords a splendid view over São Paulo. At its foot lies a small park with a lake and forest.

Pinacoteca do Estado* (State Art Collection, Av. Tiradentes 141, II, C1, ☎ 227 6329; open Tues, Wed, Fri-Sun 1:30-7pm, Thurs 1:30-9pm) contains more than 3000 works by Brazilian artists.

The outlying southern zone

This area comes to life on weekends because the Interlagos car-racing track, the Congonhas Airport, and the roads leading to the coast and to the lake-reservoirs are all here. As you drive through, you will see a cross-section of the good and bad in Brazilian housing.

The places worth visiting in this area include the following.

Parque Estadual das Fontes do Ipiranga** (Av. Miguel Stefano, Aguá Funda, I, B3-4) is a huge park about 6 mi/10 km south of the city centre. It boasts three of São Paulo's prime tourist attractions:

● **Citade da Crianca** (Rua Kara 305, São Bernardo do Campo) is a place for children, where real-life and imaginary scenes have been reproduced in miniature, rather like at Disneyland.

● **Simba Safari and Parque dos Leões**** is a wildlife park where animals roam freely. Visitors can drive through in their own car or in one belonging to the park.

Zoological Garden** contains over 2500 animal species, as well as a reference library.

Represa Billings** (Riacho Grande, I, B4) consists of an area of 321,000 acres/130,000 hectares. The *represas* are the lake-reservoirs that are being developed as tourist attractions. This site includes restaurants, fishing facilities and the Parque Municipal do Estoril with its boats, picnic areas and other amenities.

Represa de Guarapiringa (Interlagos, I, A4) is smaller than Represa Billings and includes several beaches (Praia do Sol and Praia Azul), as well as bars and restaurants. There is also a park here that was designed by Burle-Marx.

ENVIRONS OF SÃO PAULO

The outskirts

São Paulo stands on a plateau 2625 ft/800 m high and the sea is some 37 mi/60 km away. Close to the city, there are a number of small communities that you can visit on a day's outing.

Embu** is a small historical town about 15 mi/25 km west of São Paulo. It has some fine examples of 17th-century colonial architecture (see especially the church of **Nossa Senhora do Rosario**). Every Sunday afternoon there is an entertaining arts and crafts fair.

Itu**, about 68 mi/110 km north-west of São Paulo, has two interesting churches: **Bom Jesus**, dating from 1750, and **Nossa Senhora da Candelaria**, dating from 1780.

Atibaia*, is a small spa 43 mi/69 km north of São Paulo. Its location is attractive and from here you can hike up the Pedra Grande in the Serra de Itapetinga, 12.5 mi/20 km away. From Atibaia, you can also visit the tiny villages of the surrounding mountains, notably **Vila Monte Verde** and **Bragança Paulista**.

Juquitiba* is a pleasant little town 46 mi/74 km north of São Paulo, near the *represa* (lake-reservoir) of the same name.

Pirapora de Bom Jesus*, 36 mi/58 km north of São Paulo, hosts a famous fair that lasts from February until August, the **Romaria de Bom Jesus**.

São Roque* is a little village 40 mi/65 km west of São Paulo that is known for its vineyards.

Santos and the southern coast

From São Paulo, the way to the ocean either north or south is down the Serra slopes via one of the three roads leading to Santos. On this route, the altitude drops approximately 2300 ft/700 m per 6 mi/10 km. The views are magnificent, and because of the heavy traffic, there is usually plenty of time to enjoy them. Spending five or six hours going down to Santos or Guarujá is part of São Paulo's way of life. Except for weekends and holidays when roads become one-way, you can choose between the picturesque old Caminho do Mar, which twists and turns past Dom Pedro II's old hunting lodges, the Anchieta, a two-lane highway usually jammed with traffic, and the Immigrantes, a superb four-lane highway inaugurated in 1976 that is an endless string of tunnels and bridges.

Farther south, beyond Santos and São Vicente, you will see a beach so long it seems to stretch forever. All along it are tiny seaside resorts that are well worth visiting. Although the accommodation is generally modest, you can enjoy wonderfully peaceful moments here. The sandy road that follows the beach is picturesque and preferable to the large asphalt road inland.

Santos**, 43 mi/70 km south-east of São Paulo, is a large city that stands on a island. It is São Paulo's harbour — the most important one in Brazil — and handles over 15 million tons of goods per year (i.e., 50% of Brazilian exports and 40% of imports). Despite its stifling summer heat, it remains the favourite resort of most residents of São Paulo.

Sights to see in Santos include the **Nossa Senhora do Monte Serrat**, dating from 1603, which sits on top of the hill of the same name and offers lovely views, the **municipal aquarium;** and the **Orquidário**, which is especially worth visiting between March and November when all the orchids are in bloom. A trip to the top of Santa Teresinha, at 656 ft/200 m, is also worthwhile.

From Santos, you can take many sea excursions as far as the bays of Santos, São Vicente, Guarujá and Bertioga. You can also go ocean-fishing from the Praticos Bridge or the Praia Bridge (☎ 31 2898).

The beaches at Boqueirão, Embaré, Gonzaga and José Menino form one long stretch of sand, but the proximity of the harbour and a nearby industrial zone known to Brazilians as 'Death Valley' because of heavy pollution make swimming unadvisable.

São Vicente** is 45 mi/72 km south-east São Paulo and looks like an extension of Santos, even though it has a character of its own. It is less industrialized and its natural setting has more appeal than that of Santos. The town was founded in 1532 by the Portuguese Martin Afonso de Souza upon his return from an expedition along the coast of Argentina. The prettiest beaches here are the ones at Prainha and Itararé. The latter stretches as far as the celebrated Ilha Porchat, one of the most picturesque sights in town.

Itanhaém**, 68 mi/110 km south-east of São Paulo, is a historical town. Among its sights is the **Convent of Nossa Senhora da Conceição**, dating from 1561. The most attractive of its beaches is **Praia do Sonho**, which is set among magnificent rocks.

Peruíbe** is 87 mi/140 km south-east of São Paulo and has two stunning beaches, **Guaraú** and **Arpoador. Morro do Guaraú**, 2 mi/3 km away, and **Cochoeira do Paraíso**, 9 mi/15 km away, are great places for walking in the vicinity.

Praia Grande* is 50 mi/80 km south-east of São Paulo and 5 mi/8 km from São Vicente. It is the largest of the beaches that serves as a playground for the multitudes of São Paulo.

Guarujá and the northern coast

Guarujá is a trendy weekend spot for residents of São Paulo, and the stretch of coast to its north leads to Rio via Parati and the Costa Verde (see p. 95). This entire region is being developed for tourism now that the entire length of the Estrada Rio-Santos has been paved. The last stretch to be paved, between Bertioga and São Sebastião, is still quite wild and picturesque.

Guarujá*** is 58 mi/90 km south-east of São Paulo. It is São Paulo's most chic resort and has fairly well-developed facilities. This town, built up for the most part recently, has a handful of old forts, such as the São Felipe dating from 1532.

The beaches here are beautiful and come in all sizes. Guarujá and Pitangueiras beaches are right in town. There are several others to the north, such as Enseada, Pernambuco and Perequê. Tombo and Guaiba beaches are rocky and lie to the south. If you want a great view over the area, go to the top of the Morro do Maluf, the Morro do Pitiu or the Morro da Peninsula.

Bertioga**, 75 mi/120 km São Paulo, is a small fishermen's village that can be reached from Guarujá by ferry. It has lovely beaches, **da Enseada** and **Indaiá**. Fishing and boating are also available here, either out at sea or along the Bertioga canal. There is a fort here, São João, dating from 1547. From here to São Sebastião there are wonderful beaches, peninsulas and deserted islands.

São Sebastião**, 135 mi/217 km east of São Paulo, is a historical little town where tourism has not really been developed yet. There are various interesting colonial buildings to see here, as well as the 17th-century church of São Sebastião. Southwards 30 mi/50 km there are some sumptuous beaches — Camburi-Ilhas, Preta-Ilhas, and others.

Caraguatatuba* is a small resort near São José dos Campos that is 118 mi/190 km north-east of São Paulo.

Ilhabela*, 143 mi/230 km east of São Paulo, is a beautiful big island facing São Sebastião. This island is one of the most unspoiled and picturesque places on this part of the coast. It has lovely beaches, waterfalls, rock formations, a tropical forest and much more.

Ubatuba*, 153 mi/246 km north-east of São Paulo, is the latest 'hot spot' in São Paulo resorts. The town occupies some 52 mi/84 km of coastline with 73 different beaches, many of which remain deserted because they are so difficult to reach. The most popular now are Enseada and Tenorio. Toninhas is a great surfing beach, while Lazaro and Perequê-Açu are peaceful and quiet. If you enjoy fishing, the best beaches are Flamengo and Ponta Grossa.

The mountains around São Paulo

If Guarajá is the favourite seaside haunt of São Paulo residents, Campos de Jordão is its counterpart in the mountains. The best way to reach it is to take the Via Dutra (Rio-São Paulo expressway) to São José dos Campos or to Caçapava.

Campos de Jordão★★★ is 109 mi/175 km north of São Paulo. This town consists of three villages: Abernessia, Jaguaribe and Capivari. Its invigorating climate and plant-life remind you of Switzerland, and it is full of little chalets, waterfalls and pine forests — not what you would expect to find in tropical Brazil.

Several peaks in the area beg to be explored; Pico de Itapeva (6660 ft/2030 m), Pico de Timbera (6414 ft/1955 m), and the very beautiful Pedra do Bau (6414 ft/1955 m). Other nearby places of interest include the Morro Do Elefante (cable-car from Capivari), the Duchas Chuvas de Prata, the Mirante de Boa Vista, the Palacio do Governo and the charming little villages of Monteiro Lobato, São Antônio do Pinhal and São Bento do Sapucai.

Accommodation

▲▲▲ **Casa Grande,** Av. Miguel Stefano 999, Guarujá, ☎ (0132) 86 2223. This elegant colonial-style hotel sits in a lovely park. It has two restaurants, three bars, a swimming pool and several boutiques. 160 rooms.

▲▲▲ **Toriba,** Av. Ernesto Diederichsen 7, Campos do Jordão, ☎ (0122) 62 1566. Situated in a large park, this hotel offers a wonderful view. It has a restaurant, two bars, a swimming pool and tennis courts. 34 rooms.

▲▲ **Orotour Garden,** Campos do Jordão, ☎ (0122) 62 2833. This attractive hotel, located in a park, contains a restaurant, two bars, two swimming pools and tennis courts. 61 rooms.

▲▲ **Parque Balneário,** Av. Ana Costa 555, Santos, ☎ (0132) 34 7211. A charming hotel with a restaurant, four bars, a swimming pool and various boutiques. 117 rooms.

▲▲ **Pousadas da Tabatinga,** Estr. Ubatuba, Caraguatatuba, ☎ (0124) 24 1411. On the beach, this hotel has a restaurant, two bars, a swimming pool and tennis courts. 24 rooms.

▲▲ **San Raphael Country,** Av. Tiradentes 2223, Itu, ☎ (011) 409 1821. Situated in a park, this hotel has a restaurant, four bars, two swimming pools and several boutiques. 55 rooms.

▲▲ **Vila Inglesa,** Rua Sen. Roberto Simonsen 3500, Campos do Jordão, ☎ (0122) 63 1955. The hotel sits in a lovely park and has a restaurant, two bars, a swimming pool and tennis courts. 54 rooms.

▲▲ **Village Eldorado,** Rua Dom Pedro I, Atibaia, ☎ (011) 484 2533. In a well-kept park, this hotel has a restaurant, two bars, two swimming pools, tennis courts and horseback riding. 118 rooms.

▲ **Cibratel,** Av. Atlântica 326, Itanhaém, ☎ (0132) 92 2421. This hotel is on the beach and has a restaurant and a bar. 34 rooms.

▲ **Delphin,** Av. Miguel Stefano 1295, Guarujá, ☎ (0132) 86 2111. A restaurant, two bars, a swimming pool and transportation to and from the beach are all part of a stay in this hotel. 125 rooms.

▲ **Ilhabela,** Av. Pedro Paula de Morais 151, Ilhabela, ☎ (0124) 72 1083. Although small, this hotel has many amenities, including a restaurant, three bars, a swimming pool and a gymnasium. 43 rooms.

▲ **Indaiá Praia,** Av. Tomé de Souza 10793, Bertioga, ☎ (0132) 56 1131. A little hotel on the beach. 20 rooms.

▲ **Itapemar,** Av. Pedra Paula de Morais 341, Ilhabela, ☎ (0124) 72 1329. A restaurant, two bars, a swimming pool, tennis courts and canoeing are all on offer at this modest hotel. 49 rooms.

▲ **Jequitimar,** Av. Marjory Prado 1100, Guarujá, ☎ (0132) 53 3111. This attractive hotel is on the beach. It has a restaurant, a bar, two swimming pools and tennis courts. 68 rooms.

▲ **Marazul 27,** Av. Tomé de Souza 825, Bertioga, ☎ (0132) 57 1560. On the beach, this hotel has a restaurant and a bar. 47 rooms.

▲ **Matsubara,** Rua Prof. José Paulo 80, Campos do Jordão, ☎ (0122) 62 3177. This little hotel has a restaurant, a bar and a swimming pool. 20 rooms.

▲ **Mediterrâneo,** Praia da Enseada, Ubatuba, ☎ (0124) 42 0112. On the beach, this hotel has a restaurant, three bars and a swimming pool. 29 rooms.

▲ **Mercedes,** Prainha Mercedes, Ilhabela, ☎ (0124) 72 1071. A simple, little hotel in a park with a restaurant, a bar and a swimming pool. 18 rooms.

▲ **Miramar,** Rua Itararé 94, Praia Grande, ☎ (0132) 91 6989. This is a modest, small hotel. 22 rooms.

▲ **Paulista Praia,** Av. Pres. Wilson 134, Santos, ☎ (0132) 37 4700. This hotel is simple but adequate and has a restaurant and a bar. 68 rooms.

▲ **Porto Grande,** Av. Guarda-Mor Lobo Viana 1440, São Sebastião, ☎ (0124) 52 1101. On the beach, this hotel has a restaurant, a bar and a swimming pool. 31 rooms.

▲ **Rancho Silvestre,** Estr. Votorantim 700, Embu, ☎ (011) 494 2911. This simple hotel is in a park and offers a restaurant, three bars and a swimming pool. 41 rooms.

▲ **Recanto dos Passaros,** Av. Guarda-Mor Lobo Viana 822, São Sebastião, ☎ (0124) 52 2046. A modest hotel on the beach, it has a restaurant, a bar and a swimming pool. 64 rooms.

▲ **Solemar,** Rua Lima Barreto 395, Praia Grande, ☎ (0132) 93 1116. This is a tiny hotel. 12 rooms.

▲ **Sol e Vida,** Praia da Enseada, Ubatuba, ☎ (0124) 42 0188. This hotel is on the beach and contains a restaurant, two bars and a swimming pool. 41 rooms.

▲ **Terrazza,** Av. Sen. Roberto Simonsen 1071, Campos do Jordão, ☎ (0122) 63 1255. This pleasant hotel is in a park and has a restaurant and two bars. 28 rooms.

▲ **Timão,** Estr. Bertioga, São Sebastião, ☎ (0124) 63 1130. This is a modest hotel with a restaurant, a bar and a swimming pool. 28 rooms.

▲ **Ubatuba Palace,** Rua Cel. Domiciano 500, Ubatuba, ☎ (0124) 32 1500. This comfortable hotel offers a restaurant, a bar and a swimming pool. 62 rooms.

Food

** **Canto Bravo,** Estr. Bertioga, São Sebastião. This modest restaurant has a wonderful view, as well as a good variety of seafood. Open daily 1-4pm, 8pm-midnight.

** **Casa d'Irene,** Rua Raul Mesquita 83, Campos do Jordão, ☎ (0122) 63 1115. French cuisine in a charming ambience. Open daily 11am-3pm, 7pm-midnight.

** **Cassino Sol e Vida,** Hotel Sol e Vida, Estr. Caraguatatuba, Ubatuba, ☎ (0124) 42 0188. Very good seafood in a welcoming atmosphere. Open daily 11am-4pm, 6-11pm.

** **Deck,** Av. Alm. Tamandaré 805, Ilhabela, ☎ (0124) 72 1489. This restaurant offers a wonderful view and delicious seafood. Open noon-1am.

** **Malibu,** Estr. Caraguatatuba, Ubatuba, ☎ (0124) 42 0830. International cuisine in a lovely dining room with a view. Open daily 11am-midnight.

** **Old Harbor,** Hotel Parque Balneário, Av. Ana Costa 555, Santos,

☎ (0132) 34 7211. International cuisine and live music in a charming dining room. Open daily noon-3pm, 7pm-midnight.

** **Penhasco,** Al. Paulo Gonçalves 68, São Vicente, ☎ (0132) 68 4050. International cuisine in a lovely dining room with a view. Open daily 7pm-4am.

** **Steiner,** Rua Paula Souza 575, Itu, ☎ (011) 482 4284. Live music and international cuisine in a welcoming restaurant. Open daily 11am-midnight.

* **Atibaia,** Rua José Bim 119, Atibaia, ☎ (011) 484 3707. This modest restaurant offers good Chinese food. Open daily 11:30am-2:30pm, 6-10pm.

* **Le Arcate,** Av. Dom Pedro I, Guarujá, ☎ (0132) 55 2556. Simple but delicious Italian cuisine. Open daily noon-4pm, 6pm-1am.

* **Café Paulista,** Praça Rui Barbosa 8, Santos, ☎ (0132) 33 4500. A good choice of seafood in a comfortable setting. Open Mon-Sat 11am-8:30pm.

* **Cantina Italia,** Rua Br. do Itaim 211, Itu, ☎ (011) 482 4206. Simple Italian fare in this lively restaurant. Open 11am-3pm, 6pm-midnight.

* **Davo's,** Av. Macedo Soares 340, Campos do Jordão, ☎ (0122) 63 1824. This charming little restaurant specializes in Swiss cuisine. Open Mon-Sat 11am-midnight.

* **Orixas,** Rua N.S. do Rosario 60, Embu, ☎ (011) 494 5123. This restaurant offers simple Brazilian fare. Open daily 11am-6pm.

* **Panela de Barro,** Rua 11 de Junho 104, São Vicente, ☎ (0132) 68 3894. This modest restaurant serves a good variety of seafood. Open daily 11-4am.

* **Patacão,** Rua Joaquim Santana 95, Embu, ☎ (011) 494 2051. Good Brazilian cooking in this family-style restaurant. Open daily 11am-4pm, 7pm-midnight.

* **Pirata,** Rua Euclides Figueiredo 700, Praia Grande, ☎ (0132) 91 1559. A lively *churrascaria.* Open Mon-Sat 6pm-midnight.

* **Riviera,** Av. Dois, Bertioga, ☎ (0132) 56 1265. Simple seafood in a restaurant with a lovely view. Open daily noon-midnight.

* **Robalo,** Av. Europa 12, Itanhaém, ☎ (0132) 92 1155. This restaurant offers a good choice of seafood. Open daily 11am-midnight.

* **Rufino's,** Estr. do Pernambuco 111, Guarujá. This simple little restaurant serves very good seafood dishes. Open daily noon-1am.

SÃO PAULO STATE

Traveling in São Paulo state is made easy by a network of fine roads. If you are interested in visiting the interior, perhaps the best place to begin is the **Paraíba valley**.

Behind the impressive range of Serra do Mar the valley of the Paraíba River stretches almost all the way from São Paulo to Rio. Although this part of the Via Dutra (Rio-São Paulo expressway) has become heavily industrialized, some pretty villages remain.

Guararama* is 46.5 mi/75 km north-east of São Paulo on the Paraíba River. Sights of interest include the lovely **Pau d'Alho island**, which sits in the middle of the river, and the 16th-century church, **Nossa Senhora da Freguesia da Escada**.

São José dos Campos* is a large provincial city 60 mi/97 km north-east of São Paulo. It is famous for being the home of Embraer, the Brazilian aeronautics manufacturer of such aircraft as the Bandeirantes and the Xavantes.

São Luís de Paraitinga*, 111 mi/177 km north-east of São Paulo, is a small historical village that was the birthplace of Oswaldo Cruz, the well-known Brazilian doctor who was responsible for setting up Brazil's medical system.

Cunha*, 141 mi/227 km north-east of São Paulo, is the departure point for visits to the *fazenda* (farm) of Santa Rosa, 17 mi/27 km away.

Aparecida*, 108 mi/173 km north-east of São Paulo, is a sanctuary and a place of pilgrimage in honour of Nossa Senhora Aparecida, the Black Virgin, Brazil's patron saint. The town has two basilicas in her honour. The older **Basilica Vellia**, dating from 1745, is by far the more beautiful. **São Francisco dos Campos do Jordão*** is 155 mi/250 km north-east of São Paulo. It is a lovely natural site with mineral springs and waterfalls.

Another interesting trip into the interior of São Paulo state is to the **Serra da Bocaina National Park****. This is a magnificent natural reserve of forests, waterfalls and fruit groves. It lies on the border with Rio de Janeiro state at 5709 ft/1740 m. There are several villages worth visiting in its surroundings.

São José de Barreiro*, 168 mi/270 km north of São Paulo, is an excellent stopping-off point for a visit to the park. Close to the town (2 mi/3 km) is a *fazenda* (farm) named **Pau d'Alho**, which dates back to colonial days.

Bananal* is 199 mi/320 km north of São Paulo and only 31 mi/50 km from São José de Barreiro. The town centre merits a visit, as do the various *fazendas* (farms) in the area, which have been declared national treasures. Particularly noteworthy are the **Fazenda do Resgate**, 6 mi/10 km out of town, and the **Fazenda Rialto**, 5 mi/8 km away.

Silveiras*, 140 mi/225 km north of São Paulo, is the site of an old prison that is now classed as a national treasure.

A third option for visiting the interior is to head for the far south of São Paulo state. This area is wedged between the Serra Paranapiacaba and the sea and is crisscrossed by the São Paulo-Curitiba expressway. Places of interest in the area include the following.

Iguape**, 130 mi/210 km south of São Paulo, is a small seaside resort with vestiges of colonial architecture, including the Basilica de Bom Jésus, dating from 1772, and the Gruta de Bom Jésus. There are also lovely beaches here.

Cananéia*, 170 mi/275 km south of São Paulo, has pretty beaches and islands to visit.

La Caverna do Diabo*** lies in the Serra da André Lopes, 133 mi/215 km south of São Paulo. Also called Gruta da Tapagem, this is one of Brazil's most remarkable grottos, over 3 mi/5 km long. Guided tours are available, ☎ (0122) 42 3233.

La Caverna de Santana* is 217 mi/347 km south of São Paulo, located between Apiaí (14 mi/23 km away) and Iporanga (12.5 mi/20 km away). This is another lovely grotto with a natural pool that can be visited on a guided tour.

Another touring option in São Paulo state is a visit to one of its spas. Several that we recommend in the area follow below.

Serra Negra** sits at an altitude of 3148 ft/960 m, about 95 mi/150 km south of São Paulo. Besides the spa facilities, you can take advantage of numerous excursions to parks in the area.

Águas de Lindóia*** is 112 mi/180 km south of São Paulo, at an altitude of 2965 ft/904 m. This is the most fashionable spa, with up-to-date facilities.

Águas da Prata* is 140 mi/226 km south of São Paulo, at 2683 ft/818 m. The town has extensive tourist facilities (pools, saunas, boutiques).

Águas de São Pedro**, 115 mi/185 km south of São Paulo, is farther west than the other spas in the valley of the Piracicaba River, at 1541 ft/470 m. This spa is different from the spas previously cited and has a special charm. Close by is the **Serra de Santo Antônio** and the small community of **São Pedro*** (4.5 mi/7 km away), which are worth visiting.

Two other small and pleasant spas are **Amparo** (93 mi/150 km south of São Paulo) and **Monte Alegre** (90 mi/145 km south of São Paulo).

Several other towns in the interior of São Paulo state warrant a look if you find yourself in their area.

Barra Bonita★★, 192 mi/310 km north-west of São Paulo, is the site of a lock on the Tieté River. From here, it is possible to take a four-hour excursion on the river (departures 9:30am, 1pm and 2:30pm; Av. Pedro Ometo, ☎ 0146 41 2422).

Analandia★ (143 mi/231 km north-west of São Paulo) and **Nuporanga★** (243 mi/391 km north-west of São Paulo) are two health resorts

Águas de Santa Barbara★ (193 mi/311 km north-west of São Paulo) and **Ibira★** (256 mi/413 km north-west of São Paulo) are two very small spas.

Presidente Epitácio★ (422 mi/680 km north-west of São Paulo) and **Panorama★** (425 mi/684 km north-west of São Paulo) are situated on the Paraná River. From either of these towns, you can take a three-hour boat trip, including lunch, on the river (departures Sat, Sun and holidays at noon; ☎ 0188 21 1666).

Accommodation

▲▲ **Estância Barra Bonita**, Estr. da CESP 2700, Barra Bonita, ☎ (0146) 41 0400. Situated in a particularly lovely park, this hotel offers a restaurant, two bars, three swimming pools, tennis courts and horseback riding. 110 rooms.

▲ **Cananéia Glória**, Av. Luis Wilson Barbosa, Cananéia, ☎ (0138) 51 1377. This small hotel has a marvelous view, as well as a restaurant, a bar and two swimming pools. 27 rooms.

▲ **Estância**, Rua Cap. José Inacio 325, Monte Alegre, ☎ (0192) 99 1206. Modest little hotel with a swimming pool. 11 rooms.

▲ **Fazenda Club dos 200**, Estr. Bananal. São José do Barreiro, ☎ (0125) 77 1211. This hotel is located in a charming park and has a restaurant, a bar, a swimming pool, tennis courts and horseback riding. 24 rooms.

▲ **Fazenda São João**, Av. Paschoal Antonelli 800, São Pedro, ☎ (0194) 81 1411. Lying in a pleasant park, this hotel offers a restaurant, a bar, a swimming pool and horseback riding. 73 rooms.

▲ **Fazenda Vale do Sol**, Estr. Lindóia, Serra Negra, ☎ (0192) 92 3500. An enormous hotel, with a restaurant, four bars, six swimming pools, tennis courts, horseback riding and a cinema. 261 rooms.

▲ **Grande Hotel Amparo**, Praça Br. do Rio Branco 33, Amparo, ☎ (0192) 70 2093. This is a modest little hotel. 23 rooms.

▲ **Grande Hotel São Pedro**, Parque Dr. Otávio Moura Andrade, Águas de São Pedro, ☎ (0194) 82 1211. This hotel is situated in a lovely park and has a good restaurant, four bars, two swimming pools and tennis courts. 115 rooms.

▲ **Hotel Brasília**, BR-116, Jacupiranga, ☎ (0138) 64 1063. This is a modest and comfortable hotel. 40 rooms.

▲ **Jerubiaçaba**, Av. Carlos Mauro 168, Águas de São Pedro, ☎ (0194) 82 1411. This average hotel has a restaurant, a bar, two swimming pools and tennis courts. 130 rooms.

▲ **Majestic**, Praça Dr. Vicente Rizzo 160, Águas de Lindóia, ☎ (0192) 94 1812. This charming hotel has a restaurant, two bars, a swimming pool and tennis courts. 102 rooms.

▲ **Maré Alta**, Av. Beira-Mar, Iguape, ☎ (0138) 42 1135. This is a lovely hotel with a restaurant, two bars, a swimming pool and tennis courts. 40 rooms.

▲ **Nova Lindóia Vacance**, Av. das Naçoes Unidas 1374, Águas de Lindóia, ☎ (0192) 94 1191. This is an extremely attractive hotel set in a park offering a lovely view, as well as a restaurant, four bars, two swimming pools and tennis courts. 209 rooms.

▲ **Panorama**, Rua Dr. Hermani G. Correa 45, Águas da Prata, ☎ (0196) 42 1511. This is a comfortable hotel with a restaurant, a bar and a swimming pool. 52 rooms.

▲ **Radio**, Rua Cel. Pedro Penteado 387, Serra Negra, ☎ (0192) 92 3311. This attractive hotel has a restaurant, two bars, two swimming pools and tennis courts. 85 rooms.

Food

* **Arrastão**, Av. Biera-Mar 9, Iguape ☎ (0138) 42 1259. This seafood restaurant is extremely well situated. Open daily 11am-10pm.

* **Barracão do Doca,** Praça Adolfo Bragaia 991, São Pedro, ☎ (0194) 81 1083. This is a lively *churrascaria*. Open daily 11am-3pm, 6:30-10pm.

* **Caiçara,** Praça Martim Alfonso de Souza, Cananéia, ☎ (0138) 51 1174. This is a modest seafood restaurant. Open daily 11am-3:30pm, 6-11pm.

* **Canoa Grande**, Barra Bonita, ☎ (0146) 41 1998. An attractive seafood restaurant with live music and parking. Open daily 11am-3pm.

* **Do Lago,** Saida Piracicaba, Águas de São Pedro, ☎ (0194) 82 1638. In a pleasant location, this restaurant serves a good variety of seafood. Open daily 11am-5pm.

* **Engenho das Aguas,** Grande Hotel São Pedro, Parque Estância, São Pedro, ☎ (0194) 82 1211. An excellent restaurant offering French cuisine and live music. Open daily 9pm-2am.

* **Fazenda Club dos 200,** Hotel Fazenda Club dos 200, Estr. Bananal, São José do Barreiro, ☎ (0125) 77 1211. Mixed cuisine in this hotel dining room. Open daily noon-2:30pm, 7:30-9:30pm.

* **Pinheirinho,** Rua Rio de Janeiro 403, Águas de Lindóia, ☎ (0192) 94 1196. Portuguese cuisine in a simple setting. Open daily 11am-10pm.

* **Recanto Português,** Praça Br. do Rio Branco 29, Amparo, ☎ (0192) 70 5346. Modest restaurant offering Portuguese cooking. Open daily 11am-3pm, 6-11pm.

* **Taco-Taco,** Saida Amparo, Serra Negra. This *churrascaria* has music and parking. Open daily 11:30am-4pm.

* **Universal,** Rua Cap. José Inacio 356, Monte Alegre, ☎ (0192) 99 1266. Brazilian cuisine in a lively ambience. Open daily 11am-3:30pm.

Useful addresses

Airline
Rio Sul, Av. Mal. Floriano Peixoto 4, São José dos Campos, ☎ (0123) 22 7555.

Airports
São Pedro, ☎ (0194) 81 1504.
São José dos Campos, ☎ (0123) 21 1311.

Bus terminals
Av. das Naçoes Unidas 1179, Aguas de Lindóia, ☎ (0192) 94 1128.
Praça Francisco Julianelli, Aparecida, ☎ (0125) 36 2285.
Praça 9 de Julho, Guararema, ☎ (11) 475 1039.
Rua Fortaleza 3-22, Presidente Epitácio, ☎ (0182) 81 1636.
Rua Itororó, São José dos Campos, ☎ (0123) 21 9122.
Av. dos Imigrantes, São Pedro, ☎ (0194) 81 1672.
Rua Cel. Pedro Penteado, Serra Negra, ☎ (0192) 92 1888.

Tourist office
Praça John Kennedy, Serra Negra, ☎ (0192) 92 2131.

NORDESTE

The Nordeste consist of nine states: Bahia, Sergipe, Alagoas, Pernambuco, Paraíba, Rio Grande do Norte, Ceará, Piauí and Maranhão. It covers 20% of Brazil's land area and contains 30% of the country's population. All the state capitals, with the exception of Teresina in Piauí, lie on the coast.

Despite its vast size and its climatic variations the Nordeste has a certain unity, due to a combination of geographical, social, and economic factors and a population that is highly insular.

Roughly, the Nordeste can be divided into three geographical areas. The first lies along the coast and is a narrow, fertile strip of land about 90-150 mi/150-250 km wide that is known as the *zona da mata,* literally 'the forest zone', so called for the forests that originally covered the region. Favoured by abundant rainfall, several crops such as sugarcane, cotton and cocoa are cultivated along the coastal belt.

To the west lies the *zona de agreste,* which is characterized by farming (millet, beans, tobacco and cassa) and cattle-breeding. The third geographical area is the vast and arid plateau of the *sertão.* This is a harsh and rugged place where the great riverbeds stand completely dry for six months of the year and practically the only vegetation is the *caatinga,* a scrub forest of thorn trees, cactus and bromeliads.

The northern states of Piauí and Maranhão constitute a transitional region between the *sertão* and the humid Amazon basin. Sparsely populated, the land is covered with *babaçu* palms from which a valuable vegetable oil is extracted.

The inhabitants of the Nordeste are descendants of Portuguese, Dutch, Indians and Africans. They have a reputation for being tough and unyielding, as exemplified by the mythical figure of the *vaqueiro,* the cowboy of the *sertão.* Adorned in tight-fitting leather clothing, the lone *vaqueiro* herds cattle on a share basis, daily confronting the hostile environment.

Throughout history, the Nordeste has been a breeding ground of rebellions. In the 17th century, fugitive slaves fled here, setting up *quilombos,* or fortified camps, and even establishing the short-lived Republic of Palmares (1630-1697). Maranhão was the scene of a peasant revolt in 1838.

Later in the 19th century the fanatical religious colony of Canudos in northern Bahia threatened the sovereignty of the Brazilian republic. Numerous military expeditions were sent before the government succeeded in overcoming the resistance of

---

The sugar boom

The first sugarmill in Brazil was built at São Vicente in the state of São Paulo in 1533. Gradually, plantations were formed all along the coast up to the Nordeste region. It was then discovered that the Nordeste was the most productive for sugar. Sugarmills were also established in the south of Brazil, most notably in the states of Rio de Janeiro and São Paulo.

By the middle of the 17th century, Brazil was the biggest producer of sugar in the world. Initially, captured Indians were put to work on the sugar plantations, but because they showed so much resistance, African slaves were shipped to the Nordeste region to take their place. The first official boat filled with slaves arrived in 1532, and eventually, a thriving trade developed that lasted almost to the end of the 19th century.

One of the consequences of the large influx of blacks into the region was the change in agriculture output — rice and tobacco were introduced. The traffic in slaves also had a far-reaching effect on the culture of the Nordeste, and African traditions and religious cults have been integrated into its society.

Like many other of Brazil's riches, the sugar boom came to an abrupt end. By the 18th century the country was in direct competition with Europe, where sugar beet was being cultivated, and with the Antilles. This led to a severe decline in the economy of the Nordeste, since it was almost completely dependent on the sugar trade. The abolition of slavery in 1888 ruined many plantation owners.

Today, sugar has made a spectacular comeback in Nordeste, and the region is now Brazil's second largest producer after São Paulo.

---

the enclave (and killing, in the process, all the zealots). Well into the 20th century, gangs of *cangaceiros,* half-bandits, half-idealists, roamed the Nordeste attacking the large plantations. While they were by no means revolutionaries, their fight against social injustice earned them a place in Brazilian folklore as heroes.

The social unrest in the Nordeste was largely due to upheavals in the economic structure of the region. Sugar production brought prosperity in the 17th and 18th centuries, and cotton contributed to the area's wealth in the 19th century. Tension between rich plantation owners, their slaves, and the Indian tribes was often acute. The 20th century has seen the decline of the Nordeste, which has become one of Brazil's most impoverished regions.

The economy of the *sertão* and *agreste,* in particular, is a fragile one. Droughts that sometimes last between four and 12 months cause famine and a high infant mortality rate. It would be impossible to overemphasize how crucial the Nordeste region's rivers are to its economy. The powerful São Francisco River serves as a waterway, supplies the region's prime source of energy with the Paulo Afonso hydroelectric plant, and is used in large-scale irrigation schemes.

Today, Bahia has become the major petroleum-production region of Brazil, supplying 80% of the country's petroleum and practically all of its natural gas. The coastal road between Rio and Salvador in Bahia has made the Nordeste more accessible, and the various projects of the Superintendency for Development of the Northeast (SUDENE) are bringing new hope to the region.

For the tourist, the Nordeste offers many appealing features. If you have sufficient time, try to visit all the state capitals. If your stay is short, only four or five days, you should probably choose Salvador and two or three other capitals, such as Recife or Natal. Salvador is a city with unique customs and traditions. Recife is the cultural and economic centre of the region and one of Brazil's largest cities. Another option is to concentrate on a single state — each has distinctive characteristics. Bahia is rich in contrasts, Pernambuco is full of historical reminders, and Maranhão offers an introduction to the Amazon basin.

PRACTICAL INFORMATION

When to go

To avoid the heat, the best period to visit the Nordeste region is between July and October. Be aware that during the rainy season, which lasts from March to August, the routes are sometimes flooded and certain areas can be temporarily inaccessible.

Access

The most practical means of getting to the Nordeste is by plane. There are several departures daily from Rio, Brasília and São Paulo to Salvador and Recife. Avoid the lengthy flights that make too many stops en route (some stop in nine capitals).

Unless an economical means of transport is a major concern, we suggest you avoid the long and tiring trip by bus from distant regions of Brazil.

Getting around the Nordeste

The major airlines (in particular, **Varig** see p. 138) have several flights a week between all the capitals of the Nordeste plus Campina Grande, Petrolina, Juazeiro de Norte and Imperatriz. In addition, the regional airline **Nordeste** (see p. 138) offers flights in Bahia to Bom Jesus da Lapa, Guanambi, Ilheus, Itabuna, Paulo Afonso, Porto Seguro; in Pernambuco to Petrolina and Caruaru and to Campina Grande in Paraíba.

Buses link many of the smaller towns of the region, but if you want to leave the major cities and go where you please, a car is the only solution.

SALVADOR

See maps pp. 144, 145, 148, 149.

Bahia state covers 216,612 sq mi/561,026 sq km, one third of the Nordeste region. It is a land of sharp contrasts, with thriving coastal areas and the impoverished ones of the interior.

Tradition states that the Bay of All Saints (Bahia de Todos os Santos) was first discovered by Amerigo Vespucci on November 1, 1501 — All Saints Day. Salvador, or Bahia as it was then called, was founded in February 1549 by Tomé de Souza. On the orders of Dom João III, he turned it into the seat of Brazil's colonial government.

The earliest settlers built homes around the Vitória and Nossa Senhora da Graça churches in Vila Velha and gradually the city expanded around the Jesuit church of Nossa Senhora da Ajuda. In 1558, the first shipload of slaves arrived to work in the sugarcane fields and Bahia's economy continued to be based on slave labour until the abolition of slavery in the 19th century.

In 1580, when Portugal became Spanish, the city of Bahia suffered dreadfully at the hands of the Inquisition. The Dutch invaded and colonized the city in the 1620s, but Bahia reverted to the Portuguese in 1640.

Bahia's early prosperity was based on the cultivation of sugarcane. As sugar production spread to other areas of Brazil, Bahia began to lose its economic importance. In 1763, when Rio de Janeiro became Brazil's

NORDESTE

N

Ilha Fernando de Noronha

Camocim
is Correia / Jericoacoara
naiba Granja
gua   Sobral
curuca
P. N. Ubajara
I. de Sete Cidades   Mondubim
ipiri   Ipu   Caninde
dro II   Araras   Açude
Crateus   *Serra de Baturité*   Baturité

FORTALEZA
Aquirás
Cascavel
Beberibe
Maranguape
Aracati
Tibau
Areia Branca
Quixadá
Macau
Mossoró Açu
CEARA
Rio Jaguaribe

RIO GRANDE
DO NORTE
NATAL
Iguatu   Catolé do Rocha
Currais
Novos
Caicó
Baia da Traição
Juazeiro
do Norte   Sousa   Pombal   Guarabira
Crato   Cajàzeiras   Sta Luzia   Areia   **PARAIBA**
Cabedelo
Chapada do Araripe   Patos   JOÃO PESSOA
Campina Grande
Serrita   Gameleira   Triunfo   Boqueirão   Tracuhhaém   Goiana
Salguero   Taquaritinga   Itamaracá
Igaraçu
PERNAMBUCO   Serra   do Norte   Limoeiro   Olinda
Talhada   Fazenda Nova   Gravatá   RECIFE
Cabrobo   Arcoverde   Caruaru   Jaboatão
Rio São Francisco   Palmares   Muribeca dos Guararapes
rragem   Garahuns   Catende   S. José de Coroa Grande
obradinho   Petrolina   União dos   Maragoji
Juazeiro   *P.N. de*   Paulo Afonso   Palmares   Barra de Santo Antônio
Sobradinho   *Paulo Afonso*
Piranhas   **ALAGOAS**   MACEIÓ
SERGIPE   Arapiraca   Marechal Deodoro
Praia Porto do Francês
hor do Bonfim   Euclides da Cunha   Propria   Barra de São Miguel
ta dos Brejoes   Carrapicho   Penedo
Neópolis
Laranjeiras
Salgado   ARACAJU
Jacobina   Ribeira   São Cristovão
do Amparo   Estância

Itaberaba   Feira de   Alagoinhas
cois   Santana
Sto Amaro
Cachoeira   Candeias
Camaçari
co   Nazare   SALVADOR
s Almas   Jaguaripe   *B. de Todos Os Santos*
50   Valença
nado   Jequié
Barra   Itabuna
Ilheus
ria da Conquista   Olivença
Itapetinga

ATLANTIC

OCEAN

Sta Cruz Cabrália
Porto Seguro
N Sra da Ajuda
Mte Pascoal
P.N. de Monte Pascoal
lanuque   Alcobaça
Caravelas
PIRITO   Nova Viçosa
NTO *Vitoria, Rio*

Railway |—|—|

0   150   300 km
0   100   200 miles

capital, the period of affluence was definitely over. The economic difficulties that followed led to a number of revolts and separatist movements — the Inconfidência Baiana in 1797 (see p. 33), the Alfaiates revolt in 1798, the slave uprisings of 1835 and the Sabinades uprising of 1837 — all of which were mercilessly put down.

The abolition of slavery in 1831 further contributed to the economic decline of the region. Today, the sugarcane industry is experiencing a resurgence. Tourism and petrochemical production are being developed, too, and great efforts have been made to irrigate large-scale agrarian projects in the São Francisco River valley. While pockets of extreme poverty persist in the interior of Bahia, the state is the most dynamic area of the Nordeste.

Salvador, the capital of the state of Bahia, has a population of over one million. It lies at the northern tip of the gigantic Bahia de Todos os Santos and, today, has a booming economy, thanks to the tourist industry and the new industrial complex at Aratu.

Brazilians think of Salvador as a sort of paradise on earth. Its charming, easy-going atmosphere attracts poets, painters and musicians. Notwithstanding its industrial development, Salvador retains its colour and traditions. Its food, music, religious practices and customs are highly distinctive. Its well-preserved historical heritage is framed in a magnificent natural setting — bright blue skies, a dark blue sea, a warm red soil, pure white dunes and brilliant green vegetation.

Telephone area code: 071

When to go

Salvador is warm, humid and rainy all year. The climate is most pleasant between June and September, when temperatures tend to be mild. This period, though, is also the height of the rainy season, which begins in April and lasts until September. You might want to consider going to Salvador specifically for one of its unique festivals (see p. 141), in particular those of Boa Viagem (Jan 1), Nosso Senhor de Bonfim (end of Jan), and Yemanjá (Feb 2).

Access

Plane

Salvador's **Dois de Julho** airport, I, B1, is located 20 mi/32 km from the city centre. There are several flights daily to Salvador from Brazil's main capitals and from the major cities of the Nordeste. ☎ 49 2811/204 1010.

From the airport, take the bus marked Aeroporto-Politeama to Av. 7 de Setembro in Salvador.

Nordeste, Av. Dom João VI 259, ☎ 244 7533.
Pan Am, Rua Visconde do Rosário 3, ☎ 243 8066.
Tap, Av. Estados Unidos 10, II, D1, ☎ 243 6122.
Transbrasil, Rua Carlos Gomes 616, II, A2, ☎ 241 1044.
Varig, Rua Carlos Gomes 616, II, A2, ☎ 243 1344.
Vasp, Rua Chile 27, II, B2, ☎ 243 7044.

Bus

You can get to Salvador by bus from most of the major cities of Brazil, although we don't recommend that you make the lengthy trip from Rio (28 hours), São Paulo (30 hours) or other distant capitals. Extensive bus service is available between Salvador and all the main cities of the Nordeste as well as the town of Bahia.

Bus terminal, Av. Antonio Carlos Magalhães, Pituba, I, A2, ☎ 231 5711.

Accommodation

Hotels have been springing up all over Salvador in response to the huge influx of tourists in the last few years. It is not difficult to find accommodation here, except perhaps during Carnival. The best hotels are expensive and are mostly located in the districts of

Barra, Ondina and Rio Vermelho. Swimming pools, restaurants and air-conditioning are the norm here. The hotels located in the area from Campo Grande to Vitória along the Avenida 7 de Setembro are all good, but are far from the beaches. They also lack the life that the centre or Barra have to offer — but there's always a taxi. The beach area on the northern side of Salvador is distant from the centre, and the hotels here are not outstanding. On the other hand, Amaralina, Pituba and Boca do Rio are neighbourhoods with flourishing nightlife. In the centre, there aren't many good hotels, but there are efforts underway to improve the situation.

▲▲▲▲ **Da Bahia**, Praça 2 de Julho 2, Campo Grande, III, CD1, ☎ 237 3699. This handsome hotel has a restaurant, two bars, two swimming pools and various boutiques. 292 rooms.

▲▲▲▲ **Méridien Bahia**, Rua Fonte do Boi 216, Rio Vermelho, I, A2, ☎ 248 8011. This lovely hotel is on the beach and all its rooms offer a sea view. It has a restaurant, three bars, a swimming pool and many boutiques. 426 rooms.

▲▲▲▲ **Quatro Rodas Salvador**, Rua Pasargada, Farol de Itopõa, I, B2, ☎ 249 9611. Near the airport, this hotel is ideal for families because of its many attractions, including a restaurant, three bars, two swimming pools, tennis courts and a gymnasium. 195 rooms.

▲▲▲ **Luxor Convento do Carmo**, Largo do Carmo 1, Santo Antônio, II, 2, ☎ 242 3111. This is an 18th-century convent that was turned into a hotel. Situated in the heart of the old town, this hotel has a restaurant, a bar and a swimming pool. 70 rooms.

▲▲▲ **Salvador Praia**, Av. Pres. Vargas 2338, Ondina, I, A2, ☎ 245 5033. This charming hotel gives onto the beach and contains a restaurant, two bars, two swimming pools and various boutiques. 164 rooms.

▲▲ **Enseada das Lajes**, Av. Pres. Vasgas 511, Morro da Paciência, II, A2, ☎ 237 1027. A former private home transformed into a small and warm hotel with a wonderful view, a restaurant, a bar and a swimming pool. 8 rooms.

▲▲ **Grande Hotel da Barra**, Rua Forte de São Diogo 2, Porto da Barra, III, A1, ☎ 247 6011. This comfortable hotel offers a restaurant, two bars and a swimming pool. 117 rooms.

▲▲ **Hotel do Farol**, Av. Pres. Vargas 68, Barra, III, A2, ☎ 247 7611. A modest hotel with a restaurant, a bar and a swimming pool. 80 rooms.

▲▲ **Marazul**, Av. 7 de Setembro 3937, Barra, III, A2, ☎ 235 2110. This is a simple hotel with a restaurant, a bar and a swimming pool. 124 rooms.

▲▲ **Praiamar**, Av. 7 de Setembro 3577, Porto da Barra, III, A1, ☎ 247 7011. This hotel is simple, with a restaurant, a bar and a swimming pool. 174 rooms.

▲ **Atlântico**, Av. Otávio Mangabeira 3319, Jardim de Ala, I, A1, ☎ 231 6166. This small, modest hotel has a restaurant, a bar and a swimming pool. 49 rooms.

▲ **Bahia do Sol**, Av. 7 de Setembro 2009, Vitória, III, C1, ☎ 247 7211. This simple hotel has a restaurant and a bar. 84 rooms.

▲ **Bahia Praia**, Av. Pres. Vargas 2483, Ondina, I, A2, ☎ 247 4122. This modest hotel has a restaurant and a bar. 40 rooms.

▲ **Ondiva Praia**, Av. Pres. Vargas 2275, Ondina, I, A2, ☎ 247 1033. A simple hotel with two bars and a swimming pool. 100 rooms.

▲ **San Marino**, Av. Pres. Vargas 889, Barra, III, A2, ☎ 235 4363. A modest hotel with a restaurant, a bar and a swimming pool. 59 rooms.

▲ **Vila Velha**, Av. 7 de Setembro 1971, Vitória, III, C1, ☎ 8911920. This modest hotel has a restaurant and a bar. 98 rooms.

Camping

If you join the **Camping Clube do Brazil**, you will find lovely sites available at the Praia do Forte and the Parque Pituaçu. For information on joining the club, contact **Bahiatursa** (see p. 147). Addresses of camping sites include:

Cabana da Praia, Praia do Flamengo, Itapoã ☎ 2480023.
CCB-BA-02, Praia do Flamengo, Itapoã, ☎ 2492001.
De Pituaçu, Rua Prof. Pinto de Aguiar, Parque Pituaçu, ☎ 231 7413.

Entertainment and cultural life

The arts play a central role in Salvador and many artists have settled here, drawing on Bahia for inspiration. Jorge Amado lives in Rio Vermelho, and the famous poet Vinicius de Morais used to live in Itapoã. Artists like Yora Aguiar in Campo Grande, Rubico in Nazaré, Scaldaferri in Graça, and Caribé in Boa Vista open their studios to visitors.

Theatres

Teatro Castro Alves, Praça 2 de Julho, Campo Grande, II, C1, ☎ 2357616.
Teatro do Instituto Goethe, Av. 7 de Setembro 1809, Vitória, III, C1, ☎ 2370120.
Teatro do Senac, Largo do Pelourinho, Pelourinho, II, D2, ☎ 2425503.
Teatro Gamboa, Rua Gamboa de Cima 3, Newton Prado, Aflitos, III, D1.
Teatro Santo Antônio, Rua Araujo Pinho 27, Canela, I, A1, ☎ 2478162.
Teatro Vila Velha, Passeio Público, II, C1, ☎ 245 7324.

Cinemas

There is usually a very good selection of films to be seen in Salvador, particularly in certain speciality cinemas, such as the following:
Capri, Largo 2 de Julho 33, Centro, II, A3
Instituto Brazil-Alemanha, Av. 7 de Setembro 1809, Vitória, III, C1, ☎ 2370120.
Rio Vermelho, Rua João Gomes, Rio Vermelho, I, A2.
União Culturel Brazil-Estados Unidos, Rua Oscar Porto 208, Vitória, III, C1

Festivals

Carnival

Salvador's Carnival, which usually takes place in February, is less organized and more spontaneous than Rio's. Throughout the streets of Salvador, you can watch and join the neighbourhood groups, the samba schools and the *afoxés* (*candomblé* groups dressed in African costumes). Typical of Salvador's Carnival are the *trio elétricos* — musicians on the back of trucks who cruise the streets blasting their music through loudspeakers, followed by costumed and dancing crowds. The most festive areas of the city are around Praça da Sé and Praça Castor Alves.

For information about specific events, contact **Bahiatursa** (see p. 147).

Festivals play a significant part in the lives of Salvadorans and are a reflection of their cheerful, spiritual outlook. From late November through August, life in Salvador resembles one uninterrupted festival. Stalls spring up all over selling every imaginable sort of food and drink. Barely has one celebration come to an end than another begins on the other side of town. The following is a list of the best-known festivals:

The 'Sons of Gandhi' parade during Salvador's Carnival.

Jan 5-6	Lapinha (or Santos Reis)
Jan 20	São Sebastião
Epiphany	Nosso Senhor de Bonfim
Feb 2	Yemanjá
Feb 6	Nossa Senhora da Purificação
Feb 8	Banco de Rio Vermelho (or Nossa Senhora de Santana)
Two weeks before Carnival	Pituba
Feb	Itapoã
	Arembepe
Mar 19	Senhor dos Passos
Holy Thursday and Friday	Caxixis
After Lent	Micareta
June 17	Corpus Christi
June 23-24	São João
June 29	São Pedro
Aug 13-15	Nossa Senhora da Boa Morte
Aug 16	São Lazaro
Nov 24-25	São Nicodemus de Cachimbo
Nov 30	Oxum, goddess of fresh water
Dec 2	*Noite do Samba* (night of samba)
Dec 4-6	Iansà (Santa Barbara, protector of merchants)
Dec 5-8	Nossa Senhora da Conceição da Praia
Dec 10-13	Santa Luzia
Dec 18-25	Christmas
Dec 31-Jan 1	Bóa Viagem (or Nosso Senhor dos Navegantes)

Secular festivals

July 2	Bahia Independence Day
Sept 7	Brazilian Independence Day

Salvador: festivals, folklore and fetishes

Salvador celebrates its traditions more than any other place in Brazil. The influences of African cults, the burden of slavery and the vestiges of colonial occupation have left their mark on Salvador. The Salvadorans revel in all kinds of festivities and celebration has become a way of life.

Candomblé is a cúlt very similar to Haitian voodoo that was brought to Brazil by African slaves. It has developed into a full-scale religion with a hierarchy of divinities, a liturgical calendar and many ceremonies. The word *candomblé* is African in origin and means 'dance', because the gods were invoked by song and dance. Ceremonies take place at a *terreiro* (a place of worship) and offerings, consisting usually of elaborately prepared foods, drinks or candles, are placed here for the gods. Tourists may attend but are expected to do so with all the respect due to a religion.

Carnival is the main tourist attraction in Salvador. People come from all over, and the entire population flocks into the streets. The party lasts for four days and nights.

These are just several of the Salvadoran traditions. There are many more — all of which are jealously guarded by inhabitants. You can see women in the traditional costume of long, full skirts of flower prints and blouses with short wide sleeves *(baiananago)* or in billowing long white gowns and a turban *(baianamuçulmana)*. These women can be seen everywhere seated behind their trays bearing pastries, sweets and other Bahian specialities. You can also see fishermen hauling in their nets from their strange-looking boats, the *jangada* and the *saveiro*.

Food

Food plays a leading role in the traditions and folklore of Salvador. Bahian cuisine requires technical skill and love and can be prepared successfully only by highly experienced cooks. The cuisine's distinctiveness stems in part from its being a combination of African and Brazilian cooking with Portuguese ingredients. Fish, pork and chicken are stewed in palm oil *(dendé)* and lavishly spiced with pimentos *(malagueta)*. If this cuisine is new to you, it is best to go slowly at first — you may find it hard to digest. The best-known dishes are:

- *Vatapa:* a stew made of bread, milk, coconut, peanuts, cashews, shrimp and *dendé.*
- *Caruru:* a combination of *quiabo* (a sticky vegetable), shrimp, peanuts, cashews and *dendé.*
- *Xinxin de galinha:* chicken cooked in stock and seasoned with pimentos, garlic, shrimp and *dendé.*
- *Muqueca:* either fish, lobster or shrimp, cooked first in water and oil, then in a sauce made of coconut milk, tomatoes and onions.
- *Feijão de leite:* a puree of brown beans and coconut milk, which accompanies *muqeca.*
- *Efo:* a hybrid vegetable between lettuce and cabbage, known popularly as *lingua de vaca* (cow's tongue). It is cut into strips and cooked with herbs.
- *Sarapatel:* a dish made of offal and pork tripe.
- *Frigideira de caranguejo* or *de camarões:* crabmeat or shrimp sauteed with herbs.
- *Acarajes:* crushed beans rolled into little balls with various seasonings and served with a spicy sauce made with shrimp. These are sold everywhere on the street.

Bahia's desserts are also well known, and these are Portuguese in origin. The most common include:

- *Quindins:* small pastries made from shredded coconut.
- *Bolos de coco:* a coconut concoction that is served with pineapple strawberries, plums, etc.
- *Cocadas:* kind of jam made from coconut, either white or brown in colour.
- *Pudins:* a variety of custard.

Beverages include the celebrated *sucos* (juices made from the many different kinds of local fruit) and *batidas* (cocktails made from fruit juices).

**** Di Liana, Estr. do Coco, near the airport, I, B1, ☎ 891 1088. An excellent Italian restaurant specializing in Venetian cuisine. Open daily noon-3pm, 7pm-midnight.

*** Agda, Rua Orlando Moscoso 1, Boca do Rio, I, A2, ☎ 231 2851. A modest restaurant serving very good regional specialities. Open Mon-Sat noon-5pm, 7pm-midnight.

*** Baby Beef, Av. Antônio Carlos Magalhães, Pituba, I, A2, ☎ 244 0811. This is an excellent *churrascaria.* Open daily 11:30am-midnight.

*** Bargaço, Rua P., quadra 43, Jardim Armação, Boca do Rio, I, A2, ☎ 231 5141. A seafood restaurant offering great variety and excellent quality. Open daily noon-3pm, 7pm-midnight.

*** Chaillot, Av. Pres. Varga 3305, Ondina, I, A2, ☎ 237 4621. This comfortable restaurant serves very good international cuisine. Open daily noon-3:30pm, 7:30pm-midnight.

** Adega d'Alfama, Av. Otávio Mangabeira, Pituba, I, A2, ☎ 248 8999. A lively restaurant with good Portuguese cuisine. Open Mon-Sat noon-4pm, 7-11pm.

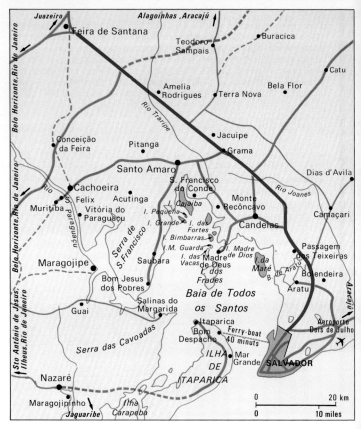

Environs of Salvador.

** **Bella Napoli,** Rua Nova de São Bento 194, Centro, II, B2, ☎ 243 5125. This modest restaurant serves simple Italian cuisine. Open Mon-Sat 11:30am-2:30pm, 6:30-10:30pm.

** **Casa da Gamboa,** Rua Gamboa de Cima 51, Campo Grande, III, C1, ☎ 245 9777. A lively restaurant with an excellent view and good regional cuisine. Open Mon-Sat noon-3pm, 7-11:30pm.

** **Chez Bernard,** Rua Gamboa de Cima 11, Aflitos, III, D1, ☎ 245 9402. This very good French restaurant has a wonderful view. Open Mon-Sat noon-2:30pm, 7pm-midnight.

** **Enseada das Lajes,** Av. Pres. Vargas 511, Rio Vermelho, I, A2, ☎ 237 1027. A restaurant with a great view and good international cuisine. Open Mon-Sat noon-3:30pm, 8-11pm.

** **Frutos do Mar,** Rua Alm. Marques de Leão 415, Barra, III, AB1, ☎ 245 6479. A simple restaurant offering a wide choice of seafood. Open daily noon-4pm, 6pm-midnight.

** **O Marisco,** Rua Euricles de Matos 123, Rio Vermelho, I, A2, ☎ 237 3910. A good seafood restaurant. Open daily 11am-3pm, 6pm-midnight.

** **Tiffany's,** Rua Br. de Sergy 156, Porto da Barra, III, A1, ☎ 247 4025. A lively, good French restaurant. Open daily 7pm-1am.

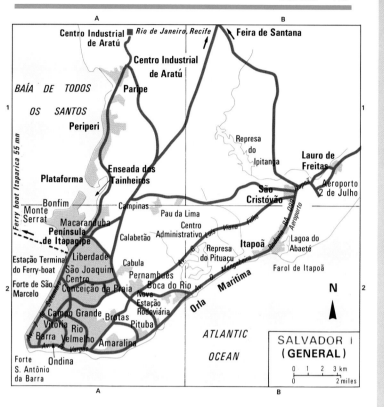

* **Camafeu de Oxossi,** Mercado Modelo 1, II, C1, ☎ 2429751. This hearty restaurant serves good regional cuisine. Open Mon-Sat 11am-8pm.

* **Iemanjá,** Av. Otávio Mangabeira, Boca do Rio, I, A2, ☎ 2315069. There is a good choice of regional cuisine in this little restaurant. Open Mon-Sat noon-4pm, 7pm-midnight.

* **Roda Viva,** Av. Otávio Mangabeira, Jardim dos Namorados, I, A2, ☎ 2483499. A cheerful *churrascaria* serving excellent meat. Open daily 11-1am.

* **Senac,** Largo do Pelourinho 13, Pelourinho, II, D2, ☎ 2425503. Very good regional cuisine in this self-service restaurant. Open Mon-Sat 11:30am-3:30pm, 6:30-9:30pm.

Getting around Salvador

Orientation

Salvador is situated on the Bahia de Todos os Santos. The centre is divided between the upper town on a plateau and the lower town along the bay, which are connected by an elevator and cable car. Outside the city centre are the residential districts on the plateau behind the upper town (Campo Grande to Vitória), the Itapagipe peninsula to the north and the beaches along the ocean (from Barra, near the centre, to Itapoã, near the airport).

On foot

Walking is the ideal way to visit the historical centre of Salvador. To reach the upper town it's best to use the Elevador Lacerda (between Praça Tome de Sousa and Praça Visconde de Cairu, II, C1) or the cable car Plano Inclinado do Gonçalves (between Av. Gonçalves and Praça Ramos de Queiros, II, C2).

By bus
Buses can be useful for getting from your hotel to the centre or the beaches. They tend, however, to be uncomfortably crowded and hot.

By taxi
Taxis are easy to find and inexpensive. They are perfect for visiting the more distant areas of Salvador.
Chametaxi, ☎ 241 2266.
Comtas, ☎ 245 2344.
Teletaxis, ☎ 247 9988.

By car
You will not need a car for the city centre. If you prefer driving to the areas on the outskirts of Salvador, there are numerous agencies in the city and at the airport.
Avis, Av. 7 de Setembro 1796, Vitória, III, BCD1, ☎ 237 0154.
Hertz, rua Baependi 1, Ondina, I, A2, ☎ 245 8599.

Nightlife

Nightclubs
Most nightclubs are located near the beach in the major hotels.
Buall'Amour, Av. Otávio Mangabeira, Corsário, ☎ 231 9775.
Close Up, Av. Pres. Vargas 84, Barra, III, AB1, ☎ 245 5763.
Tropical, Hotel da Bahia, Praça 2 de Julho, Campo Grande, III, C1, ☎ 237 3699.

Bars featuring live music
Berro d'Argua, Rua Barão de Sergy 27, Centro, ☎ 235 2961.
Bistrô do Luis, Rua Cons. Pedros Luis 369, Centro, ☎ 247 5900.
Canoa, Méridien Hotel, Rua Fonte do Boi 216, Rio Vermelho, I, A2, ☎ 248 8011.
New Fred's, Rua Visconde de Itaborai 125, Amaralina, ☎ 246 4166.
Quintal do Roso Catarina, Rua 7 de Setembro 1370, Vitória.
Segredo do Noite, Rua Gamboa de Cima, Campo Grande, III, C1, ☎ 245 5267.
Vagão, Rua Barroso 315, Centro, ☎ 237 1227.

Dinner dancing
The best places to go dancing are the bars and restaurants along the coast between Barra and Itapoã, I, AB2.

Shopping
You can buy practically anything in Salvador — from Bahian handcrafts to more sophisticated goods that have appeared with the recent influx of tourists. Handcrafts in Salvador consist mostly of jewelry and other articles made of silver, ceramic utensils and figurines and tapestries. Salvador is also famous for its cigars.

Mercado Modelo
The Mercado Modelo (see p. 150) is a shopping complex of over 200 shops. Here, you can find necklaces, African-style jewelry, articles used in the *candomblé* ceremonies, wooden carvings, pottery, hammocks, cigars and all the other things usually sold in shopping complexes. There are also restaurants and bars here.

Feira do Artesanato
The Feira do Artesanato, or handcrafts fair, is held every Sunday from 8am-1pm in Terreiro de Jesus, II, C2. You can buy typical Bahian handcrafts here.

Markets

The markets in Salvador are very colourful, lively places where just about anything can be found. The most popular are:

● **Feira do Cortume** (Rua Luis Maria, Urugai): animals and goods are bartered here.

● **Feira de São Joaquim** (Av. Frederico Pontes, Jequitaia): open every day except Sunday, you can find lots of surprises here.

● **Mercado do Ouro** (Praça Marechal Deodoro).

● **Mercados da Baixa dos Sapateiros** (Rua Dr. Seabra, II, BC2): this is three different markets, **Santa Barbara**, **Sete Portas** and **São Miguel.**

Useful addresses

Banks

Banco da Bahia, Rua Miguel Calmon 32, Comércio, II, C1.
Citibank, Rua Miguel Calmon 555, Comércio, II, C1, ☎ 241 5555.

Consulates

Britain, Av. Estados Unidos 4, Edificio Visconde de Cairu, II, CD1 ☎ 241 3120.
United States, Av. Pres. Vargas 1892, III, AB2-3, ☎ 245 6691.

Currency exchange

Salomão Fainstein, Av. Estados Unidos 379, Comércio, II, CD1 ☎ 242 0837.

Emergencies

Pronto Socorro, ☎ 192

Post office

Correio Central, Praça da Inglaterra, Comércio, open Mon-Fri 8am-7pm, Sat, Sun and holidays 8am-1pm.

Railway terminal

Estaçao Ferroviaria, Largo da Calçada, ☎ 242 2294.

Tourist office

Bahiatursa, Palácio Rio Branco, Rua Chile, Praça Municipal, II, B2 (open 8am-6:30pm), ☎ 131 (recorded announcement).

Travel agencies

Alameda, Av. Magalhães Neto 20, Pituba, I, A2, ☎ 248 2977.
Conde, Rua Santos Dumont 4, ☎ 242 8000.
Itaparica Turismo, Av. Pres. Vargas 2338, III, AB2-3 ☎ 245 1455.
J. Leonardo, Rua Frederico Castro Rabelo 1, Comércio, ☎ 243 7766.
Rumundi, Rua da Grécia 8, Comércio, ☎ 243 3011.

▬ *GETTING TO KNOW SALVADOR*

The city centre

Salvador's centre is divided between the lower town *(cidade baixa)* that streches along the bay, II, A-E1, and the upper town *(cidade alta)* that lies on a plateau, II, B-E2.

Start your visit in the lower town, an area comprising the commercial district, the harbour, and many sights of interest to tourists. The streets teem with colourful throngs of people. If you enjoy watching crowds, there is no better place.

Set off at the northern side of Praça Cairu and cross Praça Riachuelo on the way to Rua do Pilar. Along the way there are the following sights:

Forte de São Marcelo***, II, B1, stands facing the harbour inside the bay. It was built between 1605 and 1623. Its round construction, framed by coconut trees, makes it a very picturesque spot for a promenade. It can be reached by boat from Praça Cairu, but its interior is closed to the public.

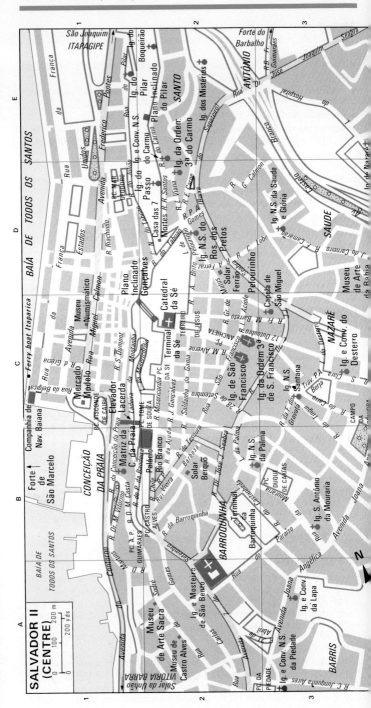

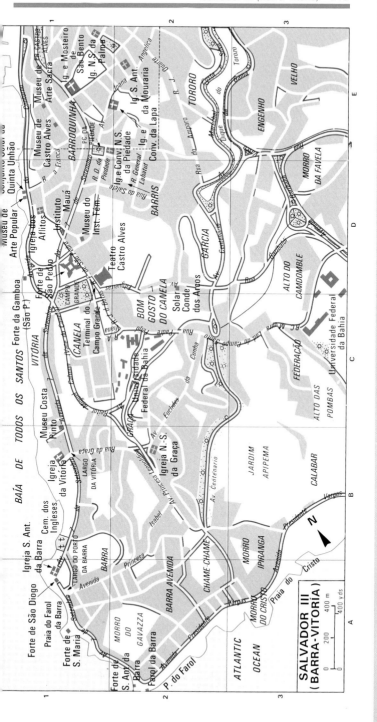

SALVADOR III
(BARRA-VITÓRIA)

Nossa Senhora da Conciçeão da Praia*** (Largo da Conceição, II, B1, ☎ 2420545; open Mon-Sat 7-11am, 3-5pm, Sun 7-11:30am) is a church that dates from the days of Tomé de Souza's arrival in Brazil and stands on the site of a former monastery. The stones with which it was built between 1735 and 1852 were brought from Portugal. The paintings in the cupola are by José Joaquim da Rocha. Together with Nossa Senhora de Bonfim, this church is one of Salvador's main sites for religious celebrations. It has two statues of Nossa Senhora da Conceição. One of them dates from 1856 and is paraded through town every year on December 8 (Feast of Yemanjá), and the other dates from 1732 and has stood in the chancel since that time. The church's organ, dating from 1868, is used during masses on Saturday and Sunday mornings at 8am.

Mercado Modelo*** (II, C1 ☎ 2423683) was formerly the customs building. Rebuilt after a fire, it now houses the city's main centre for arts and crafts. This is also the site of the huge, modern illuminated **fountain**** (Praça Cairu), which was designed by Mario Cravo and faces the harbour.

Santa Luzia do Pilar** (Rua do Pilar, II, E1, ☎ 2420462; open daily 7:30am-noon, 2-4pm) is a church that was originally built in 1752. Rebuilt in 1845 after a fire, it contains many interesting works of art.

Elevador Lacerda** (Praça Cairu, II, C1) is a vast system of elevators between the upper and lower towns. It has been in operation since 1872 and is now an integral part of the landscape.

Casa dos Azulejos* (Praça Cairu, II, C1) is a house prettily covered with multi-coloured tiles.

Riachuelo Monument* (Largo do Riachuelo, II, D1) stands in commemoration of a naval battle (Riachuelo) during the war with Paraguay.

Plano Inclinado do Gonçalves* is a funicular railway that runs between the upper and lower towns. The terminal is in the Praça da Sé, II, C2.

Plano Inclinado do Pilar* is another funicular railway that runs between the Rua do Pilar and the Rua Joaquim Tavora, II, E2.

From the lower town, the way to get to the upper town is by the Elevator Lacerda, the *Plano Inclinado* or, if you don't mind a good walk, through a variety of picturesque little alleyways. The upper town is the historical heart of Salvador. It is best to remember that all of the important crossroads run parallel to the bay. Armed with this information, you can wander at will — up to Rua Dr. José Joaquim Seabra, also known as *Baixa dos Sapateiros*, which is the area's boundary.

If you cross the upper town from south to north, you will pass **Praça Castro Alves**, II, B2, with its crowds, **Praça Tomé de Souza**, II, C2, where the seat of the state government is located and the Elevador Lacerda ends; the vast **Praça da Sé**, II, C2, with the bus terminal and more crowds; the mysterious square known as **Terreiro de Jesus**, studded with churches (the da Sé cathedral among them); **Praça Anchieta**, II, C2, which leads to the renowned Convent of São Francisco, and **Largo do Pelourinho**, II, D2, which has recently been restored. Finally, you will come to **Largo do Carmo**, II, E2, bordered by a church, a museum and a fortress. Each of these places has its own special atmosphere, its points of interest and its history — things that the inhabitants of Salvador take pride in and enjoy keeping up. The following are sights that you should be sure to see:

São Francisco*** (Praça Anchieta, II, C2, ☎ 2432367; church open daily 7-11am, 2-5pm; convent is closed to the public) is a church and convent that was constructed on the site of an earlier chapel dedicated to St Francis, which was given to the Franciscans on their arrival in Salvador in 1587. The convent was built between 1686 and 1708, and the church between 1708 and 1712. The church's interior is one of the country's most beautiful examples of Baroque decoration. There is so much gold here that the church is sometimes referred to as *Igreja* *de Ouro* — 'church of gold'. Also inside the church stands a beautiful rosewood sculpture of São Pedro de Alcantara, by Manuel Inacio da Costa. There is a library here devoted to the convent and the city. This is the most important monument in Salvador.

Catedral Basilica da Sé★★★ (Terreiro de Jesus, II, C2, ☎ 2434573; open Tues-Sun 7-11am, 2-6pm) is Salvador's largest church. Completely covered with Portuguese marble, it was constructed between 1657 and 1672. It contains 13 altars and its sacristy is arguably the most beautiful in Brazil. It also houses a museum of sacred art.

Ordem Terceira de São Francisco★★★ (Rua Ignacio Aciole, II, C2, ☎ 2427046; open Mon-Fri 8-11:30am, 2-5pm) stands next door to São Francisco and dates from 1703. It has a highly elaborate and ornate façade, which an electrician discovered accidentally under a plaster covering. In the interior, in the **Casa dos Santos**, there are 25 statues of saints by Joaquim Francisco do Matos.

Conjunto do Pelourinho★★★ (Largo do Pelourinho, II, D2) is the square where slaves were tortured and executed. Legend has it that the stones of the square are black because of all the blood that was spilled on them. Now all the buildings around the square have been restored and form an architectural whole in the colonial style. Hotels, restaurants, shops and museums have been successfully integrated. This entire area stands in the shadow of the church of Nossa Senhora do Rosário dos Pretos.

Nossa Senhora do Rosário dos Pretos★★ (Largo do Pelourinho, II, D2) was built in the 17th century by slaves. It is filled with many interesting statues.

Ordem Terceira de São Domingos★★ (Terreiro de Jesus, II, C2, ☎ 2428145; open Mon-Fri 7-11am, Sat and Sun 8-9am) is a church that contains many handsome statues and paintings. Begun in 1731, it was only completed in 1888.

Igreja e Museu do Carmo★★ (Ladeira do Carmo, II, DE2, ☎ 2420182; open daily 8am-noon, 2-6m) was originally built in 1592. It was destroyed by fire in 1788 and then rebuilt in 1803. The church contains statues dating from 1588 and large catacombs. In 1625, the convent served as the headquarters for the Dutch. The museum houses items that once belonged to the Jesuits. It also displays some well-known sculptures, such as the Christ by Francisco Manuel das Chagas, who was known as O Cabra.

Ordem Terceira do Carmo★★ (Ladeira do Carmo, II, DE2, ☎ 2422042; open Mon-Sat 8:30am-noon, 2-5:30pm, Sun 10am-noon, 2-5:30pm) is situated next to the Carmo church. It was built between 1644 and 1786 and contains numerous statues,' a Baroque altar and an organ dating from 1808.

Santa Casa da Misericordia★★ (Rua da Misericordia, II, C2, ☎ 2434722; church open Mon-Fri 7-9am, 2-5pm, Sat and Sun 7am-9pm; museum open Mon-Fri 2-5pm) is a church and a museum. The church was completely overhauled starting in 1654 and underwent modification until 1938. The museum houses religious paintings and manuscripts of Bahian literature and poetry.

Fonte do Terreiro de Jesus★★ (Praça 15 de Novembro) is a fountain symbolizing Bahia's four main rivers.

Solar do Ferrão★★ (Rua Gregório de Matos 45, II, CD2, ☎ 2426155; open Mon-Fri 9am-noon, 2-5:30pm, Sat and Sun 2-5pm) is a lovely residence that was built in 1709. It houses a museum with a fine collection of sacred art.

Casa dos Sete Candeeiros★★ (Rua São Francisco 32, II, C2) is a lovely 18th-century house that has been completely renovated.

Other sites worth seeing include the **statue of Castro Alves★** (Praça Castro Alves), **Paço church** (Rua do Paço), **São Pedro dos Clerigos church** (Terreiro de Jesus), **São Miguel chapel** (Rua Frei Vicente), **Ajuda church** (Rua da Ajuda), **Casa de Rui Barbosa** (Rua Barbosa) and the **Rio Branco Palace** (Praça Tomé de Souza).

North from the city centre II, E2-3

If you head north from the centre, you will reach first the **Santo Antônio district** and then the **Barbalho district**. Sights here include the following.

Forte do Barbalho** (Rua Emidio dos Santos) is an imposing 17th-century fortress that was constructed to defend the northern flank of the city.

Cruz do Pascoal** (Rua do Carmo) is an oratory that dates from 1743 and was built by Marquis Pascoal de Almeida in honour of Nossa Senhora do Pilar.

Forte do Santo Antônio Além do Carmo* (Praça Barão do Triunfo) is a fortress that dates from the 17th century. It now serves as a prison.

Soledade* (Praça Maria Quiteria) is a church and convent that dates from the late 17th century and early 18th century. They figured prominently in the struggle against the Dutch.

Other sights in these districts include the **Mistérios church** (Praça 15) and the **Lapinha church** (Largo da Lapinha).

East from the city centre II, C3

If you head east from the centre, you will arrive at the **Nazaré district**, which lies between the Rua Dr. José Joaquim Seabra and the Tororo section. Sights here include the following.

Museu de Arte da Bahia*** (Museum of Bahian Art, Av. 7 de Setembro 2340, ☎ 235 9492; open Tues-Sat 2-6:30pm) houses a large collection of paintings and sculptures, both secular and religious. It also has interesting displays of ceramics, items in gold and furniture from the 16th, 17th and 18th centuries.

Nossa Senhora de Santana* (Ladeira de Santana, ☎ 241 1165; open Sun-Fri 8-11am, Sat 7am-5pm) is a church that was consecrated in 1752.

Desterro* (Rua Santa Clara do Desterro) is a church and convent built in the colonial style. The convent was the first to be built in Brazil.

Other places of interest in Nazaré include the **Saude e Glória church*** (Largo da Saude), the **Nazaré church*** (Largo de Nazaré), the **Rui Barbosa courthouse*** (Largo da Plovora), the **Otávio Mangabeira Stadium*** (which can seat 110,000) and the **Dique de Torozó*** (a large artificial lake).

South from the city centre III, E4

To the south of the centre is **Barroquinhá**, a transitional district between the lively working-class areas of the centre and the elegant, quiet neighbourhoods of the south. As soon as you turn into Rua 7 de Setembro you will notice the luxury surrounding you, whereas in Rua do Sodré, old Bahia still predominates. Places of interest to see in this district include the following.

Museu de Arte Sacra*** (Museum of Sacred Art, Rua do Sodré 276, ☎ 243 6310; open Mon-Fri 1-5:30pm) was formerly a convent dedicated to St Teresa. It was transformed into a museum in 1958 and contains art that has come from several Salvador churches, as well as a number of private collections, including sculpture, paintings and silverware. The convent was built between 1666 and 1697 and was once inhabited by an order of Carmelite nuns.

Museu Castro Alves** (Rua do Sodré), the former home of a wealthy Brazilian family, houses furniture and jewelry.

Mosteiro de São Bento** (Largo de São Bento, ☎ 243 6922; open daily 7-10am, 5-7pm) is a monastery that is architecturally very impressive. It was built in 1581.

Lapa* (Av. Joana Angelica, ☎ 243 0948; open daily 6:30-7:30am) is a church and convent that date from the 18th century.

Other places of interest in Barroquinhá include the 18th-century **Santo Antônio da Mouraria church** (Rua da Mouraria), the **Nossa Senhora da**

Colourful façades line a street in the Pelourinho area of Salvador.

Piedade church and convent (Praça da Piedade), **Barroquinhá church** (Rua da Barroquinhá), **Palma church** (Praça da Palma) and the **Bahia Museum of Geography and History** (Av. 7 de Setembro, ☎ 241 2453; open Mon-Fri 2-5pm).

Itapagipe peninsula

North of the lower town lies the large **Itapagipe peninsula**. It is here that the famous Bonfim cathedral stands as a shrine for all Salvadorans. The peninsula has handsome beaches stretching around the bay, surrounded by residential neighbourhoods. The northern part of the peninsula is flat and has a small cove called **Anseada**. This area is inhabited by a destitute population that live in huts on stilts.

Forte de Monte Serrat*** (Ponta de Monte Serrat) was built in 1586 and has been modified several times. It is generally held to be the best example of colonial military architecture in Brazil. For a long time it confined political prisoners. The interior of the fort is closed to the public but the view of the surroundings from its grounds is magnificent.

Nosso Senhor do Bonfim*** (Adro de Bonfim, ☎ 226 0196; open daily 6am-noon, 2:30-6pm) is Salvador's main centre of religious activities and festivals. Built between 1746 and 1754, it is an example of formal, classical architecture with the odd Baroque feature. It is known for its many ex-voto offerings, which can be seen in the **Sala dos Milagres.** The statue of Nosso Senhora do Bonfim comes from Portugal.

Boa Viagem** (Largo de Boa Viagem) is a church built in the 18th century by Franciscan monks that contains lovely Portuguese tilework.

Feira de São Joaquim** (Av. Frederico Pontes) is Salvador's most picturesque market. It is located near the ferryboat pier.

Other churches you can visit on the Itapagipe peninsula include **Nossa Senhora da Penha** (Ponta da Ribeira), **São Joaquim** (Av. Jequitaia) and **Mares** (Largo dos Mares).

Campo Grande, Canela, Vitória and Graça

These mostly residential areas lie south of the centre of Salvador on either side of the Rua 7 de Setembro. Constructed on a hill with the sea close by, some of the houses and hotels here betray the opulence of Brazil's days of glory.

Solar do Unhão*** (Av. do Contorno, III, D1) is a complex comprising master's quarters, slaves' quarters and a chapel. It now houses the **Museu de Arte Moderna**** (☎ 243 6174; open Tues-Fri 11am-5pm, Sat and Sun 1-6pm), with works by Brazilian painters.

Museu Costa Pinto*** (Av. 7 de Septembro 2490, III, B1, ☎ 247 6081; open Wed-Mon 2:30-6:30pm) is one of Salvador's most interesting museums and contains the municipal collection of jewelry, crystal and furniture, dating from the 17th to the 19th centuries. The objects and the house formely belonged to the collector Costa Pinto.

Praça 2 de Julho**, III, D1, contains a park that is one of the few public spots of greenery in Salvador. Located here are the **Caboclo Monument,** which commemorates independence, and the large, modern theatre, **Teatro Castro Alves.**

Igreja da Vitória (Largo da Vitória, III, B1; open daily 6:30-10am, 4:30-6pm) is one of the oldest churches in Brazil, dating from 1552. It contains lovely 18th-century Portuguese tilework.

Nossa Senhora da Graça* (Largo da Graça, III, B2; open daily 7am-5pm) dates from the 16th century and has paintings depicting the life of Caramuru, an Indian who converted to Catholicism, as well as the tomb of his wife.

Other sights to visit in this area include the **Aflitos** church (Largo dos Aflitos, III, D1), the **Forte de São Pedro** (Rua do Forte de São Pedro, III, D1), the **Forte de São Paulo** (Av. do Contorno, III, C1), the **Palácio do Aclamação** (Av. 7 de Setembro) and the **statue of Edgar Santos** (Av. Padre Feijo).

The beach neighbourhoods

The most fashionable beaches in the southern part of Salvador lie between Barra and Rio Vermelho. There are several old forts here, and Barra contains a number of interesting shops. The beaches tend to be small and surrounded by rocks.

Porto da Barra, III, A1, lies between the Santa Maria and the São Diogo lighthouses. It is the first beach that you will come to as you leave town and head toward the bay — which explains its popularity.

Farrol da Parra, III, A2, lies on the open ocean after the Santo Antônio lighthouse. The ocean is extremely rough here, making swimming inadvisable.

Ondina and Rio Vermelho, I, A2, are the sites of **Patiença, Santana,** and **Mariquita** beaches. They are good for swimming and for watching fishermen at work. If you prefer strolling, you can visit the following sights.

Forte Santo Antônio da Barra*** (Praia da Barra, III, A2) was completed in 1602. In 1705, St Anthony became the fort's patron saint. During the ensuing years, a lighthouse was added in its centre.

Forte de Santa Maria** (Praia da Barra, III, A1) was built around 1630 as a reinforcement to the Forte de Santo Antônio in the defense of Vila Velha. Forte de Santa Maria was abandoned around 1883. The interior is closed to the public.

Forte de São Diogo* (Porto da Barra, III, A1) was built in 1626 and completely overhauled in 1704. Tomé de Souza landed in Salvador behind the site of this fort. The interior is closed to the public.

Santo Antônio da Barra* (Av. 7 de Setembro, III, A1, ☎ 247 9042; open daily 9-11:30am, 3-7pm) is a church built in 1560. There is a panoramic view of the bay from here.

Parque de Ondina (Ondina, I, A2; open daily 8am-5pm) was formerly the site of the governor's summer residence. It now contains the **Getúlio Vargas zoological garden.**

The beaches in the northern part of Salvador are known collectively as **Orla Maritima** ('the seaside'). Scheduled expansion of the city is to take place here. The area is becoming more and more fashionable and crowded. It consists of the neighbourhoods of **Amaralina, Armação, Pituba, Boca do Rio, Piatã** and **Itapoã**. Two roads run through it — the Avenida Otávio Mangabeira, along the beaches, and the Avenida Luis Viana Filho (also called Avenida Paralela), a little inland. These neighbourhoods are known for their restaurants and their nightlife.

Amaralina, I, A2, is a very large and very popular beach, but also dangerous for swimming.

Pituba, I, A2, is an equally popular beach that is smaller and good for swimming and fishing. The water is warm here but full of rocks.

Jardim dos Namorados, or **Chaga-Negro**, I, A2, is a very dangerous beach for swimming, but it is good for fishing.

Jardim de Allah, I, A2, is one of Salvador's most beautiful beaches, surrounded by coconut trees. It is possible to camp here.

Armação, I, A2, is a large and barren beach, where in keeping with years of tradition, you can see fishermen pulling in their nets every evening.

Boca do Rio and **Pituaçu**, I, AB2, are beaches that are very popular with surfers.

Piatã and **Placa Norte**, I, B2, are very crowded, beautiful beaches surrounded by coconut trees. The water is smooth and clear here.

Itapoã and **Farol d'Itapoã**, I, B2, are lovely beaches that have been immortalized in poems and songs. The water is smooth, the sand is soft, and there is shade from the many coconut trees.

Flamengo is an inhospitable beach with choppy water that lies behind the airport. It is good for fishing.

Once you are in this area, don't miss a visit to **Lagoa do Abaeté***** and **Itapoã dunes**, I, B2. They are among the most famous landscapes in Salvador. The tiny lagoon is a pleasant place to spend an afternoon and is crowded with street peddlars selling all kinds of Bahian specialities. Note that it is dangerous to swim here. At night, in the moonlight, it is a splendid, romantic place, with the pure white dunes standing out against the black water.

Bahia de Todos os Santos

See map p. 144.

This magnificent bay is studded with some 30 islands. Boats can constantly be seen crossing it because they remain the best form of transportation between the various cities in the *Reconcavo baiano* (bay area). You should be sure to take at least one boat trip.

Compania de Navegação Baiana (Av. da França, ☎ 242 9411), organizes tours, including the following two options.

● **Veja do Mar a Cidade do Salvador** itinerary: as its name suggests (view from the sea of the city of Salvador), this itinerary offers a fabulous view of Salvador. The route passes the Barra lighthouse, Itaparica island and heads out to the Itapagipe peninsula and back.

● **Tour of the islands:** this excursion takes an entire day with a three-hour stopover on Itaparica island for lunch, a swim, and time for a nap if you want one. Other visits on this tour include the following islands.

Ilha da Maré** is full of beautiful flowers, trees and plants and is the site of the lovely little church of **Nossa Senhora das Neves.**

Ilha dos Frades*** is one of the prettiest islands with fresh-water springs and coconut trees. According to legend, two brothers who survived a shipwreck landed here, and were then eaten by Tupinambas Indians.

Ilha da Madre de Deus* is the site of the Petrobas oil refineries.

Ilha das Vacas** is one large *fazenda* (farm).

Ilha do Capeta* is covered only with sparse vegetation.

Ilha de Maria Guarda* is a mountainous island with a tiny fishermen's village.

Ilhas de Bimbarra* and **Fontes*** are two islands that are covered with lush vegetation.

Ilha de Bom Jesus dos Passos** is the site of a small shipyard and shops selling interesting handcrafts.

Ilha de Santo Antônio* is allegedly the site of many hidden treasures.

Ilha de Itaparica*** is the largest of the islands in the bay and the most populated. It is covered with greenery and has up-to-date tourist facilities. **Itaparica*** is the island's resort. Things to see include **mineral springs**, a **fort** and the **church of São Lourenço**. The island's east coast, which faces the ocean, is fairly dangerous for swimming because of its currents. There is a bridge that links Itaparica to the mainland at Nazaré. The island is also connected to the mainland by regular ferries.

▬ *ENVIRONS OF SALVADOR*

See map p. 144.

The Reconcavo

The area surrounding the Baia de Todos os Santos is called *Reconcavo* (bay area). It was here that sugarcane was first cultivated on a scale large enough for it to become the mainstay of the colonial regime. Today, the sugarcane has mostly been replaced by tobacco, and oil deposits have been found under the bay. It was also here that the struggle for independence first took hold. Starting from Salvador and heading north-west around the bay, you will come upon the following towns.

Candeias* is 27 mi/44 km north of Salvador. It is a small town with many reminders of its colonial past.

São Francisco do Condé* is 56 mi/91 km north-west of Salvador. This town contains several noteworthy colonial buildings, including the 17th-century **São Francisco** church and convent. It is possible to take excursions from here to neighbouring islands like Cajaiba, Fontes, Pati and Bimbarra.

Santo Amaro** is 50 mi/81 km north-west of Salvador. You will be able to see many interesting colonial buildings and fountains here. There are also several striking churches, such as **Nossa Senhora da Purificação** and the 18th-century **Recolhimento dos Humildes**. This latter church houses a museum of sacred art. In the nearby town of **Oliveira dos Campinhos** (7 mi/12 km), there is the church of **Nossa Senhora Oliveira dos Campinhos** and, at **Sambara** (14 mi/22 km), there is the little church of **São Domingos**.

Cachoeira*** is 74 mi/120 km north-west of Salvador. After Salvador, this is the most important city in Bahia. It was founded by descendants of Caramuru, an Indian converted to Christianity. During the 17th and 18th centuries, the town developed quite rapidly because it became the place from where people left to go to Minas Gerais. It developed further when refugees fleeing Portuguese oppression in Salvador arrived, and it was in Cachoeira that the most crucial resistance operations against the Portuguese were planned. Besides the opulent homes built by wealthy Reconcavo landowners, many other sights present themselves.

● **Ordem Terceira do Carmo***** (open Mon-Fri 8-11am, 1-5pm, Sat and Sun 9-11:30am) is a lovely 18th-century church, with wood carvings and wonderful paintings.

● **Nossa Senhora do Rosário**** (open Tues-Sat 9am-noon, 2-4pm, Sun 8am-noon) is a church with interesting blue ceramic towers.

● **Nossa Senhora da Conceição do Monte**** offers a magnificent view.

● **São de Ajuda**** is a church dating from 1595 — the oldest in Cachoeira.

Fishing boats and bathers share one of the lovely sand beaches in the Bahia de Todos os Santos.

- The cigar *(charutos)* factory** (Rua Rui Barbosa 19, ☎ (075) 724 1150) still manufactures its cigars using old-fashioned methods. It is in **Muritiba,** 6 mi/10 km away.
- **Santo Antônio de Paraguaçu**** (26 mi/42 km) was a convent that is now in ruins. It dates from the 17th century.
- The **sugarmills**** *(engenhos)* can be visited at **Cabonha** (5 mi/8 km), Guaiba (8 mi/12 km) and **Vitória** (19 mi/30 km).
- **São Felix*** is only 0.5 mi/1 km from Cachoeira and faces it on the other shore of the Paraguaçu River. There are lovely views from here.

Nazaré* is 37 mi/60 km west of Salvador and can be reached by ferry-boat. This small town has an intersting colonial past and is known for its ceramics fair *(Feira de Caxixis)* held during Holy Week. There are several noteworthy churches here, including **Nossa Senhora da Conceiçaõ,** dating from 1762, the **Nazaré church,** dating from 1801, and **Saõ Roque,** dating from 1649.

Jaguaribe* is a small town 13 mi/21 km from Nazaré. Sights include the **Paço Municipal,** dating from 1697, the **Casa dos Ouvidores** and **Nossa Senhora da Ajuda,** dating from 1612.

Aratu

Aratu is a completely new industrial and residential city about 12 mi/20 km north of Salvador that owes its existence to the latter's recent economic boom.

Reconcavo Museum***, also know as the Wanderley Pinho Museum, is located in a former sugarmill, the Engenho da Freguesia. Its displays concern sugar cultivation and the area's social and economic history, mostly during colonial times. The architectural compound includes a chapel that dates from around 1522. Outdoors, all of the tools used in the processing and transportation of sugar are on display. Indoors, there are exhibitions on the role played by blacks in the region's economy and on Reconcavo's history and economy up to the time of independence. A good view from here of the bay and Ilha de Maré.

Aratu harbour** is South America's most important modern industrial port.

Aratu industrial centre** covers an area of 168 sq mi/436 sq km. Not far away lies the important petrochemical plant of Camaçari.

Dias d'Ávila* is 35 mi/56 km north-east of Salvador. It is a tiny and pleasant spa town. Beyond Dois de Julho Airport is the north coast. The beaches here are completely deserted thus very appealing. The most noteworthy beaches are **Buscavida, Java, Sapato, Guaratuba** and **Tacimirim.**

Accommodation

▲ **Balneário Dias d'Ávila,** Rua Severino Vieira, Dias d'Avila, ☎ (071) 825 1001. This charming hotel sits in a park and contains a restaurant, a bar and a swimming pool. 45 rooms.

▲ **Pousada do Convento,** Rua Inocêncio Boaventura, Cachoeira, ☎ (075) 724 1151. This small hotel has a restaurant, a bar and a swimming pool. 26 rooms.

▲ **Pousada do Coronel I,** Praça da Purificaçao 45, Santo Amaro, ☎ (075) 241 1375. A very simple accommodation, with a very modest restaurant. Not all rooms have baths. 12 rooms.

▲ **Pousada do Guerreiro,** Rua 13 de Maio 14, Cachoeira, ☎ (075) 724 1203. This very simple accommodation offers no amenities. 10 rooms.

Food

* **Cabana do Pai Tomás,** Rua 25 de Junho 4, Cachoeira, ☎ (075) 724 1288. Small restaurant serving regional food. Open daily 11am-midnight.

* **Cabana Gaúcha**, Rua Lomanto Júnior, Dias D'Ávila, ☎ (071) 825 1108. Hospitable *churrascaria*. Open daily noon-3pm and 6-9pm.

BAHIA STATE

One of the best ways to see the interior of Bahia is to take a trip down the São Francisco River. Small vessels, known as *barranqueiras*, ply the river between Pirapora in Minas Gerais and Juazeiro in Bahia.

This area was, in days gone by, a refuge for Indians driven from the coast, for fugitive slaves and for all kinds of bandits. It was also a waterway into the interior for slave-hunters, adventurers and people dreaming of gold, diamonds and emeralds. The São Francisco River was the scene of many bloody confrontations before landowners finally settled here and turned to cattle-raising. Today, this area is being considered as the site for huge agricultural projects.

If you are interested in going down the river, you must make your reservations at least two weeks in advance. Contact the **Companhia de Navegação do Rio São Francisco** (see 'Useful addresses' p. 161).

On your way downstream, you will pass the following towns and villages.

Pirapora* is in Minas Gerais, about 267 mi/430 km north of Belo Horizonte. Other villages in Minas Gerais, near the border with Bahia, include **São Francisco***, **Januaria*** and **Manga***.

Bom Jesus da Lapa* is 490 mi/790 km west of Salvador. From May to October, pilgrimages of as many as 100,000 people come here to visit its sacred grottos, in particular **Gruta Sanchiário***** and the nearby **Nossa Senhora da Soledade**, **Ressureição** and **Santo Luzia**.

Juazeiro* is 320 mi/515 km north-west of Salvador. Since the construction of the Sobradinho dam, the Juazeiro harbour has been moved to Nova Sento Sé. Visit the historical museum, **Regional do São Francisco** (Praça Imaculada Conceiçao; open Tues-Fri 8am-12:30pm, 2-6pm, Sat 8:30am-noon, 2:30-5:30pm).

About 193 mi/310 km from the river's mouth, you can explore the **Paulo Afonso waterfalls***. Four of the waterfalls are 260 ft/80 m high, a remarkable sight in the heart of a tropical forest. For a permit to visit the neighbouring hydroelectric plant, its park and lake, contact the **Centro Informação Turistica**, Av. Getúlio Vargas, ☎ (075) 281 1321.

Going farther into the interior, you will come on the national park of **Chapada Diamantina***. This is a moutainous ridge in the centre of Bahia that was once the scene of a gold rush. Legends of hidden treasure abound here, as do grottos in the rocks. Nearby are the towns of **Lençóis***, 279 mi/449 km west of Salvador, and **Jacobina***, 209 mi/336 km west of Salvador.

If, instead of traveling in the interior, you decide to take the coast from Salvador to Rio de Janeiro, you will pass through many towns with worthwhile sights.

Valença* is 170 mi/273 km south of Salvador. This small, historical town is famous for its fishing-boat repairs industry. There are several noteworthy buildings, such as the **Paço Municipal** and **Nossa Senhora do Amparo church**, but Valença's main appeal is its magnificent beaches. You can also make an excursion to the island of **Tinharé** with its Fortaleza and Presidio do Morro São Paulo or to the island of **Cairu** with its Santo Antônio convent, dating from 1661.

Ilhéus**, 292 mi/470 km south of Salvador, is the cocoa capital of Brazil. The setting of the well-known novel, *Gabriela, Clove and Cinnnamon*, by Jorge Amado, Ilhéus is becoming one of the main tourist centres of Brazil. Visit the **São Jorge church** (open Sun-Fri 4-5 pm), dating from 1534, and the wonderful beaches. There is a tiny spa called **Olivença**, 22 mi/36 km away.

Porto Seguro* is 451 mi/726 km south of Salvador. This town was constructed on the very spot where Alvares discovered Brazil in 1500.

Many colonial buildings have survived in the upper town, including **Nossa Senhora da Penha**, dating from 1535, **Senhor dos Passos**, dating from 1549, and **São Benedito**, dating from 1549. There are beautiful beaches to the north of the town.

Arraial da Ajuda★ is 4 mi/6 km from Porto Seguro. This village was founded in 1549. Its **Nossa Senhora da Ajuda** church is the site of pilgrimages in August.

Trancoso★ is 15 mi/25 km from Porto Seguro and is a village that has grown popular with tourists.

Santa Cruz Cabrália★★ is 15 mi/25 km north of Porto Seguro. This beach witnessed the first mass ever to be said on Brazilian soil. A cross serves as a memorial to this event.

Alcobaça★ is 478 mi/770 km south of Salvador. There are lovely beaches here and fishing and boating excursions are available.

Nova Viçosa★ is 569 mi/916 km south of Salvador. Here, you can explore the coral reefs of the **Da Coroa Vermilho** and **Arquipelago dos Abrilhos★★★** — permission from the navy needed to visit the latter, ☎ (071) 242 1577.

Accommodation

▲▲ **Porto Seguro Praia**, BR- 367, Porto Seguro, ☎ (073) 288 2321. This lovely hotel in a park has a restaurant, two bars, two swimming pools and various sports facilities. 106 rooms.

▲▲ **Pousada de Lençois**, Rua Altina Alves 747, Lençois, ☎ (075) 334 1102. This hotel is situated in an attractive park and contains a restaurant, a bar and a swimming pool. 36 rooms.

▲▲ **Serra do Ouro**, Largo Monte Tabor, Jacobina, ☎ (075) 621 2324. This little hotel offers a wonderful view, as well as a restaurant, a bar and a swimming pool. 32 rooms.

▲ **Canoeiros**, Av. Salmeron 3, Pirapora, ☎ (037) 741 1946. A restaurant, a bar and two swimming pools will be found here. 84 rooms.

▲ **Grande Hotel de Paulo Afonso**, Acampamento da Chesf, Paulo Afonso, ☎ (075) 281 1914. This nice hotel sits in a park and has a restaurant, a bar and a swimming pool. 40 rooms.

▲ **Grande Hotel do Juazeiro**, Rua José Petitinga, Juazeiro, ☎ (075) 811 2710. A modest hotel with a restaurant, a bar and a swimming pool. 42 rooms.

▲ **Ilhéus Praia**, Praça D. Eduardo, Ilhéus, ☎ (073) 231 2533. This comfortable hotel in the town centre has a restaurant, a bar and a swimming pool. 64 rooms.

▲ **Pousada da Lapa**, Av. Lauro de Freitas, Bom Jesus da Lapa, ☎ (073) 481 2248. A simple hotel with a restaurant and a bar. 32 rooms.

▲ **Rio Una**, Rua Maestro Barrinha, Valença, ☎ (075) 741 1614. This little hotel provides a restaurant, a bar and a swimming pool. 36 rooms.

▲ **Sul Americano**, Av. Atlântica 1101, Alcobaça, ☎ (073) 293 2171. This modest hotel has a simple restaurant. 50 rooms.

Food

★ **Cabanas do Mirante**, Rua Madre Thais, Ilhéus, ☎ (073) 231 2533. Offering a magnificent view, this restaurant serves good regional cuisine. Open daily 11-2am.

★ **Canoeiros**, Hotel Canoeiros, Av. Salmeron 3, Pirapora, ☎ (037) 741 1946. This restaurant offers international cuisine and a lovely view. Open daily 11am-3pm, 7-11pm.

★ **Os Velhos Marinheiros**, Av. 2 de Julho, Ilhéus. Seafood restaurant near the centre of town in a very nice location. Open daily 11am-midnight.

* **Saldanha Marinho**, Rua Juvêncio Alves, Juazeiro, ☎ (075) 811 2587. An attractive restaurant with a wonderful view and regional cuisine. Open daily noon-3pm, 6-11pm.
* **Travessia**, Praça dos Pataxos, Porto Seguro, ☎ (073) 288 2403. This good seafood restaurant is very pleasantly located. Open daily 11:30am-midnight.

Useful addresses

Airlines

Nordeste, at airport, Porto Seguro, ☎ (073) 288 2108; at airport, Ilhéus, ☎ (073) 231 3949.
Rio-Sul, Hotel Porto Seguro Praia, Porto Seguro, ☎ (073) 288 2321.
Varig, Rua Ernesto Sa 12, Ilhéus, ☎ (073) 231 1862.
Vasp, Praça Antônio Muniz 22, Ilhéus, ☎ (073) 231 3185.

Airports

Ilhéus, ☎ (073) 231 3015.
Juazeiro, ☎ (075) 961 3530.
Porto Seguro, ☎ (073) 288 2400.

Bank

Banco do Brasil, Rua Mq. de Paranagoa 112, Ilhéus, ☎ (073) 231 2341.

Boat line

Companhia de Navegação do Rio São Francisco, Av. São Francisco 1396, Pirapora, ☎ (037) 741 1744; Av. Dr. Raul Alves, Juazeiro, ☎ (075) 811 2340.

Bus terminals

Rua Otávio Carneiro, Pirapora, ☎ (037) 741 1544.
Praça dos Pataxos, Porto Seguro, ☎ (073) 288 2239.

Car rental

Budget, Rua do Bonfim 268, Ilhéus, ☎ (073) 231 4672.
Localiza, at airport, Ilhéus, ☎ (073) 231 2171.

Tourist offices

Bahiatursa, Praça Visc. de Porto Seguro, Porto Seguro, ☎ (073) 288 2126.
Ilhéustur, Praça Castro Alves, Ilhéus, ☎ (073) 231 1861.

Travel agencies

BPS, Av. dos Navegantes, Porto Seguro, ☎ (073) 288 2335.
Freitas, Rua Mq. de Paranagua 50, Ilhéus, ☎ (073) 231 4915.

▬ *ARACAJU AND THE STATE OF SERGIPE*

See map pp. 136-137.

Sergipe is Brazil's smallest state, with an economy based on petrol production and the cultivation of rice, coconuts, tobacco and sugarcane. It is known for its lovely climate, its folk dances, its rodeos and its wonderful beaches. **Aracaju*** is a quiet little town practically unknown to tourists. It has been the capital of Sergipe state since 1855.

São Cristóvão*** lies 16 mi/26 km south of Aracaju. It was founded in 1590 by Cristovão de Baros and was the first capital of Sergipe. Many colonial buildings have survived, such as the **Ordem Terceira do Carmo convent**, dating from 1693, the **Rosário de São Francisco church**, the **Imaculada Conceição church** and the **Matriz church**. There are also many museums. The most important sights are the **Senhor dos Passos church****, dating from 1743, and the **Museum of Sacred Art**** inside the São Francisco convent (☎ (079) 261 1240; open Tues-Sun 1:30-6pm). This museum displays objects dating from the 16th-19th centuries.

Laranjeiras** is 12 mi/20 km north of Aracaju. This small colonial village is noted for its traditional dances and for its seven churches built on the tops of seven nearby hills; hence its name, 'little Rome'. Several museums and the **Comanda Roba church**, dating from 1734, are worth a look. There is a cultural information centre, the **Centro de Tradiçoes**, located in a former warehouse.

Propria* is 63 mi/102 km north of Aracaju. This is a charming little river port on the São Francisco River.

Carrapicho* lies 25 mi/40 km north of Propria, also on the São Francisco River. This little community is known for its handmade pottery.

Estancia* is 43 mi/70 km south of Aracaju. This town was formerly an agrarian community that was founded by Jesuits. Dom Pedro II described it as 'Sergipe's garden'. There are a handful of colonial houses left in the centre of town.

Salgado* is 42 mi/68 km west of Aracaju. This is a health resort with lots of pleasant greenery.

Telephone area code: 079

Accommodation

▲▲ **Parque dos Coqueiros**, Rua Francisco Rabelo Leite Neto 1075, Aracaju, ☎ 223 1511. This hotel is in wonderful location and has a restaurant, three bars and two swimming pools. 74 rooms.

▲ **Balneário de Salgado**, Rua da Estância 1, Salgado, ☎ 622 1011. In a lovely park, this hotel contains a restaurant, a bar and a swimming pool. 38 rooms.

▲ **Beira-Mar**, Av. Rotary, Aracaju, ☎ 223 1921. A comfortable hotel with a restaurant, three bars and a swimming pool. 75 rooms.

▲ **Grande Hotel**, Rua Itabaianinha 371, Aracaju, ☎ 222 2112. This modest hotel has a restaurant and a bar. 67 rooms.

▲ **Palace de Aracaju**, Praça Gen. Valadão, Aracaju, ☎ 224 5000. A hotel that offers comfort, a restaurant, three bars and a swimming pool. 70 rooms.

Food

** **Taberna do Tropeiro**, Av. Oceânica 6, Aracaju, ☎ 233 1466. A lively restaurant with very good regional cuisine. Open daily 11-3m.

* **Adega do Antônio**, Rua José Sotero 235, Aracaju, ☎ 222 6844. This restaurant offers an interesting assortment of international dishes. Open daily 11am-2:30pm, 6pm-1am.

* **Parque da Cidade**, Av. Corinto Leite, Aracaju. A lively *churrascaria* situated in a pleasant park and with a lovely view. Open daily 11am-11pm.

Useful addresses

Airlines
Transbrasil, Rua São Cristóvão-14, Aracaju, ☎ 222 2133.
Varig, Rua João Pessoa 71, Aracaju, ☎ 222 7800.
Vasp, Rua São Cristóvão 79, Aracaju, ☎ 224 1801.

Airport
Santa Maria, Aracaju, ☎ 223 1929.

Banks
Banco do Brasil, Praça Gen. Valadão 341, Aracaju.
Banco do Estado Sergipe, Largo do Esperanto, Aracaju.

Bus terminal
Av. 37 de Março, Contorno, ☎ 221 1376.

Car rental
Interlocadora, Av. Monteiro Lobato 2357, Aracaju, ☎ 223 2284.
Locarauto, Av. Beira-Mar 1450, Aracaju, ☎ 223.2379.

Post office
Correio Central, Av. Laranjeiras 229, Aracaju.

Tourist office
Emsetur, Av. Pres. Tancredo Neves, Aracaju; at airport.

MACEIÓ AND THE STATE OF ALAGOAS

See map pp. 136-137.

Alagoas is among the smallest of Brazil's states and yet is one of Brazil's largest producers of sugarcane. It also owes its prosperity to the cotton that grows on the slopes of the Planalto and to an abundant production of pineapples. Because of its pleasant climate (69-82° F/20-28° C), Alagoas is said to have the most enjoyable beaches in all of the Nordeste region.

For a long period, Alagoas was a breeding ground for all sorts of unrest. The turmoil stemmed from invasions by the French and the Dutch, conflicts with the Indian population, runaway slaves and various revolutionary movements. Alagoas was one of the first states to attempt to gain independence from Portugal.

Maceió**, the capital of Alagoas, is virtually enclosed by the magnificent **Mundau lagoon**. Starting as a small community built around a sugarmill, Maceió became a city in 1830. One of its most appealing features is its beachfront, lined with coconut trees twisted by the wind. Several beaches are protected from the open sea by coral reefs. You can take wonderful boat excursions on the Mundau lagoon.

A beautiful stretch of coast lies north of Maceió with some charming little villages. The best known beaches include:

Pajuçara** is 2 mi/3 km from Maceió. There are lovely natural pools in the sea here encircled by reefs.

Garça Torta*** is 7 mi/11 km from Maceió. There is a little fishing village close by.

Pratagi*** is 11 mi/17 km from Maceió. Here again, there are lovely natural pools and coral reefs.

Barra Santo Antônio** is 25 mi/40 km from Maceió. This is the limit of what are considered Maceió's northern beaches. Sea excursions are available from here.

The very large and very beautiful beaches on the southern side of Maceió are farther away. The best known of these is **Do Frances*****, 15 mi/25 km from Maceió. This magnificent beach was the scene of decisive battles against French smugglers.

Pontal da Barra* is a little fishing village 7.5 mi/12 km from Maceió, known for its handmade lace. Excursions are available from here to the Mundau and Manguaba lagoons.

Marechal Deodoro** is 43 mi/69 km from Maceió. A former capital, this small town on the shores of the Manguaba lagoon has lost none of its colonial character. Several noteworthy churches remain, including **São Francisco**, dating from 1684, **Nossa Senhora da Cinceição**, dating from 1755, and the 16th-century **Nossa Senhora de Bonfim**. Make sure to visit the **Porto do Frances** (Frenchmen's harbour), once a smuggler's lair. There are excursions available from here on the lagoon.

Among the interesting towns in the interior of Alagoas are:

Penedo** is 112 mi/180 km south-west of Maceió. This is a small colonial town that sits on the banks of the São Francisco River and contains several churches that are worthy of a visit like **Nossa Senhora dos Anjos**, dating from 1660, **Nossa Senhora da Corrente**, dating from 1764, and **São Gongalo Garcia**, dating from 1758. The **São**

Francisco convent is renowned for its colonial architecture. It is possible to take excursions from here on the São Francisco River, either upstream as far as Piranhas, or downstream as far as the estuary at Brejo Grande. Two towns to visit on the other side of the river from Penedo are **Carrapicho*** and **Neopolis***.

Poxim*, **Pontal do Coruripe*** and **Piaçabuçu*** are tiny villages that lie on the coast on the way to Penedo. There are few signposts, so you will have to ask for directions.

União dos Palmares* is 56 mi/90 km north-west of Maceió. This town is famous as the former site of the legendary Quilombo dos Palmares, a camp built by rebel slaves (the subject of a recent movie, *The Mission*). There is hardly anything left of it today.

Arapiraca* is 8 mi/13 km west of Maceió. The world's most important centre for black tobacco, the factory can be visited on request. The **Feira Livre*** market, where you can find regional produce and handcrafts, is held on Mondays (open 5am-6pm).

Telephone area code: 082.

Accommodation

▲▲▲ **Jatiúca**, Rua Lagoa da Anta 220, Maceió, ☎ 231 2555. An attractive hotel in a pleasant location with a restaurant, three bars and two swimming pools. 95 rooms.

▲▲ **Luxor**, Av. Dq. de Caxias 2076, Maceió, ☎ 221 9191. A comfortable hotel with a wonderful view, a restaurant, a bar and a swimming pool. 98 rooms.

▲ **Beiriz**, Rua João Pessoa 290, Maceió, ☎ 221 1080. This modest hotel offers a restaurant, a bar and a swimming pool. 75 rooms.

▲ **Pajuçara Othon**, Rua Jangadeiros Alagoanos 1292, Maceió, ☎ 231 2200. A comfortable hotel with a restaurant, a bar and a swimming pool. 117 rooms.

▲ **São Francisco**, Av. Floriano Peixoto, Penedo, ☎ 551 2273. This modest hotel has a restaurant, a bar and a swimming pool. 52 rooms.

Camping
Camping Clube do Brasil, Jacarecica beach, Maceió, ☎ 231 3600.

Food

** **Gstaad**, Av. Robert Kennedy 2167, Maceió, ☎ 231 1780. Excellent French cuisine and a magnificent view. Open daily 7pm-1am.

* **Do Alipio**, Av. Alipio Barbosa 321, Maceió, ☎ 221 5186. A wide variety of seafood in an attractive setting. Open Mon-Sat 11-1am.

* **Lagostão**, Av. Dq. de Caxias 1384, Maceió, ☎ 221 6211. This lively and attractive restaurant serves a large selection of seafood. Open daily 11am-11pm.

Useful addresses

Airlines
Transbrasil, Rua Barão de Penedo 213, Maceió, ☎ 223 4830.
Varig, Rua Dr. Luis de Miranda 42, Maceió, ☎ 223 7334.
Vasp, Rua do Comércio 56, Maceió, ☎ 221 2655.

Airport
dos Palmares, Maceió, ☎ 242 1410.

Bank
Banco do Brasil, Rua Barão de Penedo 61, Maceió.

Bus terminal
RFFSA, Rua Br. de Aradia 121, Maceió, ☎ 223 4432.

Car rental
Avis, João Davino 297, Maceió, ☎ 231 4289.
Locarauto, Gabino Bezouro, Maceió, ☎ 221 1819; at airport, ☎ 242 1461.

Emergencies
Pronto Socorro, Av. Siqueira Campos, Maceió, ☎ 221 5939.

Post office
Correio Central, Rua Dias Cabral 338, Maceió.

Railway terminal
Av. Leste-Oeste, Maceió, ☎ 221 4615.

Tourist office
Ematur, Praça do Centenario 1135, Maceió, ☎ 243 6868. There are also tourist information desks at the **Pajuçara Othon Hotel** (see p. 164) and the airport.

Travel agencies
Alatur, Av. Dq.de Caxias 1456, Maceió ☎ 221 1307.
Dreamar Turismo, Av. Cons. Lourenço Albuquerque 261, Maceió.

▬ RECIFE AND THE STATE OF PERNAMBUCO

See map pp. 136-137.

The small state of Pernambuco, with an area of 37,946 sq mi/98,281 sq km and a population of seven million inhabitants, has a culture, a tradition and a folklore all its own.

This region is said to have been explored by the Phoenicians as early as the 12th century BC. From AD 1500 onwards, piracy and smuggling were rife along the coast. When the Portuguese settled here in 1534, they launched the cultivation of sugarcane and founded the then capital, Olinda. From 1630 to1654, the Dutch were the colonial overlords and brought further prosperity and cultural development so that at this time Recife began to overshadow Olinda. Today the decline in the sugar industry has left this region at an economic disadvantage vis à vis Bahia.

Recife, the capital of Pernambuco, is one of the largest cities in Brazil and the region's economic centre. Situated at the confluence of the Capiberibe and Beberibe rivers, Recife is often referred to as Brazil's Venice. The city's name comes from the Portuguese term for *reefs:* a barrier of them extends along the coastline forming pools on the beaches when the tide is low. Sometimes when the water rises, parts of Recife are flooded. The city is one of the major gateways to Brazil, thanks to its international airport.

Carnival

Recife's Carnival lasts almost 10 days. Here, and in the nearby city of Olinda, Carnival offers the visitor a perfect opportunity to witness the rich folklore of Pernambuco state. The *samba* is replaced by the *frevo*, a typically Pernambuco dance form accompanied by an accordion and with a faster tempo than the *samba*. Among the other specifically regional presentations you can see are the *maracatu* (costumed performers act out an African theme concerning Congo royalty) and the *ursos* (a dance based on the theme of a bear, its trainer and hunter).

Spectator seating is set up along Avenida Dantas Barreto for the main parades and the major nightclubs organize balls. Contact **Empetur** (see p. 169) for more information on carnival events.

The city consists of four districts: Santo Antônio in the middle, surrounded by São José, Recife and Boa Viagem. There are many bridges connecting these areas.

Santo Antônio

Santo Antônio is Recife's oldest section and contains many noteworthy buildings.

Capela Dourada and Museu Franciscano de Arte Sacra*** (Rua do Imperador 206, ☎ (081) 224 0530; open Mon-Fri 8-11:30am, 2-5pm, Sat 7-11:30am) dates from 1695. The interior of the chapel is covered with gilded wood paneling framing large paintings. The ones on the ceiling represent the life of Francis. The museum has a fine collection of 17th- and 18th-century religious objects.

Nossa Senhora do Rosário dos Pretos** (Rua Estreita do Rosário, ☎ (081) 224 0409; open daily 7am-noon, 2-6pm) is a church that was built by slaves in 1725. It contains lovely statues of the Virgin.

Nossa Senhora do Carmo** (Av. Dantas Barreto 646, ☎ (081) 224 3359; open Mon-Fri 2-5pm, Sat 7am-noon, 2-6pm) is a church and convent that was built in 1675 on the ruins of a palace.

São Pedro dos Clerigos** (☎ (081) 224 2954; open Mon-Sat 8am-noon, 2-6pm) is a large cathedral dating from 1728. The ceiling's *trompe l'oeil* treatment was the work of the painter Deus Sepulveda. There is also a handsome sacristy here. The cathedral is situated on **Patio São Pedro***, an attractive little plaza where many festivities take place.

Nossa Senhora da Conceição dos Militares** (Rua Nova 309, ☎ (081) 224 3106; open Mon-Fri 7-11am, 1:30-4pm, Sat 7am-noon, Sun 10am-6pm) is a Baroque church that dates from 1757. It is an imposing edifice with paneling in the nave and an interesting painting of the pregnant Virgin. In its annex is a small museum devoted to sacred art.

Casa da Cultura** (Rua Floriano Peixoto, ☎ (081) 224 2084; open Mon-Sat 9am-8pm, Sun 3-8pm) was a prison in the mid-19th century. It has now become an important centre for handcrafts and folklore. Its architecture, with beautiful staircases and wrought-iron balconies, is impressive.

Governor's Palace* is set in gardens on the fringe of Santo Antônio.

São José

São José is a southern expansion of Santo Antônio. Sights to see here include the following.

Forte das Cinco Pontas* is a fort that was built by the Dutch in 1630.

Mercado São José** (Praça São José; open Mon-Sat 6am-5pm, Sun 6am-noon) is a lively market where you can find all kinds of regional products (handcrafts, herbal medicines, Afro-Brazilian cult objects and food).

Among the churches you can visit here are **Nossa Senhora da Penha***, **Nossa Senhora do Livramento*** and **Nossa Senhora do Terço***.

Recife

The district of Recife is, in fact, an island that sits in the estuary of the two rivers. Sights to see here include:

Madre de Deus** (Open Mon-Fri 8-11am, Sun 10-11am) is a church that was constructed in 1715 of arenite taken from the reefs.

Forte do Brum** (Praça Luso-Brasileiro, ☎ (081) 224 4334; open Tues-Fri 10am-5pm, Sat and Sun 2-5pm) was built by the Portuguese in 1677 and houses a military museum.

The outlying districts also contain worthwhile sights.

Museu Homen do Nordeste** (Casa Forte, ☎ (081) 268 2000; open Tues, Wed and Fri 11am-5pm, Thurs 8am-5pm, Sat and Sun 1-5pm) was created by the well-known sociologist Gilberto Freyre. It consists of four sections:

● **Museu Açucar** contains everything there is to know about the cultivation of sugarcane. The emphasis is on both the technical and cultural aspects.

● **Museu Antropologia** deals with the everyday life of Nordeste's farmers.

● **Museu Arte Popular** focuses on the traditions, customs and folklore of the people of Nordeste.

● **Museu Joaquim Nabuco** contains the archives of this famous jurist.

Museu Estado de Pernambuco** (Av. Rui Barbosa 960, ☎ (081) 222 6694; open Tues-Fri 9am-6pm) relates the history of the art of Pernambuco. It is located in the former mansion of the Barão de Bereribe.

Other interesting visits a bit farther away are to be found.

Horto Dois Imãos* is 6 mi/10 km from Recife. This is a lovely park full of all the flora and fauna particular to the Nordeste region.

Nossa Senhora dos Prazeres** is a chapel 9 mi/14 km from Recife. It is set in the Parque Nacional Historico dos Guararapes and was built in 1656 by General Francisco Barreto to commemorate victories won against the Dutch. It is beautifully decorated.

Museu Francisco Brennand* (☎ (081) 271 2623; open Mon-Fri 8-11:30am, 2-5pm, Sat 8-11:30am) is located in the Engenho São João Varzea 10 mi/16 km from Recife. It contains a lovely collection of ceramics.

Boa Viagem beach

Although the centre and the areas around São Pedro are lively and full of interest, it is the *zona sul* — the **Boa Viagem beach area** — that has become the main residential quarter for Recife. It is also here that you will find the best hotels, restaurants and nightclubs.

Telephone area code: 081

Access

Plane

Flights originating in North America, Europe and the major cities of Brazil arrive at the international airport of **Guararapes**, 7 mi/12 km from Recife, ☎ 341 1888.

To get to the city centre, you can take the bus marked Aeroporto or a taxi.

Transbrasil, Av. Dantas Barreto 191, Santo Antônio, ☎ 224 6166
Varig/Cruzeiro, Av. Guararapes 120, Santo Antônio, ☎ 224 3235.
Vasp, Av. Manoel Borba 488, Santo Antônio, ☎ 222 3611.

Bus

Recife is linked with all the main cities of Brazil and the Nordeste by bus. We recommend, however, that you avoid the long bus trips from distant cities.

Terminal Integrado de Pallageiros, acesso pela BR-232, Curado, ☎ 251 4666.

Train

Recife is on the train route that runs from Cinco Pontas and Maceió in the south to Natal and Paraiba in the north. Trains tend to be slow.

RFFSA, Av. Sul, São José, ☎ 224 8013.

Accommodation

▲▲▲ **Mar**, Rua Br. de Souza Leão 451, Boa Viagem, ☎ 341 5433. This handsome hotel includes three restaurants, three bars and three swimming pools. 207 rooms.

▲▲▲ **Miramar**, Rua dos Navegantes 363, Boa Viagem, ☎ 326 7422. An attractive hotel that has a restaurant, two bars and two swimming pools. 173 rooms.

▲▲▲ **Othon Palace**, Av. Boa Viagem 3722, Boa Viagem,

☎ 326 7225. This large, fashionable hotel contains a restaurant, three bars and two swimming pools. 264 rooms.

▲▲▲ **Recife Palace,** Av. Boa Viagem 4070, Boa Viagem, ☎ 325 4044. The best hotel in Recife. It has two restaurants, two bars and a swimming pool. 294 rooms.

▲▲ **Jangadeiro,** Av. Boa Viagem 3114, Boa Viagem, ☎ 326 6777. A comfortable hotel that offers a lovely view, as well as a restaurant, two bars and a swimming pool. 100 rooms.

▲▲ **Vila Rica,** Av. Boa Viagem 4308, Boa Viagem, ☎ 326 5111. This hotel faces the beach and has a restaurant, two bars and a swimming pool. 103 rooms.

▲ **Grande Hotel,** Av. Martins de Barros 593, Santo Antônio, ☎ 224 9366. This comfortable hotel comes with a restaurant and a bar. 106 rooms.

▲ **Quatro de Outubro,** Rua Floriano Peixoto 141, Santo Antônio, ☎ 224 4477. A modest but adequate hotel that has a restaurant and a bar. 52 rooms.

▲ **São Domingos,** Praça Maciel Pinheiro 66, Boa Vista, ☎ 231 1404. This is a quiet, simple hotel with a restaurant and a bar. 84 rooms.

Food

*** **Cantinho do Camões,** Rua 48, Espinheiro, ☎ 222 3249. A lively restaurant serving excellent Portuguese cuisine. Open daily noon-11pm.

*** **Canto da Barra,** Av. Bernardo Vieira de Melo 9150, Candeias, ☎ 361 2168. This is a charming restaurant that offers a wide variety of seafood. Open daily noon-3pm, 7pm-midnight.

*** **Edmilson,** Av. Maria Irene 311, Jordão, ☎ 341 0644. Very good regional cuisine. Open daily 11-1am.

*** **Marruá,** Rua Ernesto de Paula Santos 183, Boa Viagem, ☎ 326 1656. The best *churrascaria* in Recife. Open daily 11am-midnight.

*** **Seridó,** Rua José Osório 270, Madalena, ☎ 227 1087. This restaurant serves simple but good regional cuisine. Open daily 11am-3pm, 6pm-midnight.

** **Lobster,** Rua Bruno Veloso 200, Boa Viagem, ☎ 326 7593. Live music and an amazing assortment of seafood. Open daily noon-midnight.

** **O Laçador,** Rua Visc. de Jequitinhinha 138, Boa Viagem, ☎ 326 3911. This is a lively *churrascaria*. Open daily 11:30-11pm.

Getting around Recife

On foot
Walking is a fine way to visit specific neighbourhoods, but you will need to use other means of transportation to get from one district to another.

By underground
Recife's underground runs from 5am-11pm and goes from São José to the railway terminal in the suburb of Jaboatão and the bus terminal in Curado.

By taxi
Taxis are expensive and can be flagged in the street or ordered by telephone.
Coopertaxi, ☎ 224 8411.
Radiotaxi Recife, ☎ 222 0625.
Tele-Taxi, ☎ 231 7533.

By car
You might want to rent a car to reach some of the sights and beaches on the outskirts of the city or to visit the environs of Recife.
Avis, Av. Mal. Mascarenhas de Morais 5174, ☎ 326 5730.
Budget, Rua Des. João Paes 300, Boa Viagem, ☎ 325 0110.
Hertz, Av. Cons. Aguiar 4212, Boa Viagem, ☎ 325 2907.

Useful addresses

Banks
Banco do Brasil, Av. Rio Branco 240, Centro, ☎ 224 2500.
Citibank, Av. Mq. de Olinda 126, Recife, ☎ 224 7922.

Consulates
Great Britain, Av. Mq. de Olinda 200, Recife, ☎ 224 0650.
United States, Rua Gonçalves Maia 163, Boa Vista, ☎ 221 1412.

Emergencies
Geral de Urgência, Av. Caxangá 4477, Iputinga, ☎ 271 2044.

Post office
Embratel, Av. Magalhaes 1114, Parque Amorim, ☎ 221 4149.

Tourist office
Empetur, Av. Cruz Cabuga 553, ☎ 231 7941.

Travel agencies
Kontik-Franstur, Rua da Concórdia 278, Santo Antônio, ☎ 224 9888.
Moturismo, Rua Rosário de Boa Vista 159, ☎ 231 1197.

▬ *PERNAMBUCO STATE*

See map pp. 136-137.
There are many lovely towns outside Recife that retain traces of their colonial past, as well as villages worth visiting that are scattered in the foothills of the Serra.
Olinda*** is only 4 mi/6 km north of Recife. The former capital of Pernambuco state, this city was designated one of 'mankind's treasures' by UNESCO in 1982. It remains entirely colonial in character. Sights to be admired include the following.
● **São Francisco convent*****, with its **Nossa Senhora das Neves church,** was the first Franciscan monastery in Brazil; it was built in 1585. Looted by the Dutch, it was rebuilt between 1715 and 1755 and now has a sumptuous interior.
● **São Bento monastery**** (Rua São Bento; open daily 8-11am, 1-5pm) was founded in 1599 and includes a church, which was built in the late 18th century. Its principal chapel is one of the most beautiful in Brazil.
● **Nossa Senhora de Graça***, once part of a former college for Jesuits, was founded in 1561. Lovely views from the grounds.
● **Mercado da Ribeira*** (Rua Bernardo Vieira de Melo; open daily 9am-6pm) was once the slave market and is now occupied by painters' studios and handcraft boutiques.
● **São Roque chapel** (open daily 8-11:30am, 2-4:30pm) dates from 1811 and contains fine examples of Portuguese tilework.
● **São João Batista dos Militares***, constructed in 1580, is the only church that survived the great fire that accompanied the Dutch attack on Olinda.
Igaraçu** is 22 mi/36 km north of Recife. This is a small town that has retained many elements of its colonial past.
● **Santo Antônio convent** was founded in 1588 but was practically demolished by the Dutch in 1632. You can visit what is left. Its church dates from 1705 and its cloister from 1654.

● **São Cosme e Damião church**** is reputed to be the oldest church in Brazil, dating from 1535. Its interior is lavish and it contains so many interesting items it is almost a museum.

● **Engenho Monjape*** is a colonial estate with a sugarmill, dating from 1750, a large house and a chapel. It was once visited by Dom Pedro II.

Itamaraca** is 29 mi/47 km north of Recife. This is a lovely island full of coconut trees with a village that contains several historical buildings. Note the **Engenho Ampara sugarmill***, which is now in ruins, and **Forte Orange***, which dates from 1630. The ancient harbour of **Vila Velha***, constructed in 1526, is also in ruins. There are lovely beaches and good fishing here.

Tracunhaém* is 25 mi/40 km north of Recife. This little village is renowned for its handcrafts and ceramics. There is a fair on Sundays.

Goiana* is 47 mi/75 km north of Recife. This is another small colonial town. Among its interesting sights are the **Carmo church***, dating from 1717, and the 18th-century **Nossa Senhora do Amparo**, which houses a museum of sacred art. You can take excursions from here to **Tejucopapo**, a historic battlefield where the Dutch were once defeated.

There are a string of magnificent beaches that stretch from the south of Recife towards **São José da Coroa Grande***. They are **Cabo***, 20 mi/32 km from Recife, **Ipojuca***, 25 mi/41 km from Recife, and **Sirinhaem***, 45 mi/72 km from Recife. São José da Coroa Grande itself is 68 mi/110 km from Recife.

Heading inland, you enter the Serra foothills. Here you will find several charming small resorts, including **Gravatá** (53 mi/86 km west of Recife), **Salgadinho** (75 mi/120 km west of Recife) and **Taquaritinga do Norte** (106 mi/170 km west of Recife).

Caruaru** is 78 mi/126 km west of Recife. This is the capital of a region known as the Agreste and the birthplace of the famous artisan, Mestre Vitalino. UNESCO has named Caruaru the most important site for South American figurative art. There is a wonderful fair on Wednesdays and Saturdays where you can buy examples of it. Lots of artisans work in the Alto do Moura neighbourhood and you can visit their studios. Two sights worth a visit are the **Mestre Vitalino Museum** (open daily 8am-5pm) and the **Casa da Cultura José Conde** (open Mon-Fri 9am-noon, 2-5pm, Sat 9am-1pm). There is a spectacular view from the nearby **Morro do Bom Jesus**.

Fazenda Nova** is 115 mi/185 km west of Recife. This tiny village is right next to **Nova (new) Jerusalem**, a reconstruction of the ancient city of Jerusalem, where every year over 500 actors participate in a re-enactment of the principal scenes of the Passion.

Garanhuns** is 150 mi/241 km west of Recife. This is a lovely little resort at an altitude of 2950 ft/900 m in the Borborema Mountains. It has a pleasant climate. Close by is Mount Alto Magano, 3380 ft/1030 m high.

Arcoverde*, 158 mi/254 km west of Recife, is known as the gate to the Sertão.

Serrita** is 342 mi/550 km west of Recife. On the third Sunday in July a huge crowd gathers here to celebrate a mass, the Missa do Vaqueiro. *Vaqueiro* means 'cowhand', and more than 1000 of them are on hand for this event. Festivities start the Friday before.

Triunfo* is 280 mi/450 km west of Recife. This is a green little mountain village located at an altitude of 3280 ft/1000 m.

Petrolina* is 450 mi/725 km west of Recife. This little town straddles the São Francisco River.

Fernando de Noronha Archipelago

The Fernando de Noronha Archipelago consists of 21 volcanic islands that lie about 224 mi/360 km off the coast of Pernambuco, 326 mi/525 km from Recife. This area is administered as a federal territory by the Brazilian armed forces. Only one of the islands is inhabited, and it is a paradise for tourists. It has gorgeous beaches, crystalline water, an unspoiled natural setting and plentiful fishing. During World War II this was a base for the United States Army.

Telephone area code: 081

Accommodation

▲▲▲▲ **Quatro Rodas Olinda**, Av. José Augusto Moreira 2200, Olinda, ☎ 431 2955. This fabulous hotel is on the beach and includes an excellent restaurant, two bars and two swimming pools. 195 rooms.

▲▲▲ **Tavares Correia**, Av. Rui Barbosa 296, Garanhuns, ☎ 761 0900. An attractive hotel that sits in a park and contains a restaurant, a bar and a swimming pool. 123 rooms.

▲▲ **Hotel do Sol**, BR-104, Caruaru, ☎ 721 3044. A restaurant, a bar and a swimming pool. 62 rooms are offered by this comfortable hotel.

▲▲ **Marolinda**, Av. Beira-Mar 1615, Olinda, ☎ 429 1699. A little hotel with a restaurant, two bars and a swimming pool. 48 rooms.

▲ **Grande Hotel**, Av. Poeta Carlos Pena Filho, Fazenda Nova. This modest hotel sits in a park and has a restaurant, a bar and a swimming pool. 60 rooms.

▲ **Hotel do Grande Rio**, Rua Pe. Fraga, Petrolina, ☎ 961 4722. A comfortable hotel that includes a restaurant, a bar and a swimming pool. 47 rooms.

▲ **Orange Praia**, Av. do Forte, Itamaraca, ☎ 544 1170. An extremely attractive hotel with a restaurant, two bars, two swimming pools and various sports facilities. 52 rooms.

▲ **Pousada dos Quatro Cantos**, Rua Prudente de Morais 441, Olinda, ☎ 429 0220. A modest but agreeably located little hotel. 12 rooms.

▲ **Pousada Triunfo**, Av. Frei Fernando, Triunfo. This is a very simple hotel offering no amenities. 10 rooms.

Food

**** L'Atelier, Rua Bernardo Vieira de Melo 91, Olinda, ☎ 429 3099. An attractive restaurant serving excellent French cuisine. Open daily 7pm-2am.

*** Buraco da Gia, Rua Pe. Batalha 100, Goiana, ☎ 626 0150. This restaurant serves a good variety of delicious seafood. Open daily 11:30am-10pm.

** Fornalha, Av. Beira-Mar 4381, Olinda, ☎ 431 1507. Excellent pizzas. Open daily noon-2am.

** Itapoã, Av. Beira-Mar 998, Olinda, ☎ 429 1713. A simple but very good seafood restaurant. Open daily 11am-midnight.

Useful addresses

Airlines
Transbrasil, Av. Maciel de Freitas 51, Caruaru, ☎ 721 4742.
Varig, Rua 7 de Setembro 50, Caruaru, ☎ 721 2886.
Vasp, Rua da Conceição 50, Caruaru, ☎ 721 1649; Av. Pres Getúlio Vargas 275, Olinda, ☎ 429 0495.

Bus terminal
Av. José Pinheiro dos Santos, Caruaru, ☎ 721 3869.

Car rental
Freebug, José Augusto Moreira 2200, Olinda, ☎ 431 2955.

Emergencies
Pronto Socorro Municipal, Av. Santos Dumont, Olinda, ☎ 429 0277.

João Pessoa, capital of the state of Paraíba

Railway terminal
RFFSA, Praça Dr. Silva Filho, Caruaru, ☎ 721 3114.

Tourist office
Secretaria de Turismo, Rua 13 de Maio 322, Olinda, ☎ 429 0397.

Travel agency
Evatour, Rua Manõel Santos Moreira 133, Olinda, ☎ 431 1225.

▬ *JOÃO PESSOA AND THE STATE OF PARAÍBA*

See map pp. 136-137.
Paraíba is another small state, with a surface area of less than 21,770

sq mi/56,400 sq km. Nevertheless, it is Brazil's largest producer of pineapple, while the mainstay of its economy is sugarcane. Although its economy was damaged by the drought that started in 1979, it is slowly on the mend. Paraíba is most famous for the glorious Tambaú beach.

In 1585, João Tavares founded the village of Filipeia as a base of operations against smugglers. The Dutch were expelled in 1654 and the locals began a drive against the Indians. This led to so much trouble that Portugal was forced to intervene and by 1684 Paraíba was controlled by the Portuguese. Filipeia was renamed João Pessoa after the former governor was assassinated in Recife in 1930.

João Pessoa**

João Pessoa, the capital of Paraíba, is a quiet and peaceful city with some stunning landmarks, such as the **Santo Antônio Convent***** with a superb Rococo façade. The convent complex also contains the 16th-century **São Francisco church,** a magnificent square and a handsome cloisters. Other sights in the town are the **Praça São Pedro Gonçales** and the handcrafts market, the **Mercado Artesanato** (open daily 8am-8pm).

About 3 mi/7 km from town is the famous **Tambaú beach.** This beach is simply enchanting, with its boats, fishermen's cottages, and one of the best hotels in Nordeste. To the north 5 mi/8 km is another beach, **Manaira.** The **Cabo Branco beach** is 9 mi/14 km south of Tambaú and is the easternmost point of land in the western hemisphere. If you enjoy shellfish, make a point of tasting the local crab soup — it's delicious!

Traveling around João Pessoa you will come to several towns worth noting.

Cabedelo** is 14 mi/23 km north of João Pessoa. This is a harbour where you can catch a boat or bus to **Costinha*,** a whaling community (the season lasts from July to November). In Cabedelo, there is also a boat going to **Nossa Senhora da Guia,** an interesting church.

Baia da Traição** is 53 mi/85 km north of João Pessoa. This is a pretty beach where a Portuguese contingent was massacred by Indians in 1501. It was also here that in 1625 the Portuguese scored a famous victory against the Dutch.

Leaving the coast and heading into the interior, you will come across the following towns and villages:

Campina Grande* is 81 mi/130 km west of João Pessoa. This town is famous for its market where you can buy handmade leather goods and pottery. The tourist centre, **Centro Turistico Cristiano Lauritzen,** is located in a former railway station. Several excursions are possible from Campina Grande. You can visit **Itaquatiaras do Inga,** 22 mi/35 km away, to see a menhir 56 ft/17 m tall or travel to **Areia,** 29 mi/46 km away, a colonial village with a **Rosário church** dating from 1866 and the home of the painter, Pedro Americo.

Catole da Rocha* is 280 mi/450 km west of João Pessoa. This little village is known for its handmade batik.

Brejo das Freiras* is 310 mi/500 km west of João Pessoa. This is the Nordeste's most agreeable spa resort with extensive tourist facilities, fountains of mineral water and a natural sulphur pool with a constant temperature of 96° F/35.5° C.

Telephone area code: 083

Accommodation

▲▲▲ **Tambaú,** Av. Alm. Tamandaré 229, João Pessoa, ☎ 226 3660. A fabulous hotel located on Tambaú beach. It contains a restaurant, three bars and three swimming pools, as well as many other services. 175 rooms.

▲ **Estância Termal Brejo das Freiras,** Brejo das Freiras, ☎ 521 2478. This comfortable hotel is situated in a lovely park and contains a restaurant, two bars and two swimming pools. 60 rooms.

▲ **Manaira Praia,** Av. Flavio Ribeiro 115, João Pessoa, ☎ 226 1550. A modest hotel that offers a simple restaurant, a bar and a swimming pool. 50 rooms.

▲ **Ouro Branco,** Rua Cel. João Lourenço Porto 20, Campina Grande, ☎ 321 4304. This comfortable little hotel runs a restaurant and a bar. 57 rooms.

▲ **Rique Palace,** Rua Venâncio Neiva 287, Campina Grande, ☎ 321 4207. A modest hotel with a restaurant and a bar. 40 rooms.

▲ **Sol-Mar,** Av. Rui Carneiro 500, João Pessoa, ☎ 226 1350. This is a comfortable little hotel with a restaurant, a bar and a swimming pool. 38 rooms.

Food

** **Badionaldo,** Rua Vitorino Cardoso, João Pessoa, ☎ 228 1442. This is an attractive restaurant offering a wide selection of very good seafood. Open Mon-Sat 11am-midnight.

** **Cassino da Lagoa,** Prq. Solon de Lucena, João Pessoa, ☎ 221 4275. Very good seafood restaurant. Located in a lovely park. Open daily 11am-midnight.

** **O Cearense,** Rua Sto. Elias 228, João Pessoa, ☎ 222 0267. This restaurant serves very good regional cuisine. Open daily 11am-11pm.

* **Peixada do João,** Rua Corácão de Jesus 147, João Pessoa. Delicious seafood. Reasonably priced. Open daily 11am-midnight.

Useful addresses

Airlines
Varig, Praça João Pessoa 11, João Pessoa, ☎ 221 3055.
Vasp, Av. Camilo de Holanda 530, ☎ João Pessoa, ☎ 222 0715.
Transbrasil, Rua Gen. Osório 177, João Pessoa, ☎ 221 1822.

Airport
Pres. Castro Pinto, ☎ 229 1415.

Bank
Banco do Brasil, Praça 1817, 129, João Pessoa, ☎ 221 9121.

Bus terminal
Rua Francisco Londres, Varadouro, ☎ 221 9611.

Car rental
Belauto, Av. Epitácio Pessoa 4910, Tambaú, ☎ 226 3866.
Interlocadora, Av. Alm. Tamandaré 229, Tambaú, ☎ 226 1371.
Locarauto, Rua Tito Silva 23, Miramar, ☎ 224 3979.

Post office
Praça Pedro Americo João Pessoa.

Taxi
Teletaxi, ☎ 222 3765.

Tourist office
TB Tur, Av. Getúlio Vargas 301, João Pessoa, ☎ 221 7220.

Travel agency
Planetur, Rua das Trincheiras 146, João Pessoa, ☎ 221 5109.

▬ *NATAL AND THE STATE OF RIO GRANDE DO NORTE*

See map pp. 136-137.
Rio Grande do Norte is one of the Nordeste's most beautiful states, with gorgeous beaches, pink coral reefs and salt marshes. Although modest in size — 20,500 sq mi/53,000 sq km — it lies in one of the world's most strategic spots in South America's easternmost corner.

Its predominantly agrarian economy (cotton, coconut and sugarcane among other crops) was hard hit by the drought of 1979, but it is also Brazil's leader in salt and tungsten production. Lobster fishing is another important activity of this area.

Natal**

Natal is the capital of Rio Grande do Norte. Founded on Christmas Day 1599, its name comes from the Portuguese word for *Christmas*. During World War II, the Allies had a base in Natal from which they monitored operations in Africa. Natal now boasts the first Brazilian space research facilities, known as *Barreira do Inferno*, or 'the gate to hell'.

Places to visit in Natal include the **Forte dos Reis Magos**** (Fort of the Wise Men; open Tues-Sun 8am-5pm), so named because its construction began during Epiphany, and the **Museum of Popular Art*** inside the fort. Another interesting museum is the **Camera Cascudo*** (Av. Hermes da Fonseca 1398, ☎ (084) 222 2860; open Tues-Fri 8-11am, 2-4pm), with its displays of native art. There is a tourist centre in what used to be the prison and a municipal market, the **Mercado do Alecrin**. There are shops and peddlars everywhere selling handcrafts made of leather, wood, even coconut. The farthest point of the city lies at the mouth of the Potengi River and is sheltered by reefs. Among Natal's beaches, **Areia Profeta*** is the best for swimming, while **Ponta Negra**, **Cotovela** and **Pirangi** have impressive dunes.

In the outskirts of Natal, there are several interesting places to visit.

Barreira do Inferno Eduardo Gomes** is 12 mi/20 km west of Natal. There is a rocket-launching facility here, which can be visited provided you have a permit (☎ (084) 222 1638).

Lagoa de Bonfim* is 28 mi/45 km west of Natal. This is a beautiful, unspoiled lagoon.

Going farther into the interior of Rio Grande do Norte, you will find the following:

Mossoro* is 174 mi/280 km west of Natal. You can visit salt marshes, which are at some distance from Mossoro — **Macau** is 95 mi/153 km north and **Areia Branca** is 205 mi/330 km north.

Tibau* is 202 mi/325 km west of Natal. This area is known for its beaches, which are covered in multi-coloured sand. The local people sell bottles of it.

There are aquamarine deposits at **Equador**, **Parelhos** and **São Tomé**.

Telephone area code: 084

Accommodation

▲▲ **Luxor**, Av. Rio Branco 634, Natal, ☎ 221 2721. The Luxor is situated in the centre of town and contains a restaurant, a bar and a swimming pool. 170 rooms.

▲▲ **Termas de Mossoro**, Av. Lauro Monte 2001, Mossoro, ☎ 321 1200. A handsome hotel with a restaurant, a bar, several swimming pools and various spa facilities. 61 rooms.

▲▲ **Vila do Mar**, Via Costeira, Natal, ☎ 222 3755. A pretty hotel that stands on the beach and has a fabulous view. It includes a restaurant, two bars and two swimming pools. 154 rooms.

▲ **Barreira Roxa Praia**, Via Costeira, Natal, ☎ 222 1093. This little hotel is very nicely situated and offers a wonderful view, as well as a restaurant, two bars and two swimming pools. 42 rooms.

▲ **Marsol Natal**, Via Costeira 1567, Natal, ☎ 221 2619. An attractive hotel offering a wonderful view, a restaurant, two bars and two swimming pools. 60 rooms.

▲ **Natal Mar**, Via Costeira 8101, Natal, ☎ 236 2121. This hotel is in a fabulous location, offering a splendid view as well as a restaurant, a bar and a swimming pool. 150 rooms.

▲ **Pousada do Sol**, BR-101, Natal, ☎ 272 2211. Located in a pleasant park and including a restaurant, a bar and a swimming pool. 44 rooms.

▲ **Reis Magos**, Av. Pres. Café Filho 822, Natal, ☎ 222 2055. A modest restaurant, three bars and a swimming pool are offered by this comfortable little hotel.

▲ **Sambura**, Rua Prof. Zuza 263, Natal, ☎ 221 0611. This modest hotel is located in the centre of town and contains a restaurant and a bar. 72 rooms.

Food

** **Carne Assada do Lira**, Rua Miramar 165, Natal, ☎ 221 3389.

A little restaurant serving very good regional cuisine. Open daily 11am-11pm.

** **Mil e Uma Noites**, Centro de Convencões, , Via Costeira, Natal, ☎ 236 2011. Very good Arab cuisine, a fine view and live music are found here. Open daily noon-3pm, 7pm-midnight.

* **O Crustaceo**, Rua Apodi 414 A, Natal, ☎ 223 3810. This modest restaurant serves a good variety of seafood. Open daily 11:30-2am.

Useful addresses

Airlines
Transbrasil, Av. Deodoro 363, Natal, ☎ 221 1805.
Varig, Av. João Pessoa 308, Natal, ☎ 221 1537.
Vasp, Av. João Pessoa 220, Natal, ☎ 222 2290.

Airport
Augusto Severo, Natal, ☎ 272 2811.

Banks
Banco do Brasil, Av. Rio Branco 510, Natal.
Banco Brasiliero de Descontos, Av. Rio Branco 692, Natal.

Bus terminal
Rua Cap. Gouveia 1237, Natal, ☎ 231 1170.

Car rental
Dudu, Av. Rio Branco 420, Natal, ☎ 222 4144.
Interlocadora, at airport, ☎ 222 7717.

Post office
Correiro Central, Av. Engenheiro Hidelbrando de Gois 221, Natal.

Tourist office
Centro de Turismo, Av. Deodoro 249, Natal, ☎ 221 1451.

Travel agencies
Nataltur, Av. Deodoro 424, Natal, ☎ 222 5401.
Solis, Av. Deodoro 755, Natal, ☎ 221 1150.

FORTALEZA AND THE STATE OF CEARÁ

See map pp. 136-137.

Ceará covers an area of 57,150 sq mi/148,000 sq km. This region is said to have been explored by the Portuguese as early as the 16th century. It was fought over by the Portuguese and the Dutch until the Portuguese took the Dutch fort of Nossa Senhora de Assunção in about 1660 and settled in Ceará for good. In 1799, Ceará split off from Pernambuco, and in the mid-19th century, the region really began to develop when its harbour facilities were improved. Ceará was the first Brazilian state to abolish slavery. Like the other states of Nordeste, Ceará's agrarian economy (cotton, sweet corn and sugarcane) was severely hit by the drought of 1979.

Fortaleza**

Fortaleza is the third largest city in Nordeste. It was the birthplace of José de Alençar, a 19th-century writer who developed the historical novel as a literary genre. The name 'Fortaleza' comes from the Portuguese word for fortress and refers to Nossa Senhora de Asunção, the fortress taken from the Dutch in the mid-17th century, around which the city originally grew.

Fortaleza has the most active harbour along Brazil's northern coast. Its main focus is on lobster fishing and canning.

The city is in the midst of a commercial boom, and you will be amazed at how well ordered it is. The seaside districts are the most attractive.

Iracema beach is crowded; **Volta de Jurema** and **Mucuripe** beaches are cluttered with boats, and **Futuro** beach has lovely dunes, with samba nightclubs that are the favourite haunt of the younger crowd. There is a lively trade in handcrafts here, especially at the **municipal market** (open Sun-Sat 8am-6pm) and the **Centro do Turismo do Ceará** (open Mon-Sat 8am-6pm, Sun 8am-noon). This last is also known as the **Casa de Cultura** and is located in a former prison (which is, however, quite picturesque). These handcrafts include handmade lace and bottles filled with multi-coloured sand.

Other sights include the **Ceará Historical Museum** (Av. Br. de Studart 410, ☎ (085) 224 4688; open Tues-Sun 8am-5pm), the **José de Alençar theatre** (open Mon-Fri 8-11am, 2-6pm) and, of course, the fort of **Nossa Senhora de Asunção**. You can also visit the **home of José de Alençar** at **Messajana**, 8.5 mi/14 km away.

Heading south-east along the coast from Fortaleza, you will come across several interesting towns.

Aquiraz★★ is 19 mi/31 km from Fortaleza. Once the capital of the state, this tiny town has many reminders of its colonial past. You can visit the **Sacro São José do Ribamar Museu**, the **São José do Ribamar church** and the **Mercado da Carne** (meat market).

Prainha★ is a small fishing village 3 mi/5 km from Aquiraz that is renowned for its handmade lace.

Cascavel★ is 38 mi/61 km from Fortaleza. This town is known for its handcrafts, particularly lace and pottery. There are also lovely beaches and strange multi-coloured rock formations here.

Beberibe is 50 mi/80 km from Fortaleza. Its name means 'where the sugarcane grows' and this is what you will see here.

Aracati★★★ is 90 mi/145 km from Fortaleza. A tiny colonial town on the banks of the Jaguribe River, it is a thriving centre for handcrafts, including lace and coloured sand. Sights include the **Jaguaribano Museum** (Av. Col. Alexanzito 743; open Tues-Sat 7:30-11:30am, 1:30-5:30pm, Sun 8am-noon) in the Casa do Barão de Aracati, the **Nossa Senhora do Rosário church** and various colonial buildings in the town centre such as the **Casario Colonial**.

Heading inland are the following places of interest.

La Serra de Baturité★★ is a small mountain range that covers more than 500 sq mi/1300 sq km of Ceará. It is all around you as you visit the places already mentioned and you cross it by train on the *Trem Turistico* (tourist train) that leaves from Fortaleza every Sunday (for reservations, telephone Bec Turistico, see 'Useful addresses' p. 182).

Maranguape★ is 25 mi/40 km south-west of Fortaleza. This is a pleasant little town. Close by are waterfalls that form little pools in the rocks. You can also visit a brandy distillery at Ipioca, 4 mi/6 km away.

Baturité★ is 65 mi/105 km south-west of Fortaleza. This was once the capital of the Serra de Baturité; the range's highest peak is at **Guaramiranga**, 12 mi/19 km from here. The main square of the town is delightful. Make sure to see the **Nossa Senhora da Palma church**, dating from 1764, the **Palácio Entre-Rios** and the **Pelourinho**, the public square where slaves were punished by whipping.

Caninde★ is 81 mi/131 km south-west of Fortaleza. This city is the site of pilgrimages and feasting during the Feast of Saint Francis (Sept 2-Oct 4). Sights include the **São Francisco basilica**, the **Casa dos Milagres** (house of miracles) and the street where religious processions are held, the **Passo da Via Sacra**.

Quixadá★ is 106 mi/170 km south-west of Fortaleza. This small town lies on a plateau covered with cotton plants. From here you can visit the **Acude do Cedroa**, a dam built in 1880. You can swim and fish, in the lake behind the dam.

Parque Nacional de Ubajara★★ is located in Ubajara, 217 mi/350 km south-west of Fortaleza. It lies at an altitude of 2788 ft/850 m. This park, with its forest and celebrated grotto (containing limestone formations, stalactites and an underground lake), is located in the Serra da Ibiapaba, one of Ceará's greenest areas. You can visit the grotto and take a tour of its nine caverns.

Ipu★ is 50 mi/80 km west of Fortaleza. This is the site of the **Bicu do Ipu** (328 ft/100 m waterfalls). About 15 mi/25 km away is the huge **Araras lock**, which irrigates some 62,000 acres/25,000 hectares.

Sobral★ is 15 mi/24 km west of Fortaleza. This town has some interesting colonial buildings and the **Museu Dom José** (open Tues-Sat 1-5pm, Sun 8am-noon).

Tianguá★ is 205 mi/330 km south of Fortaleza. This former Indian settlement (its name means 'where water is always present') is an entrance point to the park.

Juazeiro do Norte★★ is 329 mi/530 km south of Fortaleza. This town is a religious shrine to Padre Cicero, who is buried here and who is believed to have been responsible for several miracles earlier in this century. On March 24 and November 1-2, pilgrims flock here to visit his grave. The **Logradouro do Horto** has 14 scenes from the sacred way. There is a **statue** of Padre Cicero that is 89 ft/27 m high. The **Capuchinho basilica** and the **church of Perpetuo Socorro** containing the grave of Padre Cicero are also worth visiting.

Crato★ is 338 mi/545 km south of Fortaleza. This is a little colonial town famous for the *vaqueiros* (cowboys) who ride in every Monday dressed in leather from head to toe. There is also a museum, the **José e Figueiredo Filho** (Rua Sen. Pompeu 502; open Tues-Sat 8-11am, 1-5pm), that contains religious objects and regional handcrafts.

Jericoaquara★★ is a large nature reserve at the northern tip of the state. It has lovely beaches, dunes and lagoons. You can reach it by boat from the town of **Camocim**★.

Telephone area code: 085

Accommodation

▲▲▲ **Esplanada Praia**, Av. Pres. Kennedy 2000, Fortaleza, ☎ 244 8555. This attractive hotel has a lovely view, as well as a restaurant, two bars and a swimming pool. 244 rooms.

▲▲▲ **Imperial Othon Palace** Av. Pres. Kennedy 2500, Fortaleza, ☎ 224 7777. A lovely hotel offering a wonderful view, a restaurant, three bars and two swimming pools. 264 rooms.

▲▲ **Novotel Magna Fortaleza**, Av. Pres. Kennedy 2380, Fortaleza, ☎ 244 9122. This hotel has a wonderful view, a restaurant, a bar, and a swimming pool. 150 rooms.

▲▲ **Praiano Palace**, Av. Pres. Kennedy 2800, Fortaleza, ☎ 244 9333. This attractive hotel has a lovely view, a restaurant, two bars and two swimming pools. 189 rooms.

▲ **Beira Mar**, Praia de Majorlândia, Arcati, ☎ 134. A very small and modest hotel. 11 rooms.

▲ **Municipal**, Praça Sen. Figueira, Sobral, ☎ 611 2454. This simple little hotel has a restaurant and a bar. 42 rooms.

▲ **Palace**, Rua Alm. Alexandrino 1000, Crato, ☎ 521 1200. A modest little hotel where only half of the rooms offer baths. There is a simple restaurant. 29 rooms.

▲ **Panorama**, Rua Sto. Agostinho 58, Juazeiro do Norte, ☎ 511 2666. This charming hotel has a restaurant, a bar and a swimming pool. 75 rooms.

▲ **Pousada da Neblina**, Estrada do Teleférico, Ubajara, ☎ 634 1270. A simple little hotel with a restaurant, a bar and a swimming pool. 42 rooms.

▲ **San Pedro**, Rua Castro e Silva 81, Fortaleza, ☎ 211 9911. This

The jangadeiros, *fishermen in the Nordeste, travel in their boats, which are little more than open rafts.*

modest hotel in the town centre offers a restaurant and a bar. 65 rooms.

▲ **Savanah**, Praça do Ferreira, Fortaleza, ☎ 211 9299. A comfortable hotel in the centre of town with a restaurant and a bar. 136 rooms.

▲ **Serra Grande**, BR-222, Tianguá, ☎ 621 1301. A modest hotel with a restaurant, a bar and a swimming pool. 111 rooms.

▲ **Sol**, Rua Br. do Rio Branco 829, Fortaleza, ☎ 211 9166. Situated in the town centre, this hotel has a restaurant, a bar and two swimming pools. 68 rooms.

Food

** **Sandra's**, Av. Eng Luis Vieira 555, Fortaleza, ☎ 234 0503. A lively restaurant offering an excellent view and seafood. Open daily 11-1am.

** **Trapiche**, Av. Pres. Kennedy 3956, Fortaleza, ☎ 244 4400. This charming restaurant serves a great variety of seafood. Open daily 11-2am.

* **Cirandinha**, Av. Aquidaba 789, Fortaleza, ☎ 226 9245. A lively *churrascaria*. Open daily 11am-11pm.

* **O Osmar**, Rua São João 147, Fortaleza, ☎ 234 4712. This is an attractive restaurant that serves a large assortment of seafood. Open daily 11am-3pm, 6:30pm-midnight.

* **Sorriento**, Av. Pres. Kennedy 3080, Fortaleza, ☎ 224 3789. Simple but delicious Italian food. Open daily 11-2am.

Jangadas

All along the north-east coast from Bahia to Maranhaò you will see *jangadas*, strangely shaped vessels that skim through the water. Originally used by the Indians and made simply of logs, by colonial days they had gained a mast, a triangular sail and a sternpost. Today, they are constructed of balsa wood, which is even lighter than cork, hence the swiftness with which they travel. Because balsa wood rots easily, it is starting to be replaced with fibreglass.

The *jangadeiros*, the men who own these vessels, are famous throughout Brazil for their toughness and bravery. In colonial times they helped slaves escape to Ceará, a state where slavery was abolished long before the national law abolishing it in 1888 was passed.

Today, the *jangadeiros* fish for lobster along the coast but, unlike in olden days, rarely go out to sea. Sadly, the conditions under which they now work are so harsh that they are forced to rent their crafts for tourist excursions.

Useful addresses

Airlines
Transbrasil, Rua Br. do Branco 1251, Fortaleza, ☎ 231 3500.
Varig, Rua Maj. Facundo 631, Fortaleza, ☎ 226 3654.
Vasp, Rua Br. do Rio Branco 959, Fortaleza, ☎ 244 6222.

Airport
Pinto Martins, Fortaleza, ☎ 247 1711.

Bank
Banco do Brasil, Av. Duque de Caxias, Fortaleza, ☎ 231 3444.

Bus terminal
Rua Oswaldo Studart, Fortaleza, ☎ 227 1566.

Car rental
Locatur/Hertz, Av. Br. de Studart 3330, Fortaleza, ☎ 227 4433.
Nobre, Av. Abolição 3850, Fortaleza, ☎ 244 4062.

Consulates
Canada, BR-116, Fortaleza, ☎ 229 1811.
Great Britain, Av. Dr. João Moreira 163, Fortaleza, ☎ 231 6006.

Emergencies
Pronto Socorro, Av. Des. Moreira 2283, Fortaleza, ☎ 244 2144.

Post offices
Av. Mister Hull 5063, Fortaleza.
Praça Capistrano de Abreu, Fortaleza.

Railway terminal
RFFSA, Praça Castro Carreiro, Fortaleza, ☎ 211 4127.

Taxi
Radiotaxi, ☎ 221 5744.

Tourist office
Rua Sen. Pompeu 350, Fortaleza, ☎ 231 3566.

Travel agencies
Bec Turistico, Av. Br. de Studart 1071, Fortaleza, ☎ 244 6982.
Lazartur, Rua Floriano Peixoto 137, Fortaleza, ☎ 226 5577.
Mundialtur, Rua Gonçalo Soto 100, Fortaleza, ☎ 227 6629.

▬▬ TERESINA AND THE STATE OF PIAUÍ

See map pp. 136-137.

Piauí and its neighbouring state, Maranhão, form a transitional area between the Amazon basin and the arid zones of Nordeste. Piauí is one of Brazil's largest states but one of its poorest, owing to its hot, dry climate.

For a long time, the Parnaíba River was the only route to the interior of the state, which is why so many of the principal cities lie close to the river. Cattle-breeding occupies approximately 60 % of the state's working population. The region's principal agricultural activities are the cultivation of babaçu and carnauba palms, which yield valuable commercial products. Recently, Piauí farmers have increased the cultivation of such staple crops as rice, beans and sweet corn. During the drought of 1979, Piauí lost almost 75 % of its production.

Teresina*

Teresina is the capital of Piauí. Founded in 1852, it is the only inland capital in the Nordeste region. It lies at the confluence of the Parnaíba and Poti rivers, on the right bank of the Parnaíba, more than 185 mi/300 km from the coast.

Interesting sights in Teresina include the **Mercado Central** (central market; open daily 8am-6pm), the **Karnak Palace,** the seat of government, the **Museu Piauí** (Praça Mal. Deodoro, ☎ (086) 22 6027; open Tues-Fri 8am-5pm, Sat and Sun 8-10:30am, 3-5:30pm) and the modern **Nossa Senhora de Lourdes,** which was constructed in 1961. This church has carved wooden panelling by Mestre Dezinho and a painting, *Stations of the Cross,* by Afranio Branco.

Outside Teresina, the banks of the Parnaíba River offer many pleasant beaches and places to fish. You can take a boat to the village of **União,** 37 mi/60 km north of town, or to **Timon*** in Maranhão state, on your way to **Roncador park*.** There are equally good beaches along the Poti River, some 6 mi/10 km away.

Farther into the interior of Piauí, you will come across the following places:

Piripiri* is 109 mi/175 km north-east of Teresina and **Piracuruca*** 130 mi/210 km north-east of Teresina. These cities make good bases for visiting the **Parque Nacional das Sete Cidades***** (Seven Cities National Park). Trains, buses, rental cars, taxis, guides and information are all available here. The park is 12.5 mi/20 km from Piripiri and 16 mi/26 km from Piracuruca. The park is enormous, covering an area of 2970 sq mi/7700 sq km. It contains seven groups of eroded rocks that look like ancient ruins and cover an area of around 8 sq mi/20 sq km. Some of these gigantic rock formations are very beautiful. The park also offers accommodation and, because of its large size, it is best to spend a night. While in the area, try to visit the **Açude Calderão waterfalls,** 7 mi/11 km from Piripiri.

Parnaíba** is 230 mi/370 km south of Teresina. This is a charming river port, 18 mi/29 km from the mouth of the Parnaíba River. Alongside the quays, there are often large ships from London, Lisbon or New York. The area has some nice beaches, including **Pedra do Sol, Atalaia** and **Coqueiro.** The writer Humberto de Campos used to live here in the Casa Grande.

Picos* is 205 mi/330 km south of Teresina. This small city lies at the crossroads between Salvador, Recife, Natal and Belem. It is the site for major regional fairs.

Bão Esperança* is an impressive dam that lies 217 mi/350 km south of Teresina.

São Raimundo Nonato*, 342 mi/550 km south of Teresina, is an Indian cemetery with a museum that displays bones over 3000 years old.

Telephone area code: 086

Accommodation

▲▲▲ **Luxor do Piauí,** Praça Mal. Deodoro 310, Teresina, ☎ 222 4911. This comfortable hotel is in the town centre and contains a restaurant, two bars and a swimming pool. 85 rooms.

▲ **Abrigo do I.B.D.F.,** Parque Nacional de Sete Cidades, Piripiri, ☎ 232 1142. A simple hotel in the national park, with a modest restaurant, a bar and two swimming pools. 121 rooms.

▲ **Atalaia Panorama,** Av. Brasil, Picos, ☎ 422 1826. A small hotel offering a modest restaurant and a swimming pool. 25 rooms.

▲ **Fazenda Sete Cidades,** Parque Nacional de Sete Cidades, Piripiri, ☎ 261 3642. Attractively situated, this hotel includes a restaurant, a bar and two swimming pools. 35 rooms.

▲ **Sambaiba,** Rua Gabriel Ferreira, Teresina, ☎ 222 6711. This little hotel is located in the centre of town and includes a restaurant and a bar. 38 rooms.

Food

** **Chez Matrinchan,** Av. N.S. de Fátima 671, Teresina, ☎ 232 6529. This bustling restaurant serves very good French cuisine. Open daily 11am-midnight.

* **Camarão do Elias,** Av. Pedro Almeida 457, Teresina, ☎ 232 5025. A variety of excellent seafood. Open Mon-Sat 5pm-2am.
* **Rio Poty,** Av. Mal. Castelo Branco 616, Teresina, ☎ 222 1954. This is a lively *churrascaria*. Open daily 11-2am.

Useful addresses

Airlines
Varig, Rua Des. Freitas 1177, Teresina, ☎ 223 4427.
Vasp, Av. Frei Serafim 1826, Teresina, ☎ 223 3222.

Bank
Banco do Brasil, Rua Alvaro Mendes 1313, Teresina.

Bus terminal
BR-343, Teresina, ☎ 222 9901.

Car rental
Belauto, ☎ 225 1534.
Localiza, ☎ 225 1333.
Unidas, ☎ 225 2904.

Emergencies
Getúlio Vargas, Av. Frei Serafim 2352, Teresina, ☎ 222 5553 (pronto socorro).

Post office
Av. Antonio Freire 1471, Teresina.

Taxi
Teletaxi, ☎ 222 2747.

■ SÃO LUÍS AND THE STATE OF MARANHÃO

See map pp. 136-137.

The state of Maranhão extends over 127,000 sq mi/329,000 sq km. It is a very humid place, not unlike the Amazon basin.

Maranhão was first colonized by the French, at a time when Portugal was ruled by Spain (1578-1640). By 1615, the French had been expelled by the Portuguese with a bit of help from the Tupinamba Indians. From 1640-1644 the area was briefly settled by the Dutch, and from 1830-1840, the Portuguese were engaged in war against the advocates of independence.

In colonial days, Maranhão's economy was based on sugarcane. Today, rice and corn are grown and it is Brazil's largest producer of babaçu from which vegetable oil is extracted. The local economy has been stimulated by the development of harbour facilities at São Luís and iron and aluminium industries at Itaqui.

São Luís**

São Luís is the capital of Maranhão. It lies on an island, was founded by the French in 1612, and was named after Louis XIII.

Since the end of the boom in sugarcane, the city's economy has been stagnant, but with the creation of Ponta Madeira harbour, it seems to be stirring again. The harbour was inaugurated in 1986 when the railroad from Carajas to São Luís was completed and one of its puposes is to carry the iron ore between the Serra dos Carajas and Para.

São Luís retains its colonial atmosphere, with winding streets and old buildings, many along the tiny Avenida Dom Pedro II. Other streets worth seeing are Rua do Giz, Rua Formosa and Rua Portugal. Praça Gonçalves Dias, Praça do Desterro and Praça São Lisboa are lovely. Many handsome landmarks dot the areas.

Palácio dos Leões* (Av. Dom Pedro II, ☎ (098) 222 0355; open Mon,

Wed and Fri 3-6pm) was built in 1776 by the French. This is the seat of the state government.

Palácio Arquiepiscopal** is also interesting, as are the **Teatro Arthur Azevedo***, the **Fonte de Ribeirão*** and the **Prefeitura Municipal***.

Several churches merit a visit, including the 17th-century **Desterro**, **Santo Antônio*** and, especially, the **Catedral da Sé****, dating from 1763 with a marvelous Baroque interior.

Museu Historico Maranhão** (Rua do Sol 302, ☎ (098) 2214537; open Tues-Fri 12:45-6pm, Sat and Sun 3-6pm) is most interesting, with displays of items from colonial days.

There are beautiful beaches just minutes away. They include **Calhau**, **Ponta d'Areia** with its ruined **São Antônio fortress** and **Olho d'Agua**.

Outside São Luís there are several places worth visiting.

Alcântara*** is a very beautiful, historical city that sits opposite São Luís. It was inhabited by Tapui and Tupinamba Indians before the arrival of the Portuguese in 1621. Following the sugarcane boom, Alcântara flourished as the residential city of rich landowners, in contrast to São Luís, which remained a commercial centre. During the 19th century, cotton production contributed to the continuing development of São Luís, while Alcântara's prosperity declined. The town slid into decay with the abolition of slavery in 1888 and has never revived.

There are, however, several sights worth visiting here. On Praça Gomes de Castro there are the ruins of the 17th-century **São Matias church***, the **Pelourinho**** and the **Cadeia Publica****, which now serves as an administration building. The church of **Nossa Senhora do Carmo***, with its Baroque altar, the **Mercés chapel** and the **Museu Alcântara**** (open daily 9am-2pm) are also of interest.

São José de Ribamar* is 20 mi/32 km east of São Luís and has lovely beaches.

Imperatriz* is 397 mi/640 km south of São Luís. This is a good place to stop on your way to Brasília — it is only about 375 mi/600 km south of Belém. You can take excursions by boat from here on the Tocantins River.

Telephone area code: 098

Accommodation

▲▲▲▲ **São Luís Quatro Rodas**, Praia do Calhau, São Luís, ☎ 2270244. This is a fabulous hotel with a splendid view, as well as restaurant, two bars, a swimming pool and various sports facilities 112 rooms.

▲▲▲ **Vila Rica**, Praça Dom Pedro II 299, São Luís, ☎ 2224455. This attractive hotel provides a restaurant, two bars and two swimming pools. 213 rooms.

▲▲ **São Franciso**, Rua Dr. Luís Serson 77, São Luís, ☎ 2271155. Attractively situated and with a lovely view, this hotel has a restaurant, a bar and three swimming pools. 90 rooms.

▲ **Posseidon**, Rua Paraíba 740, Imperatriz, ☎ 7214466. This comfortable hotel has a swimming pool. 120 rooms.

Food

* **Base do Germano**, Av. Wenceslau Bras, São Luís, ☎ 2223276. This attractive restaurant serves good regional cuisine. Open daily 11am-4pm, 6pm-1am.

* **Mag's**, Rua Rio Branco 437, São Luís, ☎ 2321936. Excellent Brazilian cuisine. Open daily 11am-3pm, 6pm-midnight.

* **Ricardão**, Praia do Araçaji, São Luís. This restaurant offers an outstanding variety of seafood. Open daily 11am-5pm.

* **Solar do Ribeirão**, Rua Isaac Martins 141, São Luís, ☎ 2223068. A pretty little restaurant that serves very good regional cuisine. Open daily 11:30am-3pm, 7-11pm.

Useful addresses

Airlines
Transbrasil, Praça João Lisboa 432, São Luís, ☎ 232 1414.
Varig, Av. Dom Pedro II 268, São Luís, ☎ 221 5066.
Vasp, Rua do Sol 43,São Luís, ☎ 222 4655.

Airport
Tirirical, São Luís, ☎ 225 0044.

Bank
Banco do Brasil, Av. Dom Pedro II 76, São Luís.

Bus terminal
Av. do Franceses, Santo Antônio, ☎ 223 2616.

Car rental
Belauto, Av. dos Franceses 18, Apeadouro, ☎ 223 2471.
Hertz, Praça Dom Pedro II 299, São Luís, ☎ 221 1779.
Localiza, Av. Getúlio Vargas 2414, São Luís, ☎ 221 1104.

Post office
Praça João Lisboa 290.

Taxis
Coopertaxi, ☎ 225 2335.
Rodotaxi, ☎ 223 5904.

Tourist office
Maratur, Rua 14 de Julho 88, São Luís, ☎ 221 1276.

Travel agencies
Martur, Rua do Sol 141, São Luís, ☎ 221 4658.
Turismar, Praça Benedito Leite 6, São Luís, ☎ 232 1075.

BRASÍLIA

Situated in the state of Goiás (but not under its administration), Brasília rises up from a vast plain in the heart of Brazil like some strange city from another world. Designed by Lucio Costa, a disciple of Le Corbusier, the city is laid out in the shape of an airplane or, as some see it, a bow and arrow. Brasília's residential areas fall neatly into two parts: the *Asa Sul* and *Asa Norte* (north and south wings). These consist of large six-storey apartment blocks called *super-quadras*. These quadras are separated by roads lined with shops, and in between lie schools, parks and cinemas. The overall effect is one of wide open spaces and greenery.

The idea of building a capital in the centre of Brazil was not conceived in the 20th century. Ever since the 18th century there had been talk of transferring the seat of power from the coast to the interior of the country — the principal reason at that time was to protect it against attacks from the sea. The idea remained only a dream until 1956 when President Kubitschek came to power. The economy was suffering badly because practically all of Brazil's activities were concentrated around Rio de Janeiro. This hurt the rest of the country, especially many unexploited areas believed to be rich in minerals. Aware of the urgency of the situation, President Kubitschek launched a competition to design a new capital. Lucio Costa won the competition, and Brazil's leading architect, Oscar Niemeyer, was commissioned to design the principal buildings.

Work on the city began in 1957, with President Kubitschek's now-famous pronouncement, 'Brazil will advance 50 years in five years'. This was no empty promise.

From 1957 to its inauguration in 1960, around-the-clock shifts worked on the site. It was certainly a fantastic undertaking, not least because all the building materials, as well as the workers, had to be air-lifted onto the plain since, at that time, there was no other way to reach the area.

Despite Brazil's fascinating architecture, expanses of greenery and abundance of flowers, Brasília has a reputation as an empty, soulless place. Even many of its inhabitants feel little warmth towards it. This is hardly surprising, since Brasília was at first populated by people from Rio — the lively city of beaches, blue sea and Carnival. They were understandably reluctant to exchange all this for a dusty plain and many only did so after considerable pressure from the government.

Lucio Costa

Brasília's avant-garde design is the work of Lucio Costa, heir to the rationalist tenets of Le Corbusier, who held that the specific functions (living, working, etc.) given to a design's different areas must not overlap. Costa designed Brasília with the automobile in mind — thus, distances were no object and landscaping was all. It is for this reason that the first thing to strike a visitor is the city's abundance of greenery and space.

Brasília's layout has been interpreted by some as an airplane, a bird in flight, a bow and arrow. In fact, it is laid out in the form of a cross with two main arteries crossing at the city's centre. The one that runs north-south is called Eixo Rodoviario and is designed for high-speed traffic between the residential sectors. The other is called Eixo Monumental. On one side of it are the districts designed for hotels, municipal buildings, banks, hospitals and so forth. On the other side are the districts for administrative offices, cultural centres, recreational centres and buildings catering to the food trade. At their intersection stands the bus terminal. The residential areas are divided into super-quadros of housing and shopping facilities. At the junction of four super-quadros stand a church and a school.

There are three kinds of road in Brasília: one for pedestrians, one for cars and one for trucks and buses. Because none of them cross each other, getting around Brasília is easy and pleasurable.

Brasília now has more immediate problems. Designed to accommodate 500,000 people, the population already exceeds 1.5 million inhabitants. The temporary housing projects set up on the outskirts of the capital for the labour force that built Brasília have now become permanent suburban towns.

Nevertheless, with the construction of Brasília, Brazil has achieved the near impossible — it has built a thriving capital in an empty wasteland within a few years and has, as a result, brought prosperity to many of its regions. As for those who say the city has no character, its young inhabitants and their children will see to that.

▬ PRACTICAL INFORMATION

See maps p. 189.

Telephone area code: 061

When to go

Brasília sits high on a plateau and tends to have very cold winters. Rainfall is fairly heavy from November to March and the dry season runs from May to September. Nights are cool here all year long.

Access

Plane

Brasília's **International Airport** is located 7.5 mi/12 km from the city centre. It is served by all of the large Brazilian airline companies and offers regular flights to the principal Brazilian cities. ☎ 248 5131.

The distance between Brasília and São Paulo is 630 mi/1015 km and the distance between Brasília and Rio de Janeiro is 755 mi/1215 km. The proximity and the regularity of flights make it possible to fly for a morning's sightseeing to Brasília and return in the afternoon. This is, however, very expensive.

National and international airlines

Aerolineas Argentinas, SHS Hotel Nacional, II, A5, ☎ 224 0461.

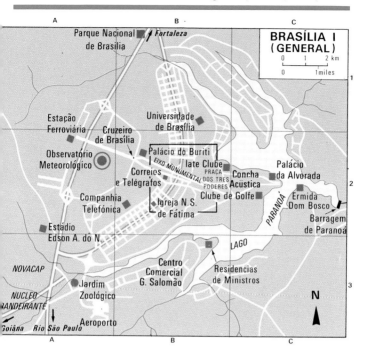

BRASÍLIA I
(GENERAL)

0   1   2 km
0   1 miles

Parque Nacional
de Brasília

Fortaleza

Estação
Ferroviária   Cruzeiro
de Brasília

Universidade
de Brasília

Observatório
Meteorológico

Palácio do Buriti
EIXO MONUMENTAL   Iate Clube
PRAÇA
DOS TRES
PODERES
Correios
e Telégrafos   Concha
Acústica   Palácio
da Alvorada

Companhia
Telefónica   Clube de Golfe   Ermida
Dom Bosco

Igreja N.S.
de Fátima   Barragem
de Paranoá

Estádio
Edson A. do N.   LAGO

NOVACAP   Centro
Comercial
G. Salomão   Residencias
de Ministros

NUCLEO   Jardim
Zoológico

BANDEIRANTE

Goiâna   Rio São Paulo   Aeroporto

N

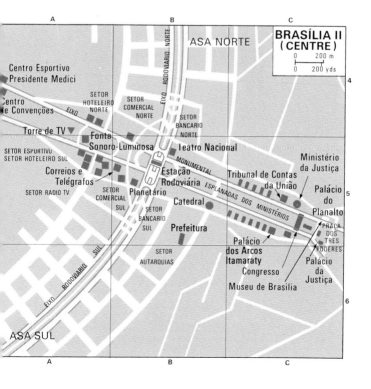

BRASÍLIA II
(CENTRE)

0   200 m
0   200 yds

ASA NORTE

RODOVIARIO NORTE

Centro Esportivo
Presidente Medici

Centro
de Convenções   EIXO   SETOR
HOTELEIRO
NORTE   SETOR
COMERCIAL
NORTE   SETOR
BANCARIO
NORTE

Torre de TV   Fonta
Sonoro-Luminosa   Teatro Nacional

SETOR ESPIRTIVO
SETOR HOTELEIRO SUL   MONUMENTAL   Ministério
da Justiça

Correios e
Telégrafos   Estação
Rodoviária   Tribunal de Contas
da União   Palácio
do
Planalto

SETOR RADIO TV   SETOR
COMERCIAL
SUL   Planetário   ESPLANADAS DOS MINISTÉRIOS

SETOR
BANCARIO
SUL   Catedral

Prefeitura   PRAÇA
DOS
TRES
PODERES

Palácio
dos Arcos
Itamaraty

SETOR
AUTARQUIAS   Palácio
da
Justiça

Congresso

Museu de Brasília

EIXO RODOVIARIO SUL

ASA SUL

Air France, Hotel Nacional, II, A5, ☎ 223 4299.
Swissair, Hotel Nacional, II, A5, ☎ 223 2102.
Tam, Hotel Nacional, II, A5, ☎ 223 5168.
Transbrasil, Comércio Local Norte, Quadra 102, II, B4, ☎ 223 4568.
Varig/Cruzeiro, Comércio Local Sul, Quadra 306, II, A6, ☎ 242 4111.
Vasp, Hotel Nacional, II, A5, ☎ 226 4115.
Votec, Setor Diversões Sul, ☎ 225 9528.

Train
You can travel from São Paulo to Brasília by train via Campinas, but it is very slow. A train leaves Brasília every weekday evening for São Paulo, arriving the next evening.

RFFSA, Eixo Monumental, Parque Ferroviário, Setor Nordeste, II, A4, ☎ 33 7800.

Bus
Several buses a day leave for all of Brazil's main cities. The bus terminal is next to the railway terminal.

Eixo Monumental, Parque Ferroviário, Setor Nordeste, II, A4, ☎ 233 7200.

Accommodation
Brasília has good hotels at every level of comfort and price. They are either in the northern sector or the southern sector and are all near the heart of the city.

Southern sector
▲▲▲ **Carlton**, Setor Hoteleiro Sul, Q 5, bl G, II, A5, ☎ 224 8819. This comfortable hotel has a bar, one restaurant, a swimming pool and a coffee shop. 197 rooms.

▲▲▲ **Nacional**, Setor Hoteleiro Sul, lote 1, II, A5, ☎ 226 8180. This centrally located hotel includes two bars, three restaurants, a swimming pool and several attractive boutiques. 346 rooms.

▲▲ **Hotel das Américas**, Setor Hoteleiro Sul, Q 4, bl D, II, A5, ☎ 223 4490. Located in the hotel sector, this hotel has one bar and one restaurant. 148 rooms.

▲▲ **Hotel das Naçaoes**, Setor Hoteleiro Sul, Q 4, bl I, II, A5, ☎ 225 8050. This medium-size hotel offers a pleasant restaurant and a bar. 129 rooms.

▲▲ **Phenicia**, Setor Hoteleiro Sul, Q 5, bl J, II, A5, ☎ 321 4342. This hotel has a travel agency for tourist information, two bars and a restaurant. 130 rooms.

▲▲ **Saint Paul**, Setor Hoteleiro Sul, Q 2, lote 5, bl H, II, A5, ☎ 321 6688. A good choice for businesspeople, this hotel has two bars, a restaurant and a swimming pool. 274 rooms.

▲▲ **San Marco**, Setor Hoteleiro Sul, Q 5, lote C, II, A5, ☎ 321 8484. A comfortable hotel with two bars, two restaurants and a swimming pool. 256 rooms.

▲ **Alvorada**, Setor Hoteleiro Sul, Q 4, bl 1, II, A5, ☎ 225 3050. Basic comfort, in a hotel with one bar and one restaurant. 116 rooms.

▲ **Continental**, Setor Hoteleiro Sul, Q 3, bl J, II, A2, ☎ 225 7071. This modest but comfortable hotel has one restaurant. 32 rooms.

Northern sector
▲▲ **Aracoara**, Setor Hoteleiro Norte, Q 5, bl C, II, A4 ☎ 321 9222. A comfortable hotel with a bar and restaurant. 132 rooms.

▲▲ **Eron Brasília**, Setor Hoteleiro Norte, Q 5, lote A, II, A4, ☎ 321 1777. This pleasant hotel has a bar, restaurant, coffee shop and several boutiques. 186 rooms.

▲▲ **Garvey Park Hotel**, Setor Hoteleiro Norte, Q 2, bl J, II, A4,

☎ 223 9800. Centrally located, this hotel offers three bars, a restaurant and a swimming pool. 205 rooms.

▲▲ **Torre Palace**, Setor Hoteleiro Norte, Q 5, bl A, II, A4, ☎ 321 5554. This hotel offers two bars, two restaurants and a travel agency. 165 rooms.

▲ **Casablanca**, Setor Hoteleiro Norte, Q 3, lote A, II, A4, ☎ 321 8586. A modest hotel with a bar and restaurant. 58 rooms.

▲ **Diplomat**, Setor Hoteleiro Norte, Q 2, bl L, II, A4, ☎ 225 2010. A small hotel with a bar and restaurant. 44 rooms.

Camping

The main camping site is 2.5 mi/4 km from the city centre near the Asa Norte sports centre. It has 3100 individual campsites. There is another site, the **Agua Mineral Parque**, 4 mi/6 km northwest of the city. Other sites that we recommend are **ABC**, located 12 mi/19 km from Brasília on Route BR 050, and **Bela Vista**, 29 mi/47 km from Brasília on Marilia Road. For further information, ☎ 223 6561.

Entertainment and cultural life

Brasília doesn't offer much in cultural events, although the situation is improving. There are numerous cinemas in the city's recreational centres (*centros de diversões*), three theatres and several art galleries. Nightlife in Brasília is not extraordinary either. There are several nightclubs in the Centro Comercial Gilberto Salomão (L'escalier's, Papillon), I, B3, and the following clubs are also interesting:

Chateau Noir, ☎ 225 7598
Kako, ☎ 248 3222
Tendinha's, ☎ 225 0050

Food

*** **Gaf**, Setor Habitações Individuais Sul, bl c, ☎ 248 1103. This is considered the best French restaurant in Brasília. Open daily noon-4pm, 7pm-2:30am.

** **Le Français**, Comércio Local Sul 404, bl B, lj 27, II, AB6, ☎ 225 4583. A lively French restaurant providing quality food. Open Mon-Sat noon-3pm, 7-11pm.

** **Hoffman Confalonieri**, Comércio Local Norte Q 102, bl A, II, B4, ☎ 224 9051. Traditional Brazilian meals. Open Mon-Sat noon-4pm, 7pm-midnight.

** **Lake's Baby Beef**, Setor Habitações Individuais Sul Q 9, bl E, ☎ 248 3426. This is one of the best restaurants in Brasília, serving the traditional *churrasco* . Open daily noon-3pm, 7pm-midnight.

** **Piantella**, Comércio Local Sul 202, bl 1, II, B6, ☎ 224 9408. This restaurant offers an interesting selection of international cuisine. Open daily noon-4pm, 7pm-2am.

** **Le Vieux Chalet**, Comércio Local Sul 405, bl JA, II, A6, ☎ 243 9311. International cuisine in a simple, pleasant atmosphere. Open daily noon-3pm, 7-11pm.

* **Chamas**, Setor de Indústrias Gráficas Sul 3, bl B, ☎ 225 6071. A good-quality *churrascaria*. Open Mon-Sat noon-1am.

* **Florentino**, Comércio Local Sul 402, bl C, II, B6, ☎ 223 7577. This lively restaurant serves international cuisine. Open daily noon-2am.

* **Intervalo**, Comércio Local Sul 302, bl A, II, A5, ☎ 226 9619. This is a conveniently located restaurant specializing in international cuisine. Open Mon-Sat 11:30am-4pm, 6pm-midnight.

* **La Mamma**, Comércio Local Sul 201, bl C, II, B6, ☎ 226 5416. A simple but consistently good Italian restaurant. Open daily noon-midnight.

Getting around Brasília

The best way to see Brasília is by car. It is so large that trying to see the sights on foot is out of the question. Taxis and buses are in plentiful supply if you don't have a car. If you are only going to be in Brasília a short while, take an organized tour. Most of these leave from the lobby of the Hotel Nacional. For further information, contact any tourist office.

Shopping

Brasília is not a paradise for shoppers — the prices tend to be very high. It boasts eight large shopping centres, including the **Conjunto Naçional** (north of the Rodoviário) and the **Conjunto Venencio**. Make sure to visit the latter — it's the biggest in South America.

Useful addresses

Banks
Banco do Brasil, Setor Bancario Sul, II, B5, ☎ 212 2211.
First National City Bank, Av. W3, Quadra 502, ☎ 225 6710.

Car rental
Hertz, Hotel Eron Brasília, II, A4, ☎ 225 8654.
Le Mans, Av. W2 Sul 502, ☎ 224 7288.
Unidas, Hotel Nacional, II, A5, ☎ 225 5191.

Consulates
Australia, SH15, QI 9, cj. 16 casa 1, ☎ 248 5569.
Canada, SE5, Av. das Nações Q 803, lote 16, ☎ 223 7515.
Great Britain, SE5, Av. das Nações Q 801, cj. K lote 8, ☎ 225 2710.
United States, SE5, Av. das Nações, lote 3, ☎ 223 0120.

Post office
7 Av. W3, Quadra 508, Setor Comercial Sul.

Tourist office
Centro de Convenções Brasília, ☎ 225 5710. The tourist office also has an information desk at the airport.

Travel agencies
Presmic, Hotel Nacional, II, A5, ☎ 225 5515.
Toscano, Hotel Nacional, II, A5, ☎ 225 4288.
Valetur, Hotel Nacional, II, A5, ☎ 224 7166.

▬ GETTING TO KNOW BRASÍLIA

The choice of Oscar Niemeyer as the architect for all of Brasília's official buildings not only guaranteed the unity of the design, but also contributed to the success of the enterprise and to its fame abroad. If Brasília continues to attract so much attention, it is largely due to this unity, which stands as a benchmark for 20th-century architecture.

The novelty of the design lies both in its disregard for the notion that function and technique must dictate form, and in an imaginative use of concrete. A precedent for such innovative thinking had already been set in Le Corbusier's spectacular design for the Ronchamp chapel. As Niemeyer wrote, 'architecture is not merely a question of engineering and technique; it also draws on imagination and the poetic impulse'. What Niemeyer did in Brasília was to use size as a formula for dignity and harmony, and to create a unified complex free of monotony. The repeated use of colonnades, rendered all the more effective by their reflection in water, makes for a formal ensemble in the Greek tradition.

Diversity was achieved by varying the shapes of the columns: 'I created distances between columns and façades, using both curves and straight lines, so that people walking between them would be constantly surprised by the changes in perspective'. Differences in proportion,

The Ministry of Justice in Brasília.

volume, level and perspective are constantly brought into play and result in a harmony that does justice to Niemeyer's grasp of classical forms and to his grandiose vision of the future.

The best way to take a comprehensive look at the city is to drive down the Eixo Monumental from the television tower to the congressional complex. Two or three days will suffice to see Brasília and its surroundings. It is best to visit during the week, because many buildings close on weekends. Organized tours of the city almost all follow the same itinerary and include the following sights.

Fatima church* (Entrequadra Sul 307, ☎ 242 0149; open Mon-Sat 8am-noon, 2-6pm, Sun 8am-noon, 3-8pm) is also known as Igrejinha. It was the first church to have been built in Brasília and is constructed in the shape of a nun's headdress.

Cathedral*** (Eixo Monumental, II, B5, ☎ 224 4073; open Tues-Sun 8:30-11:30am, 2:30-6pm) is a circular building, shaped to resemble a crown of thorns. It is one of Oscar Niemeyer's major achievements. On the square in front of it stand statues of Saint Luke, Saint Mark, Saint Matthew and Saint John by Alfredo Ceschiatti. In the interior three angels made from aluminium by the same artist hang from the ceiling.

Esplanado dos Ministerios** II, C5, is the name given to the stretch of the Eixo Monumental, where all the ministries and the Congresso stand, II, BC5. According to the original design they were all to be identical, but the Ministry of Foreign Affairs and the Ministry of Justice are particularly noteworthy.

● **Ministry of Foreign Affairs***** is also known as the Palácio dos Arcos. It stands surrounded by water and is considered to be one of Brasília's most beautiful buildings. It contains sculpture by Bruno Giorgi and a garden by Burle-Marx.

● **Ministry of Justice**** sits on the other side of a green expanse from the Ministry of Foreign Affairs. Gargoyles spout water into a basin from various levels among the colonnades.

● **Congresso***** is the symbol of the nation. It houses the Chamber of Deputies and the Senate, which are symbolized by twin cupolas. It also contains administrative offices in twin buildings 28 floors high in the form of the letter *H*.

Praça dos Três Poderes*** II, C5, the square of three powers, is Brasília's most famous square. It lies behind the Congresso and between the Palace of Justice and the Planalto Palace. Brunio Giorgi's celebrated statue called *Guerreiros* (Warriors) stands in the square, as does a gigantic flagpole flying an enormous flag.
● **Palace of Justice**** is a handsome building surrounded by water. It was landscaped by Burle-Marx.
● **Historical Museum**** (open daily 9am-5pm) houses all there is to know about the city's construction. On its façade there is sculpted a bronze head of President Kubitschek.
● **Monument to Juscelino Kubitschek***** (open daily 8am-6pm) honours this famous Brazilian figure.
● **Planalto Palace***** is the executive mansion. You can see the changing of the guard here Monday to Friday at 7:40am and 5:40pm.

Embassy district** II, B6, is interesting because of the variety of architectural styles that have been used here. Every country commissioned its own architect.

Alvorada Palace***, on the shores of Lake Paranoá, I, C2, is the presidential residence. It was built in 1958 before the city's layout had been decided on, which explains why it doesn't stand on the Eixo Monumental.

Television tower** (Eixo Monumental, II, A4) is of no particular architectural interest but remains a favourite with tourists because it offers a splendid view of the city from its platform. It also contains a restaurant.

Santuário Dom Bosco*** (Av. W-3 Sul Q702, II, A5, ☎ 223 6542; open daily 8am-6:30pm) is a lovely church with dark-blue stained-glass windows, a crystal chandelier and an enormous wooden crucifix.

Teatro Nacional** (Eixo Monumental, II, B6, ☎ 223 5620) is shaped like a pyramid and has two halls.

Paranoá Lake** I, BC1-3, is a beautiful artificial lake that was created for aesthetic purposes and also to humidify the air. Boat excursions available.

Cruzeiro de Brasília** I, B2, translates as 'the cross of Brasília'. The first mass was held here on May 3, 1957.

Jardim Zoo-Botânico* (Av. das Nações, I, A3, ☎ 242 9535; open Mon-Sun 9am-5pm) is an interesting zoo and botanical garden with areas for shows of trained animals.

Ermida Dom Bosco* I, C2, is a tiny chapel on the banks of Lake Paranoá dedicated to Dom Bosco, the city's patron saint. From here there are wonderful views of the city.

Centro Comercial Gilberto Salomão* I, B3, boasts many tourist attractions, including cinemas, nightclubs, restaurants and bars.

Parque Nacional** (I, B1, ☎ 233 4055; open daily 8:30am-5pm) is a huge area, measuring 81,510 acres/33,000 hectares. Part of it can be visited, part of it is for ecological research and part of it is a wildlife reserve. The country's three river basins (Amazon, Paraná and São Francisco) can be clearly distinguished here. The entrance is on the road to Formosa, about 5.5 mi/9 km from the city centre.

Parque Rogério Pitho Farias** measures 1037 acres/420 hectares and is full of recreational and sports facilities.

▬ *ENVIRONS OF BRASÍLIA*

If you have a little extra time during your visit to Brasília, you can go and have a look at some of its satellite communities or a colonial town in the interior.

Satellite communities

Built to house the labourers employed in the construction of the new capital, these towns were originally supposed to disappear after the work was finished. Not only have they not disappeared, they have actually spread and today have satellite communities of their own.

● **Taguatinga** is 15.5 mi/25 km south of Brasília. It was built in 1958 and consists of collective housing and many temples celebrating spiritualism. The working-class town of **Ceilândia** was constructed nearby as a satellite of Taguatinga to prevent the spread of shantytowns there.

● **Sobradinho** is 12.5 mi/20 km north of Brasília. This appealing residential town was created in 1960. It is the most urban of all the satellite communities.

● **Gama** is 23.5 mi/38 km from Brasília. Its streets were laid out in a hexagonal pattern. On your way into town you can see the first presidential mansion, **Catetinho★**. It is built of wood and set in a splendid garden.

● **Nucleo Bandeirantes** was created in 1956. It is a bedroom community with wooden houses.

● **Guará** was built in 1969. By 1979 its population had grown to 40,000.

Environs

Planaltina★ is 25 mi/40 km north of Brasília. A small town founded in 1859, it was here that the committees met to plan the new capital. The **Pedra Fundamental★** marks Brazil's exact geographical centre. The stone was laid during a historical ceremony that took place on September 7, 1922 for the centennial of Brazilian independence. A plaque describes it as the first stone laid for the country's future capital.

Luziânia★ is 37 mi/60 km south of Brasília. It is a lovely little colonial town with a charming church, **Rosário,** an adobe structure that was built by slaves.

Cristalina★ is 62 mi/100 km south of Brasília. This town is known for its jewelry made from semi-precious stones.

Formosa★ is 47 mi/80 km north of Brasília. A small rural town, it contains a lake, **Freia,** and a waterfall, **Salto de Itiquira.** There is also a camping site nearby.

Lagoa Bonita is 23.5 mi/38 km north of Brasília. This is a lovely natural lake.

Saia Velha waterfall★ lies 22 mi/35 km south of Brasília. One of Brazil's first hydro-electric plants is located here.

▬▬ *GOIÁS STATE*

See map p. 197.

The state of Goiás sits on a high plateau that sprawls across the centre of Brazil. It is one of the country's most rapidly expanding agricultural areas — a considerable achievement, given its slow start. On its northern side it stretches into the Serra do Estrondo, an enormously wide and flat ridge along which runs a road linking Belém to Brasília, Rio de Janeiro and São Paulo. The state of Goiás can be divided into three parts:

● The historic south where the capital, **Goiânia,** lies.

● The **Araguaia valley,** which makes up the western region. This area is still largely unexplored. It lies close to Amazonia and is inhabited by Indians.

● The **Tocantins basin,** which makes up the eastern region.

The adventurer Bartolomeu Bueno da Silva was the first to make an expedition to Goiás. In 1682, spurred on by rumours that the territory was rich in gold, he decided to find it. Coming across Indians covered with sparkling gold ornaments, he tricked them into telling him the source of their treasure.

Word spread quickly, and soon the state of Goiás was consumed by gold fever. This fever quickly stripped the region of all its precious metal. Not long after, the state fell into decline. It only began to recover in the 20th century, particularly with the construction of Brasília, capital of Goiás since 1937. The city lies 126 mi/202 km north-east of Goiânia.

Goiânia** was founded in 1933 and is a spacious, modern-looking town with lots of greenery and plants dotted along its sleek highways.

In some respects, the town was a prototype for the design of Brasília. Goiânia doesn't offer much that will interest the tourist but it is a perfect place to begin visits into the state, especially to Goiás Velho, the former capital.

Goiás Velho*** is 93 mi/150 km north-west of Goiânia. Founded in 1727 on the shores of the Vermelho River by *bandeirantes* and gold-miners, it is still very much a colonial town. Hardly changed since its foundation, it is a charming mix of narrow, twisting streets and uneven pavements. Its single-storey houses with their tiled roofs give a strong sense of what this area was like in Brazil's pioneering days. Several interesting sights are here.

● **Abadia church**** (Rua Sen) dates from 1790 and has handsome woodwork.

● **São Francisco de Paula**** (Praça de Castro), built in 1761, is another impressive church. There is a panoramic view from here.

Other interesting churches include **Boa Morte***, **Carmo*** and **Santa Barbara**, all built in the 18th century.

● **Museum of Boa Morte**** (open Tues-Sat 7:30-11am, 1-5pm, Sun 7:30am-noon) is in the church of the same name. It is dedicated to sacred art and contains sculptures by José Joacquim de Veiga Valle and a collection tracing the history of the search for gold.

● **Museum das Bandeiras**** (open Tues-Sat 7:30-11am, Sun 7:30am-noon) is housed in the former prison. It is concerned with the days of gold fever.

Interesting 18th-century colonial buildings include the **Conde dos Arcos Palace**, the **Chafariz de Calda**, the **Quartel do 20**, the **Mercado** and others clustered in the old colonial centre.

Pirenópolis** is 80 mi/128 km north of Goiânia. Standing on the lovely slopes of the Serra dos Pirineus, this tiny colonial town was founded in 1723 when gold was first discovered. It owes a large part of its fame to the Festa do Divino (45 days after Easter). This festival lasts three days and involves the entire population. Its high point is a cavalcade, *Cavalhadas*, during which armed riders representing Christians and Moors re-enact a medieval battle. The Christians always win. Interesting sights include the **Carmo church**, dating from 1750 and its **museum** of sacred art (open daily 1-5pm), the **Matriz church**, dating from 1728, the **church of Nosso Senhor do Bonfim**, dating from 1750, and the **Fazenda Babilônia**, the town's first building. About 16 mi/26 km away from town is the highest point (4540 ft/1385 m) of the Serra dos Pirineus. There is a place of pilgrimage here, but there are also many other reasons to visit this spot. There are wonderful rock formations, waterfalls and papiro trees.

Caldas Novas** is 121 mi/195 km south-east of Goiânia and is a well-known little spa. It stands at an altitude of 2250 ft/686 m, not far from the border with Minas Gerais, and has a very pleasant climate (66-80° F/-18-27° C). Its hot springs (104° F/40° C) were discovered in 1722 and are claimed to help cure arthritis and neurological problems. There are other springs at **Lagoa de Piratininga** (4 mi/7 km away) and at **Rio Quente** (17 mi/28 km away). The landscape all around here is lush and beautiful.

Down the Araguaia River***

The **Araguaia River**, 1633 mi/2630 km long, runs the entire length of the

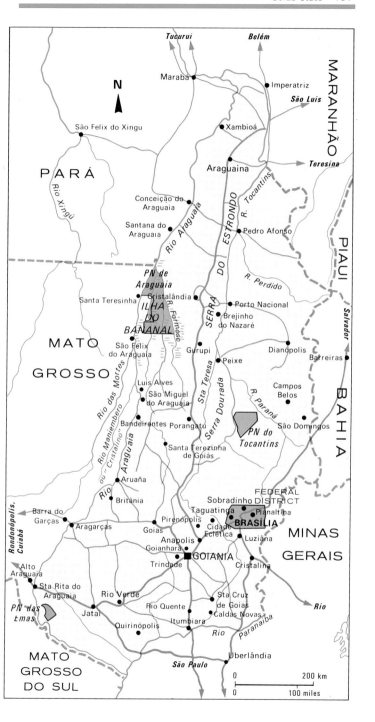

Goiás state.

state of Goiás from its source in the Serra dos Calapos (Parque Nacional das Emas) to the area surrounding the city of Macapá in the state of Pará, where it joins the Tocantins River. Once an inland sea, it is still somewhat salty and is a habitat for sardines. It is navigable for its entire length, but in spite of this, one virgin stretch remains that is relatively well protected. The beauty of the landscape is accentuated when its waters are low. Then the lovely white sand emerges along the river's shores. Many wading birds, leopards and tapirs live on its banks. The average daytime temperature is 77° F/25° C.

The Araguaia River is best known for its abundant fish, such as the *jau* and the *piratininga*, which sometimes weigh as much as 300 lb/150 kg, the *pirarucu*, which are often over 6 ft/2 m long, and the *boto*, a fresh-water dolphin. During the rainy season (October-May), the river's waters turn dark and muddy and flood the whole area. During the tourist season (June-September), the water level drops and the river again becomes clear and smooth. This is also when the birds do their nesting.

Start your journey downstream from Aruana (the starting point of many excursions) and continue to Bananal Island. You will pass though the most rewarding areas of this river valley. Several sights present themselves along the way.

Aruanã** is 197 mi/318 km north-west of Goiânia. It is a small town that is one of the best places from which to enter the Araguaia valley. If you are interested in taking an excursion on the river, there are several available here. There are small hotel-boats that ply the river as far as Santa Terezinha, and there are spots close by that you can reach by boat that offer fishing and camping (*Acampemento Sol do Araguaia*, ☎ (062) 225 3727; *Clube de Pesca do Araguaia*, in Britania).

São Miguel do Araguaia** is 298 mi/480 km north of Goiânia. This town is connected to Goiás by a road called the *estrada do boi*. Here you can run into vast herds of cattle, some of which may number over 4 000 head. These herds cover enormous distances (over 600 mi/1 000 km) on their way to the state of São Paulo. If you want to take a fishing expedition on the Cristalino River, you will have to start from São Miguel, even though it is 30 mi/50 km from the river (for further information, ☎ (011) 457 3277 in São Paulo).

Bananal Island** is the largest river island 7 722 sq mi/20,000 sq km in the world. It is a nature preserve that is now called the **Parque Nacional do Araguaia**. It also serves as an Indian reserve, particularly for the Karaja Indians, known for their method of fishing with bow and arrow and their spectacular feathered headgear. Excursions to the island leave from São Miguel, São Felix and Santa Terezinha.

São Felix do Araguaia is a little village that stands at the confluence of the Araguaia and das Mortes rivers. It can be reached by air or by boat. If you are traveling by car, it can only be reached by traversing Mato Grosso.

Santa Terezinha is 186 mi/300 km north of São Felix. From here, it is possible to travel by hotel-boat on the Tapirape River (for further information, Goiânia, ☎ (062) 261 2323; Brasília, ☎ (061) 248 3746).

Telephone area code: 062

Accommodation

▲▲▲ **Castros' Park**, Av. República do Lobano 1520, Goiânia, ☎ 223 7707. One of the best hotels in Goiânia, offering three bars, two restaurants and two swimming pools. 177 rooms.

▲▲ **Parque das Primaveras**, Rue do Balneário, Caldas Novas, ☎ 453 1355. This particularly attractive hotel is situated in a park. It has a bar, restaurant, two heated swimming pools, and three unheated swimming pools. 18 rooms.

▲▲ **Pousada do Rio Quente**, Route GO507, Caldas Novas, ☎ 421 2244. This charming hotel located in a park has three bars, a restaurant, seven heated swimming pools, and several boutiques. 237 rooms.

▲▲ **Tamburi,** Rua Eça de Queiros 10, Caldas Novas, ☎ 453 1455. An intimate hotel with two bars, a restaurant and four heated swimming pools. 20 rooms.

▲▲ **Vila Boa,** Lorro do Chapeu do Padre, Goiás Velho, ☎ 371 1000. This hotel offers a panoramic view of the old city. It has a bar, a restaurant and two swimming pools. 33 rooms.

▲ **Alegrama,** Rua Moretti Foggia, Goiás Velho, ☎ 371 1360. A modest but acceptable hotel. No restaurant or bar. 56 rooms.

▲ **Augustus,** Praça Antonio Lizita 702, Goiânia, ☎ 224 1022. This pleasant, centrally located hotel has a bar and a restaurant. 117 rooms.

▲ **Caldas Termas Club,** Av. Orcalino Santos 219, Caldas Novas, ☎ 453 1515. This is a pleasant hotel in the hot spring area, with three bars, a restaurant and five heated swimming pools. 129 rooms.

▲ **Do Sesi,** Av. Altamiro Caio Pacheco, Aruanã, ☎ 376 1221. This is the best hotel in the town, with three bars, a restaurant and two swimming pools. 44 rooms.

▲ **Meridional,** Av. Bartolomeu Palhas 52, Porto Nacional, ☎ 863 1020. A small but comfortable hotel with a bar, restaurant and swimming pool. 18 rooms.

▲ **Pousada das Cavalhadas,** Praça da Matriz 1, Pirenópolis, ☎ 331 1313. This modest hotel has one bar but no restaurant. 21 rooms.

▲ **Samambaia,** Av. Anhanguera 1157, Goiânia, ☎ 261 1444. Located in the university area, this hotel has a bar restaurant and swimming pool. 90 rooms.

▲ **Trans-Hotel,** Route BR153, Araguaia, ☎ 821 1233. The most comfortable small hotel in the town, with a bar, restaurant and swimming pool. 61 rooms.

Camping

Itanhangá, Av. Princesa Carolina, Goiânia, ☎ 261 1977.

Quente, Lagoa Quente, Caldas Novas, ☎ 453 1250.

Tangará, Jardim Rosa do Sul, Goiânia, ☎ 225 7214.

Food

*** **Centro de Tradições Goianas,** Rua 4 515, Goiânia, ☎ 225 4606. This centrally located restaurant serves excellent regional cuisine. Open Mon-Sat 11am-3pm, 6-11:30pm.

** **Cliff,** Rua 23 72, Goiânia, ☎ 241 7888. A lively restaurant that is one of the best in the town and offers international cuisine. Open daily 11:30am-3pm, 8pm-3am.

, **Novo Forno de Barro, Rua Henrique Silva 570, Goiânia, ☎ 224 7155. This restaurant offers a taste of the regional cooking. Open daily 11-2am.

** **Papaula,** Av. 31 de Marco 497, Goiânia, ☎ 241 5607. International cuisine in a lively atmosphere. Open Mon-Sat 7pm-2am.

* **Baco,** Av. T 9/R 9 105, Goiânia, ☎ 241 6084. This is a pleasant restaurant that serves international-style food. Open daily noon-3pm, 7pm-midnight.

* **Dom Quixote,** Rua 5 710, Goiânia, ☎ 225 4048. An attractive restaurant that offers international cuisine. Open 11:30am-3pm, 7pm-midnight.

An ipé (black ebony) in bloom near Jatai, in Goiás.

Useful addresses

Airlines
Varig, Av. Goías 287, Goiânia, ☎ 224 5049.
VASP, Rua 3 569, Goiânia, ☎ 223 4266.

Airport
Santa Genoveva Airport, Goiânia, ☎ 261 1600.

Bank
Banco do Brasil, Rua 3 860, Goiânia.

Bus terminals
Rua Antônio Coelho de Godoy, Caldas Novas, ☎ 453 1408.
Rodoviária, Av. Anhanguera 4602, Goiânia, ☎ 224 7078.
Praça Vinicius Fleury, Goiás Velho, ☎ 371 1510

Car rental
Belauto, Av. Anhangüera 4050, Goiânia, ☎ 225 7519.
Localiza, Rua 6 608, Goiânia, ☎ 224 3666.
Nobre, Av. Anhangüera 4270, Goiânia, ☎ 223 2550.

Post office
Correio Central, Praça Civica 11, Goiânia.

Railway terminal
Ferroviária, Praça do Trabalhador, Goiânia, ☎ 223 1764.

Tourist office
Goiastur, Estadio Serra Dourada, Goiânia. The tourist office also has an information desk at Santa Genoveva Airport.
Praça Mestre Orlando 182, Caldas Novas, ☎ 453 1540.

Travel agencies
Cardealtur, Av. Goiás 382, Goiânia, ☎ 225 8633.
Incatur, Av. Goiás 151, Goiânia, ☎ 225 2622.
Transworld, Galeria Central, Goiânia, ☎ 224 4340.

IGUAÇU FALLS AND SOUTHERN BRAZIL

The southern region of Brazil, the *sul,* stretches from the Brazilian border with Uruguay and Argentina to the boundaries of São Paulo state. It comprises the states of Paraná, Santa Catarina and Rio Grande do Sul. This is non-tropical Brazil, with well-defined seasons, and because much of the area lies at an altitude above 660 ft/200 m, it sometimes snows here.

The region is dominated in the north by the Paraná plateau, which is covered with pine woods, while vast tracts of open prairie, *pampas,* are found in the south. Cattle-breeding is the main economic activity in the pampas where large ranches are worked by *gauchos* (cowboys of the pampas of Brazil, Argentina, Uruguay and Paraguay). Hence the southern region of Brazil is also known as gaucho country.

The three states of the south are among the wealthiest in Brazil. The temperate climate is well suited to wheat, soy bean and potato farming and wine is produced in Rio Grande do Sul. The fertile land attracted German and Italian immigrants in the early 19th century, and Poles and Russians later on in the century. Although their numbers were proportionally small, the European influence was significant; they brought to the region a European style of owner-operator farming that differed greatly from the Brazilian *fazendas.*

The resources of the south include the pine forests, with timber constituting one of the region's major export commodities, and the Indian herbal tea, *maté,* extracted from the wild trees of the region. All of Brazil's coal production originates in the south, and the hydro-electric potential of its rivers is enormous.

For the tourist, the south's single greatest attraction is Iguaçu falls. Thousands of Brazilians and foreigners visit the falls every day. If you have sufficient time, we suggest that you explore each of the southern states. The forests of Paraná, the coastal towns of Santa Catarina, the wine-growing communities of Rio Grande do Sul and much more make this one of the loveliest regions of Brazil.

▬ IGUAÇU FALLS*** (Foz do Iguaçu)

See map p. 209.

The Iguaçu falls are among the grandest and most awe-inspiring phenomena of nature in the world. They are five times larger than Niagara Falls. There are 275 falls that lie in a semi-circle among lush vegetation and drop a distance of 236 ft/72 m. The region surrounding the falls has been designated a protected area and comprises two nature reserves.

The falls were discovered in 1541 by Alvar Nunez Cabeza de Vaca, governor of the Rio da Prata Spanish colonies. *Iguaçu* is a Caigangue Indian word meaning 'great waters'. According to Indian legend, these falls were formed as an expression of the wrath of Mboi, the serpent-god who inhabited the Igaçu River. When Mboi learned that his betrothed, Naipi, was being unfaithful, he roared in anger and hunched his back, causing the river bed to uproot. He then threw Naipi in the chasm as she tried to flee with a young warrior, Taroba. Casting a spell, he changed Taroba into a tree and Naipi into a rock. Mboi finally went back to his cavern, which is known as *Garganta do Diablo* (Devil's Gorge). Even today, this cavern belches continual clouds of steam, and there is almost always a rainbow here.

Telephone area code: 0455.

When to go

The falls are most magnificent when the waters are high, from August to November. October and November are undoubtedly the best months to visit the falls, since it can be quite cold from July to September.

Access

Plane
There are numerous daily flights from São Paulo, Rio, Brasília, Curitiba, Porto Alegre and Campo Grande in Brazil and from Asunción in Paraguay and Buenos Aires in Argentina to the **Foz do Iguaçu International Airport** (☎ 74 1744). Weather permitting, the pilot will fly directly above the falls before landing.

Airlines
Transbrasil, Av. Brasil 1225, Foz do Iguaçu, ☎ 74 3671.
Varig, Av. Brasil 821, Foz do Iguaçu, ☎ 74 1424.
Vasp, Av. Brasil 845, Foz do Iguaçu, ☎ 74 2999.

Bus
There are direct buses to Foz do Iguaçu from Rio, São Paulo and the main cities of southern Brazil. While you can purchase a separate bus ticket, we recommend that you go through a travel agent who can also book your hotel room.
Estação Rodoviário, Av. Brasil 99, Foz do Iguaçu, ☎ 73 3595.

Car
Take the BR 116 from Rio to Curitaba, capital of Paraná, and then the BR 277 via Cascavel to Foz do Iguaçu. The trip is long (930 mi/1500 km from Rio and 651 mi/1050 km from São Paulo), but the roads are excellent and you can take advantage of the voyage to do some sightseeing.

Accommodation

▲▲▲ **Bourbon**, Rod. das Cataratas, Foz do Iguaçu, ☎ 74 1313. A first-class hotel with two bars, a restaurant and two swimming pools. 180 rooms.

▲▲▲ **Das Cataratas**, Rod. das Cataratas, Foz do Iguaçu, ☎ 74 2666. A lovely hotel located in a park, with two bars, a restaurant, a swimming pool and various boutiques. 200 rooms.

▲▲▲ **Internacional Foz**, Rua Alm. Barroso 345, Foz do Iguaçu, ☎ 73 4240. This is one of the best hotels near the falls, with a bar, restaurant and two swimming pools. 211 rooms.

▲▲ **Carima**, Rod. das Cararatas, Foz do Iguaçu, ☎ 73 3377. This lovely hotel is a good place for families and offers three

The spectacular Iguaçu Falls lie on the border between Brazil and Argentina.

bars, a restaurant, two swimming pools and various sports facilities. 421 rooms.

▲▲ **Dom Pedro I Palace**, Rod. das Cataratas, Foz do Iguaçu, ☎ 74 2011. Many sports facilities and tourist services distinguish this hotel. One bar, a restaurant and two swimming pools are also here. 184 rooms.

▲▲ **Mirante**, Av. Rep. Argentina 892, Foz do Iguaçu, ☎ 74 3166. An attractive hotel with a bar, restaurant and two swimming pools. 165 rooms.

▲▲ **Panorama**, Rod. das Cataratas, Foz do Iguaçu, ☎ 74 1200. This well-situated hotel has a bar, restaurant and two swimming pools. 164 rooms.

▲▲ **Rafahin Palace**, Route BR277, Foz do Iguaçu, ☎ 73 3434. This hotel has a bar, restaurant, two swimming pools and various tourist facilities. 164 rooms.

▲▲ **San Martin**, Rod. das Cataratas, Foz do Iguaçu, ☎ 74 3030. This hotel offers many facilities for a family visit. A restaurant, two bars, and two swimming pools are here. 142 rooms.

▲ **Estoril**, Av. Rep. Argentina 892, Foz do Iguaçu, ☎ 74 3911. A modest hotel with a restaurant and swimming pool. 130 rooms.

▲ **Salvatti**, Rue Rio Branco, Foz do Iguaçu, ☎ 74 2727. This comfortable hotel has two bars, a restaurant and two swimming pools. 177 rooms.

▲ **San Rafael**, Rue Alm. Barroso 683, Foz do Iguaçu, ☎ 74 3311. A simple but comfortable hotel with a bar, restaurant and swimming pool. 97 rooms.

Camping
CCB, Rod. das Cataratas, Foz do Iguaçu, ☎ 74 1310.
Das Cataratas, Rod. das Cataratas, Foz do Iguaçu, ☎ 74 3369.

Food

* **Abaeté**, Rua Alm. Barroso 893, Foz do Iguaçu, ☎ 74 3084. International cuisine in a lively atmosphere. Open daily 11am-3pm, 6:30pm-midnight.

* **Cabeça de Boi**, Av. Brasil 1325, Foz do Iguaçu, ☎ 74 1168. Live musical entertainment at this traditional *churrascaria*. Open daily 11:30am-3pm, 6:30pm-midnight.

* **Rafahin**, Rod. das Cataratas, Foz do Iguaçu, ☎ 74 2720. This is one of the better *churrascarias*. Live music nightly. Open 11am-4pm, 6pm-midnight.

Getting around

By bus
Buses marked Cataratas and Parque Nac. do Iguaçu go to the falls daily from 8am to 6pm.
Bus terminal, Av. Brasil 99, ☎ 73 3595.

By helicopter
Helisul offers a breathtaking tour of the falls and the surrounding area.
Departures from the airport, ☎ 74 2414.

Excursions
All of the travel agencies in Foz do Iguaçu and most of the hotels in the area offer organized trips to the falls. This is the most convenient and practical way to visit them.
Cataratas, Rua Jorge Sanways 683, Foz do Iguaçu, ☎ 74 3948.
Frontur, Av. Brasil 97, Foz do Iguaçu, ☎ 74 2752.
Gatti, Av. Brasil 688, Foz do Iguaçu, ☎ 72 1717.
Salvatti, Rua Rio Branco 577, Foz do Iguaçu, ☎ 74 2727.

Useful addresses

Bank
Banco do Brasil, Av. Brasil 1365, Foz do Iguaçu, ☎ 72 1434.

Car rental
Interlocadora, Av. Brasil 437, Foz do Iguaçu, ☎ 72 3311.
Solemar, Av. Georges Schimmelpfenning 600, Foz do Iguaçu, ☎ 74 1188.

Currency exchange
Iguaçu, Av. Brasil 1281, Foz do Iguaçu, ☎ 74 2900.

Post office
Rua Edoardo Barros 281, Foz do Iguaçu.

Tourist office
Praça Getúlio Vargas 56, Foz do Iguaçu.

▬ ENVIRONS OF IGUAÇU FALLS

If you have enough time, try to see the falls from the Brazilian and Argentinian side — the views are completely different. On the Brazilian side you visit the falls at the bottom, and on the Argentinian side you cross them at the top. It takes at least two or three hours to see the

Brazilian side and about five hours to see the Argentinian side. Take your passport along to cross the border into Argentina. A visa is not necessary.

The falls are not the only sights to see here. The city of **Foz do Iguaçu*** has grown slowly to accommodate the tourist trade. Now that the great Itaípu dam has been built on the Paraná River, people have been coming to the area in greater numbers.

Another important feature of this region is the confluence of the Iguaçu and Paraná rivers, where the boundaries of three countries meet. This area is known as the **Marcas das Três Fronteiras** (three fontiers) and comprises the boundaries of Brazil, Paraguay and Argentina. There are magnificent views from here.

The Itaípu dam and reservoir** is only a few miles from Iguaçu. In order to tap the energy potential of the enormous volume of water rushing down the Paraná River over the Sete Quedas ('Seven Waterfalls'), Paraguay and Brazil have just completed the construction of a giant hydro-electric power plant. The dam is one of the largest in the world — five times the size of Egypt's Aswan dam. You can visit the dam and power plant (departures from Foz do Iguaçu, ☎ 73 3133).

PARANÁ STATE

See map p. 207.

Paraná measures 77,048 sq mi/199,554 sq km. It is a wealthy state with the most productive agrarian economy in Brazil and magnificent forests.

Until the 18th century Paraná's development stopped at Curitiba and Paranaguá. Throughout its history, it has welcomed waves of immigrants, and the territory has been progressively opened up. Since 1960 its agriculture and lumber production have expanded rapidly. Now this area accounts for 20% of Brazil's exports.

Paraná's main tourist attraction is Iguaçu Falls (see p. 202). Other places to visit include:

Curitiba* is 522 mi/840 km south-west of Rio de Janeiro. Founded in 1693, it is the capital of Paraná. We recommend Curitiba as a departure point for excursions to the south; it has several good hotels with a charming European atmosphere.

Among the sights to see in the capital are the aquarium, the playground and lake on the **Passeio Público** (open Tues-Sun 7am-8pm), and the **Museum of Contemporary Art** (Rua Des. Westphalen 16, ☎ (041) 222571; open Mon-Tues, Fri-Sat 9:30am-6pm, Thurs 9:30am-10pm, Sun 2pm-6pm).

From Curitiba, you can take a lovely train excursion, the *viagem de trem para Paranaguá******** (departures from the bus terminal, ☎ (041) 225 6622; reservations five days in advance). It is a spectacular two-hour trip across the Serra passing such marvelous sights as the Marumbi peak and the Veu da Noiva waterfall.

Vila Velha** is 59 mi/95 km west of Curitiba. This is a national park located in the very centre of the large Campos Gerais plateau. It is known for its beautiful wind-hewn rock formations.

Paranaguá** is 56 mi/90 km east of Curitiba. This small seaside resort is the final destination of the scenic train from Curitiba. The town has a couple of museums, several churches and lovely beaches.

Antonina* (58 mi/94 km east of Curitiba), **Caiobá-Matinhos*** (78 mi/126 km from Curitiba) and **Guaratuba*** (83 mi/124 km east of Curitiba) are all small communities near the coast with fine beaches and traces of colonial architecture.

Telephone area code: 041

Accommodation

▲▲▲ **Iguaçu Campestre,** Route BR116, Curitiba, ☎ 262 5313. A particularly lovely hotel in a charming setting. Three bars, a restaurant and two swimming pools (one heated). 47 rooms.

▲▲ **Caravelle Palace,** Rue Cruz Machado 282, Curitiba, ☎ 223 4323. This hotel has a bar, a restaurant and a convenient location. 98 rooms.

▲▲ **Colonial,** Rue Commendador Araujo 99, Curitiba, ☎ 222 4777. This is a conveniently located hotel with a bar and restaurant. 81 rooms.

▲▲ **Del'Rey,** Ermelino de Leão 18, Curitiba, ☎ 224 3033. Centrally located, this hotel has a bar and restaurant. 153 rooms.

▲▲ **Mabu,** Praça Santos Andrade 830, Curitiba, ☎ 222 7040. This is one of the more comfortable hotels in the town, with a bar, restaurant and heated swimming pool. 150 rooms.

Food

**** **Le Doyen,** Rua Sen. Alencar Guimarães 50, Curitiba, ☎ 222 8722. An elegant restaurant offering first-rate international cuisine and live music. Open daily noon-midnight.

*** **Ile de France,** Praça 19 de Dezembro 538, Curitiba, ☎ 223 9962. This is a truly excellent French restaurant in the centre of the city. Open Mon-Sat 7pm-1am.

** **Alpendre,** Av. Visc. do Rio Branco 1046, Curitiba, ☎ 224 5694. Good Portuguese cooking and live music in a friendly atmosphere. Specialities include baked *bacalhau*. Open daily 11:30am-2:30pm and 7pm-midnight.

* **Pinheirão,** Rua João Negrão 400, Curitiba, ☎ 224 1661. Try this restaurant for a traditional *churrasco*. Open daily 11am-11:30pm.

Useful addresses

Airlines
Transbrasil, Rua Mal. Deodoro 410, Curitiba, ☎ 223 2614.
Varig/Rio-Sul, Rua 15 de Novembro 614, Curitiba, ☎ 222 2522.
Vasp, Rua 15 de Novembro 537, Curitiba, ☎ 224 3303.

Airport
Afonso Pena, Curitiba, ☎ 292 1143.

Banks
Banco de Boston, Praça Tiradentes 410, Curitiba.
Lloyds Bank, Rua 15 de Novembro 317, Curitiba.

Bus terminal
Av. Afonso de Camargo, Curitiba, ☎ 225 6622.

Car rental
Hertz, Rua Emiliano Perneta 420, Curitiba, ☎ 223 0023.
Interlocadora, Rua Chile 1284, Curitiba, ☎ 224 1242.
Nobre, Rua Dr. Pedrosa 453, Curitiba, ☎ 233 0033.

Emergencies
Pronto Socorro Municipal, Av. São José 738, ☎ 262 1121.

Post office
Praça 15 de Novembro, Curitiba.

Tourist office
Rua da Paz 54, Curitiba.

Travel agencies
ABC, Rua Buenos Aires 178, Curitiba, ☎ 222 3485.
Onetur, Rua Emilaino Perneta 861, Curitiba, ☎ 223 7976.

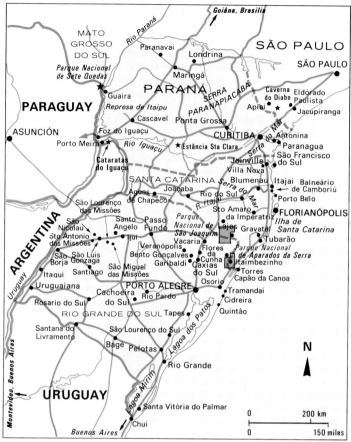

Southern Brazil.

▬ SANTA CATARINA

See map this page.

Santa Catarina is a tiny state (37,059 sq mi/95,985 sq km) that lies wedged between Paraná and Rio Grande do Sul. It has a predominantly agrarian economy — the largest producer of chicken and pork in Brazil — along with wheat, rye, beans, grapes and apples, but also important deposits of coal. The landscape is mountainous and winters tend to be very cold.

Santa Catarina was settled in the early 16th century by Jesuit missionaries and briefly — in the year 1777 — was under Spanish rule. The first German settlers arrived in 1829. They and the subsequent immigrants have left their mark on this state and helped to rejuvenate its economy.

Florianópolis* is 696 mi/1120 km south-west of Rio de Janeiro. Founded in 1726, it is the capital of Santa Catarina. Most of the town lies on lovely Santa Catarina Island, which is linked to the mainland by the newly constructed Colombo Salles Bridge. Florianópolis is very scenic, with many pleasant beaches **(Mocambique, Jurerê, Canasvieiras)**, lagoons **(Lagoa da Conceição)** and mountains **(Morro da Luz, Morro da Lagoa)**. It also has several interesting old forts **(Santana, Nossa Senhora**

da Conceição) and a Jesuit convent (**Convento Jesuita**). There are many interesting places to visit around Florianópolis in the wonderful Itajaí valley. This valley has an unmistakably German air and is best visited by car.

Blumenau** is 87 mi/140 km north of Florianópolis. This is a pleasant and typically German town that is full of flowers. You can eat German food in the restaurants and there is even a beer festival in January and February.

Joinville* is 109 mi/175 km north-west of Florianópolis. This is another typically German town. Visit the **Museu Nacional de Imigração e Colonização** (open Tues-Fri 9am-6pm, Sat. and Sun 9am-noon and 2-6pm) that recounts the history of the German settlements. Other things to see include the **Sambaqui do Rio Comprido,** an archaeological site dating from 5000 BC, the distinctive architecture at **Pirabeiraba*** 9 mi/15 km away, and the **Vila Dona Francisca***, 15 mi/24 km away.

There are many wonderful seaside resorts in this area, including **Itajaí*** (62 mi/100 km north of Florianópolis); **Camboriú*** (49 mi/79 km north of Florianópolis), **Porto Belo*** (41 mi/66 km north of Florianópolis), **Itapema*** (41 mi/66 km north of Florianópolis) and **Laguna*** (77 mi/124 km south of Florianópolis).

South of Florianópolis lie several other places worth visiting.

Gravatal* is a health resort 100 mi/162 km from Florianópolis. In addition to the extensive treatment facilities, there is a park nearby with a playground and a lake.

São Joaquim is 142 mi/228 km south-west of Florianópolis. It is a small town in the mountains inside the São Joaquim National Park. It is very cold in winter.

Finally you will come to the **Aparados da Serra National Park****. Even though this lies mainly in Santa Catarina, access is through the town of São Francisco de Paula in the state of Rio Grande do Sul (see p. 212).

Telephone area code: 0482 (unless otherwise indicated)

Accommodation

▲▲▲▲ **Plaza Itapema,** BR101 Norte, Itapema, ☎ (0473) 42 2222. This luxury hotel is beautifully situated and offers complete amenities for the discriminating tourist. Three bars, a restaurant, four swimming pools (one heated), sports facilities and various boutiques. 162 rooms.

▲▲▲ **Grande Hotel,** Av. Rio Branco 21, Blumenau, ☎ (0473) 22 0366. An attractive hotel with a bar and a swimming pool. 76 rooms.

▲▲▲ **Internacional do Gravatal,** Av. Pedro Zappelini, Gravatal, ☎ (0486) 44 2147. This particularly attractive hotel has a bar, two restaurants, two heated swimming pools and various sports facilities. 118 rooms.

▲▲▲ **Laguna Tourist,** Praia do Gi, Laguna, ☎ (0486) 44 0022. There is a panoramic view over the ocean from this highly-rated hotel. Four bars, a restaurant and two swimming pools. 98 rooms.

▲▲▲ **Plaza Hering,** Rua 7 de Setembro 818, Blumenau, ☎ (0473) 22 0366. One of the best hotels in the town, with a bar, restaurant and swimming pool. 134 rooms.

▲▲ **Florianópolis Palace,** Rua Artista Bittencourt 2, Florianópolis, ☎ 22 9633. A centrally located hotel with a bar, restaurant and two swimming pools. 93 rooms.

▲▲ **Garden Terrace,** Rua Pe. Jacobs 45, Blumenau, ☎ (0473) 22 3544. This is a comfortable hotel with a bar and restaurant. 110 rooms.

▲▲ **Jurerê Praia,** A1. 1 praia de Jurerê, Florianópolis, ☎ 66 0108. This particularly attractive hotel is very well located and offers sports facilities, three bars, a restaurant and two swimming pools. 59 rooms.

▲▲ **Tannenhof,** Rua. Visc. de Taunay 340, Joinville, ☎ (0474) 228011. A highly recommended hotel with a bar, restaurant and swimming pool. 103 rooms.

▲ **Himmelblau,** Rua 7 de Setembro 1415, Blumenau, ☎ (0473) 22 5800. This is a pleasant hotel with a bar and restaurant. 130 rooms.

▲ **Marambaia Cabeçudas,** Fraça Marco Konder 46, Itajaí, ☎ (0473) 440603. A modest hotel that offers a spectacular view of the sea. It has a bar, restaurant and swimming pool. 38 rooms.

Camping
Costa do Sol, Rua Rio do Bras 1, Florianópolis, ☎ 660499.
Rio Vermelho, Estr. do Vermelho, Florianópolis.

Food

** **Lindacap,** Rua Felipe Schmidt 178, Florianópolis, ☎ 220558. An excellent, centrally located restaurant serving international-style cuisine. Open daily 11am-midnight.

** **Manolo's,** Rua Felipe Schmidt 71, Florianópolis, ☎ 224351. Live music accompanies consistently good international cuisine. Open Mon-Sat 11am-3pm, 7-11pm.

* **Frohsinn,** Morro do Aipim, Blumenau, ☎ (0473) 222137. This charming restaurant offers German cooking and a panoramic view of the countryside. Open Mon-Sat 11am-2:30pm, 6-11pm.

* **Moinho do Vale,** Rua Paraguai 66, Blumenau, ☎ (0473) 223337. A panoramic view and live music make this one of the town's best restaurants. International cuisine, Open daily 11:30 am-3pm and 6:30pm-midnight.

* **Tante Frida,** Rua Visc. de Taunay 1174, Joinville, ☎ (0474) 220558. A consistently good restaurant serving German dishes. Open Mon-Sat 11am-3pm, 7pm-midnight.

Useful addresses

Airlines
Transbrasil, Praça Pereira Oliveira 16, Florianópolis, ☎ 220177.
Varig/Rio-Sul, Rua Felipe Schmidt 34, Florianópolis, ☎ 222811.
Vasp, Rua Osmar Cunha 15, Florianópolis, ☎ 221122.

Airport
Hercilio Luz, Bairro de Carianos, Florianópolis, ☎ 330879.

Bank
Banco do Brasil, Praça XV de Novembro 20, Florianópolis.

Bus terminal
Av. Paulo Fontes, Florianópolis, ☎ 232777.

Car rental
Interlocadora, Rua Felipe Schmidt 34, Florianópolis, ☎ 222811.
Nobre, Av. Rio Branco 110, Florianópolis, ☎ 234545.

Post office
Praça 15 de Novembro 5, Florianópolis, ☎ 223188.

Tourist office
Portal Turistico, Florianópolis, ☎ 445960.

Travel agencies
Ilhatur, Rua Felipe Schmidt 27, Florianópolis, ☎ 226333.
Turisan, Rua Dom Jaime Câmara 18, Florianópolis, ☎ 231411.

▬ *RIO GRANDE DO SUL*

See map p. 209.

Rio Grande do Sul is a cattle-breeding region. It boasts more than 13 million head of cattle and a unique cowboy culture similar to that of the gauchos of the Argentinian *pampas*. There are also vineyards here, and other produce, such as rice, soya, tobacco and fruit, is grown. Rio Grande do Sul is one of the most prosperous states in Brazil.

The Portuguese first began to settle this area around 1680, at the same time that Spanish Jesuit missionaries were penetrating the northern banks of the Rio de la Plata. The Jesuits strengthened their foothold on Brazilian soil by founding the *Sete Povos dos Missoes* (missions), which led the Portuguese to consolidate their power by founding Porto dos Casais, now known as Porto Alegre. The Jesuits were driven out in 1759 but conflicts between the Spanish and the Portuguese continued until 1801. The first German settlers arrived in 1824, the Italians in 1874.

Porto Alegre** is 963 mi/1550 km from Rio de Janeiro. Founded in 1742, it is the capital of Rio Grande do Sul. Sights to see include the handsome **Farroupilha Park** in the heart of town, the **Morro de Santa Teresa**, the **Rio Grande do Sul Museum of Art** (open Tues-Sun 10am-5pm) and the **Centre of Gaucho Tradition** ☎ (0512) 28 1711, which tells all about the region's folklore.

The surrounding areas offer an incredible variety of touring possibilities. The wine-growing communities are located in picturesque Rio das Antas valley and are especially lively at harvest time (January). They include **Caxias do Sul*** (76 mi/122 km north of Porto Alegre), **Garibaldi*** (71 mi/114 km north of Porto Alegre), **Bento Gonçalves*** (78 mi/125 km north of Porto Alegre), **Flores da Cunha*** (94 mi/151 km north of Porto Alegre) and **Veranopolis*** (102 mi/164 km north-west of Porto Alegre).

Other communities consisting of Swiss-style chalets dot the flower-filled mountains. They are very pleasant in the summertime. Three of them, which lie at an altitude of 2722 ft/830 m, are **Gramado**** (83 mi/133 km north of Porto Alegre), **Canela**** (87 mi/140 km north of Porto Alegre) and **São Francisco de Paula**** (72 ml/116 km north of Porto Alegre). At 50 mi/80 km from São Francisco de Paula you can see the steep cliffs of the Serra at **Cambara** in the Parque Nacional dos Aparados da Serra, as well as the **Itaimbezinho Canyon** (1300 ft/400 m deep).

There are also lovely beaches in the vicinity, stretching from **Torres** (6 mi/10 km from Porto Alegre) to **Tramandai** (78 mi/126 km east of Porto Alegre). This coast is stunning, with bluffs and wind-hewn rocks, in addition to the pleasant beaches. Tiny communities worth a detour in the area include: **Capáo da Canoa, Osorio, Cidreira, Pinha** and **Quintão.**

In the 17th century, this area was the site of many missions where Spanish Jesuits strove to protect the autonomous Indian cultures. Ruins of several of the missions still exist: São Miguel, Santo Antônio, Santo Angelo, São Nicolau, São Lourenço, São João Batista and São Luís Gonzaga. The only one that is really worth a visit is **São Miguel**.**

If you enjoy swimming in a lake, there are several small lakeside towns along the dos Patos lagoon between **Tapes** (69 mi/111 km south of Porto Alegre) and **São Lourenço do Sul** (128 mi/206 km south of Porto Alegre).

Finally, if you like rodeos, the place to visit is **Vacaria***, which is famous for them.

Telephone area code: 0512 (unless otherwise indicated)

> ### Accommodation
>
> ▲▲▲ **Laje de Pedra,** Av. Pres. Kennedy, Canela, ☎ (054) 282 1530. A first-class hotel offering all the amenities a discriminating tourist could want. It is in a lovely setting with a panoramic view of the valley. Two bars, a restaurant and three swimming pools (one heated). 250 rooms.

▲▲▲ **Plaza São Rafael,** Av. Alberto Bins, Porto Alegre, ☎ 216100. This is the best hotel in Porto Alegre, with two bars and two restaurants. 284 rooms.

▲▲▲ **Samuara,** RS 122, Caxias do Sul, ☎ (054) 2217733. An especially attractive hotel situated in a charming setting. It offers a bar, a restaurant and two swimming pools (one heated). 81 rooms.

▲▲ **Embaixador,** Rua Jerônimo Coelho 354, Porto Alegre, ☎ 265622. A centrally located hotel with a bar, restaurant and various boutiques. 192 rooms.

▲▲ **Serra Azul,** Rua Garibaldi 152, Gramado, ☎ (054) 2861082. A pleasant hotel with a bar, a restaurant and two swimming pools. 90 rooms.

▲▲ **Serrano,** Av. Cel. Diniz 1112, Gramado, ☎ (054) 2861332. The best hotel in Gramado, located in a lovely park. Two bars, a restaurant and a heated swimming pool. 84 rooms.

▲ **Alfred Executivo,** Praça Otávio Rocha 270, Porto Alegre, ☎ 218966. A centrally located hotel with a bar and a restaurant. 54 rooms.

▲ **Avenida II,** Av. Venancio Aires 1671, Santo Ângelo, ☎ (055) 3123011. This modest hotel has one bar. 72 rooms.

▲ **Balneario,** Av. Borges de Medeiros 1596, Gramado, ☎ (054) 2861027. A charming hotel, with a bar, restaurant and swimming pool. 37 rooms.

▲ **Rita Hoppner,** Rua Pedro Candiago 305, Gramado, ☎ (054) 2861334. An intimate hotel in a beautiful park. One bar and one swimming pool. 11 rooms.

Camping

Do Cocão, road to Viamão, Porto Alegre.

Praio do Guarujá 2875, Porto Alegre, ☎ 254743.

Food

*** **Floresta Negra,** Av. 24 de Outubro 905, Porto Alegre, ☎ 227584. An outstanding restaurant well worth the trip. German cuisine. Open Mon-Sat 7-11:30pm.

** **Napoleon,** Praça Otávio• Rocha 47, Porto Alegre, ☎ 218825. This consistently good, centrally located restaurant serves international cuisine. Open daily 11-1am.

** **Santo Antonio,** Rua Dr. Timoteo 465, Porto Alegre, ☎ 223130. One of the best *churrascarias* in the town. Open daily 11am-3pm, 7pm-midnight.

** **Quero-Quero,** Praça Otávio Rocha 49, Porto Alegre, ☎ 218825. Centrally located, this *churrascaria* has live music. Open daily 11-1am.

* **Santa Teresa,** Av. Assis Brasil 2750, Porto Alegre, ☎ 412251. Live music and delicious food make this *churrascaria* a worthwhile stop. Open daily 11am-3pm, 7pm-midnight.

Useful addresses

Airlines

Transbrasil, Av. Borges de Medeiros 410, Porto Alegre, ☎ 258300.
Varig/Rio-Sul, Rua dos Andradas 1107, Porto Alegre, ☎ 216333.
Vasp, Av. Borges de Medeiros 267, Porto Alegre, ☎ 216611.

Airport

Salgado Filho, Porto Alegre, ☎ 435638.

Bank

Banco de Boston, Rua dos Andradas 1250, Porto Alegre, ☎ 263633.

Bus terminal
Lgo. Vespasiano Julio Veppo, Porto Alegre, ☎ 21 2599.

Car rental
Interlocadora, Av. Azenha 85, Porto Alegre, ☎ 23 5509.
Nobre, Av. Sertório 1480, Porto Alegre, ☎ 43 5252.

Consulates
Great Britain, Rua Pedro Chaves Barcelos 309, Porto Alegre,
☎ 31 2745.
United States, Rua Cel. Genuino 421, Porto Alegre, ☎ 26 4288.

Emergencies
Pronto Socorro Municipal, Av. Osvaldo Aranha, Porto Alegre,
☎ 31 5900.

Post office
Rua Arauja Ribeiro 100, Porto Alegre.

Railway terminal
Av. dos Estados, Porto Alegre, ☎ 43 6680.

Taxis
Coptaxi, Porto Alegre, ☎ 34 7444.
Tele-táxi, Porto Alegre, ☎ 26 1919.

Tourist office
Epatur, Porto Alegre, ☎ 25 4744.

Travel agencies
Gaúcha Tur, Av. Farrapos 45, Porto Alegre, ☎ 26 5074.
Laçador, Rua Garibaldi 165, Porto Alegre, ☎ 25 4757.

MINAS GERAIS

This vast south-eastern state was once described as having a heart of gold and a breast of iron. Two gold mines are still in operation here today, while more than half of the mineral production of Brazil, including practically all its iron ore, comes from this region.

Until the late 16th century, the territory was populated only by a small number of Indians. Then *bandeirantes,* groups of adventurers from São Paulo, began threading their way through the region's mountains and valleys in search of its legendary treasures. For many years they were only moderately successful, returning to São Paulo with bagfuls of semi-precious stones. In 1700, however, strange black granules were discovered in a riverbed in the south of the region. These turned out to be a type of mineral rich in gold. Soon prospectors were stampeding into the area — which was given the name Ouro Preto meaning 'black gold.'

When news of this gold discovery reached Portugal, a huge number of people rushed to Minas Gerais. Greatly alarmed, the Portuguese government imposed a tight system of control on the gold mines (and on the mining of diamonds and emeralds, which had also been discovered in the territory), taxed the output, and took a large percentage of the proceeds. But this didn't stop the mania, and towns continued to spring up around Ouro Preto, by now the capital of the region.

In the lust for wealth little thought was paid to cultivating the land. Predictably, famines and epidemics resulted. By 1725, the situation had stabilized, mainly through the development of cattle-breeding — by then, vast herds had begun to fill the plains. The next 30 years or so were extremely prosperous for Minas Gerais; after that, the production from the mines began to drop off.

In 1788, in response to the continuing Portuguese restrictions, a group of revolutionaries conspired to bring about Brazil's independence from Portugal. The *Inconfidencia* movement, led by José Joaquim da Silva Xavier (known as Tiradentes), gained considerable popular support. It was crushed in 1789, and Tiradentes was executed a few years later. Brazilians had to wait until 1822 for independence.

In 1897 a new state capital was built to replace Ouro Preto. Belo Horizonte was the first modern planned town in the country. In the 20th century, the area around Belo Horizonte grew as a result of iron and steel mining. Ouro Preto became a ghost town, an ancient monument with such an abundance of Baroque treasures that, in 1980, UNESCO declared it a World Historical Monument.

The gold era: 1680-1770

Toward the end of the 17th century, groups of adventurers known as *bandeirantes* set out regularly from São Paulo in their search for gold, silver and precious minerals. They also hunted down Indians, in particular the tribes living among the Jesuit missions in Paraguay, to use as labourers.

Between 1692 and 1695, the *bandeirantes* discovered large deposits of gold in Minas Gerais, Goiás and Mato Grosso. Huge numbers of people began to migrate here, causing a veritable gold rush. Precious minerals were discovered at about the same time, specifically emerald deposits around Ouro Preto and in the Diamantina area. Production rose steadily until the middle of the 18th century.

After an initial period of chaos, these various deposits were mined under strict Portuguese supervision: foundries were run by the government and a tax known as the *quinto* (or 'fifth') was levied on all production. At the same time, there was a lively black market.

The need to feed the mining population led to the development of cattle-breeding. Vast herds filled the plains, tended by herdsmen on horseback, known as *gauchos.*

It was a century of great wealth in the state of Minas Gerais. New towns sprung up and the elaborate churches and houses that were constructed bear witness to this period. In the meantime, the Nordeste region, already experiencing a decline in its sugar production, was further impoverished as the gold rush drained a sizeable part of its population.

Brazilian mining techniques, especially for alluvial gold, were rudimentary and required the services of an enormous work force — over 100,000 blacks worked in these mines when production was at its peak. Once the top layers containing the gold nuggets and gold dust were depleted, production fell sharply. By the end of the 18th century, the richest deposits had been used up.

An entire century spans the period from the days of the *bandeirantes* to those of the *gauchos,* a century full of violence and adventure. However, it was also a century that stands out for its creative spirit, and for positive developments such as the first stirrings towards independence.

Of principal interest for tourists are the colonial towns of this region, in particular Ouro Preto. Other towns renowned for their rich colonial treasures include Mariana, São João del Rei, Congonhas do Camp, and Diamante. Altogether, a tour through this area offers a glimpse of an architectural heritage unique in South America.

■ PRACTICAL INFORMATION

See map p. 225.

Telephone area code: 031

When to go

Minas Gerais is on the highest part of Brazil's central plateau. The climate is dry and pleasant all year round with warm days giving way to sometimes chilly nights. Temperatures average between 59° F/15° C and 68° F/20° C

Access

Situated in the centre of the state of Minas Gerais, Belo Horizonte is the usual point of arrival and a good base for visiting the surrounding region.

Plane

There are numerous daily flights from Rio de Janeiro, São Paulo, Brasília and Salvador to **Confins airport,** 25mi/40 km from Belo Horizonte, ☎ 689 2747.

From the airport, you can take a bus or a taxi to Belo Horizonte.
Transbrasil, Rua Tamoios 86, Belo Horizonte, ☎ 226 3433.
Varig, Rua Espírito Santo 643, Belo Horizonte, ☎ 224 1611.
Vasp, Rua Carijós 279, Belo Horizonte, ☎ 226 3282.

Bus

Buses arrive in Belo Horizonte's central bus terminal from the major cities of Brazil.
The bus terminal is on Praça Rio Branco, ☎ 201 8111.

Train

An overnight train runs twice a week between Rio de Janeiro and Belo Horizonte (Fri and Sat).
RFFSA, Rua Aarãi Reis, ☎ 222 3169.

Car

If you are coming from Rio de Janeiro, take the BR040 to Belo Horizonte. The road is excellent until Juiz de Fora, after which driving becomes more difficult.

Getting around Minas Gerais

By bus

There is extensive bus service between Belo Horizonte and every town of interest in the area, with buses leaving for Ouro Preto every half an hour. Traveling by bus is a good solution if you want to go to only one or two towns. There are, however, only limited connections between the towns themselves.

By plane

The regional airlines, Nordeste and BRC, operate flights to some of the smaller airports in the area, including Governador Valadares, Ipatinga, Passos de Caldas, Juiz de Fora, Montes Claros, Uberaba, Uberlandia and Varginha.
Pampulha airport in the suburbs of Belo Horizonte is the point of departure, ☎ 441 2000.
BRC, Aeroporto de Pampulha, ☎ 443 5742.
Nordeste, Av. Olegário Maciel 1801, ☎ 337 2411.

By car

Since planes and buses travel only between each town and the capital, driving offers the advantage of allowing you to visit several towns without returning to Belo Horizonte.
Avis, Rua Aimorés 1043, Belo Horizonte, ☎ 226 3886; Aeroporto de Confins, ☎ 689 2714; Aeroporto de Pampulha, ☎ 443 5647.
Hertz, Av. João Pinheiro 341, Belo Horizonte; Aeroporto de Confins, ☎ 689 2713; Aeroporto da Pampulha, ☎ 441 4457.

Excursions

All of the local travel agencies organize regional sightseeing trips to the main historical places around Belo Horizonte.
Franstur, Rua Espírito Santo 1204, ☎ 273 1288.
Revetour, Rua Espírito Santo 1482, ☎ 337 2500.
Unitur, Rua Tupis 171, ☎ 201 7144.

BELO HORIZONTE

Belo Horizonte, the capital of Minas Gerais, is the third-largest city in Brazil. Modeled after Washington DC, it is a city of verdant squares, multi-storeyed buildings and wide avenues. It is one of Brazil's largest industrial centres as well as the traditional centre of mining and diamond cutting. Its dense cluster of skyscrapers gives it the appearance of a large, rather nondescript North American city. Among the sights well worth visiting in the city itself are the **Parque Municipal**** (open 6am-6pm), the **Historical Museum**** (Rua Bernardo Mascarenhas, ☎ 212 1400, open Wed-Mon 10am-5pm), the **Mineralogical Museum***** (Rua da Bahia 1149, ☎ 271 1666, open Tues, Wed and Fri 12:30-6:30pm, Thurs 12:30-9pm, Sat-Sun 10am-4pm) and the handsome building designed by Oscar Niemeyer in 1960 at the corner of Avenida Brasil and the Praça da Liberdade.

Also worth a visit is the suburb of **Pampulha****, 5 mi/8 km from the city centre. Oscar Niemeyer is the architect of the complex of modern buildings that includes the glass and marble **Museum of Art**** (☎ 443 4533, open daily 9am-6pm). There is a botanical garden, a zoo, a lake, a casino and a dance hall-cum-restaurant. Don't miss the renowned church of **São Francisco***** (open Mon-Fri 8:30am-4:30pm, Sat 8:30-11am, 2-5pm, Sun 10am-8pm), which contains the famous *Stations of the Cross* painted by Candido Portinari.

Telephone area code: 031

Accommodation

▲▲▲ **Belo Horizonte Othon Palace,** Av. Alfonso Pena 1050, Belo Horizonte, ☎ 226 7844. Centrally located, this very good hotel offers a multitude of facilities. Two bars, a restaurant, two swimming pools and boutiques. 303 rooms.

▲▲ **Brasilton,** BR381, Belo Horizonte, ☎ 351 0900. Located outside the city, this hotel has a bar, restaurant and swimming pool. 141 rooms.

▲▲ **Dela Rey,** Praça Afonso Arinos 60, Belo Horizonte, ☎ 273 2211. A comfortable hotel with a bar and a restaurant. 230 rooms.

▲▲ **Real Palace,** Rua Espírito Santo 901, Belo Horizonte, ☎ 273 3111. Conveniently located, it has two bars, a restaurant and a swimming pool. 256 rooms.

▲▲ **Wembley Palace,** Rua Espírito Santo 201, Belo Horizonte, ☎ 201 6966. Located in a popular tourist section, the hotel offers a bar and a restaurant. 107 rooms.

▲ **Normandy,** Rua Tamoios 212, Belo Horizonte, ☎ 201 6166. A centrally located hotel with a bar and restaurant. 130 rooms.

▲ **Serrana Palace,** Rua Goitacazes 450, Belo Horizonte, ☎ 201 9955. One of the advantages here is that a travel agent is available to assist the tourist. Bar, restaurant and swimming pool. 129 rooms.

Food

*****Café Ideal,** Rua Claudio Manoel 583, ☎ 226 6019. You can expect consistently excellent food in this French restaurant. Open Mon-Sat 7pm-2am.

*** **Dona Derna,** Rua Tomé de Souza 1380, ☎ 223 6954. Considered one of the best Italian restaurants in town. Open daily 11am-midnight.

** **Maria das Tranças,** Rua Estoril 938, ☎ 441 1103. Known for its Brazilian specialities. Open daily 11am-10pm.

** **Nini e Familia,** Rua Cristovão Colombo 631. An excellent Brazilian restaurant. Open Mon-Sat 11:30am-3:30pm, 7pm-midnight.

** **Tavernaro,** Rua Antônio de Albuquerque 889, ☎ 221 8283. A restaurant serving consistently good Italian food. Open daily 11:30am-2:30pm, 6:30pm-1:30am.

** **Verde Gaio,** Rua Guajajaras 606, ☎ 224 5331. A lively, centrally located Portuguese restaurant. Open Mon-Sat 11-1am.

* **Minuano,** Rua Prof. Morais 635, ☎ 225 3600. This is a good *churrascaria.* Open 11am-midnight.

Useful addresses

Banks
Banco do Brasil, Rua Rio de Janeiro 750, ☎ 212 1055.
Citibank, Rua Espírito Santo 872, ☎ 224 1922.

Consulate
Great Britain, Edificio Guimaraes, Av. Afonso Pena 952, ☎ 222 6318.

Post office
Correio Central, Av. Afonso Pena 1270, ☎ 201 9833.

Taxis
Coopertramo, ☎ 443 2288.
Tele-taxi, ☎ 442 2424.

Tourist office
Belotour, Av. Contourna 8471, ☎ 337 7711.

OURO PRETO

See map p. 220.

Ouro Preto, the most interesting of Minas Gerais's colonial towns, lies 60 mi/100 km south of Belo Horizonte. At an altitude of 3600 ft/1075 m and nestled among greenery in the lovely Ribeiro do Fonil valley, Ouro Preto is a most appealing place. Along its steep and winding streets stand houses with magnificent balconies in wood or wrought iron, ornately carved fountains, and innumerable churches.

Progress has bypassed Ouro Preto, and what you will find are living reminders of the past. It is one of the most beautiful Baroque towns in South America. You will be well rewarded if you spend a day or two seeing its sights. The best way to see Ouro Preto is on foot. Local children love to act as guides. Taxis are also available and can be rented for an hour at a fixed rate.

Among the most impressive sights in Ouro Preto are its churches — 13 crown its steeply climbing streets. The most impressive is **São Francisco de Assis*****, C1-2 (open Tues-Sun 8-11:30am, 1-5pm), which was built between 1777 and 1799 and is considered one of Aleijadinho's masterpieces. Its relief showing St Francis, its altar and

---

Aleijadinho

Minas Gerais was famous in the 18th century not only for its gold but also for the abundance of artists who worked there. By far the greatest of these was the sculptor Antônio Francisco Lisboa. The son of a Portuguese architect and a mulatto slave, he was a man of exceptional intelligence, sensibility, humanity and religious conviction. Indeed, his faith in God and passion for his work were no doubt what kept him going when, around 1778 at the age of 40, he contracted a crippling disease — probably polio or leprosy. From this time until his death at 77 he worked on his knees with carving instruments strapped to his forearms. As a result he was called *Aleijadinho* (little cripple).

His work can be found in towns throughout the region, such as Sabara and São João del Rei. It is most prominent in Ouro Preto, which has many churches full of his superb Rococo carvings. His most famous work, however, is his group of apostles, which stands at the entrance to the church of Bom Jesus do Matozinho at Congonhas do Campo. These 12 dramatic statues carved in soapstone with a brilliant sense of movement are among the finest works of art of their period in the world.

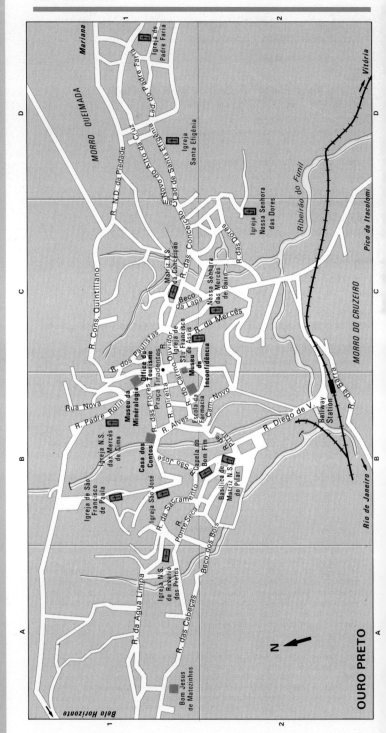

OURO PRETO

Ouro Preto represents the height of Brazilian Baroque during the 18th century.

pulpits and its superb Baroque carvings in wood and soapstone all exhibit Aleijadinho's masterful touch. **Nossa Senhora do Carmo****, C1 (open Tues-Sun 1-5pm) has a magnificent façade and sculptures by the same master. His work can also be seen in the lovely **Nossa Senhora da Conceição*****, C1, which contains the **Museu Aleijadinho** (open Tues-Sun 8-11:30am, 1-5pm).

Another inspiring church is **Nossa Senhora do Pilar*****, B2 (open Tues-Sun noon-5pm), built between 1711 and 1733 in a curious decagonal shape and with elaborate gold carvings inside.

Other churches worth visiting include **Nossa Senhora do Rosário***, A1, dating from 1784, the **Padre Faria Chapel****, D1, with its sumptuous interior, and **das Mercês de Cima**, B1, built between 1771 and 1820.

There are two beautiful churches that afford splendid views of Ouro Preto. Sitting on the Piedade hill is the church of **Orden Terceira da São Francisco de Paula****, B1, dating from 1804. It is closed to the public but on the plaza in front of the church are several ceramic statues.

In the old quarter of Alto da Cruz is the **Santa Efigenia church*****, D1 (open Tues-Sun 8am-noon) with a clock dating from 1762 on the outside and fine sculpture inside.

Ouro Preto is also the home of several interesting museums. The **Mineral Museum*****, B1 (open daily noon-5pm, closed holidays) is housed in the former town hall and the **Museum of Silver*** (open Tues-Sun noon-5pm) retraces the mining history of the region. Note that the main police station was once the gold foundry. Among the town's many fountains are some that were carved by Aleijadinho.

In the immediate outskirts of Ouro Preto you can visit the remains of the **Arraial de Ouro Padre*** (a former goldminers' camp) and the **Ouro de Passagem*** (☎ (031) 557 1255, open daily 9am-6pm), which dates from 1719 and has 3740 ft/1140 m of underground caverns.

Ouro Preto.

Telephone area code: 031

Accommodation

Except for a single night's stay, you would be advised to stay in a hotel in Belo Horizonte (see p. 218), because accommodation is extremely limited in Ouro Preto. If you want to stay here, you must make reservations — even the largest hotel has no more than 35 rooms.

▲▲▲ **Estrada Real,** Rod. dos Inconfidentes, C2, ☎ 551 2122. A lovely hotel with a panoramic view of the region. Three bars, a restaurant and two swimming pools. 30 rooms.

▲▲ **Grande Hotel Ouro Preto,** Rua Rocha Lagoa 164, B1, ☎ 551 1488. This a small, attractive hotel but without a bar or a restaurant. 35 rooms.

▲▲ **Luxor Pousada,** Rua Dr. Alfredo Baeta 287, C1, ☎ 551 2244. An intimate hotel with a restaurant. 16 rooms.

▲ **Pouso Chico Rey,** Rua Brig. Mosqueira 90, ☎ 551 1274. A small hotel offering basic comfort for the tourist. 7 rooms.

▲ **Quinta dos Barões,** Rua Pandiá Catalógeras, C2, ☎ 551 1056. A simple hotel with a bar and a restaurant. 7 rooms.

Food

** **Taberna Luxor,** Rua Dr. Alfredo Baeta 10, C1, ☎ 551 2244. This is one of the better restaurants in the town. International cuisine. Open daily 11am-3pm, 7-10pm.

* **Calabouço,** Rua Conde de Bobadela 132, B1, ☎ 551 1222. Regional cuisine is served in a pleasant setting. Open Mon-Sat 11am-3:30pm, 7-10:30pm.

* **Casa do Ouvidor,** Rua Conde de Bobadela 10, B1, ☎ 551 2141. A consistently good restaurant featuring regional cuisine. Open daily 11am-3pm, 6:30-10pm.

Useful addresses

Bank
Banco do Brazil, Rua São José 195, B1, ☎ 551 2663.

Bus terminal
Rua Pe. Rolim 661, ☎ 551 3166.

Emergencies
Pronto Socorro Municipal, Rua Pe. Rolim 344, ☎ 551 1585.

Post office
Rua Conde de Bobadella 180, B1.

Railway terminal
RFFSA, Praça Cesário Aluim 102, B2, ☎ 551 3100.

Tourist office
Associaçaõ de Guias, Praça Tiradentes 41, C1, ☎ 551 2655.

▬ *ENVIRONS OF MINAS GERAIS*

See map p. 225.

The historical towns of Minas Gerais are all situated in the vicinity of Belo Horizonte. Sabará, Caeté and Santa Barbara are the closest to the capital. To the south, besides Ouro Preto, you can visit Mariana, Ouro Branco, Congonhas, São José del Rei and Tiradentes. To the north are Diamantina and Serro.

Mariana*** is 7 mi/11 km east of Ouro Preto and 69 mi/111 km from Belo Horizonte. It was founded in 1711 and classed as a national monument in 1945. Two churches, **do Carmo,** dating from 1783, and **São Francisco de Assis,** dating from 1777, are especially interesting.

The Carmo church has a striking façade and, in the interior, carvings and paintings. São Francisco is also striking and houses pulpits and an altar by Aleijadinho. Other sights include the **former prison** with a handsome 18th-century winding staircase and the **Museum of Sacred Art** in the former Bishop's Palace, which houses works by Aleijadinho, furniture and an ivory cross.

Sabará★★★ is 17 mi/27 km north-east of Belo Horizonte. Sights to see in Sabará include the church of **Nossa Senhora do Carmo,** which was built in 1763 and has a doorway and interior carved by Aleijadinho and a ceiling painted by Joaquim Conçalves da Rocha; **Nossa Senhora da Conceição,** dating from 1710; and **Nossa Senhora da Ó,** dating from 1717 with medallions painted with chinoiseries in the interior. Also worth visiting is the celebrated **Museum of Gold** (open Tues-Sun noon-5pm) housed in the former foundry dating from 1720. It contains furniture and tools used by gold miners. The town is also full of lovely 18th-century fountains.

Caeté★, 16 mi/25 km east of Sabará, was once painted by Aleijadinho. It lies nestled among banana trees and magnificent cedars. While in Caeté, be sure to see the church of **Nossa Senhora do Bom Sucesso,** built in 1756 by the father of Aleijadinho. Aleijadinho, as a young man, worked on the decoration of its interior. Also worth visiting nearby, at 11 mi/17 km, is the 5800 ft/1770 m high **Serra da Piedade.**

Santa Bárbara★ is 45 mi/73 km east of Sabará. You can visit the **Matriz of Santo Antônio,** begun in 1762, which houses paintings by Manuel da Costa Antaide. In the vicinity there are two interesting sights: the **Barão de Cocais★**, 9 mi/15 km away, and the **Seminário do Caraça★★**, 16 mi/26 km away.

Congonhas★★★ is 47 mi/76 km south of Belo Horizonte. To get to Congonhas, you must either take a dirt road that branches off the Rio-Belo Horizonte road or a train (Congonhas is a stop on the line between Rio and Belo Horizonte). Don't miss this small town perched on top of a hill with the magnificient basilica of **Nossa Senhora Bom Jesus de Matosinhos.** The basilica is renowned for its plaza with statues of the Apostles carved by Aleijadinho between 1800 and 1805 (see p. 219).

Ouro Branco★, 22 mi/35 km east of Congonhas, is the site of the **Matriz Santo Antônio,** dating from 1774, which may well be the purest example of Brazilian Rococo.

Baroque architecture in Minas Gerais

In Brazil, Baroque architecture can be found in two different forms: the rich, ornate variety that swept the Atlantic coast after the Europeans arrived and the variety that is prevalent in the interior of the country, in the many public buildings in the state of Goiás, and especially in Minas Gerais.

Ouro Preto, the former capital of Minas Gerais during the height of the gold rush, boasts three magnificent examples of Baroque architecture: the governor's palace, dating from 1740; the Casa do Camaro, an edifice begun in 1784 in a Baroque style bordering on the neo-Classical (it now houses the Museum of the Inconfidência); and the Casa dos Cantos, the largest building in Minas Gerais, dating from 1782.

The churches of Minas Gerais offer other outstanding examples of the Baroque style. Their beauty and originality lie in their wood carvings and the painted vaults and ceilings. The wood carvings are also gilded or painted.

The most ornate churches are those with side towers, reminiscent of churches in Italy, Germany and other parts of Central Europe. The first hints of the use of the ellipse can be seen in Ouro Preto's Nossa Senhora do Pilar. This form reached perfection during the 18th century in Ouro Preto's Nossa Senhora do Rosário.

Although Minas Gerais's Baroque architecture is more austere than that of the coastal regions, it is more breathtaking and grandiose.

São João del Rei*** is a charming little colonial town 118 mi/190 km south of Belo Horizonte. It has managed to retain its old neighbourhoods, while at the same time developing into a modern community. The most interesting of the churches is **São Francisco de Assis** with magnificent decoration by Aleijadinho. He was also responsible for the carvings on the façade of **Nossa Senhora do Carmo,** begun in 1732. Other sights worth seeing in São João are the gilded choir in the **Matriz do Pilar, Nossa Senhora do Rosário** with its Rococo wood panelling (1719), and **Nossa Senhora das Merces,** with a façade dating from 1806. The **Museum of Regional Art** (open Tues-Sun noon-5:30pm) is housed in a handsome 18th-century mansion. If you feel like an excursion, there are picturesque journeys three times a week on a little steam-engine train known as Maria Fumaça to Tirradentes or Barroso. There are also gold mines to visit in the vicinity.

Tiradentes** is 124 mi/200 km south of Belo Horizonte and 6 mi/10 km east of São João del Rei. This is the town where Tiradentes, the hero of Brazilian independence, was born (see p. 215). Its most beautiful church, **Santo Antônio,** was begun in 1736. The magnificent façade is probably Aleijadinho's last work; its interior is a mixture of Baroque (the choir) and Rococo (the organ loft). Other sights include the **São José fountain,** dating from 1749, the 18th-century **Casa de Intendencia** and the **Historical Museum.**

Diamantina**, lying 194 mi/313 km north of Belo Horizonte, is perhaps the colonial town that most retains a sense of the region's glorious past. Founded in 1729, it was the centre of a once-thriving diamond industry. At an altitude of 4133 ft/1260 m, in a beautiful mountainous landscape, the town centre contains lovely colonial buildings, such as the **Carmo church.** There is also a **Diamond Museum** (open Tues-Sun noon-5:30pm). Nearby are the **Salistre cavern** and the **Lavrinha diamond mines,** which are open to the public.

Serro*, 112 mi/180 km north of Belo Horizonte, is the site of three wonderful churches: **Nossa Senhora da Conceição, Senhor Bom Jesus de Matosinhos** and **Nossa Senhora do Carmo.** The tiny colonial town of **Conceição do Mato Dentro*** is 50 mi/80 km away.

Minas Gerais has several health resorts in the south near the border of São Paulo state that offer extensive facilities and treatments in a lovely setting. The best are the elegant **Poços de Caldas**,** 310 mi/500 km south-west of Belo Horizonte, which is popular with residents of São Paulo, and the four towns of **São Lourenço, Caxambu, Cambuquira** and **Lambari**.** **Araxa**,** 232 mi/373 km west of Belo Horizonte, is another health spa famous for its mud baths.

Telephone area code: 035 (unless otherwise indicated)

Accommodation

▲▲ Brasil, Av. João Lage 87, São Lourenço, ☎ 331 1433. This very comfortable hotel offers three bars, a restaurant and three swimming pools (two heated). 145 rooms.

▲▲ Gloria, Av. Camilo Soares 590, Caxambu, ☎ 341 1233. The best hotel in the town, with five bars, a restaurant and three swimming pools (one heated). 119 rooms.

▲▲ Grande Hotel Araxa, Estância do Barreiro, Araxa, ☎ (034) 661 2011. Beautifully situated in a park-like setting with four bars, a restaurant and three swimming pools (one heated). 168 rooms.

▲▲ Primus, Rua Cel. José Justino 681, São Lourenço, ☎ 331 1244. A wide range of tourist facilities make this hotel a pleasant place to stay. Two bars, a restaurant and two swimming pools. 129 rooms.

▲ Governador Palace, Av. Minas Gerais 550, Governador Valadares ☎ (0332) 70 0471. The most comfortable hotel in the town, with a bar, restaurant and swimming pool. 76 rooms.

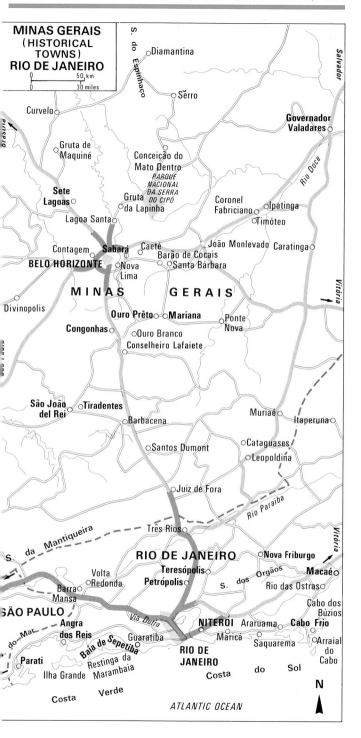

MINAS GERAIS (HISTORICAL TOWNS) RIO DE JANEIRO

0 50 km
0 30 miles

S. do Espinhaço

Diamantina

Sêrro

Curvelo

Gruta de Maquiné

Conceição do Mato Dentro

PARQUE NACIONAL DA SERRA DO CIPÓ

Sete Lagoas

Gruta da Lapinha

Coronel Fabriciano

Ipatinga

Timóteo

Governador Valadares

Rio Doce

Lagoa Santa

Contagem Sabará Caeté

Barão de Cocais

João Monlevado Caratinga

BELO HORIZONTE Nova Lima

Santa Bárbara

MINAS GERAIS

Divinopolis

Ouro Prêto Mariana

Ponte Nova

Congonhas

Ouro Branco

Conselheiro Lafaiete

São João del Rei Tiradentes

Barbacena

Muriaé Itaperuna

Santos Dumont

Cataguases

Leopoldina

Juiz de Fora

Rio Paraíba

S. da Mantiqueira Três Rios

Vitória

RIO DE JANEIRO Nova Friburgo

Volta Redonda Teresópolis

Macaé

Barra Mansa

Petrópolis

S. dos Orgãos

Rio das Ostras

SÃO PAULO

Angra dos Reis

Via Dutra

NITERÓI Araruama Cabo Frio

Cabo dos Búzios

do Mar

Guaratiba

Baía de Sepetiba

Maricá

Saquarema

Arraial do Cabo

Parati

Restinga da Marambaia

Ilha Grande

RIO DE JANEIRO

Costa do Sol

Costa Verde

N

ATLANTIC OCEAN

Salvador

Brasília

▲ **Minas Gerais,** Rua Pernambuco 615, Poços de Caldas, ☎ 7218686. This pleasant hotel has a bar, a restaurant and two swimming pools. 120 rooms.

▲ **Nacional,** Rua Barros Cobra 35, Poços de Caldas, ☎ 7212051. The largest hotel in the town, with two bars, a restaurant and two swimming pools (one heated). 226 rooms.

▲ **Nobre Palace,** Av. Francisco Sá 392, Teófilo Otoni, ☎ 5215824. This pleasant hotel has a restaurant and boutiques. 51 rooms.

▲ **Palace,** Praça Pedro Sanchez, Poços de Caldas, ☎ 7213392. Situated in a lovely setting and offering various tourist facilities, two bars, a restaurant, a heated swimming pool and boutiques, 214 rooms.

▲ **Solar da Ponte,** Praça da Merces, Tiradentes, ☎ (032) 3551255. A lovely hotel with a bar and a swimming pool. 12 rooms.

▲ **Tijuco,** Rua Macau do Meio 211, Diamantina, ☎ (037) 9311022. This modest hotel has a restaurant. 27 rooms.

Food

** **Thê,** Rua Pe. Toledo 172, Tiradentes, ☎ (032) 3551222. Reservations are recommended for this restaurant offering good French cooking. Open daily 7-11pm.

** **Chalé,** Rua Assis Figueiredo 1406, Poços de Caldas, ☎ 7212199. A lovely restaurant serving fish specialities. Open daily 11am-3pm, 6pm-midnight.

* **Cova do Daniel,** Praça da Basilica 54, Congonhas, ☎ (031) 7311834. Modest restaurant serving regional dishes. Open daily 11am-8pm.

* **Pilão,** Av. 31 de Março, São João del Rei. A small friendly *churrascaria.* Open daily 11:30am-3pm, 6-10pm.

* **Saturnino de Brito,** Represa Saturnino de Brito, Poços de Caldas, ☎ 7213575. International cooking in a restaurant located slightly outside town near the Saturnino de Brito dam. Live music Saturday evenings. Open daily 11am-midnight.

AMAZONIA

Amazonia, which covers all of northern Brazil, is made up of four states: Amazonas, whose capital is Manaus; Pará, whose capital is Belém; Acre, whose capital is Rio Branco; and Rondônia, whose capital is Porto Velho; plus the two federal districts of Amapá and Roraima. Together, these territories cover about 1,930,500 sq mi/5,000,000 sq km and account for roughly 42% of Brazil. However, because of its generally poor soil, heavy rainfall and hot climate, only 8% of the country's population lives in Amazonia, mostly around Belém and Manaus.

The region was first discovered in 1539 by the Spanish adventurer, Don Francisco Orellana, who crossed the Andes mountains from Peru. After penetrating the forests, Orellana eventually arrived at what he described as a tortuous, muddy river. Impressed by its size and strength, he called it the Rio-Mar (river-sea). What impressed him even more, however, was a tribe of women warriors he encountered. These women, he reported, were exactly like the Amazons (daughters of Mars) described in Greek mythology. Later, the river was renamed after them.

Over the past two decades, attempts by the government to settle the Amazon, while unsuccessful, have caused a great deal of damage to the tropical rain forests. Highways were constructed, opening up remote areas to cattle ranchers and farmers who then cleared the land by setting fire to the forest. It is estimated that 20% of the land has been destroyed in this way. The settlers, in turn, have profited little from their newly acquired land since much of the Amazonian rain forest lacks the necessary nutrients for farming.

Scientists in Brazil and throughout the world are concerned that the rapacious destruction of the forests, which has already greatly disrupted the region's fragile ecology, will have disastrous consequences on the world's environment. No less than 63,939 sq mi/165,602 sq km of forest went up in smoke at the end of the 1987 dry season. These yearly fires release approximately 620 million tons of carbon gases, or 10% of the world's total atmospheric pollutants. According to one environmental estimate, the amount of smoke produced is equivalent to the eruption of 100 volcanos. Scientists fear the thinning of the ozone layer, the acceleration of the greenhouse effect, and the raising of the world's temperature.

Pressured by environmental groups and encouraged by the World Bank, the Brazilian government recently put an end to the tax incentive program instituted to draw settlers to the region. Researchers are now studying methods to develop the Amazon

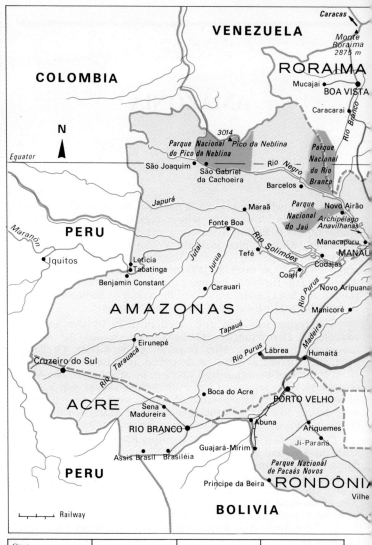

State or territory*	Amazonas	Pará	Amapá*
Surface (sm mi/sq ki)	604,032 1,564,445	481,869 1,248,042	54,161 140,276
Population 1987 (× 1000)	1833	4476	227
Capital	Manaus	Belém	Macapá
Features	Largest state in Amazonia. Manaus is a free-trade zone.	Most populated state in Amazonia. Leading gold producer. Has the largest iron ore and manganese mines in the world.	Leading producer of manganese. Smallest Amazonia state.

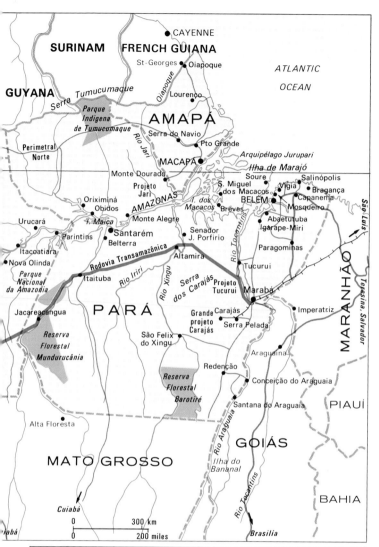

Roraima*	Rondônia	Acre	Total
88.843	93.839	58.915	1.381.659
230.104	243.044	152.589	3.578.500
112	818	374	7840
Boa Vista	Porto Velho	Rio Branco	
Least populated state in Amazonia. Its capital is the farthest from Rio and São Paulo.	Leading tin producer in Brazil (80%).	State is completely isolated during the rainy season (April-June).	

Flora and fauna

The largest variety of animals in the world live in Amazonia, including as many as 8000 indigenous species. The bird life alone is astonishing, with macaws, toucans, eagles, hummingbirds, parrots and hundreds of other species filling the forest. Monkeys swing among the branches and vines. Sumptuously coloured butterflies flash through the air in the company of a myriad of other insects, while lethal snakes coil themselves lazily around the forest's branches.

Due to the vast amount of water in the region, there is also a rich variety of aquatic animals, such as crocodiles and manatees. There are over 2000 different kinds of fish, including electric eels and legendary piranha.

As the climate here is hot and humid all year round the plant life blossoms, dies and flowers again continuously, making the forest a never-ending blaze of colour. To get the best glimpse of Amazonia's plant and animal life, rather than travel along the Amazon itself, it is best to take a boat trip through its small tributaries and penetrate deep into the forests.

without permanently destroying its wealth. Project Radam is one such successful developmental project.

In the early 1970s a huge aerial survey of the Amazon basin was completed and revealed that the region contained one of the most valuable and diverse mineral profiles in the world. Today, in the north-western district of Roraima, rock crystal, bauxite, copper, cassiterite and precious stones are mined. Elsewhere there are large deposits of manganese, uranium, iron ore, gold and diamonds. Perhaps the richest state in Amazonia is Rondônia in the far west, where huge deposits of cassiterite were discovered in the late 1960s. There are also gold mines here, and the farmland in this part of the Amazon is excellent.

▬ MANAUS AND AMAZONAS STATE

See map pp. 228-229.

The remote state of Amazonas is the largest state in Brazil but has the smallest population. Indian tribes still live in its forests, completely isolated from modern civilization. The majority of Indians today, however, work as guides, collectors of rubber and nuts, and cultivators of the forests.

Founded by the Portuguese in 1669, the capital Manaus lies on the Negro River, surrounded by jungle. It is about 780 mi/1250 km from the mouth of the Amazon River. For more than two centuries it remained a quiet village of traders, missionaries and Indians who lived on the produce of the forest. Then, in the mid-19th century, the rubber boom hit the town and changed it beyond recognition.

Rubber trees *(heveas)* had been used for practical purposes by the Indians for some time before the boom, notably to make syringes, which is why the gatherers of rubbers were later called *seringueiros*. It was in the 1840s that the American, Charles Goodyear, invented the process of vulcanization — the use of sulphur to strengthen the rubber while at the same time retaining its elasticity. Thus began Manaus's golden age.

Within a few years there was a huge demand for rubber. Because the rubber trees could be found only in Amazonia, specifically in this region, the world descended on Manaus. Overnight, roads were paved, electricity was installed, and the first tramway in South America was built. The most impressive symbol of the town's prosperity, however, was the imposing opera house, complete with domed towers and a marble interior. Artists from all over the world came here to perform.

Unfortunately, Manaus's growth came to an abrupt end around 1910, when an Englishman called Wickham managed to smuggle hundreds of *hevea* seedlings to England. These were planted in a hothouse in Kew Gardens and later shipped to Malaya. Soon that country's rubber production was in direct competition with that of Amazonia. Panic took over in Manaus. The tycoons, speculators and *seringueiros* disappeared suddenly, the opera house closed its doors and tropical weeds sprang up between the paving stones. The Indians, at least, were happy, since they had the land to themselves again, and indeed many of them went back to their old way of life in the forests.

Now only vague traces of the town's golden age remain, and these are overshadowed by its increasing number of skyscrapers. The new buildings result from Manaus's new-found wealth: in 1967 the city was declared a free-trade zone. It is today the collecting and distributing centre for all the areas of Brazil, Peru, Bolivia and Colombia along the Amazon River. New industries have been created, as well as a magnificent floating dock through which about 87% of Amazonian River traffic passes.

Although the city's economic activity has attracted people from all over Brazil, the most striking element about Manaus is its Indian flavour. Indians are omnipresent and their vast floating market, where boats slip past each other with amazing ease as vendors hawk their wares, is a dazzling sight. Far more in their element in their canoes than on the streets of Manaus, the Indians consider the river their territory. At dusk, when birdcalls and animal cries usher in the night, their pirogues leave long traces on the water's silvery surface.

The river rises with the seasons and local housing reflects this. The harbour is a floating one, and the poorer neighbourhoods consist of a mass of wooden boat-houses. Some of the boat-houses are three storeys high, with a landing stage and front door at every floor, to accommodate the river's different levels.

These houses are in stark contrast to the opulent mansions that date from the days of the rubber boom.

You may be taken aback by the large number of duty-free shops in the town centre and by the ubiquitous billboards. There is something incongruous about so much frenzied trade in such a hot and humid climate and in such an isolated place.

Telephone area code: 092

When to go

The best period to visit Manaus is when the waters are low from July to November and especially between September and November when it rarely rains. This is also high season for fishing.

The Amazon River

The dimensions of the Amazon River are so vast that it is hard to get a clear impression of this magnificent torrent. Originating in the Andes mountains, it flows across almost 4000 mi/6500 km of American continent irrigating six countries: Venezuela, Colombia, Ecuador, Peru, Bolivia and Brazil. It has more than 1000 tributaries — among the most important of which are the Xingu, the Tocantins, the Madeira, the Trombetas, the Tapajos and the Negro. The longest river after the Nile, it carries an estimated 20% to 25% of the total volume of water that runs off the earth's surface.

The Amazon has by far the strongest flow in the world. During the rainy season its volume triples and it spews out into the ocean, pushing the salt water as much as 100 mi/160 km offshore. The shock of the river hitting the Atlantic is so dramatic that its reverberations can be heard for miles around.

It is very important to remember when traveling to Manaus, or anywhere in Amazonia, that it is hot and humid. Because the rainy season lasts a long time (April-June), the rivers are high from April through October. This brings out the mosquitos, which are liable to be carrying malaria. It is wise to be vaccinated before you visit this area and to carry medicine against dysentery, as well as snake-bite serum. With this word of warning, we can then encourage you to visit an area unlike any other in the world.

Access

Plane

For the tourist, flying is the only practical way of reaching Manaus. There are numerous daily flights to Manaus from Rio (almost 4 hours), São Paulo (4h30), Brasília (2h30) and Belém (1h45). Try to avoid the lengthy flights with many stopovers. Flights originating in the major Latin American capitals and in Miami, Florida, also land at the **Eduardo Gomes International Airport,** ☎ 212 1210.

From the airport you can take a taxi or a bus to the city centre 9 mi/14 km away.

Airlines

Lloyd Aéreo Boliviano, Av. Eduardo Ribeiro 620, ☎ 232 7701.
Transbrasil, Rua Guilherme Moreira 150, ☎ 212 1356.
Varig/Cruzeiro, Rua Marcilio Dias 284, ☎ 234 1116.
Vasp, Rua Guilherme Moreira 179, ☎ 234 1266.

Bus

From Rio to Manaus, the bus trip takes a minimun of three days with transfers at Porto Velho and, sometimes, Cuiabá.
Estaçao Rodoviária, ☎ 236 2732.

Car

The distances are great and the road to Manaus, although completely paved, is often flooded, making driving difficult. On the last leg of the trip, after Porto Velho, there are six rivers that can only be crossed by ferries *(balsas)*.

If you decide to drive, make sure your car is in perfect condition and fill it up as often as possible. Drive preferably during the day and make frequent stopovers to prevent fatigue.

Belauto, Av. Constantino Neri 520, ☎ 233 2556.
Hertz, Rua Saõ Luís, ☎ 232 8155; at airport, ☎ 212 1376.
Locarauto, at airport, ☎ 212 1416.

Boat

From Belém it is possible to go up the Amazon River by boat. The 1064 mi/1713 km voyage takes at least five days. You can also take a one-week trip down the Madeira River from Porto Velho. For further information contact:

Enasa, Av. Presidente Vargas 41, Belém, ☎ 223 3011.

Accommodation

▲▲▲▲ **Tropical Manaus,** Praia da Ponta Negra, ☎ 238 5757. A luxury hotel in a beautiful location with three bars, a restaurant and a swimming pool. 378 rooms.

▲▲▲ **Novotel,** Av. Mandii 4, ☎ 237 1211. This very good hotel provides all the amenities of the French chain including a bar, a restaurant and a swimming pool. 168 rooms.

The river banks in Manaus resemble floating markets.

▲▲ **Amazonas**, Praça Adalberto Vale, ☎ 234 7679. A centrally located hotel with a bar, a restaurant and a swimming pool. 182 rooms.

▲ **Ana Cassia**, Rua dos Andradas 14, ☎ 232 6201. A simple hotel with a bar and restaurant. 88 rooms.

▲ **Da Vinci**, Rua Belo Horizonte 240, ☎ 233 6800. This hotel offers a bar, a restaurant and a swimming pool. 81 rooms.

▲ **Imperial**, Av. Getúlio Vargas 227, ☎ 233 8711. Situated in the centre of the town, this hotel has a bar, a restaurant and a swimming pool. 100 rooms.

▲ **Lord**, Rua Marcilio Dias 217, ☎ 234 9741. A centrally located hotel with a bar, a restaurant and a travel agency. 42 rooms.

Food

*** **Panorama**, Rua Recife 900, Adrianópolis, ☎ 232 3177. A seafood restaurant with a spectacular view. Open Mon-Sat 11am-3pm, 6-11:30pm.

*** **Taruma**, Hotel Tropical, Ponta Negra, ☎ 238 5757. Located outside the town, this restaurant offers international cuisine. Open daily 7pm-midnight.

** **Forasteiro**, Rua Dr. Moreira 178, ☎ 232 8162. A restaurant offering a wide selection of seafood specialities. Open Mon-Sat 11am-3pm, 6-10pm, closed holidays.

* **Fiorentina**, Praça Roosevelt 44, ☎ 232 1295. Italian cuisine is served in this centrally located restaurant. Open daily 11am-3pm, 6-11pm.

* **Mandarim**, Av. Ribeiro 650, ☎ 234 9834. A centrally located Chinese restaurant. Open Mon-Sat 11am-2pm, 6-11pm.

* **Mouraria**, Av. Efigênio Sales 2085, Parque 10, ☎ 236 6647. Located outside the town, this restaurant serves Portuguese food. Open Mon-Sat 7pm-2am.

* **Piaui**, Rua Dr. Moreira 202, ☎ 234 2133. International cuisine is served in this centrally located restaurant. Open Mon-Sat 11am-3pm, 6-10pm.

* **Roda Viva**, Av. Ajuricaba 1005, Cachoeirinha, ☎ 232 2687. A good *churrascaria*. Open daily 11am-3pm, 6-11:30pm.

Useful addresses

Banks
Banco da Amazonia, Av. 7 de Setembro 735, ☎ 232 2176.
Banco do Brasil, Rua Guilherme Moreira 315, ☎ 232 8550.

Consulates
Great Britain, Av. Ribeiro 500, ☎ 234 1018.
United States, Rua Maceio 62, ☎ 234 4546.

Emergencies
Pronto Socorro Municipal, Rua Recife, ☎ 236 0141.

Post office
Correio Central, Praça do Congresso.

Tourist office
Emantur, Av. Taruma 379, ☎ 234 5983. There is also a desk at the airport as well. For further information, ☎ 232 1646 or 234 5503.

Travel agencies
Amazon Explorer's, Rua Quintino Bocaiúva 189, ☎ 234 9741.
Selvatur, Hotel Amazonas, ☎ 234 8639.
Transamazonas, Rua Leonardo Malcher 734, ☎ 232 1454.

GETTING TO KNOW MANAUS

Originally, Manaus took up the river's northern, or left, bank; today, it is much more spread out. It consists mainly of a central district adjacent to the harbour and a northern district that is industrialized.

The best place to start a tour is the **Praça Oswaldo Cruz**, in the town centre, which contains a simple cathedral in the Jesuit style. Walking through the old streets radiating off the square, you will come upon the following sights.

Teatro Amazonas*** (Praça São Sebastião, ☎ 234 3525; open daily 9am-6pm) is the opera house that was built in 1896 in Italian Renaissance style. It seats 700 people and was designed and completely prefabricated in England. The tiles of its roof come from Alsace in France, the marble doorframes come from Verona in Italy, and the ironwork on its staircases comes from England. Frescoes and decorative panels depict life in the Amazon region. The theatre was rebuilt in 1929 and completely renovated in 1974. Today, the Teatro Amazonas is the city's most important cultural centre.

Alfândega (customs house) and the **floating harbour**** date from 1902-1906. The Alfândega was also prefabricated in England and testifies to British influence over trade in the Amazon basin in those days. The floating harbour rests on iron cylinders that permit it to rise when the river is high. This system allows large ships to enter Manaus harbour.

Mercado Municipal** (municipal market; Rua dos Bares, open daily 6am-6pm) is constructed in an Art Nouveau style and was also imported from Europe. It contains a picturesque fish market, as well as many shops selling handcrafts and local products such as medicinal herbs, roots and seeds.

Edifícios Públicos** are a collection of 19th- and early 20th-century buildings that are striking evidence of Manaus's glorious past. They include the **Palácio de Justiça**, the **Biblioteca Pública** and the **Palácio Rio Negro**.

Museu do Índio** (Indian Museum; Av. Duque de Caxias, ☎ 234 1422; open Mon-Sat 8am-noon, 2pm-5pm) displays many items from the region's native tribes. Authentic Indian handcrafts are on sale.

Pobre Diablo* (Rua Borba) is a tiny chapel in the Cachoeirinha district. It was built by a labourer known as 'Poor Devil' — hence its name.

Zona Franca** (free zone) is right in the heart of town. Created in 1967 to spur the region's economy, prices here are attractive to Brazilians, but equivalent to prices you will find in large shopping centres in Europe and North America.

ENVIRONS OF MANAUS

There are lovely beaches along some of the Amazon's tributaries. Resorts, in various stages of development, have grown up around them. Two of these are close to Manaus.

Ponta Negra** is 11 mi/18 km from Manaus. This is the region's most prestigious tourist attraction and is the site of the handsome **Tropical Hotel** (see p. 232). The height of the tourist season is between June and September. To get there, take the **Soltur** bus from Praça Matriz in Manaus. Along the way is the **Zoological Garden**, (☎ 092 238 4149; open daily 8am-5pm), which houses the Amazon forest's most representative species.

Praia Dourada** is around 14 mi/23 km from Manaus on the Estrada do Cetu. This resort is less well-known than Ponta Negra and, consequently, less developed.

While in Manaus you can take a brief excursion on the Amazon River or one of its tributaries. Every travel agency and hotel desk has information on daily excursions. Sights to see on these excursions include the following.

O Encontro das Aguas*** literally translates as 'the meeting of the waters'. It is here that the Negro River and the Solimões River meet. The waters of the Negro are black and the waters of the Solimões are yellow, and there is in addition a difference of about 12° F/5° C in temperature between the two rivers. It takes them more than 50 mi/80 km to blend together, at which time they form the Amazon River.

Igarapés*** and Igapos*** are minor branches of the Amazon and should be visited only in the course of a guided excursion. It is very easy to lose your way here! An excursion in this area is a marvelous way to see the Amazon forest. The banks are filled with giant trees, huge lianas and waterlilies. It is also a good way to see a crocodile and hear some very strange birdcalls. Sadly, the only Indian village in the surroundings has been put here for the benefit of tourists and is a sorry affair, containing only a few huts. The best time of year to visit the area is between October and April.

If you like to fish, ask your travel agent about fishing excursions. Do not go out on these rivers on your own to fish.

If the beach or an excursion on a river doesn't interest you, you can always take a bus from Manaus and see the various sights in the vicinity.

Bolivia church* is only 11 mi/18 km from Manaus.

Turumâ waterfalls* are beautiful and only 14 mi/22 km from Manaus.

Turislandia Park* is 12.5 mi/20 km from Manaus and is full of cocoa and rubber trees.

Januarilandia tourist centre* is a 40-minute boat trip from Manaus.

Manacapuru** is a little town 53 mi/80 km south-west of Manaus. It is possible to go there by boat, too.

Fazenda Porto Alegre is 31 mi/50 km from Manaus, near Lake Manury. This can only be reached by bus and boat, or hydroplane. From here, it is possible to take excursions into the forest or go fishing.

Boats leave from Manaus for the main cities in the Amazon basin, including some in neighbouring countries, such as Leiticia in Colombia and Iquitos in Peru. Boats are also available to towns on the Amazon River itself, and its tributaries.

Farther away from Manaus and in the interior of the state of Amazonas there are other interesting things to do.

Archipel das Anavilhanas** is reached from Manaus after an eight-hour boat trip on the Negro River. This is an area that offers wonderful excursions and beautiful views of the surrounding landscape.

Safaris through Amazonas state** are organized by the main travel agencies in Manaus (see p. 234) and, particularly by **Porto Nuovo Viagems** in Rio (Rua 7 de Setembro 92, ☎ (021) 242 3587). The safaris last three, six, or 13 days, and the itineraries depend on the season that you choose to travel.

Trips across the Amazon basin** can be arranged through travel agencies in Manaus (see p. 234). These trips are interesting from the point of view of landscape, but don't expect to see any Indian tribes. They are at least 300 mi/500 km from Manaus.

▬ *BELÉM AND PARÁ STATE*

See map pp. 228-229.

Traces of the oldest tribes of the Amazonian basin, the Tupis and the Aruaques, can be found in Pará state. In the Tupi language, *pará* means 'big', and the tribe named the region this because of the huge area that the mouth of the Amazon covers. It is a territory renowned for its fabulous variety of trees and plants. The density of these, however, has hindered the development of the region and as a result, Pará is sparsely populated. The majority of its people reside in its capital, Belém.

Garimperos at work in the gold mines of Serra Pelada (Pará state).

Belém*** is the most important city in northern Brazil. Founded by the Portuguese in 1616, it is situated at the mouth of the Pará River approximately 60 mi/100 km from the sea. Throughout the 19th century Belém was a relatively prosperous port, trading mainly in sugarcane and cocoa. However, towards the end of that century the rubber boom in the north changed the town dramatically.

One of the town's most attractive features is its abundance of mango trees. These line the streets, forming green tunnels that offer a welcome refuge from the heat. Noteworthy buildings to see include the **Basilica of Nossa Senhora de Nazaré****, with wonderful marble work and stained-glass windows, and the extraordinary **Teatro da Paz****, which, built in a rich, Baroque style, is one of the largest theatres in Brazil.

The **Forte do Castelo*****, constructed in 1616 to defend the mouth of the river and once the focal point of the town, is now better known for its lovely gardens. From these, there is a splendid view of the **Ver-o-Peso***** (meaning 'see the weight'), a fish market named after the huge scales on which the fish were weighed in colonial days. The **Bosque Rodrigues Alves**** (Av. Alm. Barroso 1622; open Tues-Sun 7am-noon, 2-5pm) has beautiful local vegetation around a lake as well as a small zoo, park, playground and tortoise sanctuary**, which houses 3000 tortoises.

Finally, don't miss a visit to the anthropological and archaeological **Emilio Goeldi Museum**** (Av. Magalhães Barata 376, ☎ (091) 224 9233; open Tues-Fri 8am-noon, 2-5pm, Sat 8am-1pm, 3-5pm, Sun 8am-6pm). Besides the fine collections, there is a zoo and botanical garden on the museum grounds.
Telephone area code: 091

Accommodation

▲▲▲▲ **Hilton International**, Av. Pres. Vargas 882, Praça da República, ☎ 223 6500. A luxury hotel that offers extensive facilities, including four bars, two restaurants, a swimming pool and boutiques. 361 rooms.

▲▲▲ **Equatorial Palace**, Av. Braz de Aguiar 612, Nazaré, ☎ 224 8855. This is a very comfortable hotel with three bars, two restaurants and a swimming pool. 126 rooms.

▲▲ **Novotel**, Av. Bernardo Sayão 4804, Guamá, ☎ 229 8011. You will find here the usual level of comfort standard in all Novotel hotels. Bar, restaurant and swimming pool. 121 rooms.

▲ **Excelsior Grão Pará**, Av. Pres. Vargas 718, ☎ 222 3255. A centrally located hotel with a bar and a restaurant. 138 rooms.

▲ **Regente**, Av. Gov. José Malcher 485, ☎ 224 0755. A comfortable hotel offering a bar, restaurant, swimming pool and boutiques. 117 rooms.

▲ **Sagres**, Av. Gov. José Malcher 2927, São Bras, ☎ 228 3999. Located outside the city, this hotel has two bars, a restaurant and a swimming pool. 106 rooms.

▲ **Vanja**, Rua Benjamin Constant 1164, ☎ 222 6457. A simple hotel located in the city centre with two bars, a restaurant and a swimming pool. 158 rooms.

Food

There are good restaurants in all the better hotels, but they are generally quite expensive.

*** **La Em Casa**, Av. Gov. José Malcher 982, Nazaré, ☎ 223 1212. One of the very finest restaurants in Belém, serving regional cuisine. Open daily noon-3:30pm, 7pm-midnight.

*** **Miako,** Rua 1 de Março 766, ☎ 223 4485. A Japanese restaurant conveniently located in the centre of town. Open daily noon-3pm, 6-11pm.

*** **O Outro,** Av. Gov. José Malcher 982, Nazaré, ☎ 223 1211. A lively and consistently excellent restaurant serving regional cuisine. Open Mon-Sat noon-3pm, 7pm-midnight.

*** **O Teatre,** Hilton Hotel, Av. Pres. Vargas 882, ☎ 223 6500. Live music provides entertainment in this excellent restaurant. International cuisine. Open Mon-Sat 8pm-2am.

* **Tucuruvi,** Route BR316, ☎ 235 0341. Located outside the city, this is a good *churrascaria.* Open daily noon-3pm, 6-11pm.

Useful addresses

Airlines

Transbrasil, Av. Pres. Vargas 780, ☎ 224 3677.
Varig, Av. Pres. Vargas 768, ☎ 225 4222.
Vasp, Av. Pres. Vargas 620, ☎ 224 5588.

Airport

Internacional Val de Cans, ☎ 233 4122.

Bank

Banco do Brasil, Av. Pres. Vargas 248, ☎ 222 1211.

Bus terminal

Praça do Operario, ☎ 228 0500.

Car rental

Belauto, Av. Assis Vasconcelos 175, ☎ 223 3466.
Nobre, Rue Carlos Gomes 274, ☎ 223 9900.
Unidas, Av. Gentil Bittencourt 1974, ☎ 229 2629.

Consulates

Great Britain, Rua Gaspar Viana 490, ☎ 224 4822.
United States, Rua Oswaldo Cruz 165, ☎ 223 0800.

Tourist offices

Centur, Av. Gentil Bittencourt 650.
Paratur, Praça Kennedy, ☎ 224 9633.

Travel agencies

Ciatur, Av. Pres. Vargas 645, ☎ 228 0011.
Gran Pará, Av. Pres. Vargas 882, ☎ 224 2111.
Norte, Pe. Prudêncio 43, ☎ 224 4151.

▬ ENVIRONS OF BELÉM

Belém is the best place from which to take river trips through the jungle. There are boats available to many destinations in the vicinity. Dates and schedules vary a great deal from one season to the next. For further information, contact **Enasa,** Av. Castilhos França, ☎ (091) 223 0056. Group excursions are available from: **Ciatur,** Av. Pres. Vargas 645, ☎ (091) 222 1995. Sights to see around Belém include:

The **Ilha de Marajó***** is an enormous, virtually uninhabited island near Belém. The homeland of successive Indian civilizations stretching as far back as 1000 BC, the Ilha de Marajó is one of the richest sources of Indian culture in Brazil. The island takes its name from the Marajoara Indians, the last civilization to exist here (AD 400-1300). Little is known about these people and their culture, except that they produced very beautiful, intricately designed ceramic work in red, black and white. Because this bore a certain resemblance to work by Peruvian civilizations, some archaeologists believe that the Marajoaras traveled down the Amazon from the Andes mountains, eventually settling on the island.

The vast Amazon River discharges close to 20% of the world's fresh water into the Atlantic Ocean.

Ancient objects found on the island are displayed in the excellent Emilio Goeldi Museum in Belém (see p. 238).

Ilha de Marajó offers splendid opportunities to hunt and fish. Group tours and accommodation are organized by **Metur** (☎ (091) 233 2128) and **Ciatur** ☎ (091) 228 0011. The island is reached by boat (six-hour trip) from Porto de Anasa in Belém (☎ (091) 223 3011) or by plane (45-minute trip). There are two *fazendas* (large farms) on the island that offer accommodation for tourists: **Fazenda Jilva** ☎ (091) 223 7736 and **Fazenda Bon Jardim** ☎ (091) 222 1380. Each has room for approximately 20 persons and the stay — including food and excursions — costs about US$80 per day. For further information about farm stays, contact the Gran Pará travel agency in Belém (see p. 239).

Abaetetuba* is a tiny colonial town 310 mi/500 km south-west of Belém. It is set in the midst of a virgin forest.

Santarém** is a riverside town 229 mi/369 km west of Belém at the confluence of the Amazon and Tapajos rivers. Founded in 1661, it is a place of considerable charm and historical interest. It also happens to be the third largest city on the Amazon, thanks to the discovery of gold and bauxite in the area, and its vast timber resources. You can find lovely ceramics of animals here, designed by the Tapajos Indians. Santarém is also the place where the green water of the Tapajos meets the yellow water of the Amazon, creating a spectacular mottled effect. It also has some of the most beautiful beaches in Amazonia.

Other beautiful beaches in the Belém area include **Icoaraci** (18.5 mi/30 km north of Belém), **Mosqueiro** (53 mi/85 km north of Belém), **Vigia** (65 mi/105 km north of Belém) and **Salinópolis** (142 mi/228 km north-east of Belém).

Obidos**, 683 mi/1100 km west of Belém, is a former fortified town on the Amazon River. Interesting sights include the fort and a lovely swimming spot at Curuçamba. There are boat services from here three or four times a month to Belém, Manaus and other cities along the Amazon. The Amazon is at its narrowest at Obidos: 1 mi/1.6 km wide and 230 ft/70 m deep.

Marabá* is 612 mi/985 km south of Belém. From here, you can take excursions on the Tocantins and Itacaiunas rivers. There are also boat services available to Belém, Estreito and Santarém.

Carajas*, 739 mi/1190 km south of Belém, has developed around a huge mining project for the world's richest iron deposit. In the vicinity are large deposits of manganese, nickel, copper, gold and tin.

Serra Pelada* is 30 mi/50 km from Carajas. In 1980 gold was discoverd here. Today, there is a large mine, which employs 60,000 men and is a hive of activity.

Conceição do Araguaia** is 726 mi/1170 km south of Belém. Fishing is excellent here from June to October and there are excursions available on the river.

Telephone area code: 091

Accommodation

▲▲ **Tropical,** Av. Mendoça Furtado 4120, Santarém, ☎ 522 1533. The best hotel in the area, with a bar, restaurant and two swimming pools. 122 rooms.

▲ **Santarém Palace,** Av. Rui Barbosa 726, Santarém, ☎ 522 5285. A modest hotel with a restaurant. 47 rooms.

▲ **Taruma Tropical,** Av. Beira-Rio 2120, Conceição do Araguaia, ☎ 421 1205. A simple and comfortable hotel with a bar, restaurant and swimming pool. 50 rooms.

Food

* **Beira-Rio,** Pça. Cipriano Santos, Marabá. A modest *churrascaria* with a lovely view of the river. Open daily 11am-11pm.

* **Mascote,** Pça. do Pescador 10, Santarém, ☎ 522 5997. Small restaurant specializing in fish dishes. Open daily 11am-midnight.

▬ *AMAPÁ*

See map pp. 228-229.

Amapá is a small federal district, measuring only 54,161 sq mi/140,276 sq km. Practically all of its inhabitants live along the coast. Its main source of revenue is manganese, although its forests are also a source for various resources such as cellulose and precious wood.

Amapá's capital is **Macapá***, which was founded in 1815. It is a well-run city that derives its wealth from the manganese mines. Although this area is of limited tourist interest, it is not without merit. Macapá is a charming city and you should visit the **Fort of São José***. This is also the departure point for some interesting excursions. There are boat trips on the Amazon river to Belém, Ilha de Marajó and Guyana. They leave from Porto de Santana (17 mi/28 km from the city centre). There is also a fascinating train ride from the station at Porto de Santana to the manganese mine at **Serra do Navio**** (121 mi/194 km away). You will need a permit for the trip; for information, ☎ (096) 632 6666.

Telephone area code: 096

Accommodation

▲▲▲ **Novotel,** Av. Amazonas 17, Macapá, ☎ 222 1144. A

comfortable hotel with a bar, a good restaurant and boutique. 76 rooms.

▲ **Amapaense,** Av. Tiradentes, Macapá, ☎ 222 3366. A centrally located modest hotel. 44 rooms.

Food

* **O Boscão,** Rua Amilton Silva 977, Macapá, ☎ 222 4163. A small restaurant serving international and regional cuisines. Open daily noon-3pm, 7pm-1am.

* **Peixaria,** Av. Mãe Luzia 84, Macapá, ☎ 222 0913. A centrally located fish restaurant. Open 11am-2pm, 7pm-midnight.

Useful adresses

Airlines
Taba, Av. Coriolano Juca 376, Macapá, ☎ 222 2083.
Varig, Rua Cândido Mendes 1039, Macapá, ☎ 222 1287.
Vasp, Rua Pe. Júlio Maria Lombard 115, Macapá, ☎ 222 2411.

Airport
Internacional de Macapá, ☎ 222 3155.

Car rental
Interlocadora, Av. FAB 458, Macapá, ☎ 222 0019.
Localiza, Av. Pres. Vargas 519, Macapá, ☎ 222 3596.

Emergencies
Pronto Socorro, Rua Hamilton Silva, Macapá, ☎ 192.

Post office
Av. Coriolano Juca 125, Macapá.

▬ *RORAIMA*

See map pp. 228-229.

Although 88,843 sq mi/230,104 sq km in size, Roraima is the Amazon region's least populated area. The economy currently depends on cattle-breeding, but the state has a large pool of natural resources, including gold, diamonds and uranium. Mining has not been exploited yet, but there is talk of development in the future.

Roraima was separated from Amazonas and turned into a federal district in 1937. It is made of up the Rio Branco valley, encircled by a string of mountains. Its capital is **Boa Vista***, 500 mi/800 km north of Manaus. It is practically inaccessible during the rainy season.

Boa Vista is situated on the banks of the Rio Branco and, unlike most of Brazil, lies in the northern hemisphere. Boats travel to Manaus once every two weeks, and there are many excursions possible: **Caracaraná lagoon** (124 mi/200 km away), **Pedra Pintada rocks** (75 mi/120 km away) and the beaches at **Ponte de Cauamé** (6 mi/10 km away).

Telephone area code: 095.

Accommodation

▲▲ **Praia Palace,** Av. Floriano Peixota 352, ☎ 224 8110. A lovely hotel with a bar, restaurant and swimming pool. 81 rooms.

▲ **Eusébio's,** Rua Cecilia Brasil 1107, ☎ 224 1846. A centrally located hotel with a bar, restaurant and swimming pool. 30 rooms.

▲ **Tropical,** Praça Centro Cívico 53, ☎ 224 4850. Situated in the centre of town, this modest hotel has a bar, restaurant and swimming pool. 43 rooms.

Food

* **Senzala,** Av. Castelo Branco 1313, ☎ 224 1079. Located in a

lovely park, this restaurant serves a variety of international dishes.
Open Tues-Sun 11am-2pm, 6pm-1am.
* **Varanda Tropical**, Rua Cap. Bessa 74, ☎ 224 4734. A modest
fish restaurant situated on the banks of the river.

Useful addresses

Airlines
Varig, Av. Getúlio Vargas 242, ☎ 224 2226.
Venezuelana, Av. Benjamin Constant 285, ☎ 224 9300.

Airport
Internacional, ☎ 224 3680.

Bus terminal
Av. das Guianas 1627, ☎ 224 3547.

Car rental
Localiza, Av. Maj. Williams 538, ☎ 224 3786.

Emergencies
Pronto Socorro, Av. Cap. Júlio Bezerra, ☎ 224 2380.

Post office
Praça Centro Cívico.

▬▬ *ACRE*

See map pp. 228-229.
Acre is a small state, measuring only 58,915 sq mi/152,589 sq km.
After being Bolivian, Acre passed to Brazil in 1912. This area is not
really geared to tourism, but it is interesting in that it typifies the truly
Amazonian character. It is an integral part of the Amazon forest and is
rich in latex, Brazil nuts, and many kinds of wood. A few years ago, a
study found that its soil was outstandingly fertile. This has led to an influx
of settlers from the south, leading to unemployment and a good deal of
social strife.
Acre's capital is **Rio Branco***, which lies on the banks of the river of the
same name. It was founded in 1882. Boats ply the river to Manaus and
Boca do Acre, and buses are available to Brasília and Assis Brasil. There
are still some *seringueiros* to be seen at Sena Madureira, 93 mi/150 km
away.

Telephone area code: 068

Accommodation

▲ **Inácio Palace**, Rua Rui Barbosa 72/82, ☎ 224 6397.
A simple hotel with a restaurant located in the centre of the town.
87 rooms.

▲ **Rio Branca**, Rua Rui Barbosa 193, ☎ 224 1785.
Centrally located, this modest but comfortable hotel has a
restaurant. 46 rooms.

Food

* **Trevo**, Boulevard Augusto Monteiro 1254. A small friendly
churrascaria. Open daily 11am-3pm, 6pm-1am.
* **Tu canaré**, Av. Ceará 868. A modest fish restaurant. Open daily
11am-3pm, 6pm-midnight.

Many Indigenous tribes still live isolated in the heart of Amazonia.

Useful addresses

Airlines
Taba, Rua Quintino Bocaiúva 94, ☎ 224 6883.
Varig, Rua Mal. Deodoro 115, ☎ 224 2226.
Vasp, Rua Mal. Deodoro 89, ☎ 224 6585.

Airport
Internacional Pres. Medici, ☎ 224 6692.

Bus terminal
Estaçio Rodoviária, ☎ 224 1182.

Tourist office
Secretaria de Industria e Comercio, Av. Getúlio Vargas 659, ☎ 224 3997.

▬ RONDÔNIA

See map pp. 228-229.

Rondônia extends over 97,525 sq mi/252,589 sq km. This state is in the midst of frantic development as a consequence of the agrarian boom in neighbouring Mato Grosso. Its natural resources consist mostly of tin and gold. The tin mines are Brazil's most productive, and the working conditions in the gold mines are notoriously harsh. The state also contains precious wood.

Today, the government is seeking to provide large-scale support for industries that wish to relocate here. Thus far, the state has been unable to do much for settlers because the infrastructure has not been able to keep up with immigration. In 1950 Rondônia's population was a mere 37,000; today it is 818,000.

Rondônia was settled originally in the 17th century as a result of an overflow from settlement in Mato Grosso. Modern development did not begin until the rubber boom in the mid-19th century. Finally, the area is opening up to the outside world, thanks mostly to a new road between Cuiaba and Porto Velho.

Porto Velho★★ is Rondônia's capital and lies on the banks of the Madeira River. You can visit the **Rondônia museum★** (☎ (069) 223 3835; open Mon-Fri 8am-noon, 2-5pm, Sat and Sun, 8am-noon) and the **Ferroviário museum** (☎ (069) 221 3835; open Mon-Fri 8am-6pm). This latter museum houses the mementos from the building of the railway that was constructed to transport latex. The railway was known as the 'train of death' because of the huge mortality rate among the labour force employed to build it.

Besides frequent boats to Manaus, there are lovely excursions on the Madeira and Jamari rivers. Places to visit include the **São Antônio waterfalls** (4.5 mi/7 km away) and the tiny fishing community at **Teotônio★★** (31 mi/50 km away). About 250 mi/400 km away at **Guajara-Mirim** fishing and hunting expeditions are available. Also from here it is possible to enter Bolivia.

Telephone area code: 069

Accommodation

▲▲▲ **Vila Rica**, Av. Carlos Gomes 1616, ☎ 221 2286. A centrally located hotel with a bar, restaurant, swimming pool and boutiques. 115 rooms.

▲▲ **Floresta**, Rua Prudente de Morais 2313, ☎ 221 5669. A comfortable hotel with a bar, restaurant and swimming pool. 65 rooms.

▲▲ **Rondon**, Av. Gov. Jorge Teixeira, ☎ 221 3166. Another comfortable hotel with a bar, restaurant and two swimming pools. 138 rooms.

Food

** **Caravela do Madeira**, Rua Ariquemes 104, Arigolândia, ☎ 221 6641. A good fish restaurant situated along the banks of the Madeira River, 3 mi/5 km outside Porto Velho. Live music in the evenings. Open Mon-Sat 11am-3pm, 6:30pm-midnight.

* **Oriente**, Av. Amazonas 1280, ☎ 221 6071. A modest Chinese restaurant. Open Wed-Mon 11:30am-2:30pm, 7-11:30pm.

Useful addresses

Airlines
Taba, Rua Prudente de Morais 39, ☎ 221 5493.
Varig, Av. Campos Sales 2666, ☎ 221 8555.
Vasp, Rua Tenreiro Aranha, ☎ 223 3755.

Airport
Belmont, ☎ 221 3935.

Bus terminal
Av. Pres. Kennedy, ☎ 221 2141.

Car rental
Belauto, Av. Calama 2468, ☎ 221 3805.
Localiza, Rua Dom Pedro 1208, ☎ 221 4187.

Post office
Av. Pres. Dutra 1701.

Tourist office
Detur, Av. Pinheiro Machado 326, ☎ 221 1565.

MATO GROSSO, MATO GROSSO DO SUL AND PANTANAL

The states of Mato Grosso and Mato Grosso do Sul, covering more than 494,600 sq mi/1,281,000 sq km, lie in the centre of Brazil with the state of Goiás to the east and Bolivia and Paraguay to the west. The Portuguese sailor, Alexio Garcia, was the first to explore the area when he sailed up the Paraguai River in 1522 — the only means of reaching the territory at that time. Because it was so inaccessible, few attempts were made at colonization and it was not until 1748 that Mato Grosso (the name given at the time to the whole area) was declared a captaincy and incorporated into the Portuguese crown.

Later, when rubber trees *(heveas)* were discovered in the region, traders settled along the Guaporé River, west of Cuiabá, which was to become the capital of Mato Grosso. However, the fierce resistance of the Indian tribes of the region, coupled with the area's remoteness, hindered the development of Mato Grosso for centuries. It was only in the 1950s, when trains began to link its towns with principal cities in Brazil, that the territory started to grow in importance.

In 1977, the Brazilian government divided Mato Grosso into two states, Mato Grosso and Mato Grosso do Sul. Their respective capitals are Cuiabá, founded in 1718 and made the capital of Mato Grosso in 1825, and Campos Grande, inaugurated in 1899. Combined, the states now represent one of the richest areas of Brazil, with their extensive cattle breeding, coffee and rice plantations, important manganese mines, and rich mineral and metal beds, which have yet to be fully exploited.

Although both Cuiabá and Campo Grande have their share of fine buildings — the government palace in Cuiabá is particularly impressive — and are certainly pleasant cities to visit, they and other towns in the region have a very modest appeal compared to the fabulous architecture found in regions affected by the gold rush. On the other hand, in terms of natural beauty, Mato Grosso is one of the most exciting areas to visit in the world.

Pantanal is a vast flood plain that lies between Cuiabá and Campo Grande. Home to myriad rare animals, it is considered one of the greatest wildlife preserves in the world. There are also hundreds of bird species here, and the area is plentifully supplied with fish.

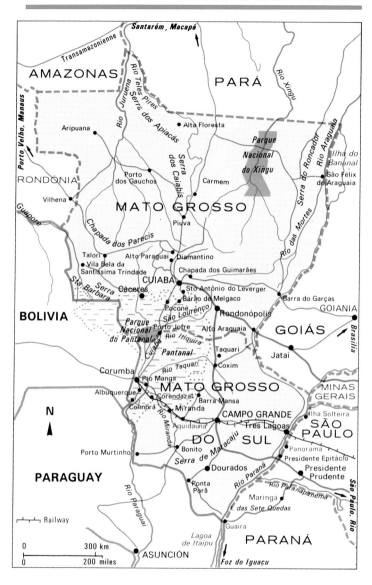

Mato Grosso and Mato Grosso do Sul states.

The plain, which stretches over approximately 88,800 sq mi/230,000 sq km, is protected by the National Parks Authority and zealously guarded by local farmers. Bear in mind that you are not allowed to hunt here, although fishing is permitted all year long.

Pantanal has a rainy season and a dry season. During the rainy season (January to June) the Paraguai River and its tributaries flood the entire area. During the dry season (July to the beginning of October) the birds return to build their nests.

▬ PRACTICAL INFORMATION

See map p. 249.

Telephone area code: 065   (Cuiabá),
067 (Campo Grande, Corumbá).

When to go
The dry season, from July to the beginning of October, is the best time to visit this region simply because you will stay dry. Don't forget, however, that the best time to see all the flowers in bloom is during the rainy season. If you are interested in fishing or photography, July, August and September are the best months to visit.

Access

Plane

The easiest, and most common, way of getting to this remote region is by plane. The airport in Cuiabá, **Marechal Rondon,** is located 5 mi/8 km from the centre of town. In Campo Grande, the airport is located on Avenida Pedrossian.

Taba, at airport, Cuiabá, ☎ 381 2233.
Tam, Rua Costa 728, Cuiabá, ☎ 322 3599; Av. Alfonso Pena, Campo Grande, ☎ 383 2933.
Transbrasil, Rua Barão de Melgaço 3508, Cuiabá ☎ 322 7213.
Varig/Cruzeiro, Praça Alencastro 22, Cuiabá, ☎ 321 3233; Rua Rio Branco 139, Campo Grande.
Vasp, Rua Pedro Celestino 32, Cuiabá, ☎ 321 4122; Av. Calogeras 2143, Campo Grande, ☎ 382 4091.

Train

It is possible to travel by train from São Paulo to Campo Grande but the trip takes two days. It is better to arrive by plane and then take trains around the area.

Av. Calogeras, Campo Grande, ☎ 383 2762.

Bus

There are direct buses from São Paulo to Campo Grande and Cuiabá (length of trip 18 and 30 hours, respectively). If you take a bus from Rio, it will stop in São Paulo.

Rua Joaquim Nabucco 200, Campo Grande, ☎ 383 1678; Av. Marechal Rondon, Cuiabá, ☎ 321 4703.

Car

The distance from Rio to Campo Grande is 900 mi/1449 km, to Corumbá 1176 mi/1892 km, and to Cuiabá 1308 mi/2105 km.

Accommodation
We strongly advise against setting off without reservations. A journey to Mato Grosso or Pantanal should be properly planned before departure; otherwise you risk finding yourself without accommodation or, worse yet, lost.

Hotels

These only exist in the larger cities, and by and large they leave something to be desired.

▲▲ **Aurea Palace,** Av. Gen. Mello 63, Cuiabá, ☎ 322 3377. A centrally located hotel offering a bar, restaurant and swimming pool. 72 rooms.

▲▲ **Campo Grande,** Rua 13 de Maio 2825, Campo Grande, ☎ 383 6061. This is a very pleasant, well situated hotel with a bar and restaurant. 96 rooms.

▲▲ **Jandaia,** Rua Barão do Rio Branco 1271, Campo Grande, ☎ 282 4081. A very comfortable hotel with a bar, restaurant and swimming pool. 140 rooms.

▲▲ **Nacional,** Rua America 936, Corumbá, ☎ 231 6868. The most comfortable hotel in the town, with a bar and swimming pool. 94 rooms.

▲ **Aquidauana Palace,** Rua Manoel Paes de Barros 904, Auqidanuana, ☎ (667) 241 3596. A hotel with very basic services. 26 rooms.

▲ **Concord,** Av. Corlogeras 1624, Campo Grande, ☎ 382 3081. A pleasant hotel with a bar, restaurant and swimming pool. 84 rooms.

▲ **Excelsior,** Av. Getúlio Vargas 264, Cuiabá, ☎ 322 6322. A comfortable hotel, centrally located, with a restaurant. 153 rooms.

▲ **Fenix,** Rua dos Operarios 600, Cáceres, ☎ (065) 221 1592. This hotel offers the very basic in comfort. 11 rooms.

▲ **Gasparin,** Av. Sangradouro 162, Cáceres, ☎ (065) 221 2579. A modest hotel with a bar. 13 rooms.

▲ **Grande Hotel Corumba,** Rua Mariano 468, Corumbá, ☎ 231 1041. A very simple hotel with a bar. 66 rooms.

▲ **Hotel dos Camalotes,** Fazenda Três Barras, Porto Murtinho, ☎ (067) 382 5361. A comfortable hotel for the region, with a bar, restaurant and swimming pool. 34 rooms.

▲ **Ipanema,** Rue Gen. Osorio 540, Cáceres, ☎ (065) 221 1676. This is a small, simple hotel. 15 rooms.

▲ **Las Velas,** Av. Filinto Muller 62, Cuiabá, ☎ 381 1422. Conveniently located near the airport, this hotel has a bar and restaurant. 42 rooms.

▲ **Piracema,** BR163, Coxim, ☎ (067) 291 1610. A hotel offering simple lodging, restaurant. 42 rooms.

▲ **Pousada do Cachimbo,** Rua Alan Kardec 4, Corumbá, ☎ 231 4833. An attractive and beautifully located hotel with a panoramic view of the port. Bar, restaurant, swimming pool. 22 rooms.

Fazendas and pesqueiros

Fazendas are cattle farms. They often accommodate guests, and do it in a satisfactory way, providing them with everything needed to go out on the rivers for a photographic or fishing expedition. *Pesquieros* are temporary camps offering rudimentary accommodation. Their advantage lies in the fact that they are close to fishing areas and that their atmosphere is almost always congenial.

Acampamento Pirigara 40 mi/65 km from Poconé on the São Lourenço River. Fishing, excursions, 6 apartments that sleep 4. Reservations, call Cuiabá, ☎ 322 8961.

Baranquinho, 45 mi/72 km from Cáceres on the Jauru River. 10 apartments that sleep 4. Reservations, call Cuiabá, ☎ 322 0513.

Cabana da Lontra, 62 mi/100 km from Corumbá. Excursions and fishing on the Miranda River, camping equipment for rent, 20 apartments. Reservations, call Aquidauana, ☎ (067) 241 2405.

Cabana do Pantanal, 26 mi/42 km from Poconé at Porto Cerado on the Cuiabá River. Fishing, excursions, photo-safaris, 11 apartments that sleep 2 to 5. Reservations, call São Paulo, ☎ (011) 34 4245.

Cabana do Pescador, 35 mi/60 km from Aquidauana. Excursions, fishing, 8 apartments. Reservations, call Aquidauana, ☎ (067) 241 3697 or São Paulo, ☎ (011) 283 5843.

Fazenda Cachoeira dos Palmeiras, 19 mi/30 km from Coxim on the BR163. Camping.

Fazenda Santa Rosa Pantanal, 90 mi/145 km from Poconé at

Porto Jofre on the Cuiabá River. Fishing, excursions, photo-safaris, 10 apartments and 24 chalets that sleep 4. Reservations, call Cuiabá, ☎ 321 5514.

Pesqueiro do Severinho, 45 mi/72 km from Corumbá. Fishing, excursions, 38 apartments that sleep 2 to 6. Reservations, call Corumbá, ☎ 231 1532.

Pesqueiro Taruma, 43 mi/70 km from Corumbá. Excursions and fishing on the Paraguai River, 9 apartments that sleep 2 to 6. Reservations, call Corumbá, ☎ 231 4197.

Pousada do Barão, 1.5 hour trip by boat from Barão de Melgaço. Photo-safaris, accommodates 15 to 20. Reservations, call Onlytur in Rio, ☎ (021) 257 7733.

Pousada do Pantanal, 68 mi/110 km from Corumá. Fishing, excursions, horseback riding, 9 apartments that sleep 2 to 4. Reservations, call Corumbá, ☎ 231 5797.

Pousada Pixaim, 35 mi/55 km from Poconé. Fishing, excursions, 10 apartments that sleep 2. Reservations, call Cuiabá, ☎ 322 0513.

Safari Foto e Pesca, 93 mi/150 km from Cáceres. Fishing, photo-safaris, accommodates 8. Reservations, call Cuiabá, ☎ 321 6370.

Hotel-boats

These are boats that have been turned into floating hotels. They offer cruises that are slowly becoming popular. Their comfort levels may vary considerably, but they are practical because they make it possible to combine excursions with fishing or taking photographs.

Barco Botel. Fishing and excursions on Paraguai River, accommodates 8 to 10. Reservations, call Corumbá, ☎ 231 4473.

Barco Cabexi. Fishing, excursions, 4 cabins that sleep 2. Reservations, call Corumbá, ☎ 231 4683.

Botel Amazonas. Fishing, swimming. Reservations, call Corumbá, ☎ 231 3016.

Botel Beira-Rio. Excursions to the confluence of the Miranda and Aquidauana rivers, accommodates 40. Reservations, call Hotel Beira-Rio in Corumbá, ☎ 242 1476.

Botel Corumbi. Fishing, swimming. Reservations, call Corumbá, ☎ 231 3016.

Botel Flory. Fishing and excursions on Paraguai River, accommodates 8 to 10. Reservations, call Corumbá, ☎ 231 1968.

Botel Trans-Tur. Fishing, swimming. Reservations, call Corumbá, ☎ 231 3016.

Food

The emphasis in the cuisine is on fish of this area. The food is of average quality and reasonably priced. Other Brazilian specialities such as *churrascos* are also available.

*** **Radio Clube,** Rua Pe João Crippa 1280, Campo Grande, ☎ 382 3358. This lively restaurant is one of the best in town, serving international cuisine. Open daily 7pm-midnight.

** **Cacimba,** Rua 13 de Junho 116, Cuiabá, ☎ 741 1175. A good place to try the regional cuisine. Open Mon-Sat 8-11pm.

** **Peixaria do Queiroz,** Praça Jaime Figueiredo 130, Cuiabá, ☎ 322 6420. A restaurant serving excellent seafood. Open Sun-Fri 11am-2:30pm, 6-11pm.

** **O Regionalissimo,** Rua 13 de Junho, Cuiabá, ☎ 321 0603. Cafeteria-style restaurant specializing in regional cuisine. Open daily 11:30am-2:30pm, 7:30-11pm.

Useful addresses

Bank

Banco do Brasil, Av. Afonso Pena 2202, Campo Grande, ☎ 382 6041.

Car rental
Interlocadora, Av. Alfonso Pena 1440, Campo Grande, ☎ 382 3008.
Localiza, Av. Alfonso Pena 318, Campo Grande, ☎ 382 8786; Av. Dom Bosco 965, Cuiabá, ☎ 322 2472.
Nobre, Av. Calogeras 1932, Campo Grande, ☎ 383 1570; Av. Ponce de Arruda 980, Cuiabá, ☎ 381 1651.
Trescinco, Rua Comandante Costa/Av. Dom Bosco 1310, Cuiabá, ☎ 321 5666.
Unidas, Av. Alfonso Pena 746, Campo Grande, ☎ 383 6684; Av. Isaac Povoas 720, Cuiabá, ☎ 321 4646.

Emergencies
Pronto Socorro Municipal, Rua Gen. Valle, Cuiabá, ☎ 321 7404.

Tourist offices
MSTur, Av. Alfonso Pena 3149, Campo Grande.
Turimat, Praça República (next to the post office), Cuiabá, ☎ 322 5363, open daily 8am-6pm.

Travel agencies
Confiança, Praça República 108, Cuiabá, ☎ 321 4142
Cuiabá-Tour, Rua Barão de Melgaço 3508, Cuiabá, ☎ 322 8723.
Lion-Tour, Av. Isaac Povoas 567, Cuiabá, ☎ 321 5514.
Ouro Branco, Rua 26 de Agosto 260, Campo Grande, ☎ 383 1348.
Pantanal Express, Av. Alfonso Pena 2081, Campo Grande, ☎ 382 5333.
Selva, Rua Barão de Melgaço 3594, Cuiabá, ☎ 322 0513.
Taua-Tour, Praça do Rosário 70, Cuiabá, ☎ 322 1122.
Time-Tour, Rua 13 de Maio, Campo Grande, ☎ 382 7436.

GETTING TO KNOW MATO GROSSO, MATO GROSSO DO SUL AND PANTANAL

Mato Grosso

Cuiabá★★ lies at South America's geodesic centre. It was founded by gold hunters in 1719. It became the capital of Mato Grosso in 1835 but did not come into its own until the early 20th century, with the boom in the wholesale trade of agricultural and meat products between Pantanal, Amazonas and São Paulo. When Mato Grosso was split into two separate states in 1979, Cuiabá once again lost its economic importance.

The old parts of Cuiabá are very interesting: **Praça do Rosário, Rua de Baixa, Rua do Meio** and **Rua de Cima.** There are two noteworthy churches, **Bom Despacho★★,** which was built in 1720 and contains a small museum, and **Nossa Senhora do Rosário★.**

In the area of the university (Universidade Federal de Mato Grosso) there are several museums that are well worth visiting. The **Indian Museum★★** (also called the Marechal Rondo Museum, ☎ 361 2211, open Mon-Fri 7am-6pm, Sat 8am-2pm) is devoted to the Xavantes, Karajas and Bororos tribes. Established by FUNAI in order to protect the Indians, it has exhibitions on, and sells, their handcrafts. Items include ceramics, musical instruments and clothing. Another museum in this area is the **Museum of Popular Art and Culture★** (Museu de Arte et Cultura Popular, ☎ 361 2211, open Mon-Fri 8am-12:30pm, 2-5pm). As its name implies, this museum displays handcrafts and items of folklore.

The town centre boasts the **Ramis Bucair Museum★** (☎ 321 4624, open Mon-Fri 8am-5pm, Sat 8-11:30am), with fossil and mineral exhibits, and another museum devoted to handcrafts **(Museum do Artesanato★** (☎ 321 0603, open Mon-Fri 8am-6pm, Sat 8am-1pm).

Santo Antônio de Leverger★ is a little town 18 mi/30 km south of Cuiabá that was named after a famous Frenchman who took part in the war with Paraguay. On the Piraim River, the town has pleasant river beaches and offers excursions. Fishing and camping are also available.

Chapada dos Guimarães★★★, 37 mi/60 km east of Cuiabá, was founded in the 18th century by Jesuits. It is home to several natural 'wonders', including a magnificent formation shaped like a deep (328 ft/100 m) amphitheatre and a string of waterfalls, one of which is the 200 ft-/61 m-high **Veu da Nova**.

Other interesting towns in the vicinity of Cuiabá are **Águas Quentes*** (56 mi/90 km to the east), a spa with natural pools of hot water (104° F/40° C), **Diamantino** (84 mi/135 km north of Cuiabá) and **Alto Paraguai** (93 mi/150 km north of Cuiabá). The latter two towns have deposits of precious minerals.

If you wish to travel farther into the interior of Mato Grosso, there are wonderful excursions available on the **Rio Teles Pires***, 360 mi/580 km from Cuiabá. The excursions start in Cuiabá with a car journey to the village of Alta Floresta and then a 50 mi/80 km boat trip to an encampment of the Ilha Regina. There are also fishing excursions organized on other rivers in the vicinity including the Perxoto de Azevedo, the Cristalino and the Nhandu.

Other interesting trips are possible to the **Xingu National Park***, an **Indian reservation** (for permission to visit, contact FUNAI, see p. 49), and to the **Guaporé River***. If you are adventurous, it is possible to sail down the river, but this may be hazardous. The excursion starts in Vila Bela do Mato Grosso, a former capital founded in 1752 that is 373 mi/600 km from Cuiabá, and ends up in Guajara-Mirim. On the banks of the river you may be able to see workers tapping rubber trees.

Mato Grosso do Sul

Campo Grande* is one of Brazil's largest agricultural centres and does a brisk trade with São Paulo and other cities. Campo Grande is a good place to start an excursion to Pantanal.

In the town is one interesting museum, the **Dom Bosco Museum**** (☎ 383 3994, open daily 7-11am, 1-5pm). Its collection stresses the region's natural history and ethnology, providing exhibits of Indian hand-crafts, stuffed animals, and other items. There are also objects on sale. Close by, at 5 mi/8 km, is the **José Antônio Pereira Park***. This lovely wooded park sits on the original site of the town.

Farther into the interior of Mato Grosso do Sul is the **Paraná River,** which marks the boundaries between the states of São Paulo, Paraná and Mato Grosso. It teems with fish. Fishing expeditions can be organized from **Presidente Epitácio** (366 mi/590 km north-west of São Paulo), from **Panorama** (435 mi/700 km north-west of São Paulo) and at **Ilha Solteira** (416 mi/670 km north-west of São Paulo). There are also irregular river-boat sailings between the various towns on the Paraná. (For information, contact **Comércio de Navegação do Alto Paraná,** São Paulo, ☎ (011) 34 7359).

Another interesting exploration is to cross Mato Grosso do Sul on a train. There is a train journey between São Paulo and Bolivia that covers almost 806 mi/1297 km in a style reminiscent of the heydays of train travel in the North American Far West.

Pantanal

Corumbá*, 367 mi/590 km north-west of Campo Grande, is Pantanal's de facto capital. It is a small town that sits on the western shore of the Paraguai River on the Bolivian border. During the rainy season Corumbá is inaccessible by road.

Founded in 1775 by the Jesuit procurator Luis de Albuquerque, Corumbá was a Spanish possession from 1801 to 1865. Since then it has owed its development to the cattle trade, with Argentina in particular. It is now said to be an important centre for the international drug trade. In Corumbá, an interesting place to visit is the **Pantanal Museum *** (Rua Delamare 939), which has historical and handcraft exhibits from the region.

A seven-hour boat trip on the Paraguai River will take you to the **Coimbra Fort****, dating from 1775. You will need a permit to visit the fort (☎ 231 2861). Another excursion that we recommend is to the **manganese deposits,** the richest in the world, 15 mi/24 km south of Corumbá at Morro do Urucum. Here too, a permit is required to visit the mines (☎ 231 1661). For information on other excursions, contact the following travel agencies:

Corumbatur, 231 1532.
Pantanal Express, 231 5353.
Pantanal Tours, 231 4683.
Vagãotur, 231 5998.

Other towns of interest in Pantanal include **Aquidauana** (81 mi/131 km west of Campo Grande), the closest point of entry into Pantanal from Campo Grande, and **Bonito*** (154 mi/248 km south-west of Campo Grande). Bonito serves as a base for trips to the **caverns**** at Lake Azul and Nossa Senhora de Aparecida. The best time to visit these caverns is from November to February. It is also possible to take excursions on the **Formosa River** (7 mi/12 km from Bonito) as far as Ilha do Padre.

Porto Murtinho** (290 mi/466 km south-west of Campo Grande) lies on the border with Paraguay in Pantanal's deep south. It is famous for its rich flora and fauna. The area offers good fishing on the Paraguai River and river excursions to **Margarida Island** in Paraguay, to the **Missão Maria Auxiliadora** (a village occupied by Moros Indians), and to **Pedreiro.**

Coxim* (150 mi/242 km north of Campo Grande) is a little town that is the western point of entry into Pantanal. There are several campsites here, for members only (for further information, contact **Iate Clube Rio Verde,** São Paulo, ☎ (011) 572 7944.

If you enter Pantanal from the north, you will pass through the following towns. **Poconé*** (63 mi/102 km south-west of Cuiabá) is known as Pantanal's pink city. It lies at the beginning of the Transpantaneira Highway. **Cáceres*** (134 mi/215 km south-west of Cuiabá) offers the most characteristic Pantanal landscape. **Barão de Melgaço*** (65 mi/105 km south of Cuiabá) is the site of a fabulous natural occurrence. Whenever the river floods, a gigantic bay is formed that measures more than 300 sq mi/800 sq km, twice the size of Rio de Janeiro bay!

USEFUL VOCABULARY

General words and expressions

I	*Eu*
You (familiar)	*Tu*
You (polite)	*Vós*
He	*Ele*
She	*Ela*
We	*Nós*
You	*Vós, Você*
They (masculine)	*Eles*
They (feminine)	*Elas*
Yes	*Sim*
No	*Não*
Please	*Por favor*
Thank you	*Obrigado*
Sorry	*Desculpe*
Excuse me	*Com licença*
I don't understand	*Não entendo*
Do you speak English?	*Fala inglês?*
Does someone speak English?	*Alguém fala inglês?*
How do you say . . . in Portuguese?	*Como se diz . . . em Portugués?*
What's the Portuguese word for . . . ?	*Qual é a palavra Portugués para . . . ?*
I would like . . .	*Gostaria . . .*
It doesn't matter	*Não tem importância*
Where	*Onde*
When	*Quando*
How	*Como*
Open	*Aberto*
Closed	*Fechado*
Good morning	*Bom dia*
Good afternoon	*Boa tarde*
Good evening	*Boa noite*
Good-bye (so long)	*Até logo*
One moment	*Momentinho*
Mister	*Senhor*
Mrs.	*Senhora*
Miss	*Senhorita*
How are you?	*Como vai? como está?*
Very well, thank you	*Muito bem, obrigado*
Where is the bathroom?	*Onde fica o banheiro?*
Leave me alone	*Deixe-me tranquilo*
Go away	*Vai-te embora*

Numbers

One	*Um, Uma*
Two	*Dois, Duas*
Three	*Três*
Four	*Quatro*
Five	*Cinco*
Six	*Seis*
Seven	*Sete*
Eight	*Oito*
Nine	*Nove*
Ten	*Dez*
Eleven	*Onze*
Twelve	*Doze*
Thirteen	*Treze*
Fourteen	*Catorze*

Fifteen	*Quinze*
Sixteen	*Dezasseis*
Seventeen	*Dezassete*
Eighteen	*Dezoito*
Nineteen	*Dezanove*
Twenty	*Vinte*
Twenty-one	*Vinte e um*
Thirty	*Trinta*
Forty	*Quarenta*
Fifty	*Cinquenta*
Sixty	*Sessenta*
Seventy	*Setenta*
Eighty	*Oitenta*
Ninety	*Doventa*
One hundred	*Cem*
One hundred and one	*Cento e um*
Two hundred	*Duzentos*
Three hundred	*Trezentos*
Five hundred	*Quinhentos*
One thousand	*Mil*

Time

What time is it?	*Que horas são?*
	Tem horas?
One o'clock	*Uma hora*
Two o'clock	*Duas horas*
Noon	*Meio-dia*
Midnight	*Meia-noite*
Yesterday	*Ontem*
Today	*Hoje*
Tomorrow	*Amanhã*
Day	*Dia*
Week	*Semana*
Month	*Mês*
Year	*Ano*
Sunday	*Domingo*
Monday	*Segunda-feira*
Tuesday	*Terça-feira*
Wednesday	*Quarta-feira*
Thursday	*Quinta-feira*
Friday	*Sexta-feira*
Saturday	*Sábado*

Shopping

How much does it cost?	*Quanto custa?*
Money	*Dinheiro*
Cheap	*Barato*
Expensive	*Caro*
Large	*Grande*
Small	*Pequeno*
Blouse	*Blusa*
Cigarette	*Cigarro*
Magazine	*Revista*
Matches	*Fósforos*
Newspaper	*Jornal*
Shirt	*Camisa*
Skirt	*Saia*
Shoes	*Sapatos*
Store	*Loja*
Suit	*Terno*
Trousers	*Calças*

Health and emergencies

Call a doctor	*Chame un médico*
Hurry	*Depressa*
It's an emergency	*E urgente*
Help me	*Ajude-me*
There's been an accident	*Houve um acidente*
Ambulance	*Ambulância*
Dentist	*Dentista*
Fever	*Febre*
Pharmacy	*Farmácia*
Police	*Polícia*
Sick	*Doente*
Stomach ache	*Dor de estômago*
Hospital	*Hospital*

Driving

Attention, danger!	*Atenção, perigo!*
Blocked road	*Estrada interrompida*
Detour	*Desvio*
Fill it up	*Encha o tanque*
Filling station	*Posto de gasolina*
Litre	*Litro*
One way	*Mão única*
No parking	*Estacionamento proibído*
Slow	*Devagar*
Stop	*Pare*
Which is the way to . . . ?	*Qual é o caminho para . . . ?*

At the station, at the airport

Bus	*Ônibus*
Bus station	*Estação rodoviária*
Customs	*Alfândega*
Fare	*Preço*
Health certificate	*Atestado de saúde*
Luggage	*Bagagem*
One-way ticket	*Passagem de ida*
Passport	*Passaporte*
Railway station	*Estação ferroviária*
Round trip	*Ida e volta*
Sleeping car	*Carro-dormitório*
Suitcase	*Mala*
Taxi	*Taxi*
Ticket	*Passagem*
Travelers checks	*Cheques de viagem*
Visa	*Visto*

At the hotel

Bathroom	*Banheiro*
Bed	*Cama*
Key	*Chave*
Maid	*Arrumadeira*
Room	*Apartamento*
Shower	*Chuveiro*
Wake me up at . . .	*Acorde-me ás . . .*
What time is breakfast?	*A que horas é o pequeno almoço?*

Food and beverages

Apple	*Maçã*
Barbecue	*Churrascaria*
Beans	*Feijão*

Beer	*Cerveja*
Beverages	*Bebidas*
Bread	*Pão*
Butter	*Manteiga*
Cake	*Bolo*
Cheese	*Queijo*
Chicken	*Frango*
Cod	*Bacalhau*
Coffee	*Café*
Crab	*Caranguejo*
Dessert	*Sobremesa*
Egg	*Ovo*
Fish	*Peixe*
Fried	*Frito*
Grilled	*Grelhado*
Jam	*Geléia*
Juice	*Suco*
Lemon	*Limão*
Lobster	*Lagosta*
Meat	*Carne*
Meat balls	*Almôndegas*
Mineral water	*Água mineral*
Milk	*Leite*
Mutton	*Carneiro*
Olives	*Azeitonas*
Orange	*Laranja*
Pepper	*Pimentão*
Pineapple	*Abacaxi*
Pork chops	*Costeletas de porco*
Rice	*Arroz*
Roast	*Assado*
Salt	*Sal*
Salty	*Salgado*
Shrimp	*Camarão*
Soft drink	*Refrigerante*
Soup	*Sopa*
Steak	*Bife*
Sugar	*Açúcar*
Sweet	*Doce*
Tea	*Chá*
Wine	*Vinho*

At the restaurant

Menu	*Cardápio*
Rare	*Malpassado*
Well-done	*Bem passado*
The bill, please	*A conta, por favor*
Waiter	*Garçon*

Sightseeing

Where is . . . ?	*Onde fica . . . ?*
Near	*Perto*
Far	*Longe*
Left	*Esquerda*
Right	*Direita*
Address	*Endereço*
Avenue	*Avenida*
Beach	*Praia*
Bus stop	*Ponto de ônibus*
Cave	*Gruta*
Church	*Igreja*
City	*Cidade*

Fair/market	*Feira/mercado*
Fountain	*Fonte*
Lagoon	*Lagoa*
Monastery	*Mosteiro*
Museum	*Museu*
Neighbourhood	*Bairro*
Nightclub	*Boíte*
Street	*Rua*
Subway	*Metro*
Square	*Praça*
Trip	*Passeio*

SUGGESTED READING

History and background

Bastide, Roger. *The African Religions of Brazil* (Johns Hopkins University Press, 1978).

Botting, Douglas. *Rio de Janeiro* (Time-Life, 1978).

Bruce, G. *Brazil and the Brazilians* (Gordon Press, 1976).

Burns, E. Bradford. *A History of Brazil* (Columbia University Press, 1980).

Dos Passos, John. *Brazil on the Move* (Greenwood, 1974).

Draeger, Alain. *Brazil* (Overlook Press, 1974).

Fleming, Peter. *Brazilian Adventure* (Tarcher, 1983).

Freyre, Gilberto. *The Mansions and the Shanties: The Making of Modern Brazil* (University of California Press, 1986).

Freyre, Gilberto. *The Master and Slaves: A Study in the Development of Brazilian Civilization* (University of California Press, 1986).

Goldman, Albert. *Carnival in Rio* (Hawthorn Books, 1978).

Hemming, John. *Red Gold: The Conquest of the Brazilian Indians* (Harvard, 1978).

Pastore, Jose. *Inequality and Social Mobility in Brazil* (Wisconsin, 1982).

Parks, Gordon. *Flavio* (Norton, 1978).

Shoumatoff, Alex. *The Capital of Hope* (Coward, 1980).

Torres, Heloisa A. *Museums of Brazil* (Gordon Press, 1976).

Wagley, Charles. *An Introduction to Brazil* (Columbia University Press, 1971).

World Travel Series Map of Brazil and Bolivia (Bartholomew, 1987).

Literature

Amado, Jorge. *Gabriela, Clove and Cinnamon* (Avon, 1974).

Amado, Jorge. *Tereza Batista: Home from the Wars* (Knopf, 1975).

Bishop, Elizabeth, and Emmanuel Brasil, eds. *An Anthology of Twentieth-Century Brazilian Poetry* (Wesleyan University, 1972).

Bolt, Robert. *The Mission* (Jove, 1986).

de Castro, Josue. *Of Men and Crabs* (Vanguard, 1971).

Courter, Gay. *River of Dreams* (Houghton Mifflin, 1984).

Geld, Ellen B. *The Garlic Tree* (Doubleday, 1970).

Goldberg, Isaac. *Brazilian Literature* (Gordon Press, 1978).

Jaffe, Rona. *Away from Home* (Simon & Schuster, 1960).

Levin, Ira. *The Boys from Brazil* (Random House, 1976).

MacLean, Alistair. *River of Death* (Doubleday, 1982).

Matthiessen, Peter. *At Play in the Fields of the Lord* (Random House, 1965).

Meyer, Nicholas. *Black Orchid* (Dial, 1977).

Putnam, Samuel, et al. *Marvelous Journey: A Survey of Four Centuries of Brazilian Writing* (Century Bookbindery, 1977).

Souza, Marcio. *The Emperor of the Amazon* (Avon, 1980).

Uys, Errol Lincolin. *Brazil* (Simon & Schuster, 1986).

Vargas Llosa, Mario. *The War of the End of the World* (FS&G, 1984).

Vasconcelos, Jose Mauro de. *My Sweet Orange Tree* (Knopf, 1971).

■ *INDEX*